Gombrowicz in Transnational Context

I0593080

Witold Gombrowicz (1904–1969) was born and lived in Poland for the first half of his life but spent twenty-four years as an émigré in Argentina before returning to Europe to live in West Berlin and finally Vence, France. His works have always been of interest to those studying Polish or Argentinean or Latin American literature, but in recent years the trend toward a transnational perspective in scholarship has brought his work to increasing prominence. Indeed, the complicated web of transnational contact zones where Polish, Argentinean, French and German cultures intersect to influence his work is now seen as the appropriate lens through which his creativity ought to be examined.

This volume contributes to the transnational interpretation of Gombrowicz by bringing together a distinguished group of North American, Latin American, and European scholars to offer new analyses in three distinct themes of study that have not as yet been greatly explored— Translation, Affect, and Politics. How does one translate not only Gombrowicz's words into various languages but also the often cultural-laden meaning and the particular style and tone of his writing? What is it that passes between author and reader that causes an affect? How did Gombrowicz's negotiation of the turbulent political worlds of Poland and Argentina shape his writing? The three divisions of this collection address these questions from multiple perspectives, thereby adding significantly to little known aspects of his work.

Silvia G. Dapía is Professor of Modern Languages at John Jay College, City University of New York (CUNY), and the CUNY Graduate Center. She received her PhD degree from the University of Cologne, Germany. She is the author of *Die Rezeption der Sprachkritik Fritz Mauthners im Werk von Jorge Luis Borges* (Böhlau, 1993) and *Jorge Luis Borges, Post-Analytic Philosophy, and Representation* (Routledge, 2015), and guest editor of an issue of *The Polish Review* on Witold Gombrowicz and an issue of *Polish American Studies* on Poles in Latin America.

Routledge Studies in Twentieth-Century Literature

For more information about this series, please visit: https://www.routledge.com

Gombrowicz in Transnational Context

Translation, Affect, and Politics

Edited by Silvia G. Dapía

Routledge
Taylor & Francis Group

NEW YORK AND LONDON

First published 2019
by Routledge
52 Vanderbilt Avenue, New York, NY 10017

and by Routledge
2 Park Square, Milton Park, Abingdon, Oxon, OX14 4RN

*Routledge is an imprint of the Taylor & Francis Group, an
informa business*

First issued in paperback 2021

Library of Congress Cataloging-in-Publication Data
Names: Dapâia, Silvia G., editor.
Title: Gombrowicz in transnational context : translation, affect,
and politics / edited by Silvia Dapâia.
Description: New York, NY : Routledge, 2019. | Series:
Routledge studies in twentieth-century literature ; 61 | Includes
bibliographical references and index. |
Identifiers: LCCN 2019013724 (print) |
LCCN 2019016350 (ebook) | ISBN 9780429287152 (Master) |
ISBN 9781000004861 (Pdf) | ISBN 9781000011708 (ePub) |
ISBN 9781000018226 (Mobi) | ISBN 9780367223540 |
ISBN 9780367223540 (hardback : alk. paper) |
ISBN 9780429287152 (ebk)
Subjects: LCSH: Gombrowicz, Witold—Translations—History
and criticism. | Gombrowicz, Witold—Influence.
Classification: LCC PG7158.G6692 (ebook) |
LCC PG7158.G6692 G5935 2019 (print) |
DDC 891.8/5373—dc23
LC record available at https://lccn.loc.gov/2019013724

ISBN: 978-0-367-22354-0 (hbk)
ISBN: 978-1-03-209224-9 (pbk)
ISBN: 978-0-429-28715-2 (ebk)

Typeset in Sabon
by codeMantra

Contents

List of Illustrations

List of Contributors

Daniel Balderston is the Andrew W. Mellon Professor of Modern Languages and Chair of the Department of Hispanic Languages and Literatures at the University of Pittsburgh, where he also directs the Borges Center. Recently, he published *How Borges Wrote* (2017 by the University of Virginia Press), *Los caminos del afecto* (*The Paths of Affect*, Instituto Caro y Cuervo, 2015), and a translation of the short fiction of Silvina Ocampo, *Thus Were Their Faces* (New York Review Books, 2015).

Tul'si (Tuesday) Bhambry has a PhD in literature (University College London, 2013) and is now working on her book, *Disciplined Anarchy: Gombrowicz and the Art of Writing*. She translates from Polish and German. She won the Harvill Secker Young Translators' Prize in 2015, and has published her work in *Asymptote*, *The Paris Review* and *Words Without Borders*. She lives in Berlin.

Silvia G. Dapía is Professor of Modern Languages and Literatures at John Jay College, City University of New York (CUNY), and the PhD Program in Latin American, Iberian, and Latino Cultures (LAILAC) at CUNY's Graduate Center. She is the author of *Die Rezeption der Sprachkritik Fritz Mauthners im Werk von Jorge Luis Borges* (*The Reception of Fritz Mauthner's Critique of Language in the Work of Jorge Luis Borges*, Cologne: Böhlau, 1993) and of *Jorge Luis Borges, Post-Analytic Philosophy, and Representation* (New York: Routledge, 2015). She has been a member of the International editorial board of *Variaciones Borges* since 2006 and of *Polish American Studies* since 2017. She served as guest editor for a special issue on "Poles in Latin America" for the scholarly journal *Polish American Studies*, Spring 2012, and for a special issue of the journal *The Polish Review*, which focused on Gombrowicz, Spring 2015.

Carlos Gamerro is an Argentinean novelist, critic, and translator. Gamerro has published six works of fiction, as well as works of criticism, and scripts for film and stage. Three of his novels—*Las islas* (1998) (The Islands, 2012); *El secreto y las voces* (2002) (An Open Secret, 2012); and *La aventura de los bustos de Eva* (2004)

(The Adventure of the Busts of Eva Perón, 2015)—have been translated into English. In addition, he has translated works of William
Shakespeare, W. H. Auden, and Harold Bloom into Spanish.

Magdalena Heydel is an academic, literary translator, and critic. She
is Head of the MA Program in Literary Translation at the Department of Polish Studies at the Jagiellonian University in Kraków, and
editor-in-chief of *Przekładaniec: A Journal of Literary Translation.*
Her publications include *"Gorliwość tłumacza." Przekład poetycki
w twórczości Czesława Miłosza* (*"Translator's Zeal": Poetic Translation in the Work of Czesław Miłosz*, 2013) and *Obecność T.S. Eliota
w literaturze polskiej* (*T.S. Eliot in Polish Literature: A Study of Presence*, 2003). She is a co-editor of two anthologies, *Polska myśl prze-
kładoznawcza. Antologia* (*Polish Concepts in Translation Studies:
An anthology*, 2013) and *Współczesne teorie przekładu. Antologia*
(*Contemporary Translation Theories: An anthology*, 2009). She is
an award-winning translator of English-language literature. She has
translated into Polish the work of Joseph Conrad, T.S. Eliot, Virginia
Woolf, Ted Hughes, and Anne Fadiman, among others.

Jerzy Jarzębski is a Professor on the faculty of Polish Studies at the Jagi-
ellonian University in Kraków as well as at the Institute of Polish
Studies at the State College of Eastern European Studies in Przemyśl.
He has lectured at Harvard and the Hebrew University in Jerusalem.
His interests focus on twentieth- and twenty-first-century Polish lit-
erature, including Witold Gombrowicz, Bruno Schulz, and Stanisław
Lem. He has published more than 700 articles and 14 books including
*Gra w Gombrowicza (1982), Podglądanie Gombrowicza (Snoop-
ing Gombrowicz 2001), Gombrowicz* (2004), and *Natura i teatr:
16 tekstów o Gombrowiczu* (*Nature and Theatre: Sixteen Texts on
Gombrowicz*, 2007). His works have been translated into seventeen
languages.

Andrzej Stanisław Kowalczyk is currently the Head of the Department of
Literature of the 20th and 21st centuries at the Institute of Polish Lit-
erature at the University of Warsaw and Director of the Manuscripts
Section of the Museum of Literature Adam Mickiewicz in Warsaw.
He has authored numerous articles and books on Andrzej Bobkowski,
Witold Gombrowicz, Jerzy Giedroyc, Wojciech Karpiński, Bohdan
Osadczuk, Józef Mackiewicz, Juliusz Mieroszewski, Czesław Miłosz,
Symon Petlur, Borys Sawinkow, Jerzy Stempowski, Stanisław Vincen-
zie, and others. He edited essays and letters by Jerzy Giedroyc, Witold
Gombrowicz, Bolesław Miciński, Irene Vincenz, Stanisław Vincenz,
and Jerzy Stempowski.

Allen J. Kuharski holds the Stephen Lang Chair of Performing Arts
at Swarthmore College, where he is Chair of the Department of

Theater. He also teaches at the Pig Iron Theatre Company's School of Advanced Performance Training in Philadelphia. He has worked as an editor for *Theatre Journal, Slavic and East European Performance*, and *Periphery: Journal of Polish Affairs* and is a co-editor of the ongoing sixteen-volume Polish edition of the complete works of Witold Gombrowicz, as well as of the official website on the writer's work launched in France by his widow, Rita Gombrowicz, in 2010. His articles, translations, and reviews have been widely published in the United States, Great Britain, Poland, France, Austria, and the Netherlands. Plays that he has translated or productions for which he has served as dramaturge have been widely performed nationally and internationally.

Olaf Kühl holds a PhD in Slavic literatures. He is a writer and a literary translator from Polish, Russian, and Ukrainian. In 2015, he was awarded the Polonicum Prize of the University of Warsaw for the dissemination of Polish culture abroad, and in 2016, he received the Brücke Berlin (Berlin Bridge) Prize for the exceptional translation into German of Szczepan Twardoch's novel *Drach*. Kühl has translated works by Witold Gombrowicz, Adam Zagajewski, Andrzej Stasiuk, and Dorota Maslowska, among others. He is Senior Advisor on Russian affairs to the Governing Mayor of Berlin since 1996.

Michał Paweł Markowski is the Stefan and Lucy Hejna Family Chair in Polish Language and Literature and Head of Slavic Department at the University of Illinois at Chicago. He is also a tenured visiting professor at the Center for the Advanced Studies in the Humanities (Jagiellonian University, Kraków, Poland), which he created in 2007. Since 1997, he has published more than 30 volumes of individual books, editions, and translations on literature and philosophy, and over 400 essays. He is a co-editor of two influential Polish series in the humanities, *Hermeneia* and *Horizons of Modernity* (over 130 volumes together), and sits on editorial boards of *Teksty Drugie* and *Slavic Review.*

Daniel Pratt is an Assistant Professor in the Department of Russian Studies at McGill University, Montréal, Canada. He has written and lectured on Gombrowicz and is currently working on non-narrative constructions of personal identity and history in Central European literature and philosophy.

Piotr Seweryn Rosół is a historian and literary theorist. He did his PhD at Warsaw University and the University of Sorbonne (Paris IV). He is a faculty member at the Université Clermont Auvergne. He published, among others, in *Teksty Drugie, Konteksty, Bliza, Kresy, Twórczość*, and *Widok*, and in Polish and French collective works. He is the author of *Genet Gombrowicza. Historia miłosna.*

Jean-Pierre Salgas is Professor of Art History and Art Theory at National School of Arts (Ecole Nationale d'Arts) at Nancy, Bourges, and Marne-la-vallée. He is the author of two books on Gombrowicz: *Gombrowicz, un structuraliste de la rue* (2011) and *Witold Gombrowicz ou l'athéisme généralisé* (2000). He curated several exhibitions, among them Georges Perec at the Musée des Beaux-Arts in Nantes (2008); "Les trois mousquetaires" (Witkacy, Schulz, Gombrowicz, and Kantor; 2004) at the Musée des Beaux-Arts in Nancy.

Zofia Stasiakiewicz is currently a PhD student at the University of Girona, Spain, where she is working on her dissertation on the reception of the literary work of Witold Gombrowicz in Catalonia and Spain.

Klementyna Suchanow is an Independent Scholar. She's the author of *Argentyńskie przygody Gombrowicza* (Gombrowicz's Argentine Adventures, 2005), and she has recently published a two-volume biography on Gombrowicz, entitled *Gombrowicz: Ja, Geniusz* (*Gombrowicz: I, the Genius*), released in 2017 by Czarn, the first comprehensive biography of the writer. She is also the author of *Królowa Karaibów* (Cuba, Queen of the Caribes, 2013).

Błażej Warkocki is a faculty member in the Institute of Polish Philology at the Adam Mickiewicz University (Poznań, Poland). He is the author of a book on Gombrowicz: *Pamiętnik afektów z okresu dojrzewania. Gombrowicz – queer – Sedgwick* (*Memoirs of Affects from a Time of Immaturity. Gombrowicz—Queer—Sedgwick*) (Poznań-Warszawa, Poland: Wydawnictwo Naukowe UAM, 2018). He also wrote two other books about contemporary Polish literature in the context of queer studies: *Homo niewiadomo. Polska proza wobec odmienności* (A Queer. Polish Literature and Otherness) (Warsaw, 2007), and *Różowy język. Literatura i polityka kultury na początku wieku* (Pink Language. Literature and Cultural Politics at the Beginning of the Century) (Warsaw, 2013 Krytyka Polityczna, 2013).

Bożena Anna Zaboklicka Zakwaska is Professor of Polish Studies and Literary Translation at the University of Barcelona. She has translated the works of diverse Polish writers into Spanish; among them Witold Gombrowicz, Sławomir Mrożek, Andrzej Kuśniewicz, Tadeusz Konwicki, Jarosław Iwaszkiewicz, Andrzej Szczypiorski, Maria Wisława Szymborska, and Zofia Nałkowska.

Acknowledgments

My primary acknowledgement is to the sixteen authors of the chapters in this volume, particularly for their exciting and dedicated work. The present volume grew out of an extended period of scholarly exchanges with the authors of this volume and included lively discussions in many panels at various conferences. Their contributions frequently illuminated aspects of Gombrowicz's work that I had not considered previously and is largely responsible for any success that this volume enjoys.

I am especially grateful to Profs. Jerzy Jarzębski, Aleksander Fiut, Łukasz Tischner, and Klementyna Suchanow for their generosity in sharing with me their expertise in Gombrowicz and sending me manuscripts and detailed answers to long list of inquiries. I am particularly indebted to Rita Gombrowicz for her encouragement and for granting me permission to quote from Gombrowicz's works.

I also want to express my deepest and warmest gratitude to James Pula. Much of the exchange that took place in Gombrowicz panels (such as three that were part of the Fifth World Congress on Polish Studies, University of Warsaw, Poland, June 21–23, 2014) would not have been possible without his constant organizing of Polish Studies conferences. To him I owe especial thanks for his invaluable and continued support, faith in my work, generous friendship, and last but not least readings of complete drafts of this book that greatly improved it.

My appreciation also goes to my graduate students in a seminar about "Contagious Affectivity: Body-Affect in Witold Gombrowicz" held at the Graduate Center, City University of New York, in fall 2017. Engaging in dialogue with those perceptive graduate students often led me to revise my positions. My very special thanks go to Fabiola Fernández Adechedera, Elena Ekaterina Chávez Goycochea, Cristina Elena Pardo, Justo Planas Cabreja, Roberto Enrique Martínez Bachrich, Fátima Vélez, and Pablo Yankelevich for their enthusiasm, enlightening comments, and sense of humor.

This work was also supported by the Office for the Advancement of Research (OAR) at John Jay College via the John Jay Visiting Scholar Fellowship, which allowed me to dedicate time to completing this manuscript at Friedrich-Schiller-University of Jena, Germany, during fall 2018; and by a John Jay College Fellowship Leave, which allowed me to do research on Gombrowicz when serving as Visiting Professor at Ignatianum University, Kraków, Poland, during spring 2017.

At the University of Jena, I am particularly thankful to Prof. Claudia Hammerschmidt for her generous support and welcome as well as that of her team, including Carolin Voigt and Claudia Tomadoni, who were outstandingly helpful with logistics and facilitated diverse aspects of my research, as well as Peter Müllers-Vonwirth for friendship and his many favors. At the Ignatianum University, I must thank Prof. Piotr Świercz, who not only made my stay in Kraków more profitable but helped me develop my thinking on Gombrowicz through many conversations in formal and informal venues. I'm also especially indebted to Ms. Lisa Fretschel for showing me around Kraków and ensuring I had everything I needed to carry out my work there.

I would also like to acknowledge the three anonymous readers for Routledge Press who made valuable comments on the penultimate version of this book, and most especially to my editor at Routledge, Michelle Salyga (Senior Editor, Literature Routledge) as well as Bryony Reece (Editorial Assistant, Routledge Research) and Shina Harshavardhan (Senior Project Manager of codeMantra) for transforming my rough manuscript into a printed volume.

Earlier versions of Chapter 1 ("The Rex Café, Buenos Aires, 1947: On the Spanish Translation of Gombrowicz's *Ferdydurke*" by Daniel Balderston), and Chapter 2 ("Witold Gombrowicz in Spain" by Zofia Stasiakiewicz) appeared in Vol. 60, no. 2 (2015) of *The Polish Review* special issue on Witold Gombrowicz that I guest edited. I am grateful to the editors for permission to reprint this material.

Introduction

Silvia G. Dapía

Witold Gombrowicz (1904–1969) was born and lived in Poland for the first half of his life but spent twenty-four years (1939–1963) as an émigré in Argentina. He returned to Europe through a Ford Foundation grant in 1963, spent a year in West Berlin, and finally settled in Vence, France, where he lived until his death in 1969. Since that time, interest in his work has progressively increased.

Evidence of the interest in Gombrowicz's work is shown in the growth in Gombrowicz scholarship since 2004, "the year of Gombrowicz," as it was designated by the Polish Ministry of Culture. At least four conferences were organized in Europe in that year. Accompanying these conferences were published proceedings in Polish, French, and German, most of them between 2006 and 2010.[1] Concurrently with centenary celebrations in Poland, France, and Germany, an international conference met in the United States, at Yale University, along with a Beinecke Rare Book and Manuscript Library exhibit entitled "The World of Witold Gombrowicz."[2] In addition, three new English translations of his works appeared to celebrate his centennial.[3] Echoes of this scholarly activity surrounding Gombrowicz's work were heard again in 2014, the 110th anniversary of his birth. To celebrate the 75th anniversary of his arrival in Argentina, the "First International Conference on Witold Gombrowicz" was held at the National Library in Buenos Aires. Moreover, in June of the same year, the "Fifth World Congress on Polish Studies" sponsored by the Polish Institute of Arts & Science of America in Warsaw included two complete sessions featuring several renowned Gombrowicz scholars. Those panels, along with additional papers presented at the conference in Buenos Aires, formed the basis of a special issue of *The Polish Review* dedicated to his works.[4]

Significant scholarship on Gombrowicz has also appeared in English since 2008, including seven book-length studies. Most of the works that appeared in English examine Gombrowicz's works in comparative perspective, concerning themselves with the relationship between his work and that of other authors, such as Bruno Schulz (De Bruyn, 2008),[5] Nikolai Gogol (Oklot, 2009),[6] Joseph Conrad (Gasyna 2011),[7] and Samuel Beckett (Lutostański 2016),[8] as well as to philosophers such as Walter Benjamin (Harnesberger, 2009),[9] Gilles Deleuze (Goddard, 2010),[10] and Jean-Paul Sartre (Wojtas, 2014).[11] This collection of interpretative essays differs from these earlier studies in a number of ways but most importantly, perhaps, because this book is not comparative in approach but focuses on three main aspects of Gombrowicz's work. A path-breaking publication must be mentioned here that was originally published in English before the centennial. I am referring to *Gombrowicz's Grimaces: Modernism, Gender, Nationality* (1998), a remarkable collection of essays edited by Ewa Płonowska Ziarek. Being a multi-authored volume written in English, this work is comparable to Ziarek's format but isolating topics as yet little researched.

Regarding Gombrowicz as a transnational author means that a web of contact zones where the Polish, Argentinean, French, and German cultures meet as a result of his various border crossings has superseded the nation as the basic framework of analysis. As a result of this, the question arises: Should not Gombrowicz's work be read in a transnational context rather than being exclusively studied either in Slavic or Latin American departments? It is precisely one of the goals of this volume to break down the boundaries between Polish and Latin American studies, as well as those between North American, Latin American, and European scholarship, bringing together on this transnational author the widely varied perspectives of seventeen distinguished European, North American, and Argentinean scholars from varied academic departments.

The chapters in this book do not explore the theories of transnationalism but rather seek to explore Gombrowicz as a transnational author. Nevertheless, some explanation of how I am defining "transnationalism" appears to be in order. Most scholars accept that the term "transnational" was first used by the American author Randolph Bourne in 1916,[12] but more in the sense of the way we use the term "multicultural" today. In the 1990s, the term began to be used in conjunction with migration studies, being defined by Linda Basch, et al., as "a process by which migrants, through their daily life activities create social fields that cross national boundaries."[13] Peggy Levitt and Nina Nyberg-Sørensen[14] further refined this to specify that an understanding of transnationalism required the study of both the sending and the receiving countries. As the term became more widespread, "migrating" to different disciplines, it took on meanings specific to those disciplines as first described by Steven Vertovec.[15]

One of the definitions current among social scientists, according to Vertovec, involves social identity reflecting "multiple ties and interactions linking people or institutions across the borders of nation states."[16] What he labels "social morphology," he explains as "a kind of social formation spanning borders" that involves "systems of relationships best described as networks."[17] Although Vertovec applies this to the electronic components of the "Information Age," it can as well be applied to Gombrowicz: for example, in his use of the international translation group in Buenos Aires; his international network that led to translation of *Ferdydurke* into French, sparking the growth of his popularity in Europe; and the various international and intercultural aspects of his writing, such as the singular use of the explicitly Argentine expression "puto" in a text otherwise completely written in Polish (for these three issues, see the Translation section).

Vertovec also identifies as transnational themes (1) "type of consciousness," referring to "a kind of 'diaspora consciousness' marked by dual or multiple identifications"; (2) "mode of cultural representation" which he defines as "processes of cultural penetration and blending," such as "syncretism, creolization, bricolage, cultural translation, and hybridity"; and (3) "(re)construction of 'place' or locality," which he explains as "meanings derived from specific geographical and historical points of origin" that have been "transferred and regrounded." These types of multiple identifications and cultural blendings can clearly be seen in Gombrowicz. For example, a diaspora consciousness marked by dual or multiple identifications may be seen in Tul'si Bhambry's chapter, "'The Quieter the Louder Indeed': Silence, Space, and Subjectivity in *Trans-Atlantyk*." The second transnational theme identified by Vertovec may be seen in the aforementioned singular use of the explicitly Argentine expression "puto" in *Trans-Atlantyk*. Last but not least, also in *Trans-Atlantyk*, we see Vertovec's third transnational theme, particularly in the episode of the "Chevaliers of the Spur," where the notion of the Polish community as a dystopian fantasy of surveillance has been regrounded in Argentina. Finally, Vertovec defines "the site of political engagement" as yet another form of transnationalism, one aspect of which is the "politics of homeland" found among "members of diasporas or transnational communities." This concept is also clearly reflected in *Trans-Atlantyk*.

In her essay "Deconstructing and Reconstructing 'Transnational Cinema,'" Deborah Shaw notes that "Transnational exchanges have long been central to filmmaking" in that a large number have had an international cast and crew, and international funding and locations, and been produced for distribution to international audiences. In the same sense, we can discuss Gombrowicz as a "transnational" author – someone who wrote from exposure to multiple national cultures and languages, often with the assistance of international translators and for distribution to international audiences in various languages.[18] My approach to understanding Gombrowicz's writing in this volume reflects Shaw's thinking in that it approaches his body of work through the perspective of Gombrowicz's personal transnationalism as well as from the perspectives of scholars from various countries in several distinct fields of study, such as Slavic Literature, Latin American Literature, Translation Studies, Literary Criticism, Comparative Literature, Gombrowicz Studies, etc.

Gombrowicz's life and work crossed not only the West European-Central European border but also that between Europe and the

Americas. Poland, Argentina, Germany, and France not only correspond to nations whose borders Gombrowicz crossed at certain points in his life but also phases in his intellectual development where Gombrowicz was forced to engage in translation: to translate not only his works but also his subjectivity to others (and translate the others to himself). It is the purpose of this book to study Gombrowicz's work in connection to Translation and Affect. Moreover, in order to better understand these aspects of his work, we believe we need also to place him in a Political context. Thus, the themes of Translation, Affect, and Politics structure our approach to his work, dividing the book into these three sections.

Lost in Translation

Part I, "Lost in Translation," focuses on an examination of diverse is-sues related to the translations of Gombrowicz's work. Indeed, an issue that immediately comes to mind when discussing a transnational author is the circulation of his works by means of translations. Yet this seems to be a relatively neglected field in Gombrowicz scholarship. Translation studies seem to be here to stay. In the past twenty-five years, new jour-nals of translation studies, articles, books, encyclopedias, and conferences as well as the opening of new translation studies programs in American universities attest to the pervasive interest in this field and the consequent interest in the essays in this book. If every reading of a text implies a par-ticular interpretation of it, this is even more so for a translation. It is the goal of this section to render visible the very translations that allow Gom-browicz's works to circulate in different national and transnational con-texts, paying particular attention to its literary effects. Accordingly, this section of the volume attempts to fill a gap in the scholarship on Gombro-wicz and translation.[19] It also attempts to contribute to the interpreting of Gombrowicz's work and, last but not least, make a contribution in the field of Translation Studies. Some of the questions we shall pose in this first section are as follows: How do the translations of Gombrowicz's novels produce the "philosophical effect" of the Polish version, partic-ularly when translating his deconstructions of fundamental philosophic concepts, which in his work are tightly connected to very specific and complex erotics? Why does Gombrowicz choose to keep the Spanish word "puto" in the original Polish *Trans-Atlantyk* (1952)—a word whose con-notations are so heavily and exclusively rooted in Argentinean culture? How did the Spanish translation of *Pornografia* deal with the censorship of Franco's national, Catholic project in Spain? How does Gombrowicz convey, in his Spanish translation of *Ślub* (*El casamiento*, The Wedding), the play's embedment in the reality of pre-World War II Poland? These are some of the issues that we shall address in this section.

As is well known, in 1946, after nearly a decade of residence in Argentina, Gombrowicz decided to translate his novel *Ferdydurke*, first published in Warsaw in 1937, from Polish into Spanish. The circumstances under which this translation was made were quite unique. Gombrowicz translated his novel with the help of those who frequented the Café Rex on the Avenida Corrientes, a variable group of associates known as "the Translation Committee," whose leading figure was the Cuban writer Virgilio Piñera. In his article, "The Rex Café, Buenos Aires, 1947. On the Spanish Translation of Gombrowicz's *Ferdydurke*," Daniel Balderston examines pages of a hand-corrected typescript of this crucial Argentine translation. Through a detailed examination of these pages, he sheds light on the translation process of this work.

In the 1960s, Witold Gombrowicz, as renowned an author as he was in Europe, with his works being translated into numerous languages, including Spanish, French, English, and Italian, was still relatively unknown in Spain. The one who came to play a crucial role in the introduction of his oeuvre to the Catalan and Spanish peninsular literary world was Gabriel Ferrater (1922–1972), a Catalan poet and one of the most influential literary editors within publishers' circles in Barcelona, particularly in Seix Barral. Based on an epistolary exchange between Gombrowicz and Ferrater which began in 1965, Stasiakiewicz traces, in "Witold Gombrowicz in Spain," the process of translation of *Pornografía*, which contributed to the transnational circulation of Gombrowicz's literary work in both Catalonia and the rest of Spain.

The existence of those "untranslatable" culture-bound words that continue to fascinate translators, theorists of translation, and critics alike becomes the focal point of scholarly attention in Carlos Gamerro's article, "The 'Puto' in Argentine Literature." The word in question is the Spanish word "puto," which Gombrowicz curiously used in his Polish-language *Trans-Atlantyk*. In his article, Gamerro shows how the word "puto," as used by Gombrowicz in his Polish text, is so heavily and exclusively rooted in Argentinean culture that it makes it impossible to neglect the embedment of *Trans-Atlantyk* (1952) in its socio-cultural context of production: the Argentina of the 1950s.

Less well known than Gombrowicz's Argentine translation of *Ferdydurke* is his translation of *Ślub*, with Alejandro Rússovich, into Spanish. Gombrowicz began working on the translation in Buenos Aires during the war, and it was published first in Spanish as *El Casamiento* in 1948 before appearing in Polish in 1953 as *Ślub* (The Wedding).[20] In her article, "Are There as Many *Weddings* as Translations? On Gombrowicz's Spanish *El casamiento* (*The Wedding*)," Bożena Zaboklicka suggests that rather than a "faithful reflection" of the "original" Polish *Ślub*, Gombrowicz's Spanish *El casamiento* is a form of "rewriting" or, using André Lefevere's terminology, a "refraction" rather than "reflection" of the Polish *Ślub*.[21]

Due to its intertextuality and embedment in the reality of pre-war Poland, *Ferdydurke* is often considered untranslatable. According to Magdalena Heydel, the main difficulty, however, lies beyond the sphere of intertextuality and context-dependency: the style is the issue, and the literary impact of the novel, entrenched with overwhelming parody and mockery, is hidden in the intricacies of the author's syntax and his use of wordplay. In her essay, "Intermolecular Mockery and Derision, an Inbred Superlaugh: On English Translations of Gombrowicz's *Ferdydurke* and Their Plural Original," Heydel analyzes Danuta Borchardt's art of translating by tracing strategies employed by the translator to render the specificities of Gombrowicz's style.

Gombrowicz has always been preoccupied with forms and their deconstruction. He deconstructed not only constructs such as patriotism or "normal" sexuality but also language itself as the form "par excellence." While his subtle deconstructions may be either ignored or "overinterpreted" by the reader of Gombrowicz's original texts, they leave no choice to the translator, who has to consciously deal with them and make decisions about them. This turns out to be one of the greatest difficulties of translating Gombrowicz. It is the goal of Olaf Kühl's essay, "Translating the Secret," to explore Gombrowicz's deconstructions of fundamental philosophic concepts such as "essence" and "existence," which, in the conceptual world of the author, are tightly connected to his very specific and complex erotics.

Cartography of Affect

In an interview, Aernout Mik, a contemporary Dutch artist, internationally known for his installations and films, referring to his interest in Gombrowicz, says:

> What appeals most strongly to me about Gombrowicz, and what became a very active force in my work is what might be called a "traveling" from one object or person to the other through connections that are created almost by accident. This also happens in my work when the camera travels from body parts to objects and objects to other objects or when people assume each other's compulsive movements and emotions. There is an action of contamination or spreading out that becomes an independent force.[22]

It is precisely this "contamination" or transmission of affect[23] as it operates in Gombrowicz's work that constitutes the subject of the second section, "Cartography of Affect in Gombrowicz's Works." Interest in "affect" theory in the humanities has grown appreciably in the last decades, giving rise to talk of an "affective turn" to challenge the "linguistic turn" of the last decades of the twentieth century. It is therefore somewhat surprising that although subjectivity and form appear to be the two most dominant entry points into any discussion about Gombrowicz's work,[24] almost no critical work is dedicated to the role of affect in his work, with the exception of Błażej Warkocki's book *Pamiętnik afektów z okresu dojrzewania* (Memoirs of Affects from a Time of Immaturity), although it is not available in English for the time being. Warkocki reads Gombrowicz's short-story collection alongside Eve Kosofsky Sedgwick's work on affect and the paranoid Gothic. Yet there is still far more work to be done if we remain interested in exploring frameworks that may enable a hold on the unique density and complexity of Gombrowicz's notion of subjectivity. Accordingly, this section fosters different approaches that engage with affect and its role in Gombrowicz's work, bringing about new ways of thinking about his notion of subjectivity. Particular attention will be given to the way in which affect crosses inner-outer borders in Gombrowicz's work as well as the way in which his work performs affects such as shame, embarrassment, humiliation, disgust (the abject), and boredom. Some of the questions that we shall address in this section are as follows: How do affects circulate in the interactions of Gombrowicz's characters with other characters? How do they stick to the bodies of others? How does self-preservation function in the face of an unassimilable, abject otherness? What is the role of Immaturity in relation to Form if regarded as two symbiotic, companion forces that need each other? How do issues of subjectivity interrelate with problems of authorship in Gombrowicz? The exploration of these questions can be a venue for productive critique, both interrogating the conditions of possibility of the circulation of affect in Gombrowicz's work and at the same time refreshing the ways in which Gombrowicz scholarship looks at issues of subjectivity.

According to Michał Markowski, in his article, "'Indomitable Boredom Above the Entire World': Gombrowicz (and Other Polish Writers) on Existential Predicament," in Gombrowicz's work, boredom is not a phenomenon connected with the individual, nor is it a psychological phenomenon. Furthermore, if we accept that subjectivity is always relational because it is always established in reference to the world and the other, then boredom as a non-relational experience makes the constitution of subjectivity impossible because of the lack of any mediation. Based on "The Events on the Banbury" (Zdarzenia na brygu Banbury, 1932), Markowski demonstrates that understood ontologically, boredom makes it impossible to get beyond oneself, beyond the immediately experienced "I," in the direction of the other and thus toward the social world.

Drawing on Bruno Latour, among others, Piotr Swereryn Rosół regards Gombrowicz as a transmodernist who cannot rest content with the modernist paradigm of the excluded other. In his article, "Becoming Gombrowicz: On the Way of Trans-Subjectivity and Trans-Modernity," Rosół explores how abjection operates in Gombrowicz's work, particularly in two of his short stories: "Lawyer Kraykowski's Dancer" (Tancerz mecenasa Kraykowskiego) and "The Memoirs of Stefan Czarniecki" (Pamiętnik Stefana Czarnieckiego),[25] both contained in the volume *Memoirs from the Time of Immaturity* (Pamiętnika z okresu dojrzewania, 1933).[26] Since, in Rosół's view, Gombrowicz not only re-inforces but also hybridizes the modernist boundary between the self and the other, Rosół sees in Gombrowicz's "reinstatement of the abject" what he calls "the first scene of trans-subjectivity and the first moment of trans-modernity" in Gombrowicz's work.

In "What Really Happened Aboard the Banbury? Reading Gombrowicz with Eve Kosofsky Sedgwick," Błażej Warkocki revisits Gombrowicz's "The Events on the Banbury," questioning and develop-ing Tomasz Kaliściak's interpretation of it as a story about "homosexual panic," using Eve Kosofsky Sedgwick's understanding of this concept. Thus, drawing upon her discussion of Herman Melville's *Billy Budd*, Warkocki poses Sedgwick's question to Gombrowicz's text: "Is men's desire for other men the great preservative of the masculinist hierarchies of Western culture, or is it among the most potent of the threats against them?"[27] Warkocki attempts here to understand homosexual identity in the context of Gombrowicz's story.

The unsettling power of immaturity is the subject of Daniel Pratt's article, "Affect and Youth: Reading Gombrowicz with Deleuze." Form and immaturity have long been understood as the two major terms in Gombrowicz's work. Form has been discussed a good deal in the schol-arship and by Gombrowicz himself, but what has been less discussed, and less understood, is immaturity. This essay re-examines the role of immaturity and Form in Gombrowicz's work by reading it through the perspective of Deleuze's notion of affect.

Tul'si (Tuesday) Bhambry's essay, "'The Quieter the Louder Indeed': Silence, Space, and Subjectivity in *Trans-Atlantyk*," examines Gombrowicz's model of exilic authorship as presented in *Trans-Atlantyk*, his first work of fiction written in Argentina. Reading the allegorical con-stellations of characters within *Trans-Atlantyk* alongside Maurice Blan-chot's reflections on the role of silence in the writing process, Bhambry argues that, for Gombrowicz, the writer must not only negotiate the opposing demands of creativity and control but also confront silence. Bhambry's discussion of the interrelated problems of subjectivity and authorship contributes to current debates on artistic explorations of cre-ativity, literary self-reflexivity, and twentieth-century writers' responses to cultural and theoretical representations of authorship.

Affect is the theme of Silvia G. Dapía's "The Anatomy of Feeling in Gombrowicz's 'A Premeditated Crime' ('Zbrodnia z premedytacją')." In this essay, rather than engaging with the distinction between pre-reflective affect and culturally circumscribed emotion, Dapía prefers to think of affect and emotion as operating on a fluid line of continuity. Following Susanne Langer, a true precursor of the "affective turn," for whom feeling is nothing other than a "phase," a "mode of appearance," of the body under certain conditions,[28] Dapía provides a close reading of Gombrowicz's short story. A focus on feeling therefore allows her to avoid the problems of intentionality associated with certain restricted conceptions of affect and thus permits her to develop here a more thorough and nuanced analysis of the felt or affective dimensions of human interaction as it appears in this story.

The Political Gombrowicz

Ultimately, in the third and last part of this volume, "The Political Gombrowicz," we attempt to illuminate a relatively unexplored area in Gombrowicz studies: Gombrowicz's relationship to politics. There seems to be consensus among Gombrowicz scholars that the author did not appear to be interested in politics. Blas Matamoro (1989) insisted on the fact that Gombrowicz stayed twenty-four tumultuous years in Argentina, during which he witnessed three coups d'état (1943, 1955, 1962) and, between 1953 and 1956, the crisis and fall of Peronism, the bombing of Plaza de Mayo (June 16, 1955), and the so-called "Revolución Libertadora," and none of this seemed to have found a place in his reflections. Similarly, while in Poland, although he dedicated some articles in the newspaper *Czas* to fascism and Nazism as a result of his trip to Italy and Vienna in the late 1930s, he did not seem to consider the fascist movement in political terms. Neither Mussolini's invasion of Ethiopia in 1935 nor the Italian-German intervention in Spain appeared to arouse his interest. These events found a place in his writings in 1955, but not in the late 1930s.[29] At the time when many artists made clear political choices for or against fascism, Gombrowicz did not feel the need to engage on either side. Similarly, he appeared to have an ambivalent position in relationship to "People's Poland," appearing to accept at one point in time his inclusion in this pantheon and ultimately refusing his inclusion in it.[30] "My writing must remain what it is, particularly in its non-commitment to politics and refusal to be harnessed into its service. I pursue one policy alone: my own. I'm a separate State."[31] Although it is true that he acknowledges his "non-commitment to politics," nothing prevents us from reading his texts politically. Undoubtedly, totalitarianism was the central political feature of Gombrowicz's time, and it is true that totalitarianism still haunts our thoughts. In this chapter, we attempt to trace a topography of his ambivalent reactions, flirtations with, and rejections of fascism, including his apparent fascination with the "wild youth" that throughout Europe highlights the militarism and barbarity of pre-World War II society.

What was Gombrowicz's position toward the "Jewish question" in the interwar years? What did he mean when, speaking to an Argentine audience at the Teatro del Pueblo, he claimed that not only Italy and Germany but also Poland and the rest of Europe had developed a desire for barbarism? What does the image of the "wild youth," which appeared as early as 1939 in *Possessed* (*Opętani*) and as late as the late 1960s in *Pornografia*, stand for, and what does it tell us about subjectivities that emerged within totalitarian governments? What were Gombrowicz's reactions toward Germany when he arrived in West Berlin in the 1960s with the support of a Ford Foundation grant? How was it possible that although his name and work had been suppressed for years in "People's Poland," his plays were performed in Poland? What were the editorial policies that governed the publication of his work in and outside Poland? These questions have enormous stakes in Gombrowicz's scholarship. Moreover, given a pervasive concern with fascism and a revival of ethno-nationalism and anti-Semitism in Poland and other countries, Gombrowicz's reflections on Italian fascism, his impressions of Austria's reaction to the *Anschluss*, and his reactions to the "Jewish question" may help us achieve a deeper understanding of these transnational authoritarian movements through the opinions of an author who witnessed them and had a first-hand knowledge of them. In addition, our examination of the performance of his plays in the 1970s and 1980s, and in post-Soviet Poland will give us insight into the reception not only of Gombrowicz's work in Poland but of policies that regulated Polish theater before and after 1989.

In Jerzy Jarzębski's article, "Gombrowicz's Wild Youth: The 'Ferdydurkean Individual' Fades Away," an interrogation of Gombrowicz's relationship to politics assumes an interrogation about his attitude toward the collective. To the "Ferdydurkean individual" or generation born at the beginning of the twentieth century, Jarzębski opposes the "wild youth" model, a generation associated with "military schools," sports, the modern world, submission to a leader, and acceptance of cruelty. He traces Gombrowicz's obsessive image of a "wild youth" in his writings, with special attention to *Possessed* (1939) and *Pornografia* (1960), connecting this image with the emergence of the new individual's collective behavior in the interwar period throughout Europe.

Andrzej Stanisław Kowalczyk's article, "'Their Astounding Strength in Overcoming Their Past...': The Memory of Nazism in the Berlin Diary," discusses Gombrowicz's position toward totalitarian ideologies. In the late 1930s, the subject of Italian fascism and German Nazism appeared several times in Gombrowicz's works. Further, different versions of the same events appear in different works written in different periods of his life. After an examination of Gombrowicz's diverse reactions to fascism throughout his work, Kowalczyk focuses on the memories of Nazism in Gombrowicz's *Berlin Diary*, juxtaposing the author's own memories with those of the Berliners and the Poles.

In 1926, Gombrowicz wrote a short story about the misadventures of an accommodated Polish-Jewish youth, "Jakub Czarniecki's Memoir" (Krótkim pamiętniku Jakuba Czarnieckiego, 1926), in which he clearly shows that the development of Polishness and Jewishness as two compatible layers of one's identity was impossible in the interwar period. Gombrowicz was drawn to Polish Jews from his earliest youth. A case in point was his relationship with the Polish-Jewish writer and artist

Bruno Schulz (1892–42). In his article, "Gombrowicz-Schulz: From Duel to Double," through the description of Gombrowicz's relationship to Schulz, Jean-Pierre Salgas shows us how Gombrowicz's discourse of Jewish otherness serves as a template for his reflections on self, his attitude to Form, and Polish identity.

As a Pole living in exile, Gombrowicz's works were suspected by the communist government, although his works were published and performed during periods of liberalization, such as the Polish October era. In his article, "The Politics of Performing Gombrowicz in Communist and Post-communist Poland," Allen J. Kuharski's interest is in how various cliques or factions within Polish theatrical and cultural life before 1989 sought to claim legitimacy through identification with the performance of his works. Extending to Polish theater artists producing Gombrowicz abroad (expatriots/dissidents), this essay includes early examples of international touring of Polish productions of Gombrowicz in the 1970s and the complications around the ongoing performance of his works within Poland in the 1980s.

In her essay, "The Editorial Adventures of a Writer Without Readers," Klementyna Suchanow examines the rather complex publication history of Gombrowicz's works in the European market. Based on a rich archival source of the author's correspondence with editors, she tells us the story of his editorial adventures with emphasis on France and the Anglo-Saxon countries. Extensive correspondence between Gombrowicz and Jerzy Giedroyc, the Polish editor of Gombrowicz's works and publisher of the Paris-based Polish monthly *Kultura*, serves as a basis for Suchanow's narrative of Gombrowicz's publishing adventures in the French market. English language editors, particularly American publishers, and references to episodes of his publication history in Argentina and Spain are included in this fascinating narrative which reflects the policies and politics that surrounded the publication of Gombrowicz's works.

Notes

1 Jarzębski, *Gombrowicz: nasz współczesny*; Smorąg-Goldberg, *Gombrowicz*; Tomaszewski, *Gombrowicz*; Lawaty and Zybura, *Gombrowicz*.
2 Giroud, *World*.
3 Gombrowicz, *Memories*; Gombrowicz, *Bacacay*; Gombrowicz, *Guide*.
4 *The Polish Review*, Vol. 60, no. 2 (Spring 2015). There was also a special issue in English of *Tekstualia*, 2014, no. 1 (2) dedicated to Gombrowicz and two avant-garde Polish writers, Stanisław Ignacy Witkiewicz (Witkacy) and Bruno Schulz.
5 De Bruyn, *Literary Polemics*.
6 Oklot, *Phantasms*.
7 Gasyna, *Polish*.
8 Lutostański.
9 Harnesberger, *Sovereignty*.
10 Goddard, *Gombrowicz*.

11 Wojtas, *Translating.*

12 Bourne, "Trans-National."

13 Basch, Schiller and Blanc, *Nations Unbound*; Schiller, Basch and Blanc-Szanton, "Transnationalism."

14 Levitt and Nyberg-Sørensen, "Transnational Turn."

15 Vertovec, "Conceiving,"; Vertovec, "Transnationalism."

16 Vertovec, "Conceiving," 1. See also Bradatan, Popan and Melton, "Transnationality."

17 Bauman commented similarly that "The new migration casts a question mark upon the bond between identity and citizenship, individual and place, neighborhood and belonging." See Bauman, "Globalised City."

18 Shaw, "Deconstructing."

19 A seminar on "Gombrowicz and Translation" was held Oct. 27–28, 2003 at the University Wrocław. Organized by the Institutes of Romance Philology University of Wrocław, the Jagiellonian University, and the Centre d' Etudes de la Culture Polonaise from Université Charles de Gaulle-Lille III, it resulted in Skibińskiej's *Gombrowicz i tłumacze.* In 2014, Wojtas published a volume dedicated to Gombrowicz's translating process, *Translating Gombrowicz.* Based on deconstruction and Gadamer's hermeneutics, Wojtas's main interest lies on "the transference" of the existential content of some of Gombrowicz's Polish selected works to the English translations.

20 The title of the English translation (*The Marriage*) (like the second Spanish translation, *El matrimonio*, and the French translation, *Mariage*) is wrong. The English word "marriage" refers to the institution, while the English word "wedding" refers to the ceremony. Accordingly, the title *The Marriage* misconstrues the main point of the drama, which is not about the institution but about the ceremony.

21 Lefevere, *Translation.*

22 Maerkle, "Aernout Mik."

23 Because affect is "unformed" and "unstructured" (unlike emotions), as Brian Massumi asserts, it can be transmitted between bodies. See Massumi, *Parables*, 260. Teresa Brennan claims, "The transmission of affect means that we are not self-contained in terms of our energies. There is no secure distinction between the 'individual' and the 'environment.'" Brennan, *Transmission*, 6.

24 For a comprehensive discussion of Form in Gombrowicz, see Jarzębski, "Pojęcie," 313. For studies that explore Gombrowicz's notion of subjectivity from the perspective of gender and queer studies, see notably Ziarek, "The Scar," 213–44; Kuharski, "Witold," 267–86; and Sołtysik, "Struggle," 245–67. These articles are in Ziarek, *Grimaces.* See also Jarzębski, *Podglądanie*; Ritz, "Język pożądania," 196–261; Ritz, "Inexpressible Desire," 254–76; Grimstad, "Gender Trouble," 222–53; Grimstad, "L'homoérotisme," 231–41; Bielecki, *Literatura*; and Bielecki, *Interpretacja.*

25 In the second edition, Gombrowicz changed the protagonist's name from "Jakub" to "Stefan" and the story's title to "The Memoir of Stefan Czarniecki" (Pamiętnik Stefana Czarnieckiego).

26 In 1957, it was re-released as *Bakakaj* and included five additional stories.

27 Sedgwick, *Epistemology*, 93.

28 Langer, *Mind*, Vol. 1, 23.

29 In *Operetta*, Gombrowicz appeared to have made a reference to the events of 1935. See Jeleński, "Od bosości," 3–28. Available in English translation by Kuharski and Bukowski in Kuharski, "Theatre of Witold Gombrowicz."

30 Sandauer, "Politics," 33–39.

31 Ibid., 33.

Part I
Lost in Translation

1 The Rex Café, Buenos Aires, 1947

On the Spanish Translation of Gombrowicz's *Ferdydurke*[1]

Daniel Balderston

As is well known, the first translation of Gombrowicz into any language was the collective translation undertaken by the Polish writer with an unruly group of some twenty friends and acquaintances in the chess parlor of the Confitería Rex in 1947.[2] It was published by Editorial Argos in Buenos Aires in that year with Gombrowicz crediting Virgilio Piñera, the Cuban writer, as leading the group, which was also composed of such people as the Cuban Humberto Rodríguez Tomeu, the Argentine Adolfo de Obieta (son of Macedonio Fernández), and many others.[3] I wrote about the relations between *Ferdydurke* and Piñera's novel *Pequeñas maniobras* more than thirty years ago,[4] but could not have known then that Gombrowicz gave Piñera nineteen pages related to the project, including seventeen pages of hand-corrected typescript. These were sold by Piñera's friend and heir Antón Arrufat (along with other Piñera materials) to the Rare Books and Manuscripts Division of the Firestone Library at Princeton University.[5]

In what follows, I analyze these pages, most of which correspond to the latter part of what was to be Chapter 9 of the Argos edition. I also refer to the English translation done directly from the Polish by Danuta Borchardt and published by Yale University Press in 2000.[6] The importance of these pages is that they show some aspects of the translation process, including handwritten corrections by Gombrowicz. The pages also include a letter from Gombrowicz to Graciela Peyrou and some notes for the preface to the Spanish edition, as well as some notes on style ("Decir").

In the Argos preface, Gombrowicz explains that "Esta traducción fué efectuada por mí y sólo de lejos se parece al texto original" ("This translation was carried out by me and only distantly resembles the original"),[7] then goes on to credit Virgilio Piñera as leader of the committee[8] and Cecilia Benedit de Debenedetti for apparently material support. He concludes the discussion of the translation by saying that it was the result of "amenas discusiones ... realizadas casi todas en la sala de ajedrez de la confitería Rex bajo la enigmática y bondadosa sonrisa del director de la sala, maestro Paulino Frydman" ("pleasant discussions ... almost all of which took place in the chess hall of the Rex Café under the enigmatic and generous smile of the director of the hall, Master Paulino Frydman)."[9] Frydman was indeed a Polish-born chess player awarded the title of International Master in 1955. In his *Diary*, Gombrowicz credits Frydman with giving him money in 1943 to go to the Sierras de Córdoba to recover from a persistent fever, though the fever turned out to be the result of Frydman's thermometer which was not working correctly.[10]

There are several letters from Gombrowicz to Piñera and Rodríguez Tomeu, written in January 1947 from Cecilia Benedit de Debenedetti's house in the Sierras de Córdoba town of Salsipuedes.[11] In them Gombrowicz speaks of Benedit's hospitality and support of the translation, at the same time urging Piñera and Rodríguez Tomeu to carry on with the project. There is also the information that Gombrowicz met Benedit at the home of Antonio Berni, the notable Argentine painter.[12] Gombrowicz called Benedit "Condesa," and refers to his life at this point in Buenos Aires as oscillating between the realm of the "Condesa" and the area near the Retiro train stations (Gombrowicz's preferred cruising grounds).

In a letter to Graciela Peyrou, a writer and sister of the better-known writer Manuel Peyrou, Gombrowicz asked her to correct the Spanish translation and to make three typed copies maintaining the divisions in the text. He signed the letter "el noble y desgraciado Witoldo de Gombrowicz" (the noble and unlucky Witoldo von Gombrowicz). In his letters to Piñera and Rodríguez Tomeu, Gombrowicz refers to Peyrou as "Graziella" which seems to establish her as the typist, though perhaps of a clean copy only. This background helps us to understand the letter to Graciela Peyrou noted earlier. In this letter, Gombrowicz adds, "¿Qué hizo, Graciela, con *Ferdydurke*? Cuide de no dar un paso en falso porque ya sabe que es un escrito delicado y de mucha responsabilidad" ("Graciela, what have you done with *Ferdydurke*? Be careful not to make any false steps because you know that it is a delicate piece of writing and one on which much rests.") (Figure 1.1).

An important page of the Princeton materials is a brief and partly illegible handwritten notation called "Decir" (Figure 1.2) in Gombrowicz's handwriting. In it he says the following:

> Decir. Sacrificar la verdad a la ironía no me parece acertado. Si decimos que ?? debe entenderse que ello queda referido a lo que se ha distorsionado, o alterado misteriosamente (?) en toda interacción (?), y no a las probables gaffes que encierre la traducción, a los errores tipográficos, al cambio de letras, etc.--cosas éstas que aun en la mayoría (?) de las traducciones siempre se dan ?calireten?" ("Saying. Sacrificing truth to irony doesn't seem right to me. If we say that ??? should be understood as saying that what it tells about has been distorted, or mysteriously altered, in every interaction (?), and not the probable gaffes that the translation contains, the typographical errors, the changes of letters, and so forth, all things that happen in the majority of translations).

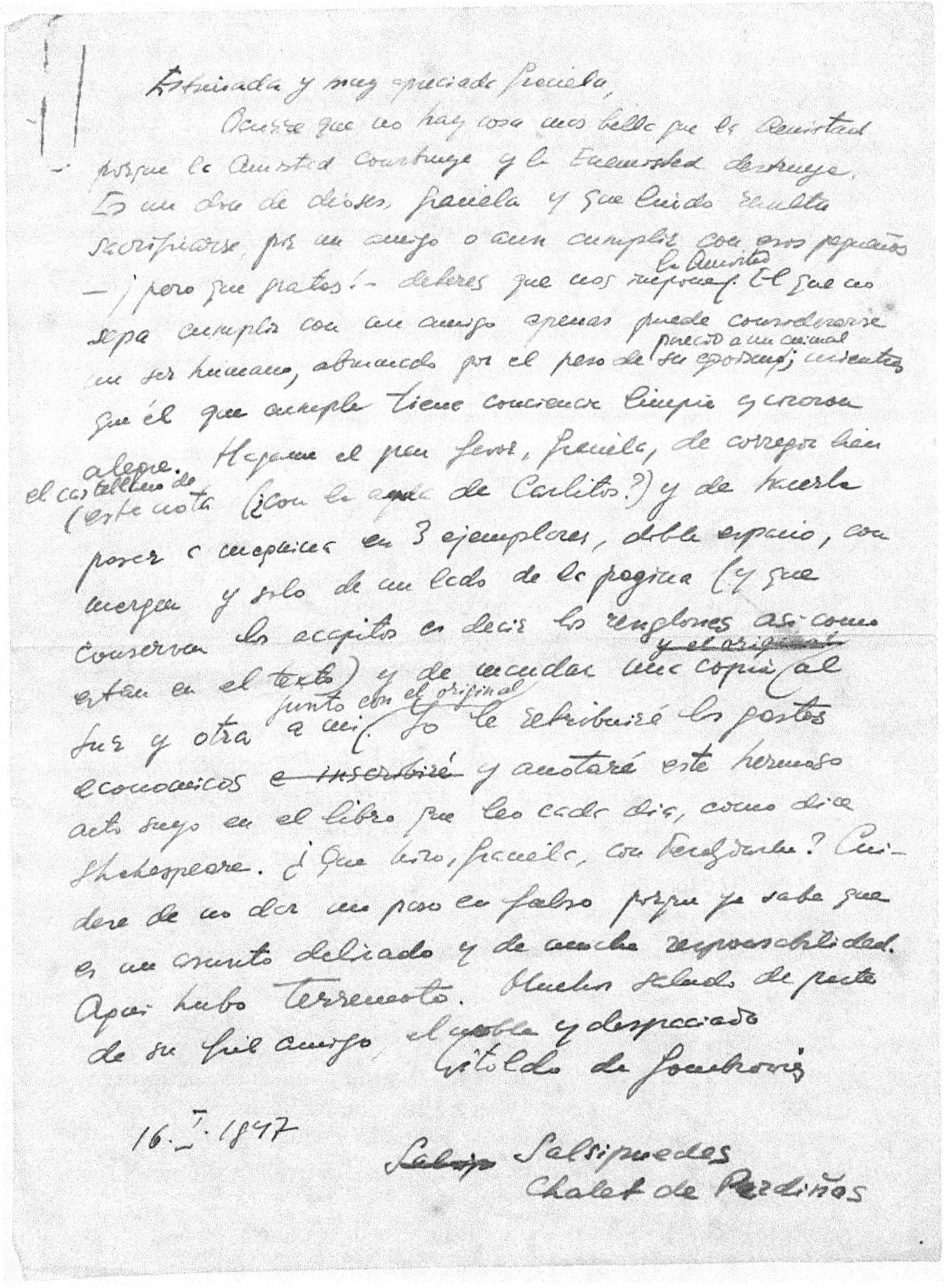

Estimada y muy apreciada Graciela,

Ocurre que no hay cosa más bella que la Amistad porque la Amistad construye y la Enemistad destruye. Es un don de dioses, Graciela y que lindo resulta sacrificarse por un amigo o aun cumplir con esos pequeños — ¡pero que gratos! — deberes que nos impone la Amistad. El que no sepa cumplir con un amigo apenas puede considerarse un ser humano, abrumado por el peso de su egoísmo; parecido a un animal; mientras que él que cumple tiene conciencia limpia y generosa alegre.

Hágame el gran favor, Graciela, de corregir bien el castellano de esta nota (¿con la ayuda de Carlitos?) y de hacerla poner a máquina en 3 ejemplares, doble espacio, con margen y sólo de un lado de la página (y que conserven los acápites es decir los renglones así como ~~y el original~~ están en el texto) y de mandar una copia al Sur y otra junto con el original a mí. Yo le retribuiré los gastos económicos ~~e inscribiré~~ y anotaré este hermoso acto suyo en el libro que leo cada día, como dice Shakespeare. ¿Qué hizo, Graciela, con Ferdydurke? Cuídese de no dar un paso en falso porque ya sabe que es un asunto delicado y de mucha responsabilidad. Aquí hubo terremoto. Muchos saludos de parte de su fiel amigo, el noble y despreciado

Witoldo de Gombrowicz

16.I.1947

~~Salsip~~ Salsipuedes
Chalet de Perdiños

Figure 1.1 Gombrowicz's letter to Graciela Peyrou in which he asks, "what have you done with *Ferdydurke*?"

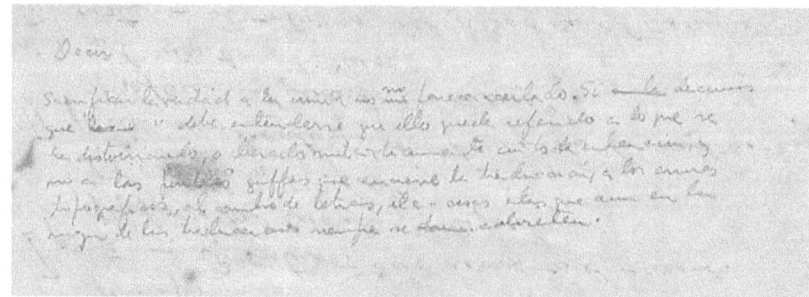

Figure 1.2 The "Decir" in which Gombrowicz indicates a concern about the accuracy and style of the translation.

In this note, written on the verso of the page in which he outlines the Spanish edition, he also notes "<u>Ojo</u>. Algunas partes del texto no están todavía corregidas y falta la última revisión" ("Attention: some parts of the text are not yet corrected and the final revision has not been done)." This indicates a concern with the accuracy and style of the translation, something that is also a concern in the note by the translators (perhaps written by Piñera).

Now it is worth examining the translation and comparing it to the Polish version and to the Borchardt translation. On page 5 of the Princeton materials (page 161 of the typescript and page 161 of the Argos edition), we read:

> La colegiala, en verdad, dormía no privada sino públicamente, no tenía vida nocturna propia y la dura publicidad de la muchacha la juntaba con Europa y América, con los campos de trabajo, con los cuarteles, las banderas, los hoteles y las estaciones, creaba perspectivas enormemente vastas, excluía la posibilidad de un rincón propio.

The typescript is identical to the Argos edition here. The Polish version reads:

> Pensjonarka spała właściwie nie prywatnie, lecz publicznie, nie miała nocnego życia prywatnego, a twarda publiczność dziewczyny łączyła ją z Europą, z Ameryką, z Hitlerem, Mussolinim i Stalinem, z obozami pracy, z chorągwią, z hotelem, dworcem kolejowym, stwarzała zasięg niezmiernie rozległy, kącik własny wykluczała.[13]

The notable change here is the exclusion in the Spanish version of the specific mention of Hitler, Mussolini, and Stalin. On the same page, there is an identical typo in the manuscript and in the Argos edition: a reference to Fred Astaire and Gingers, not Ginger, Rogers; a strikethrough eliminates a reference to two zlotys (six in the Polish version).

On this and the following pages it is clear that the handwritten corrections—in fountain pen in Gombrowicz's handwriting and in pencil in some other hand—correspond precisely to the version that was published by Argos. A minor difference appears on page 164 of the typescript: "¡Oh, el pandemaonio de la colegiala moderna!," which becomes "¡Oh, el pandemonium de la colegiala moderna!" on page 163 of the Argos edition. The Polish text reads, "O, pandemonium pensjonarki nowoczesnej!"[14] Here the correction of the spelling, in pencil, then cedes to the use of the Latin word. Later in the same paragraph "belleza" is corrected to "hermosura" and "hermosura" to "beldad," no doubt because of a prejudice in Spanish style against the repetition of words in near proximity; the English here repeats "beauty."[15] The passage is interesting in the typescript, since it shows an extended concern with questions of style (Figure 1.3):

Hay algo ultra conmovedor en eso de que sólo las personas sujetas a la disciplina de la ~~belleza~~ hermosura tienen acceso a cierta°s ~~vergüenzas~~ vergonzosos contenidos psíquicos de la humanidad. ¡Oh, la muchacha, aquel receptáculo de la ~~infamia~~ vergüenza cerrado con la llave de la ~~hermosura!~~ beldad! Aquí, ~~a~~ en este temple, cada uno, joven o viejo depositaba tales cosas que posiblemente preferiría morir tres veces seguidas y quemarse a ~~fumaza lenta (?)~~ fuego lento antes de que ~~eso~~ fuese^n dad~~o~~^{as} a la publicidad... Y el rostro del siglo – el rostro del siglo XX, del siglo de la confusión de las edades, aparecía dubitativamente como un Sileno~~,.~~ ~~desde la espesura.~~ (It's a wondrous thing that only those constrained by ~~beauty~~ loveliness have access to certain ~~shames~~ shameful psychological contents of humankind. Oh, a girl, that receptacle of ~~disgrace~~ shame, locked under ~~loveliness~~ beauty's key!" Here, ~~at~~ in this temple, each man, whether young or old brought such things that he would probably prefer to die three times and be roasted ~~slow fume~~ (?) over slow fire rather than publicize them.... And the face of this century – the face of the twentieth century, the century of all centuries gone mad, appeared dubiously like a Silenus ~~in the thicket).~~[16]

The corrected version is very close to the published one, save that "dubitativamente" (dubiously) is changed to "dudoso" (doubtful) in the latter. The Polish version here ends, "jak Sylen z gęstwiny..."[17] ("like Silenus in the thicket"), which shows that the deleted "desde la espesura" (from the thicket) corresponds to a detail in the Polish version that was left out in the Spanish translation.

In the following paragraph, there are a series of people mentioned whose names are somewhat Hispanized: "Zuta," but then "Marisita" and "Luis" and "Enrique," then "Pucho y Taco" changed to "Bobek y Hopek" (Figure 1.4).

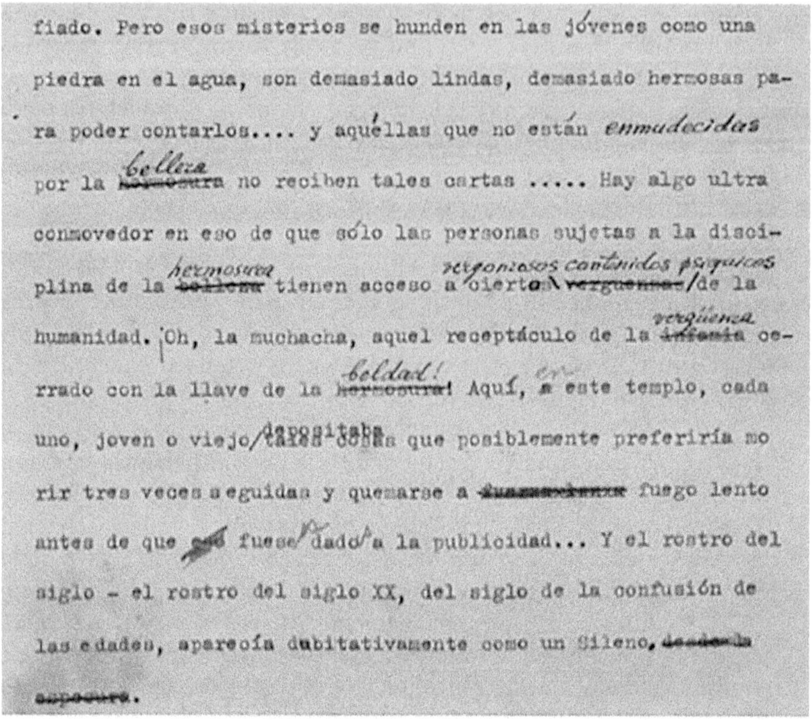

fiado. Pero esos misterios se hunden en las jóvenes como una

piedra en el agua, son demasiado lindas, demasiado hermosas pa-

ra poder contarlos.... y aquéllas que no están *enmudecidas*

por la ~~hermosura~~ *belleza* no reciben tales cartas ..... Hay algo ultra

conmovedor en eso de que sólo las personas sujetas a la disci-

plina de la ~~belleza~~ *hermosura* tienen acceso a ~~cierta~~ *vergonzosos contenidos psíquicos* ~~vergüenza~~ /de la

humanidad. ¡Oh, la muchacha, aquel receptáculo de la ~~infamia~~ *vergüenza* ce-

rrado con la llave de la ~~hermosura~~ *beldad!* Aquí, *en* este templo, cada

uno, joven o viejo/~~tales cosas~~ *deposita* que posiblemente preferiría mo

rir tres veces seguidas y quemarse a ~~fuuuuuuuu~~ fuego lento

antes de que ~~se~~ fuese dado/a la publicidad... Y el rostro del

siglo - el rostro del siglo XX, del siglo de la confusión de

las edades, aparecía dubitativamente como un Sileno, ~~deademda~~

~~aapoouue~~.

Figure 1.3 Gombrowicz's annotations on this manuscript page are a clear indication of his concern for the translation's style.

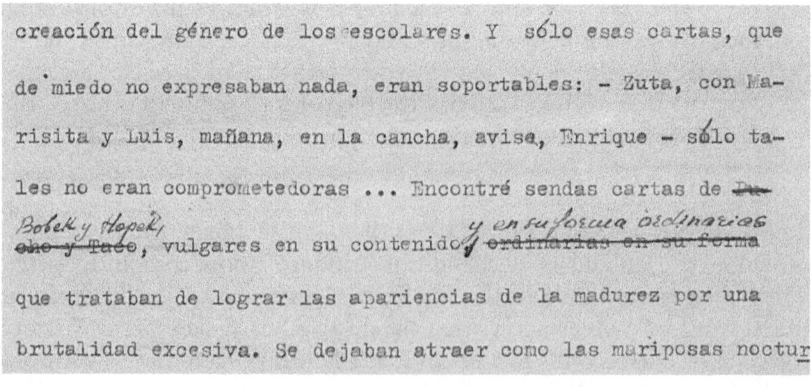

creación del género de los escolares. Y sólo esas cartas, que

de miedo no expresaban nada, eran soportables: – Zuta, con Ma-

risita y Luis, mañana, en la cancha, avise, Enrique – sólo ta-

les no eran comprometedoras ... Encontré sendas cartas de ~~Pu~~

~~cho y Taco~~ *Bobek y Hopek,*, vulgares en su contenido/ *y en su forma ordinarias* ~~ordinarias en su forma~~

que trataban de lograr las apariencias de la madurez por una

brutalidad excesiva. Se dejaban atraer como las mariposas noctu_

Figure 1.4 In this manuscript fragment, we can see Gombrowicz using typical Hispanic names but then changing the original names of "Pucho y Taco" to "Bobek y Hopek."

In the Polish, these are Żuta, Marysia, Olek, Heniek, Mizdral, and Hopek, showing that, at least in the final case, "Taco" was entertained as a possibility but then discarded in favor of the original "Hopek." Earlier in the paragraph a reference to King Sigismund Augustus (Zygmunt August) in the Polish is nowhere to be found in the Spanish, confirming a pattern that begins to emerge of the erasure of some of the Polish specificity of the text.

The following paragraph gives several examples of *lapsus linguae*, cleverly rendered in the Spanish: "trémolo de la bandera" (triumph of the flag) becomes "tremuslo de la bandera" (three thigh flag), and "el muro de la patria" (the wall of fatherland) becomes "el muslo de la patria" (the thigh of fatherland).[18] Borchardt notes the importance of the body part in question in the novel, and a bit later a whole translated poem consists of the reiteration of "calves" (Łydki); the Spanish version uses "los muslos" (thighs). Here the English version is a bit clumsier than the Spanish, with "onward, don't lag behind" becoming "onward, don't leg behind," which is fine, but then with a very forced reference to "citizens from the town of Lemno" who say "we-Legnites" instead of "we-Lemnites."[19] The bawdiness of the novel is a concern, with another example of a careful stylistic revision: "Asimismo en los escritos, ~~bastante~~, por otra parte, ^bastante^ lujuriosos" (Similarly in writings [which were] ~~rather~~ otherwise ^rather^ lascivious).[20] In fact, after the reference to the jazz age, there is an additional reference in the Spanish (but not in the Polish) to licentiousness: "la 'desnudez en la playa'" (nudity on the beach) (Figure 1.5).[21]

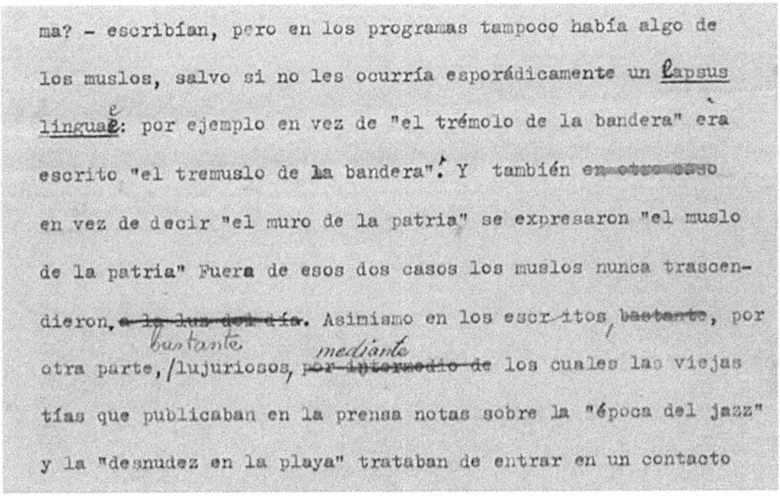

Figure 1.5 This passage provides examples of *lapsus linguae* in the translation into Spanish.

On page 167, there are dozens of corrections of lower case nouns
that were made into upper-case nouns, though the corresponding articles were mostly changed from upper to lower case. Since the novel
is known for its allegorizing of abstract qualities, Gombrowicz paid
careful attention to make sure that his team wrote "la Epoca Joven y
la Juventud en Guardia" (Young Era, and Youth on the Watch)[22] and
not (as at first) "La época joven y La Juventud en guardia." There are
handwritten insertions of "asonantes" (assonant rhyme or half rhyme)
twice here, suggesting that the group struggled with the correct rhetorical term (Figure 1.6).

The next page contains the translation mentioned earlier. A poem "El
Verso" reads (Figure 1.7):

> Los horizontes estallan como botellas
> La mancha verde cruce hacia el cielo
> Me traslado de nuevo a la sombra de los pinos
> desde allá:
> Tomo el ultimo trago insaciable
> De mi primavera cotidiana[23]
> [Horizons burst like flasks
> a green blotch swells high in the clouds
> I move back to the shadow of the pine—
> and there:
> with greedy gulps I drink
> my diurnal springtime[24]]

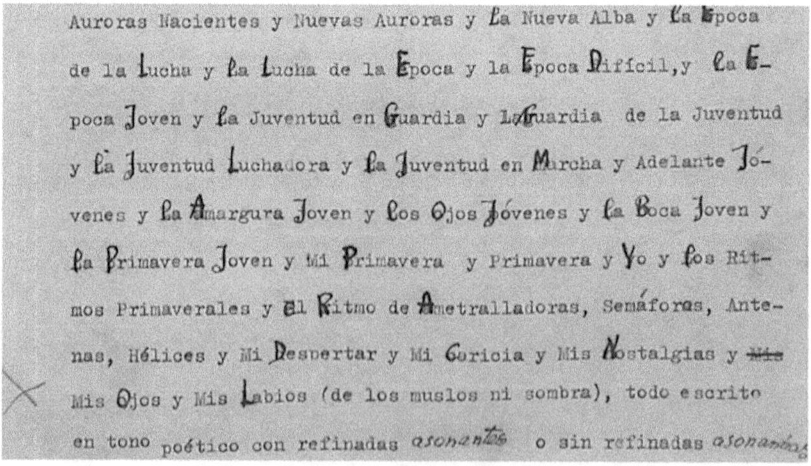

Auroras Nacientes y Nuevas Auroras y La Nueva Alba y La Época
de la Lucha y La Lucha de la Época y la Época Difícil, y La E-
poca Joven y La Juventud en Guardia y La Guardia de la Juventud
y La Juventud Luchadora y La Juventud en Marcha y Adelante Jóvenes y La Amargura Joven y Los Ojos Jóvenes y La Boca Joven y
La Primavera Joven y Mi Primavera y Primavera y Yo y Los Rit-
mos Primaverales y El Ritmo de Ametralladoras, Semáforos, Ante-
nas, Hélices y Mi Despertar y Mi Coricia y Mis Nostalgias y Mis
Mis Ojos y Mis Labios (de los muslos ni sombra), todo escrito
en tono poético con refinadas *asonantes* o sin refinadas *asonan-*

Figure 1.6 This portion of the typescript shows the particular care Gombrowicz took to give just the right written rendition to the
translation.

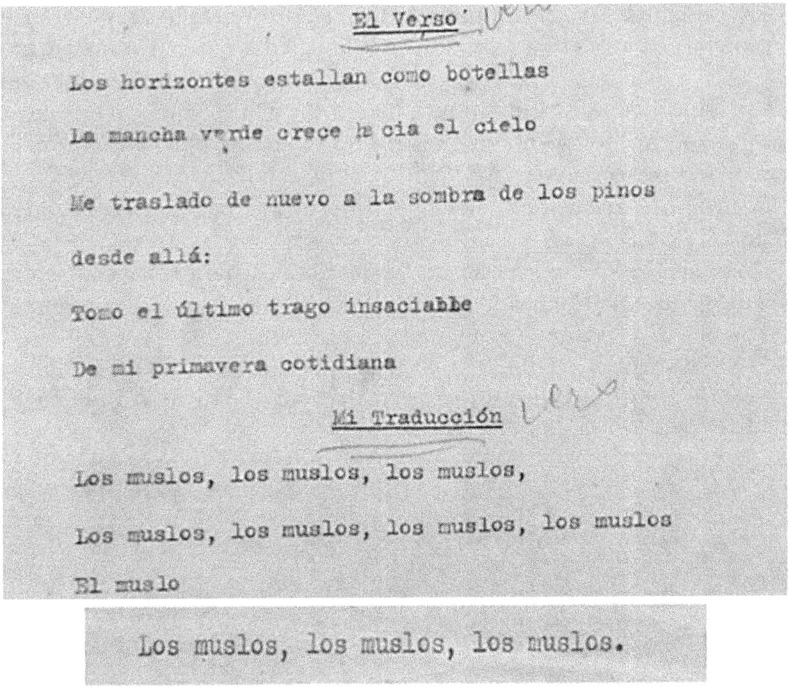

El Verso

Los horizontes estallan como botellas

La mancha verde crece hacia el cielo

Me traslado de nuevo a la sombra de los pinos

desde allá:

Tomo el último trago insaciable

De mi primavera cotidiana

Mi Traducción

Los muslos, los muslos, los muslos,

Los muslos, los muslos, los muslos, los muslos

El muslo

Los muslos, los muslos, los muslos.

Figure 1.7 Illustrations (a) and (b), from two pages of the typescript, show the poem "El Verso" and the translation.

This is translated as:

> Los muslos, los muslos, los muslos,
> Los muslos, los muslos, los muslos, los muslos
> El muslo
> Los muslos, los muslos, los muslos
> [Thighs, Thighs, Thighs
> Thighs, Thighs, Thighs, Thighs
> Thighs
> Thighs, Thighs Thighs][25]

Argentina enters the picture just afterwards, when what Borchardt translates as "urban and rural citizens"[26] becomes "estancieros" (ranch owners).[27] There is a similar reference to "hacendados" (large landowners) on the following page.

On page 170 of the manuscript the most interesting details are those in the description of the "suboficial" of the words "con calma sensual y sentimental." The English refers to his "exceptionally sensuous and lyrical soul."[28] The very odd change from "mi métrica" (my metrics) to "mi fe de nacimiento" (my birth certificate), an emendation of an obvious mistake by the committee (the English refers to "my birth certificate"[29]), is a pencil correction in a hand that is not Gombrowicz's. On this page that other person made numerous other corrections. A particularly interesting instance here is the clause "ningún ~~estanciero hacendero~~ hacendado, sino un muchacho exilado, muchacho perdido» [no ~~small landowner farmer~~ large landowner but a boy in exile, a lost boy],[30] where the first insertion is not by Gombrowicz, but the second one is (Figure 1.8).

On page 172 of the typescript, "Kopyrda" is changed to "Kopeida," which is the name that appears in the published Argentinean version, although the Polish has "Kopyrda" (Figure 1.9).

A similar phonetic detail is on page 173, where "Así" (Thus) is changed to "O si," (Or if), which suggests that the typescript is based on an oral rather than a written text.

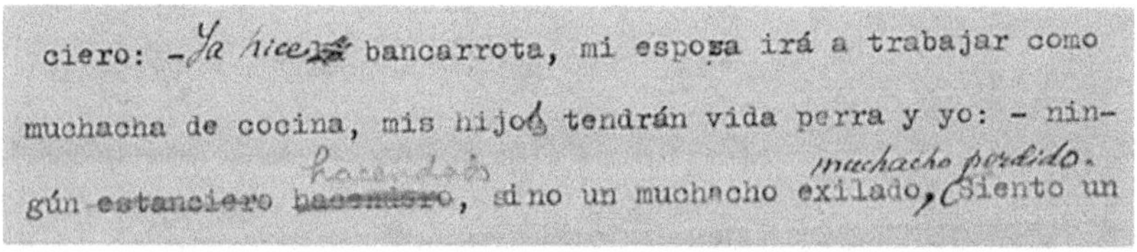
ciero: –Ya hice ~~la~~ bancarrota, mi esposa irá a trabajar como
muchacha de cocina, mis hijos tendrán vida perra y yo: – nin-
gún ~~estanciero~~ ~~hacendero~~ hacendado, sino un muchacho exilado, muchacho perdido. Siento un

Figure 1.8 In this segment of typescript, we see Gombrowicz's handwritten insertions of the phrases "hacendado" and "muchacho perdido."

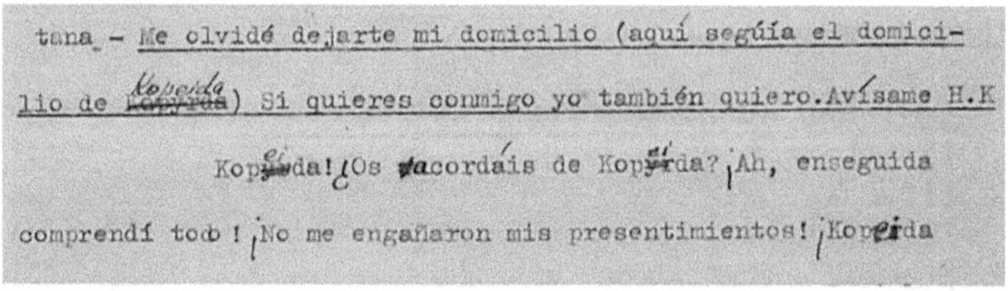
tana – Me olvidé dejarte mi domicilio (aquí seguía el domici-
lio de ~~Kopyrda~~ Kopeida) Si quieres conmigo yo también quiero. Avísame H.K

Kopeida! ¿Os acordáis de Kopeida? ¡Ah, enseguida
comprendí todo! ¡No me engañaron mis presentimientos! ¡Kopeida

Figure 1.9 Here, we can see "Kopyrda" changed to "Kopeida" along with Gombrowicz's particular attention to accents and punctuation.

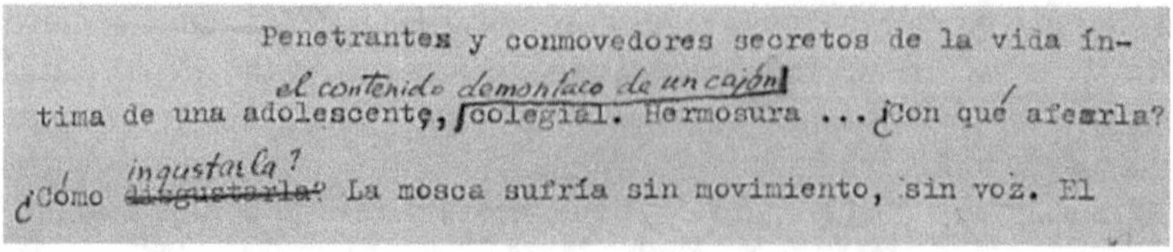
Penetrantes y conmovedores secretos de la vida ín-
tima de una adolescente, colegial. el contenido demoníaco de un cajón Hermosura ... ¿Con qué afearla?
¿Cómo ~~disgustarla?~~ ingustarla? La mosca sufría sin movimiento, sin voz. El

Figure 1.10 Gombrowicz's concern with the phonetics of the translation can clearly be seen in this fragment of the typescript.

A final example of an interesting insertion is "Penetrantes y conmovedores secretos de la vida íntima de una adolescente, el contenido demoniaco de un cajón colegial" [Penetrating and piercing secrets of the private life of an adolescent, the demonic content of a drawer belonging to a schoolgirl] (Figure 1.10).[31]

This insertion by Gombrowicz derives from the Polish original, which reads "Przenikające i przeszywające tajniki żyda osobistego siedemnastolatki, demoniczna zawartość szuflady pensjonarskiej" [The penetrating and piercing secrets of the seventeen-year-old's private life, the demonic content of the schoolgirl's drawer].[32]

In the preface to the translation, Gombrowicz writes:

> Me atrevo a creer que en todo caso la publicación de *Ferydurke* en la América Latina tiene su razón de ser. Existen varias analogías entre la situación espiritual de Polonia y la de este continente. Aquí como allá el problema de la inmadurez cultural es palpitante. Aquí como allá el mayor esfuerzo de la literatura se pierde en imitar las 'maduras' literaturas extranjeras.[33]
>
> (I dare to believe that in any case the publication of *Ferdydurke* in Latin America has its reason for being. There are various analogies between the spiritual situation of Poland and that of this continent. Here as there the problem of cultural immaturity is vibrant. Here as there every effort is wasted in literature in imitating "mature" foreign literatures.)

Gombrowicz's point is echoed by Piñera on the inside front cover of the book where he says that the translation "es una revisión especialmente valiosa para Hispanoamérica—clásico continente de la inmadurez" (it "is an especially valuable revision for Spanish America, a classical continent of immaturity)." The collective translation of *Ferdydurke*, then, was intended as an intervention in Latin American literature in 1947, echoing the impact that the book had had in Poland just before and during the war.

Sergio Romanelli, in his study of an Italian translation of Emily Dickinson, *Gênese do processo tradutório*, argues that looking at the drafts of a translation can suggest intertextual and intratextual dialogues with other translations of the same author, with the literature that is important to the author, and with texts on the theory of translation.[34] This particular case is interesting for the ways in which *Ferdydurke*, in its reflection on cultural immaturity, is profoundly concerned with destabilizing relations between the periphery and the center. It is fascinating to see in detail, then, relations not with the "center" (which, for Gombrowicz and Piñera, was undoubtedly Paris) but between periphery and periphery, surely in an uneasy dialogue with Jorge Luis Borges's ideas about the irreverence of the periphery and his defense of translation as a textual product in itself, a library of texts (as he says in his essay on the English translations of Homer's *Odyssey*).

In conclusion, then, the typescript at Princeton reveals several important things. First, it shows that, in 1947, Gombrowicz knew much more Spanish than is usually stated since the insertions in his handwriting and the avant-textes (the letter to Graciela Peyrou, the outline, and the note "Decir") are quite fluent. Second, it is not at all clear that the translation was really done by twenty people, since only two kinds of handwriting appear in the typescript, Gombrowicz's in pen and the unidentified other corrector in pencil. Third, that the translators slightly toned down the Polish context and subtly added some Argentine language, what Lawrence Venuti calls a "domesticating translation," one that makes its home in the new language and culture. Fourth, the translators were concerned with conveying the raciness of the original, occasionally adding an additional element (like the nudity on the beach) to make sure that the licentiousness of the original comes through. Fifth, that Gombrowicz selected Piñera as the recipient of at least this portion of the manuscript, and that Piñera somehow also ended up with the letter to Graciela Peyrou and with the prefatory materials (which are of undoubted importance). Sixth, it shows that for Gombrowicz the important relationships are not between periphery and center, but rather between periphery and periphery. All of these shed new light on Gombrowicz's thought process during the development of the Buenos Aires translation.

Notes

1 I am very grateful to Klementyna Suchanow, who shared with me some of her extensive archives on Gombrowicz in Argentina. An earlier version appeared in *The Polish Review*, Vol. 60, no. 2 (2015) and is used here with the permission of the editors.
2 For a bibliography of subsequent translations of Gombrowicz in Spanish, see www.gombrowicz.net/Spanish.html
3 Gombrowicz, *Ferdydurke: Novela*, with the notation "*Traducido por el autor, asesorado por un Comité de traducción*" (translated by the author with the aid of a translation committee).
4 Balderston, "Estética," 1–7.
5 Manuscript of the translation of *Ferdydurke* with associated other materials, in Antón Arrufat Papers, Princeton University, hereafter "manuscript."
6 For some interesting notes by Danuta Borchardt on *Ferdydurke* and her translation, see www.corpse.org/archives/issue_5/critical_urgencies/borchar.htm
7 Gombrowicz, *Ferdydurke* (Argos), 13.
8 Piñera's version of his role is described in "Gombrowicz en la Argentina," in Grinberg, *Evocando*, especially 30–1. See also Matamoro (especially 84–5); Piglia in Tcherkaski, *Las cartas*, especially 96–8; Gasparini, *El exilio*, especially 89–148.
9 Gombrowicz, *Ferdydurke* (Argos), 14.
10 Gombrowicz, *Diary*, 168.
11 See www.elcultural.es/version_papel/LETRAS/1447/Gombrowicz_al_completo

12 See http://witoldgombrowicz.blogspot.com/2010/06/witold-gombrowicz-la-condesa-y-retiro.html

13 Borchardt's English version reads, "The schoolgirl actually slept in public, not in private, she had no private life at night, and this hard public life united her with Europe, America, with Hitler, Mussolini, and Stalin, with labor camps, flag waving, hotels, railroad stations, giving her an immensely wide scope, eliminating the need for a room of her own." See Gombrowicz, *Ferdydurke* (Borchardt), 155.

14 "Oh, what pandemonium in the modern schoolgirl's life!" Gombrowicz, *Ferdydurke* (Borchardt), 157.

15 "It's a wondrous thing that only those constrained by *beauty* have access to certain essences of man's psychology. Oh, a girl, that receptacle of shame, under *beauty*'s lock and key!" Gombrowicz, *Ferdydurke* (Borchardt), 158.

16 Translation based mainly on Gombrowicz, *Ferdydurke* (Borchardt), 158.

17 Gombrowicz, *Ferdydurke* (Rój, 1938), 157.

18 Page 166 of typescript, 165 of Argos.

19 Gombrowicz, *Ferdydurke* (Borchardt), 159.

20 Page 166 of typescript, 165 of Argos.

21 Page 166 of typescript, 165 of Argos.

22 Gombrowicz, *Ferdydurke* (Borchardt), 160.

23 Page 168 of typescript, 166 of Argos.

24 Gombrowicz, *Ferdydurke* (Borchardt), 161.

25 Pages 168–69 of typescript, 166 of Argos.

26 Gombrowicz, *Ferdydurke* (Borchardt), 160.

27 Page 169 of typescript, 167 of Argos.

28 Gombrowicz, *Ferdydurke* (Borchardt), 162.

29 Ibid., 161.

30 Page 170 of typescript.

31 Page 174 of typescript.

32 Gombrowicz, *Ferdydurke* (Borchardt), 165.

33 Gombrowicz, *Ferdydurke* (Argos), 12.

34 Romanelli, *A gênese*, 181.

2   Witold Gombrowicz in Spain[1]

Zofia Stasiakiewicz

In the 1960s, Witold Gombrowicz, as renowned an author as he was in Europe, his works being translated into numerous languages, was still relatively unknown in Francoist Spain. The person who came to play a crucial role in the introduction of his oeuvre to the Catalan and Spanish peninsular literary world was Gabriel Ferrater, a poet and literary editor at the Catalan publisher Seix Barral in Barcelona. An epistolary exchange between the two writers started in 1965. However, the relationship began at least a few months earlier when the Catalan poet became interested in the work of the Polish writer and the idea of a Spanish edition of the novel *Pornografia* (Pornography). Thanks to this correspondence, in the Witold Gombrowicz Archive at Beinecke Library at Yale University, it is possible to trace the process of the novel's translating and editing.

Under the leadership of Víctor Seix and Carlos Barral, Seix Barral began to show interest in Gombrowicz. At that time, the Polish writer was still in Buenos Aires. Initially, the publisher asked Gombrowicz about the possibility of editing excerpts from his *Dziennik* (Diary).[2] Later, Montserrat Puig, in charge of foreign rights at Seix Barral, contacted Gombrowicz to obtain the rights to *Iwona, księżniczka Burgunda* (*Ivona, Princess of Burgundia*).[3]

In the end, *Pornografia* was the first novel by Gombowicz published on the Iberian peninsula. Ferrater, one of the editors in chief, asked Gombrowicz personally, during a meeting at the beginning of May 1965 in Vence, France, for the editing rights to *Pornografia*.[4] Seix Barral delivered the German translation of the novel (*Verführung*) to the General Directory of Information (the censorship administration) in Madrid on July 13, 1965.[5] It may seem strange that Seix Barral decided to issue the book in a German-language version instead of a more accessible French edition, but this was of necessity. In one of his letters, Ferrater told Gombrowicz that it would be difficult to find an appropriate censor-reader for the original Polish version, while French would have too many censors that could cause problems and delays.[6] Gombrowicz assured Ferrater that he would remain patient until the censorship bureau announced its decision: "I perfectly understand your difficulties with censorship and I will equip myself with patience."[7]

As stated in the censorship record preserved in the General Administration Archive in Alcalá de Henares, Spain, the publisher asked for permission to print 3,000 copies. The literary director of Seix Barral, Ferrater, in a letter dated June 11, 1965, warned Gombrowicz of possible impediments created by censorship: "The annoying thing is that as you know, in Spain there is prior censorship."[8] If *Pornografia* were rejected by the censorship bureau, Ferrater suggested another novel, *Trans-Atlantyk*.

In his letter of July 20, 1965, Ferrater assured Gombrowicz that the censor's decision would be known by the beginning of September. If it were not favorable, he proposed editing the novel at the Mexican publishing house of Joaquín Mortiz, as had been done with other authors such as Günter Grass. In the same letter, Ferrater also informed Gombrowicz that Seix Barral was equally interested in other novels: "Of course we are not interested only in *Pornography*, but also in *Trans-Atlantyk* as well as *Kosmos*. If, by chance, censorship was stupid enough to reject *Pornography*, we would immediately offer *Trans-Atlantyk*."[9] Fortunately, the whole edition was authorized on July 26 by a censor named P. Álvarez Turienzo. He concluded that the work would be understood only by a small group of readers and that it would have a very limited impact:

> The novel's meaning is difficult to grasp. Instead of perfection, it seems to propose imperfection as the ideal of life. It contains some slightly irreverent allusions against religion and Catholic religious ceremonies. Since these allusions are not serious and are contained in a text inaccessible to the common public, it can be authorized.[10]

However, the head of the Section of Readers did not issue an official authorization until January 21, 1966:

> This novel develops as a philosophical speculation about the struggle between a tendency to fullness and a tendency to immaturity, nonfulfillment. Concerns that may arise in a more popular work may be accepted in this difficult text, which aims at a small audience.[11]

He then refers to the same case in another document: "In view of the report of the Section of Readers, the current provisions, and the norms communicated by the supervisors, this office believes that the work referred to in this file may be approved."[12]

In an additional petition dated February 9, 1968, Seix Barral requested authorization to publish *Pornografia* under the title of *La Seducción* with a print run of 5,000 copies. The authorization was based on the censor's report, as well as on a previous permit issued in 1965.

Concurrently, Ferrater contacted two Polish women involved in translation. He was hoping to obtain their help and advice in translating the novel, on which he comments in one of his letters:

> I am now immersed in Polish grammar books and dictionaries and in your works. I'm beginning to be able to crack a Polish text—which, of course, does not mean that "I know Polish."... If Ms. Ciechomski is really able to read a literary text and explain to me the nuances, I think we can give a good translation of your work.[13]

This means that what Ferrater already had in mind was the idea of translating the novel himself, yet with the support of a Polish translator. Furthermore, the Catalan writer expressed his interest in the *Dziennik* as well as his hope that it was not out of print, as that would have enabled him to compare the original text with a translation. This way he could have become familiar with the Polish writer's vocabulary and basic linguistic structures.[14]

The delay in obtaining the response of the censorship bureau, which annoyed Gombrowicz, can be explained by the persecution aimed at Carlos Barral and his publishing house in 1965. These problems were eventually resolved thanks to the Catalan editor's visit to Madrid. Unfortunately, this did not prevent a delay in the issuance of the permit.

As he was awaiting the censor's response, Ferrater was comparing the Polish text to German and French translations. He spotted several differences between the original and the versions in other languages. In addition, he noticed changes in the quotations from *Ferdydurke* that he was reading at that time as well as in some of the sections of the *Dziennik*, which he was analyzing from the point of view of translation. He also identified nuances in the translations of *Pornografia* that could turn out to be problematic in the future Spanish version of the text. Gombrowicz explained the translation issues to Ferrater in a letter that, though not dated, must have been written between July and December 1965:

> No doubt there are noticeable differences between the different translations. It's impossible for me to control everything. The French version of *Pornography* was revised by me, but was a bit rushed. It may be that I simply eliminated certain words that sounded bad in French—I do not remember. *Ferdydurke*'s translation was done in 1947 by me with the help of approximately twenty collaborators. It was hard work, and many times I changed the text, thanks to my holding the copyright as the author. The German version is directly from the original. The French version is a retranslation from the Spanish, done with my participation.[15]

In a letter dated December 15, Ferrater expressed his willingness to translate another novel, *Ferdydurke*, into Catalan: "I would like to... translate *Ferdydurke* into Catalan, which is my native language. In principle, I have already found a publisher."[16] In addition, Ferrater commented that his wife, Jill Jarrell, was reading the novel at the time and "she really enjoys it."[17] Indeed, the publishing house Edicions 62 published the Catalan translation of the novel in 1968. Nonetheless, it was translated from the Spanish by Ramon Folch and not by Ferrater. Edicions 62 was, in fact, very interested in editing the translation. Anna March from the editorial department sent a letter to Gombrowicz, dated May 11, 1967, asking him for the rights to *Ferdydurke*. In yet another letter, March assured Gombrowicz of the publisher's willingness to edit the novel and presented him with the conditions of a contract for the rights to it in Catalan. In the last preserved letter from November 13, 1967,[18] March sent Gombrowicz the final contract.

Meanwhile, Ferrater asked Ciechomska to translate a book by Jan Kott, which he described as "baby talk,"[19] in order to obtain a sample of her work and to see whether she would make a good advisor for the future translation of *Pornografía*. In response, Gombrowicz agreed to the terms suggested by the publisher, but expressed doubt in Ferrater's ability to translate the novel: "I admire your heroism: to study Polish! And I fear that even your obvious linguistic ability will not easily lead you to solve the problems with translation."[20] In addition, the Polish author expressed his vivid interest in promoting his work in Spain, as well as in a campaign that should accompany the publication of the novel. He asked Ferrater to write a series of articles about his work, which could help to convince the censors to authorize publication of the book in Spain. "I'm an author who is ready to be 'discovered,'" he added in the letter on January 5, 1966.[21]

Finally, in late January 1966, a representative of Seix Barral in Madrid reported on the authorization of the entire book, and Ferrater convinced Edicions 62 to publish the Catalan translation of *Ferdydurke* a year later—a translation that the poet unfortunately never finished. At that time, Ferrater had already obtained the censor's authorization but lacked a translator from the Polish. This is when Gabriela Makowiecka recommended Sergio Pitol, who had then lived in Warsaw for two years and had already translated *Bramy Raju* (*The Gates of Paradise*) by Jerzy Andrzejewski. Ferrater, for his part, was excited by Gombwowicz's work and wanted to embark on a translation of *Dziennik* for the publisher Sudamericana, known for publishing his works in Argentina.

Since Ferrater had problems finding the right translator, he confirmed his willingness to translate the novel himself: "The only solution is that I throw myself into work on the German and French texts and the little Polish that I have gleaned from grammar books."[22] In addition, he reassured the Polish writer about the advanced stage of his work on the translation: "when I received your letter saying that Mr. Pitol is a good translator, I had already thrown myself into the translation of *Pornografia*. Two-thirds are done, and I intend to finish it in about two days—sorry! ten days!"[23] Moreover, he suggested that Pitol could translate *Trans-Atlantyk*, and he expressed his doubts about editing *Kosmos*, which he considered too controversial for the Spanish censorship. Although Ferrater assured Gombrowicz that the translation would be completed in a very short period of time, the deadline was postponed, which irritated Gombrowicz. In his letter to Ferrater on September 23, 1967, he wrote:

> But what is happening with *Pornography*? According to our contract, it was to appear in July 1966. Well, we are in September 1967. I'm afraid I cannot extend this delay much longer.... *Pornography* is not ready yet. I have not signed any contracts with Seix Barral.... Is it possible that Seix Barral does not have too much interest in publishing me?[24]

Gombrowicz asked Ferrater for the translations of his next works to be done faster, because, as he stated, "My editions in Spain are something important for me."[25] Yet, in the same letter, Gombrowicz expressed his enthusiasm for a possible translation of *Ferdydurke* into Catalan: "I received the proposal to publish *Ferdydurke* in Catalan, and I accepted it. It is an honor for me to be translated into Catalan! It is to you that I owe this honor, isn't it?"[26] Ferrater justified this delay by "a time of personal problems."[27] He also admitted having already read some of the short stories by Gombrowicz, such as "Banbury" from *Bakakaj* in a German version. This gives us a clue that he might have discovered Gombrowicz through German translations during his stay in Hamburg. Ferrater also showed great interest in Poland in general, as he questioned Gombrowicz about a book by Manfred Kridl on Polish culture. Gombrowicz showed his appreciation for Ferrater's work by asking him to write an article about himself for the *Cahier de l'Herne* that the Polish writer was preparing with Dominique de Roux. Gombrowicz characterized Ferrater as a "Spanish poet, critic, admirer, he can write an essay."[28] Carlos Barral, who kept up official correspondence with Gombrowicz, decided to write a confidential letter to the Polish author to excuse Ferrater and ensure the publication of the novel. He presented Ferrater as "one of your most enthusiastic admirers, who has a 'strong intelligence.'"[29] However, Barral stated that keeping up with a schedule was not one of Ferrater's strengths: "Ferrater, you know, is surely not a person born to take account of disciplines, including very light ones such as those in the publishing industry."[30] Finally, he also explained the whole situation to appease

Gombrowicz and convince him that his publishing house was still interested in his literary work:

> Generally when [Ferrater] handles the translations, we risk having concerns about the timeliness of his work. But *Pornography*—very probably because it is a book that he loves—was the most conspicuous victim of the neuroses of our mutual friend. He began to deliver the translation in January and half the book is already in lead [i.e., is typeset]. ...But deliveries stopped in February ... I know from Ferrater that you are worried about the progress of the Spanish editions. ...That is why I am writing this confidential letter to you.[31]

Despite this lack of discipline and all the delays, Ferrater was one of Gombrowicz's most active promoters, including his efforts to have the Pole's work recognized with the prestigious Formentor award. Despite Ferrater's intense campaign to promote Gombrowicz in 1965, the Pole came up one vote short with the Prix International de Littérature going to Saul Bellow. Two years later, Ferrater informed Gombrowicz that they decided to nominate *Cosmos* for the prize "because it seemed to us that speaking about a new book instead of insisting on the same text would refresh interest and would give us a better chance."[32] He was correct. After 1967 Gombrowicz could no longer claim, as he once had, that he had never won an award in his life.

The award was also a harbinger of other good news. At long last, Rosa Regás informed the Polish novelist that *Pornografía* was ready to be published and that it would be delivered to bookstores on January 22, 1968.[33] In fact, the novel did come out that year as part of the Biblioteca Breve Collection. The publicity campaign emphasized literary reviews and press releases sent to editors newspapers and magazines, as well as to literary critics, and the placement of printed posters in the display cases of bookstores where *Pornografía* was sold.

Gombrowicz initially disagreed with the advertising strategy and even criticized the text, the biographical note, and the photograph of him that appeared on the cover of the novel. He reproached Barral over the insufficiency of the information contained in the text since he considered that an author who was practically unknown in Spain should be introduced to the public in a more comprehensive way. In one of his letters to Barral, Gombrowicz wrote, "I deserve something better."[34] However, the publisher was pleased to be able to sell nearly 3,500 copies by February 1969. Gombrowicz was very attentive to the publication of his work in Spain, and he constantly wrote to Barral, giving him instructions and advice on how to proceed in order to make his novel more popular. In a letter dated February 18, 1968, he remarked that he had already become known in Argentina and that Sudamericana was about to publish *Diario argentino* (Argentinian Diary). He believed this could be helpful in promoting the novel in Spain, "but we must mobilize some people and prepare the ground, because people know some things but not much; no one is well aware of my affairs."[35] Gombrowicz provided the Spanish publisher with a list of names, including literary critics, publishers, and editors from both Europe and Argentina to whom he wanted the Spanish edition of *Pornografia* sent. Each copy was to have enclosed a positive review.

Sudamericana and Seix Barral had to synchronize the editions of Gombrowicz's work so as not to publish the translation of the same novel at the same time in both countries. For this reason, they agreed to add an exclusivity clause to the contract designed to guarantee that if one of the two publishing houses issued a novel by Gombrowicz the other would have to wait at least eighteen months before publishing the same work. Gombrowicz commented on this in a letter to Carlos Barral: "it is an arrangement that Sudamericana, Mr. Ferrater, and I agreed upon, when we discussed the problem of synchronizing my editions in Spain and Argentina."[36]

The enthusiasm that Ferrater felt about Gombrowicz's work was reflected in his article, published in *Presència* in 1966, entitled "Witold Gombrowicz." Its main focus was on the novel *Ferdydurke*, but Ferrater also emphasized the universal characteristics of the Polish author's creation:

> A person who possesses literary sensibility... will be fascinated to see how a very original stylistic potential develops, how it is deliberately sought: how Spanish is forced to be malleable and poured into a new mold. And in a different order of things, not related to language, form is obtained, which goes through unlimited malleability, sharp torments and the no less acute delights of the fluency and moral instability.... Gombrowicz is very enjoyable, and he is always so, even when his subjects are (and often are) atrocious.[37]

Gombrowicz was very pleased with this article and complimented Ferrater on the idea of calling him a Spanish writer:

> I'm amazed by your article. The idea that I am a Spanish writer is grand in its demagoguery! ... You have the gift, not very frequently seen, alas, of speaking in an interesting manner about books and authors. And one sees that you feel comfortable with my literary work. All my thanks, this article will do me good.[38]

From the very beginning Ferrater had a firm belief in the success of *Pornografia* in Spain. In one of his letters to Gombrowicz, as he was commenting on the edition, he stated:

> Usually the first edition of a novel is only 3,000 or 4,000 copies, but I will try to convince my boss to start in your case with 5,000

copies because I sincerely believe that your book can be a big hit with Spanish youth.[39]

Unfortunately, it is not known whether the two writers continued their correspondence since no further letters are preserved in the Gombrowicz Archive. Despite the enthusiasm Ferrater had for future translations of other Gombrowicz creations, such as parts of *Dziennik* into Spanish or of *Ferdydurke* into Catalan, he did not continue his work. However, thanks to the correspondence Gombrowicz preserved, it is possible to trace the process of this translation, understand how it was introduced into the Spanish literary market, and how it came to influence the overall reception of Gombrowicz's work in Spain. The letters also contain information on other co-workers from Seix Barral, such as Rosa Regás or Yvonne Hortet who were responsible for implementing the publication of the novel. They were also involved in the future translation of, for example, *Kosmos*—from Polish to Spanish by Sergio Pitol and published in 1969—and *Trans-Atlantyk*—translated by Sergio Pitol and Kazimierz Piekarec in 1971 for Barral.

Pitol's name appeared for the first time in one of Ferrater's letters to Gombrowicz when he suggested the Mexican writer as a possible translator for *Pornografia*.[40] Analysis of the correspondence between Gombrowicz and Pitol reveals a growing interest in the Polish writer's work among Catalan and Spanish readers. This stimulated demand for versions of his novels in those two languages. Gombrowicz, who had already "conquered" the French and German literary markets, was willing to get involved in an advertising campaign for his work in Spain.

Once Makowiecka rejected an offer to translate the second volume of *Dziennik*,[41] Pitol received the offer as he already had some experience in translating from Polish to Spanish.[42] At the same time, the Mexican writer, who lived in Warsaw in 1964–1966, was preparing an anthology of contemporary Polish short stories in which he wanted to include one of the Gombrowicz's pieces. Having translated excerpts from *Dziennik* and some of the plays for Sudamericana, Pitol had to turn down Seix Barral's offer to translate *Kosmos* due to his obligations as director of the University of Veracruz publishing house in Mexico. However, he recommended another translator, Juan Manuel Torres, whom he described as "the best Polish translator that I know of."[43]

Torres began a short correspondence with Gombrowicz on January 23, 1968. He informed him of having signed a contract to translate *Kosmos* for Seix Barral on May 20, 1968. He added, "I will do my best so that my work suits this piece and so that I can keep what is fundamental in your ideas and style even in the places where my translation is not that faithful."[44] Although he initially seemed eager to take up the translation challenge, the publishing house lost track of him in 1968. In their letters to Gombrowicz, Yvonne Hortet and Rosa Regás[45] both asked him for information on Torres's whereabouts. As Torres moved back to Mexico with his Polish wife and daughter that same year, it is possible that either he was untraceable or the correspondence failed to reach him.

Despite these false starts, Pitol finally did translate *Kosmos*. It was published in Barcelona in 1969, one year after his translation of *Diario argentino* appeared. His extensive correspondence with Gombrowicz demonstrates the Polish author's keen interest in the publication of his *Dziennik* in Spanish. Despite his initial interest in translating selected chapters, Ferrater desisted and Gombrowicz opted for entrusting Pitol with this translation. During the 1970s, Pitol also translated "Dziewictwo" ("Virginity"; 1970), *Bakakaj* (1974), and *Trans-Atlantyk* (1971). As to Torres, either he did not translate any other Gombrowicz works—which could be the case for a number of reasons—or he is not listed as the translator. Nevertheless, Pitol, who became equally fascinated with Gombrowicz's work, in an undated text called "A la sombra de Witold Gombrowicz" ("In the shadow of Witold Gombrowicz"), names Torres as his collaborator in the translation of *Kosmos* and *Bakakaj*. In the same text, Pitol confesses his absolute fascination with Gombrowicz's work and the oppositions that can be found in it: "culture and irrationality, maturity and immaturity, superiority and inferiority."[46] Furthermore, he admits to being constantly engaged in a dialogue with Gombrowicz throughout his entire literary career and cites one of his novels, *Domar a la divina garza* (*To tame the divine heron*), as an example of a tribute to Gombrowicz's literary heritage.[47]

Pitol is yet another example of the deep influence that Gombrowicz had on those who dedicated their time to translating his works. Like Ferrater, Pitol, through his enthusiasm and dedication, made room for Gombrowicz in the Spanish literary world and facilitated his gaining a strong position among other contemporary writers of that time. In a letter to Gombrowicz, besides congratulating him on winning the Prix International de Littérature, Pitol admits, "I personally congratulate myself on the enthusiasm I have felt for years for his work."[48] Both Ferrater and then Pitol, who carried on the work his predecessor did not have the time or strength to pursue, became ambassadors of Gombrowicz on the Iberian peninsula. Thanks to Ferrater, the novel *Pornografia* was translated into Spanish and published by Seix Barral. A year earlier, in 1967, Ferrater, by having influenced the other editors with his eloquence, ensured the victory of Gombrowicz at the Prix International de Littérature. Pitol continued Ferrater's work and introduced both Spanish and Latin American readers to the works of Gombrowicz.

Notes

1 An earlier version was published in *The Polish Review*, Vol. 60, No. 2 (2015) and is used with the permission of the editors. The author wishes to thank

Barbara Stasiakiewicz for translating it from Polish and Silvia G. Dapía for translating quotations from French and Spanish into English.

2 Letter from Jaime Salinas, Jan. 29, 1963, in Gombrowicz Archive.
3 Letter, Montserrat Puig to Gombrowicz, Feb. 20, 1965, in ibid.
4 He informs the publisher Sudamericana of the meeting and asks for permission to edit Gombrowicz in Spanish as the publishing house already edited *Ferdydurke* and was about to edit excerpts from *Dziennik* that referred to Argentina. See also letter to Gombrowicz, May 18, 1965, in Gombrowicz Archive.
5 The petition registration number was 5193–65.
6 Letter, Ferrater to Gombrowicz, June 11, 1965, ibid.
7 Letter, Gombrowicz to Ferrater, n.d. 1965, ibid.
8 Letter, Ferrater to Gombrowicz, June 11, 1965, ibid.
9 Letter, Ferrater to Gombrowicz, July 20, 1965, Gombrowicz Archive.
10 "Expediente de censura de la obra *La Seducción* de Witold Gombrowicz," no. 5193–65, Archivo General de la Administración, Alcalá de Henares (Spain), 1965.
11 Resolution of Jan. 20, 1966, in Archivo General de la Administración.
12 Ibid.
13 Letter, Ferrater to Gombrowicz, July 20, 1965, Correspondence, Ferrater, 3.
14 Ibid.
15 Letter, Gombrowicz to Ferrater 1965, ibid.
16 Letter, Ferrater to Gombrowicz, Dec. 15, 1965, ibid., 68.
17 Ibid.
18 Letters, March to Gombrowicz, Aug. 28, 1967, and Nov. 13, 1967, Gombrowicz Archive.
19 Letter, Ferrater to Gombrowicz, Mar. 14, 1967. Ibid., folder 92.
20 Letter, Gombrowicz to Ferrater, n.d. 1965. Ibid., folder 100.
21 Letter, Gombrowicz to Ferrater, Jan. 5, 1966. Ibid.
22 Letter, Ferrater to Gombrowicz, Mar. 14, 1967. Ibid., folder 92.
23 Letter, Ferrater to Gombrowicz, May 4, 1967. Ibid.
24 Letter, Gombrowicz to Ferrater, Sept. 23, 1967. Ibid., folder 100.
25 Ibid.
26 Ibid.
27 Letter, Ferrater to Gombrowicz, Mar. 14, 1967. Ibid., folder 92.
28 Letter, Sept. 11, 1966. Gombrowicz Archive, Writings by Others About Gombrowicz, 1960–1967, *Cahier de l'Herne*: Gombrowicz, List of persons who were considered for contributing, typescript with WG's annotations, 1966 Sept 11, GEN MSS 515 Series V, box 35, folder 1007.
29 Letter, Barral to Gombrowicz, Oct. 3, 1967. Correspondence, Editorial Seix Barral.
30 Ibid.
31 Ibid.
32 Letter, Ferrater to Gombrowicz, Mar. 14, 1967. Correspondence, Ferrater.
33 Letter, Regás to Gombrowicz, Dec. 23, 1967. Correspondence, Editorial Seix Barral
34 Letter, Gombrowicz to Barral, Jan. 19, 1968. Ibid.
35 Letter, Gombrowicz to Barral, Feb. 18, 1968. Ibid.
36 Letter, Gombrowicz to Barral, Mar. 30, 1968. Ibid.
37 Gabriel Ferrater, "Witold Gombrowicz," *Presència*, Mar. 15, 1965, 39.
38 Letter, Gombrowicz to Ferrater, Apr. 21, 1966. Correspondence, Ferrater.
39 Letter, Ferrater to Gombrowicz, June 11, 1965. Correspondence, Editorial Seix Barral.
40 Letter, Ferrater to Gombrowicz, Apr. 10, 1966. Correspondence, Ferrater.

41 Letter, Mar. 10, 1966. Gombrowicz Archive.
42 He translated *Sklepy cynamonowe*, by Bruno Schulz, into Spanish
43 Letter from Pitol, Aug. 2, 1967. Gombrowicz Archive.
44 Letter, Torres to Gombrowicz, May 20, 1968. Gombrowicz Archive.
45 Letters of July 15 and Sept. 10, 1968. Gombrowicz Archive.
46 Sergia Pitol, "A la sombra de Witold Gombrowicz," Gombrowicz Archive.
47 Ibid.
48 Letter, Pitol to Gombrowicz, May 29, 1967. Correspondence, Pitol.

3 The "Puto" in Argentine Literature[1]

Carlos Gamerro

Witold Gombrowicz's 1952 novel *Trans-Atlantyk* was written in Polish, yet he chose to consistently use the Spanish word "Puto" in the story. Why? What was there about this word that defied easy translation? I propose to address this question by beginning with four vignettes from everyday life as examples of the word's usage, then look at its appearance in four different literary texts.

Vignette 1. As a child, I spotted a group of children gathered around a child telling a joke. At least, I thought it was a joke and I moved close to listen, but I just heard the end—"And then he says to him: 'Please sign, puto.'" There was a reverential silence. No one laughed. It was not a joke. One of the listeners dared to ask, finally, "It's the worst insult, isn't it?" The narrator nodded gravely.

Vignette 2. As an adult, I was driving on an avenue. On my right a car was approaching at full speed (my memory elevates it to the dignity of a Torino, although probably it was hardly a Taunus). The car was driven by a long-haired metal rock fan who honked at me so that I would let him pass. A little maliciously, I did not let him. He pulled next to me and I saw that his face was twisted into a frown, as if by mental effort, until at last he became enlightened and before passing and cutting me off, he yelled at me "¡Puto!"

Vignette 3. Again as a grown-up, but now as a pedestrian, I threw myself into the crosswalk at a corner without traffic lights. A motorcycle came as fast as it could and I pointed, with a gesture, to the pathway inside the regular white lines as if saying that in a crossing path the pedestrian has the right of way. The motorcyclist sped up. I had to get out of his way to avoid being run over and before he vanished in the distance. To make it clear that what he did was not a mistake or through indifference but a purposeful lesson, he yelled at me "¡Puto!"

The motorcyclist, if I understood him correctly, was suggesting that here, in Argentina, to cross the street using the pedestrian crossing path, and to pretend that a driver would give way to the pedestrian, is typical of a "puto." The formula might be simplified as "to respect the law is typical of putos." In the same sense, one may say about someone who does not dare to do something beyond the norm, "Come on, don't be a *puto*." Thus, one of the uses of "puto" in Argentina applies to an individual who would not dare to step outside convention.

Vignette 4. The bus made a stop at the Rosario terminal. The passengers from various buses were many and the two or three waiters in the bus-stop bar were overwhelmed. One of them, a blond young man, strove harder to do his job than the other, coming and going, running, desperate to meet orders since the people had already paid and would not leave without their food. It would not be fair that the bus leave with all their luggage because of a miserable croissant. The passengers bitterly demanded their orders, screaming at him to hurry, berating him for lack of dedication. To all this, he responded with more speed, more anguish, and more apologies until a dark-skinned and wrinkled old man, who had not opened his mouth, pronounced the fatal word—"¡Puto!" The word reverberated through the bus terminal bringing a sudden silence as if the whole terminal, and not only the customers, had become quiet to listen to the pronouncement. The blond young man froze in the midst of his rush. He turned around slowly, untying his apron. Without going around, *he stepped over the bar* and stood in front of the old man: "What did you say to me?" The old man appeared quite surprised; he would never know how that word came out of his mouth. But he said it, and he stood up bravely. They would not say later that he backed down to a *puto*. People forgot their orders. They intervened. They stood between the two trying to calm the situation. They succeeded and the crowd dispersed, in silence, many of them without their food. What happened had been too serious, too profound, to complain about a little coffee.

The use of the signifier "puto" in the third vignette might be connected to Gombrowicz's use in *Trans-Atlantyk*. Gombrowicz defines the "puto" as follows: "A Man who, being a Man, fain would not be a Man but after Men chases, and after them Flies, admires, oh, Loves, Heats for them, Lusts for them, Hungers for them, makes up to them, simpers, adulates them, him folk hereabouts give the contemptuous name 'puto.'"[2] There can be no doubt that the phrase "folk hereabouts" refers to Argentina and that Gombrowicz is defining a specific cultural use of the word "puto" that links it to homosexuality.

I do not intend to write a history of the homosexual in Argentine literature nor to survey Argentine narrative, theatre, and poetry to determine which works present homosexuality in a tolerant or even positive way, or discriminate against or give a negative image of it. There are two main reasons for this. First, because a writer who displays, contextualizes, and tries to understand his homophobia may be much more interesting than one who conceals it and pretends to be gay-friendly, or even one who is sincerely gay-friendly. Second, because the subject of my investigation is not homophobia or homophilia but the use of the word "puto." For this reason, I do not intend to apply a gender or queer theory framework either. My more modest goal is to inquire about the particular uses of the word "puto." This is a purely personal attempt to resolve a question that has haunted me since my childhood. Why is "puto" the worst insult? What do we intend to say when we say "puto"?

Trans-Atlantyk

The first novel in Argentine literature to succumb to the fascination of the semantic and phonic aspects of the word "puto" was Gombrowicz's *Trans-Atlantyk*.[3] Originally written in Polish, it takes place in Buenos Aires during the last months of 1939. The protagonist, Witold,[4] a Polish writer on an official visit to Argentina, is surprised by news of the Nazi invasion of Poland and decides to stay in Argentina, establishing a relationship with the Polish community in Buenos Aires. He also connects with Gonzalo, the "Puto" of the novel, a millionaire who will ask his help in seducing Ignacy, a Polish young man with whom he is in love.

Ignacy is always accompanied by his father Tomasz, a man who Witold, the narrator, describes as extremely good, decent, of sober and regular features, astonishing kindness and prudence, sensible, unusually honest, extraordinarily pure and righteous, loyal in all circumstances. On this basis, the narrator feels horrified at the idea of betraying him, that is, betraying the Father and the Fatherland because of the "Puto." He decides to reveal Gonzalo's intentions to Tomasz. This leads to a fight in which the Father is injured by a mug of wine that the "Puto" throws at him. That same night Witold thinks about his shame:

> They will not forgive me that Shame and possibly I'm already ridiculed by all, condemned, a Buffoon proclaimed. And when just one, only one man who denied me not his Recognition, and perchance even some Admiration, he turned out to be a Puto.[5]

Moreover, the narrator sees in the drops of blood spurting from the Father's forehead the blood of the subjugated Fatherland. He claims,

"And when there far away, over the waters, blood, here likewise blood; and Tomasz's drops that are for my doing spilt."[6]

The following day, the Father challenged the Puto and, when Witold attempted to dissuade him, the Father responded:

> Ergo, I must challenge him. I will duel with him so that this matter in a manly manner betwixt Men is settled; to be sure, I will make a Man of him that it cannot be said that a Puto is after my Son![7]

Thereupon he asked Witold to arrange the details. Witold presented himself to Gonzalo who made the narrator hesitate in terms of his loyalties, urging him to opt for the son. And it is here that he pronounces the key word of the novel, the neologism Synczyzna ("Filistria" or "Son-land"), which will replace "Father-land." Witold is outraged:

> I would not be a Pole if I were to set a Son against a Father; know you that we Poles our Fathers respect exceedingly, and thus you do not tell a Pole that he should a Son from a Father and, moreover, for Deviation take.[8]

However, the narrator hesitates between the demands of honor and decency by supporting the Father, or giving in to the temptation by supporting the "Puto." Initially he accepts Gonzalo's proposal to fool the Father by using blanks in the duel. After each party fires two shots, the duel is interrupted by a hunt. The hounds attack Ignacy, whose life is saved by Gonzalo, and in this way Father and "Puto" reconcile. But later, in Gonzalo's country estate, Witold confesses to the Father the ruse of fake ammunition and the Father, deciding that the "Puto"'s blood would not be enough to cleanse the offense, decides to kill his own son.

Read as Polish literature, *Trans-Atlantyk* is a novel dealing with the demands of nationalism when the invasion of Poland by the Nazis makes these demands unbearable. In part, this novel may be understood as a self-justification by Gombrowicz for staying in Argentina instead of fighting for the Fatherland. The trap of patriotism appears in the memorable sequence of the Poles residing in Argentina locking themselves in a cellar, carrying bent spurs they affix to each other when one of them wants to escape or hesitates regarding their nationalist convictions. Thus, patriotism appears as an infernal circle from which everyone wants to escape but from which the group will allow no one to leave. Another figure representing patriotism is the Father who is ready to sacrifice his Son to satisfy the demands of national honor. By definition, Fatherland is filicidal and in the ritual that best defines it, that of war, Fathers send their Sons to die for their Fatherland. In this way, the old buries the new, the past devours the future, and the old people eliminate the danger represented by the Youth.

But what has the "Puto" to do with all this? He is the one who pronounces the key word "Filistria" and devises a complex plan so that by
killing his father Ignacy invests the word "Filistria" with its full meaning. The logic is clear: the "Puto" departs from the social and political
order and from the metaphorical family, the Fatherland. But there is an
evident excess surrounding the "Puto" which is contained in the word
"puto" itself. Why does the friendship with the "Puto" diminish Witold?
Why can one not challenge a "puto" to a duel? Why is a Father willing to
sacrifice his Son, not because a "puto" has seduced him but because the
son is just courted by him? I find it hard to avoid the feeling that the specifically Argentine contribution to the novel is the figure of the "Puto"
and, particularly, the excessive reactions to the obsession with the word
"puto." If *Trans-Atlantyk* is a novel about patriotism and filicide, *Trans-
atlántico* is the novel about the "Puto." It cannot be by chance that he is
the only Argentine lost in a novel populated by Polish people.[9]

Every time Gombrowicz places himself in his own work as "Witold
Gombrowicz"—and this is something he does in a systematic way—it
is not to preach but to vacillate and oscillate between good and bad,
morality and amorality, dignity and turpitude. In this case, he vacillates
between helping the Father against the "Puto" or helping the "Puto"
against the Father, and we, the readers, have a hard time in this axiological quicksand. Is it a novel that makes a mockery of the "putos,"
joyfully assuming the discriminatory attitudes typical of male-oriented
Argentine culture? Or is it a novel that mocks Argentine homophobia and takes it to the absurd? Is Gombrowicz's position regarding
homosexuality discriminatory or one of advocacy? Clearly, if it were
about determining Gombrowicz's "stance" on homosexuality, there
are many indications to be found in his diaries and correspondence:
for example, in the following letter in which Gombrowicz responds to
the allusions of his friend "Goma" (Juan Carlos Gómez) regarding his
homosexuality:

> I'm telling you, I'm not and have never been homosexual but from
> time to time I use to do it whenever I feel like it. I'm a simple person
> and, particularly in erotic matters, the people are my teacher, who
> fortunately know nothing about the terrible homosexuality and go
> to be with whom they can and in the manner they can. I would like
> it if all of you weirdos were half as healthy as those innocent and
> charming children of the army or the navy.[10]

Here, at least, Gombrowicz shakes off the label that they want to stick
on him and challenges, in only one brilliant phrase, with a very Argentine intonation, the questionable notion that sexual acts fatally determine gender identities, suggesting, instead, that it depends on each of
us to define ourselves or not to define ourselves at all. In this way, he

redirects the accusation to his accusers: "I would advise all of you that, instead of devoting yourselves to endless discussions regarding my homosexuality (the issue is apparently of interest to you), have sex among yourselves one of these days to know what it is like."[11] In the same letter, he says, "What a sad country, so 'puto' and so twisted, where no one dares to indulge oneself."

"Puto" is the person concerned about defining others as "putos." In an Argentine formula, "'Puto' is the one who says 'puto.'" With his usual ambivalence — let's be reminded that we are dealing with a *poète maudit*[12]— Gombrowicz does not legitimize the word "puto" but rather cuts the word up into slices, keeping the word's pejorative sense. He discards the sense of "homosexual" and keeps that of "chicken, repressed, who won't make a commitment." He says, "there is nothing worse than not obeying the sacred rules of the body ... learn to be courageous and free and do not let yourselves be scared."[13]

The Kiss of the Spider Woman

If Gombrowicz's *Trans-Atlantyk* represents the first literary case of the use of "puto," the second corresponds to the celebrated novel by Manuel Puig, *The Kiss of the Spider Woman* (1976). In this novel, Valentín, a revolutionary militant in the class struggle is in jail with Molina, a homosexual admirer of romantic films whose highest aspiration is becoming the mistress of the house. In the course of their daily conversations, Valentín becomes like Molina and Molina becomes Valentín. Valentín understands there are other forms of exploitation and domination, such as that of the male over the female, and other forms of struggle that do not have to be subordinated to the struggle for class revolution. On the other hand, Molina understands that he may be gay in a very feminine way and feel proud of it without being willing to accept, condone, or even desire the place of weakness and submission that the machista culture assigns to women and faggots. Their living together gives rise to company; company gives rise to exchange and meeting of minds; the latter leads to physical tenderness and eventually to a full sexual encounter. When Molina announces that he will be freed soon, Valentín suggests, "When you're out of here, you'll be free, you'll be with people. If you want you can even join up with some kind of political group." Molina responds, "That's ridiculous and you know it; they'd never trust some faggot."[14]

The whole saga of the historic misunderstanding between gay militancy, which starts in 1971 with the founding of the Frente de Liberación Homosexual (Homosexual Liberation Front; FLH),[15] and the Argentine political militancy of the 1970s fits into this exchange of views. This conversation synthesizes all the unsuccessful attempts of the FLH—among whose founding members was the same Manuel Puig—to work together with revolutionary groups.[16] In fact, the FLH was able to coordinate some common action only until a breakup not because of a dispute between the FLH and the other groups—"Who would fight with a Puto?" Witold might have said—but between right-wing Peronism and left-wing Peronism. In 1973, Lieutenant Colonel Jorge Manuel Osinde, taking advantage of the "tolerated" presence of the FLH and its flags at the inauguration of President Héctor Cámpora, and in Ezeiza for the arrival of Perón, accused the militants of Juventud Peronista (Peronist Youth, JP) and Montoneros of being homosexuals and drug addicts. The latter responded with the unfortunately memorable song: "We are not fags (putos), we are not junkies; we are soldiers of Evita and Montoneros."[17] When the males fight, the "puto" takes the blame.

Continuing in that tradition of the old left-wing, the political groups distrust homosexuals, regarding them as too weak and thus prone to become informers. Osvaldo Bazán records the following narrative: "Montoneros' executed two of their comrades who were homosexuals because they believed every homosexual is prone to become an informer."[18] Since Bazán does not give names and this episode appears after the phrase "this is what a comrade of that time told me" or "I heard this from an exiled Montonera," everything has a certain whiff of urban guerilla legend.[19] Regardless of whether it was about what the left-wing militants thought of homosexuals or what homosexuals believed the left-wing militants thought of them, the result was the same—a politically militant "puto" had to conceal being a "puto" and thus suffer double repression. The "puto" is unworthy of being a guerilla-fighter. To say "puto guerrilla-fighter" is a contradiction in terms. In the memorable wording of Fidel Castro, "The revolution does not need hair-dressers."[20]

"El Pibe Barulo"

Perhaps the most revealing literary case of the quasi-magical power of the word "puto" in Argentine literature appears in "El Pibe Barulo" by Osvaldo Lamborghini, which is worth quoting:

> I go very often to a café in Talcahuano Street. ... A plump young man (a fat-ass or *culón*) was a regular, he even used to sit at the same table where his orders were taken by the same waiter. He was always joking with the waiter; they looked like they were having a lot of fun. It was also apparent that they respected each other beyond the waiter-customer relationship. The waiter was from a small town and spoke with a strong provincial accent which made the jokes appear funnier than they really were.
>
> September 18, 1978, was a typical afternoon and the café was as quiet as usual. ... The big-bottomed (*nalgudo*), fat-ass (*culón*), or

whatever one wants to call him, arrived. He sat at the table and immediately the mutual nasty jokes started with the provincial waiter, some of them very disparaging. The butterball (*manteca*) ordered a bottle of beer and the jokes continued, all in a loud voice, with no secrets. They were the stage show of the café (I stopped going after the tragedy). The big-bottomed (*nalgudo*) made a silly and gross joke, like the ones they used between themselves. Smiling, calmly, the one from the small-town replied: "But shut up, *gordo puto*."[21]

Those of us who were close to them saw very little. The fat ass stood up and emptied the entire .45 caliber magazine into the chest of his friend, the waiter. ... [T]he one who pulled the trigger when he saw himself being called, evidently with no particular ulterior motive or grievance, "gordo puto," accepted every day, without it bothering him, expressions such as the classic "your ass is bigger than your head" or "stop bugging me," or "don't be puto."

But that afternoon two words — "gordo" and "puto" — were put together with fatal results. Why is it that a "gordo" (fat person) does not accept the term "gordo" being coupled with "puto"? It's a very interesting subject for research.[22]

The story seems memorable for two reasons. On the one hand, it is an impeccable example of montage, of how two words—and, in this case, two images—may engender, by juxtaposition, a third term which does not reduce to the sum of its parts.[23] This is also a possible definition of poetry: the juxtaposition of two more or less innocent words with lethal results.

More specific to our investigation is the way the story reveals the magic and mysterious power of certain words. The fat guy was not bothered when being called "puto." True. Perhaps he took it as an interjection or generic expletive, but when "puto" combined with the noun "gordo" (fat guy), it lost its impersonality and became an indelible characteristic of his individual personality. It is clear that the gordo of our story sees himself as fat, but not as "puto." As long as the two words were separate, he felt he had the freedom to choose—this, yes; this, no. But after the waiter subjected these words to the fatal coupling, it obliged him to see himself not only as a fat guy but also as a "puto." It is also possible that the phrase "gordo puto"—which belongs to the Argentine slang—involves a particular semantic and acoustic image which is *always* used to indicate contempt. John Searle suggests that there are words or phrases that possess what he calls "illocutionary force," indicating the way we should interpret a word, as a request, promise, threat, and so on. The problem with the use of "gordo" in Lamborghini is that we do not know whether "gordo" functions as an indicator of "puto's" illocutionary force or whether "puto" functions as an indicator of "gordo's" illocutionary force. Fortunately, we are doing literary criticism rather than philosophy of language. What is important here is that these two words, which separately may function as a sign of fraternity, taken together fatally constitute an offense that can only be redeemed by death.

"El Pibe Barulo" appears as an inquiry about the concept of tragedy. The premise is very simple: there are certain people whom Nature or God[24] equipped with particularly fat and prominent gluteus or, to say it in layman's terms, "fat asses." The fat ass (*culón*) cannot be taken seriously, not even in times of misfortune. His family "laughed at him, too, and used him to discharge their bad mood."[25] For the "wicked, sadistic and psychopathic people of all kinds," the fat ass is in this world "to suffer painful humiliations ... because something has to keep people amused."[26]

Nal's childhood was surrounded by omens; his brother invented nicknames for Nal which ended in "ulo" such as "Barulo" ("because of course it rhymes with culo [ass])."[27] The father cautioned Nal's brother that this "would end up turning him (Nal) into a *gordo puto*. He then asks Nal: 'Would you like to be a *gordo puto?*'"[28] Reacting against this way of treating the child, the mother criticized the father in front of the child: "This is the way one makes madmen, neurotics, homosexuals, and drug addicts."[29] [T]his elicits the father's response: "Wait a minute! I hope you are not accusing me of turning the fat-ass (culón) into a 'puto'?"[30] However, it was not until the mother yelled at him, "I'm fed up, you are always glued to my skirts, 'gordo puto,'" that Nal decides to change his name.[31] With a little stick, he drew on the dirt a portrait of his idol, the goalkeeper of the football[32] team "Chacarita." "Making a grimace typical of an accursed artist, he signed the drawing with the name '*Gordo Puto.*'"[33] The laws of tragedy fulfill themselves relentlessly: the more one fights against them, the more the hero strives to avoid his fate, the more he favors them. In the story "*La causa justa,*" which also revolves around Nal and his doom, Nal fantasizes about putting an end to that ongoing disgrace: "I would kill the next buttocks-toucher (nalgeador)."[34]

But the most insidious condemnation, the unappealable one due to its form and origin, comes from two street children, who are begging in the neighborhood: "Look kid, you are a *gordo puto* ... even if nobody fucks you; no way, kid, you are a *gordo puto* anyway, you are a *gordo puto*, no matter that you don't allow anybody to fuck you...."[35] From the point of view of its origin, the knowledge about deviant sex, about the inverted body, comes from below and from behind (from the bottom—culo—of society or the city, from the shanty town, the slum, the worker's suburb, from people who have sex with whom they can and in the manner they can). From the point of view of its form, the proletarian child is telling Nal that to be a puto is his essence, a *profound and secret* identity, that (alas!) one can be puto without knowing it. For *that* Argentinean culture—let's be optimistic—there was no worse destiny than to be a "puto."

Fate is relentless. To be a "puto" does not necessarily imply to have been fucked or to have fucked a "puto." Rather, it is enough that you be destined to be fucked:

> [He thought] of the cruelty of those two street children who did not intend to fuck him nor blame him for having let himself be fucked. The most terrible thing was their prophecy. He was born a fat-assed (*culón*) and destiny does not forgive this.... He recalled the words of the street child: "What are you going to do, *gordo puto*? Such is life and you have to resign yourself to it, *gordo puto*, there is no way out."[36]

Eventually, the suffering of Nal pushed Lamborghini to put into words one of his most profound reflections about life in general:

> The unbearable part of life is life itself.... The tolerable part of life is larger than one believes and its episodes many times appear disguised as "horror," as if we were to say (and we *are* actually saying it): the terrors of the Middle Ages are not the Inquisition, fanaticism, the stake, etc, but rather — nothing, absolutely nothing, or a chicken pecking corn.[37]

The statement "The unbearable part of life is life itself"—not the accidents, not the "no way out" situations, not the terminal illnesses, but the unbearable day-to-day experience, the trifle of the everyday life that Joyce intended to celebrate in his *Ulysses* to exorcize the terror that such a life provokes in us—acquires a frightening precision in Lamborghini's statement when we recall that, back in the Middle Ages, corn was absolutely unknown. Lamborghini's chicken, then, is pecking *nothing, absolutely nothing.*

The end of the story is predictable. Taking advantage of the brawl triggered during a football game, his cousin Barto dragged Nal to the bushes and there Barto raped him. And Nal loved it, feeling relieved because he finally fulfilled his destiny. Nal became a faggot (*maricón*), he referred to himself as if he were a female and walked "with a sweep of the hips, as if he were smacking his ass from inside."[38] A benevolent interpretation would be that Lamborghini gives the story a happy ending from the point of view of gender politics showing that the hell so feared by Nal, that tragic end from which he wanted to run away, was really a place of freedom, self-affirmation, *pride*—if and only if Nal were able to assume it and put aside the *machista* prejudices typical of a bourgeois society. But this would be tantamount to falling into an interpretative transvestism. The end of "El Pibe Barulo"—if we accept that there is such an end—is merely silly, a buffoonery. In fact, Lamborghini wants nothing to do with his own characters and their problems. He gets rid of them as well as he can.[39] Like Nal's mother, like Barto, Lamborghini does not know how to get the "gordo puto" off his back. Gombrowicz would probably have said in this situation, "Who would go to all the trouble to write a dignified ending to a 'puto'?"

Another problem with this ending is that it is inconsistent with what was said in Chapter 4. There we are told that Nal leads a normal life, he has married, has children, and has a minor but secure job that is well paid. It is difficult to associate Nal's present life with "the new little young lady" who leaves the scene walking "with a sweep of the hips, as if she were smacking her ass from inside."[40] "El Pibe Barulo" has, then, two possible endings, one according to which he is a "gordo puto" even though no one fucked him, and a second one, according to which he is a "gordo puto" because he was actually fucked. Both endings coexist in the same story. This coexistence transforms "El Pibe Barulo" in the first application to our literature of Ts'ui Pên's method as described in Borges's "El jardín de los senderos que se bifurcan" ("The Garden of the Forking Paths").[41]

The War of the Gyms

It is generally accepted that, in many cases, the answers are less interesting than the questions they attempt to respond to; that rarely the solution of an enigma is more interesting than the enigma itself; that when we are in search of a truth, the goal is less important than the ways pursued during the search. This inquiry will not be an exception to the rule. Answers to our main questions (Why "puto" constitutes the most horrible affront? What do we mean when we say puto?) may also be found in our fourth and last literary case, *La guerra de los gimnasios* (*The War of the Gymnasiums*), a novel written by a friend and disciple of Lamborghini, César Aira. In this novel Ferdie, the protagonist, used to go to a fitness center located in the Flores district with the aim of perfecting his body to provoke "fear to men and desire to women," only to end up involved in a ludicrous war (that of the title): "the War of the Gyms."[42] In that war, his motto "fear to men and desire to women" is adopted as a slogan. At a certain moment in the novel Ferdie realized "that what he wanted to ask Marta when she praised his figure was: 'Am I a god?' But it was a question impossible to answer, as impossible as the opposing and complementary statement: I am a 'puto.'"[43]

Ferdie struggled, not as much between god and "puto," than between "puto" and the Superman. In this way, Nietzsche's formula "the ape is to man what man shall be to the Superman" may be translated into Argentine language as "the Superman is to man what man is to 'puto.'" Or, to put it in Lamborghinean terms, "as man is to the *Tadey*"[44] (ape and puto at the same time).

Concluding Remarks

The worthless buffoonery at the end of "El Pibe Barulo" paves the way for the answer to our question: during a period in Argentine life, the individual denominated "puto" was the despicable one *par excellence*. The place of the Indian in nineteenth-century Argentine literature is occupied in the twentieth century by the "puto." The puto is the nill subject; the *musulman* of Primo Levi; the *homo sacer* of Agamben; the accursed part in Bataille's work; the one to whom everybody can cheat, lie, steal, kill without guilt, with no consequences, because after all he is a "puto." This state of affairs continues until the end of the dictatorship in 1983. After that, a kind of satiation concerning certain traditional forms of repression, regarding privileged objects of derision and discrimination, appears in Argentine society. Slowly first and dramatically later, the "puto" related subjects begin to dissolve themselves into the gay culture. The gay is accepted and the Argentine culture becomes itself gay-friendly to the extent that in 2010 the Law of Equal Marriage was approved and accepted almost without resistance from society and even the church (while the legalization of abortion is still stranded in a kind of Kafkean suspense).

Severo Sarduy, who defined forever the Neobaroque through the formula kistch-camp-gay, put in relationship the utilitarian uses of the word (referential, economical, measurable) with sex destined to procreation, while the playful, luxurious, and excessive uses are associated with non-reproductive eroticism. "All art is quite useless," said (the also "puto") Oscar Wilde.[45] Since heterosexual sex is always suspicious of utilitarianism (it can procreate even without intention), it looks as if there were a kind of natural sympathy or common feeling between homosexuality and literature. From this point of view, literature could be considered the most "puto" of all the discourses, considering both the producer and who consumes it, as represented in the immemorial graffiti: "Who reads this is a puto." Through a large part of the twentieth century, the word "puto" and the diversity of meanings associated with it did not constitute a voice of opposition but of negativity in relation to the "macho" quality and the values related to patriotism, honorable or admirable behavior, and military capability. We do not know yet which ones will be the "putos" of the twenty-first century. But something that we can take for granted is that literature will keep its role in perceiving with its "ear" the voice of the neglected beings. Or, put in other words and paraphrasing Mallarmé, to "give a more 'puto' sense to the words of the tribe."[46]

Notes

1 An extended Spanish version of this was published as "El puto en la literatura argentina," in *Facundo o Martín Fierro. Los libros que inventaron la Argentina* (Buenos Aires: Sudamericana, 2015), 365–85. This article was translated from the Spanish by Silvia G. Dapía.

2 Gombrowicz, *Trans-Atlantyk* (Karsov and French), 36. Polish original: "Mężczyznę co, mężczyzna będąc, mężczyzną być ni e chce, a za
mężczyznami się ugania i za nimi Lata jak w Koszuli, ich uwielbia ach ko-
cha, do nich się zapala, ich pożąda, na nich się łakomi, do nich się wdzięczy,
mizdrzy, im się podlizuje, lud tutejszy wzgardliwą darzy nazwa: 'puto.'"
Gombrowicz, *Trans-Atlantyk* (1988), 11. My thanks to Eva Jungman for
localizing the original quotation.

3 The word "puto" might have appeared in other literary texts before *Trans-
Atlantyk*, but this is the first work that obsessed and railed upon this word
and its meanings, and in this sense, it incorporates the term into Argentine
literature.

4 I will use "Witold" to refer to the protagonist or fictional character and
"Gombrowicz" to refer to the author.

5 Gombrowicz, *Trans-Atlantyk* (Karsov and French), 52–53.

6 Ibid., 53.

7 Ibid., 54.

8 Ibid., 56–57.

9 Although Gonzalo is described as "a Mestizo perchance, a *Portuguese* man,
born in *Libya* of a Persian Turkish mother," in the economy of the novel he
functions as an Argentine. Ibid., 37.

10 Bazán, 267.

11 Ibid.

12 *Translator's note*: a poet who receives insufficient recognition in their own
time.

13 Bazán, 267.

14 Puig, *Kiss*, 215.

15 *Translator's note*: In 1969, the first Argentine gay and lesbian organization
was created and named "Nuestro Mundo" (Our World). In 1971, they adopted a new name, "Frente de Liberación Homosexual" (FLH). Although
the new name may reflect an influence from the United States, the group
saw their fight differently from the U.S. According to the FLH, gay men
and lesbians had to be part of the process of liberation that was occurring
at the time in Argentina. They constructed alliances with the Argentine left,
especially with left wing Peronism, and they thought that it was important
to build a country free from imperialistic domination.

16 *Translator's note*: Fuerzas Armadas Revolucionarias (Revolutionary Armed
Forces, FAR), Fuerzas Armadas Peronistas (Peronist Armed Forces, FAP),
and Montoneros were three Argentine left-wing Peronist factions. Independent of these Peronist groups was the Ejército Revolucionario del Pueblo
(People's Revolutionary Army, ERP), which emerged as the arm wing of the
small Trotskyite party, the Partido Revolucionario de los Trabajadores (Revolutionary Workers' Party, PRT. "Of all these groups, the ERP alone was
Marxist. The Peronists, particularly the Montoneros, were mostly Catholics
who claimed to be Socialists but remained inveterately opposed to what they
called 'godless and international Communism.'" Rock, *Authoritarian*, 214.

17 Bazán, 322.

18 Ibid., 318.

19 Ibid., 319.

20 Ibid., 318.

21 *Translator's note*: In Argentinean Spanish, the word "gordo" is translated
as "fat" or "fat guy" but is not as taboo as it is in English. It is very common
for friends to refer to chubbier friends as "el gordito" or "la gordita" or
simply "el gordo" or "la gorda." In this sense, the term is not offensive and
accepted as nothing more than a nickname given to you by a friend. "Puto"

has different meanings in different contexts. In Spanish, the term "puta" means prostitute, and the term "puto" is the masculine form, referring to a male prostitute. "Puto" is also used as a derogatory way of referring to a homosexual (as, for example, in American English "fairy," "pansy," "faggot"). It may also be used to imply weakness or cowardice as in the expression "no seas puto" (don't be a "pussy"). In some cases, it is used similarly to "bloody" in the United Kingdom and "fucking" in the United States (el puto coche, the fucking car). As Gamerro will clarify, the combination of both in the expression "gordo puto" is always derogatory and indicates contempt.

22 Lamborghini, *Novelas*, 253–54. All translations of Lamborghini belong to the translator, Silvia G. Dapía.

23 Gamerro, "Una teoría."

24 In some contexts Lamborghini prefers to talk about "the Mad Wise Man" (Lamborghini, *Novelas*, 234). Thomas Hardy solved this in a similar manner in his tragedy *Tess of the d'Ubervilles*. Instead of talking about "God," Hardy talks about the "president of the Immortals." Hardy, 446.

25 Lamborghini, *Novelas*, 233.

26 Ibid., 234.

27 Ibid., 237.

28 Ibid.

29 Ibid., 245.

30 Ibid.

31 Ibid., 248.

32 *Translator's note:* To American readers, this would be soccer.

33 Ibid., 249.

34 Ibid., 200.

35 Ibid., 238.

36 Lamborghini, *Novelas*, 242.

37 Ibid., 252.

38 Lamborghini, *Novelas*, 269.

39 "Those who find a 'form' in destiny are only characters in a novel, one of those novels that people do not write any more. But there is no remedy; some times things get a little complicated. Some of us find no 'form' in—oh, well—destiny. If we were able to find it, we might even like to have one," says Lamborghini's narrator. The funny thing about it is that he says so in "La causa justa." In this short story, the protagonist, the Japanese Takuro, found and gave a perfect "form" to his destiny and, therefore, to the story. Lamborghini, *Novelas*, 195.

40 Ibid., 269.

41 In the "The Garden of Forking Paths," Borges says: "In all fictional works, each time a man is confronted with several alternatives, he chooses one and eliminates the others; in the fiction of Ts'ui Pên, he chooses—simultaneoulsy—all of them" (Borges, *Labyrinths*, 47). Like most of the writings that Lamborghini left unpublished when he died, "El pibel Barulo" is an "indeterminate heap of contradictory drafts" (Borges, 26).

42 Aira, 5.

43 Aira, 109.

44 Lamborghini's *Tadey* revolves around a "kind of dangerous hairless monkey which could not be domesticated and only survived in mountainous caves, normally not accessible to humans as a result of the snow." Lamborghini, *Tadey*, 109–10.

45 Wilde, *Dorian Gray*, 4.

46 Baudelaire wrote: to "give a purer sense to the words of the tribe." Mallarmé, *Selected Poetry*, 51–52.

4   Are There as Many *Weddings* as Translations? On Gombrowicz's Spanish *El casamiento* (*The Wedding*)[1]

Bożena Anna Zaboklicka Zakwaska

It is well known that Witold Gombrowicz is one of the most renowned, perhaps *the* most renowned, Polish writer of the twentieth century. However, it is not well known that some scholars also consider him a remarkable writer in the Spanish language who was able to lead the prose of his adopted language in new directions. That is the opinion shared by respected Argentine writers such as Ricardo Piglia,[2] Juan José Saer, and Alan Pauls,[3] as well as the Catalonian poet Gabriel Ferrater who also included Gombrowicz among important Peninsular Spanish literary figures.[4]

In the 1960s, Ferrater was one of the most influential intellectuals in the literary and publishing circles in Barcelona. As a member of the jury of the international literary award granted every year by the Formentor Group,[5] Ferrater advocated on two occasions for Gombrowicz's nomination for the award, which was finally given to him for his novel *Cosmos* in 1967. Ferrater was also the author of the first article on Gombrowicz published in Spain. Entitled "Witold Gombrowicz," it begins as follows:

> There is a little bit of sarcasm that, in 1966, we need to introduce Witold Gombrowicz to the Peninsular Spanish audience…. Sarcasm not because, in my opinion, Gombrowicz is without doubt the greatest prose writer of our times. … But the major issue that we ought to be concerned about is that twenty and a half years ago Witold Gombrowicz was one of the most remarkable authors writing in Spanish.[6]

Elsewhere, in the same article, Ferrater asserts, "Now, when Gombrowicz's great international fame is imminent …, it would be a good idea that we commit ourselves to the fact that Gombrowicz is a Spanish writer (although nowadays he lives in France and no longer in Argentina)."[7]

Those who consider Gombrowicz a Spanish language writer are referring to his Spanish version of *Ferdydurke* made in collaboration with his young Latin American friends. The result of this attempt to pour the novel into Spanish is so astonishing that there are writers such as Piglia who lay claim to Gombrowicz for Argentine literature. Regarding the Argentine translation of *Ferdydurke*, Piglia claims, "I know just a very few literary experiences as extravagant and meaningful."[8] Further, he asserts:

> Gombrowicz in fact rewrote *Ferdydurke*. ... Translations are of decisive importance for a history of styles. Gombrowicz's "Argentine" *Ferdydurke* is one of the most unique texts of our literature.... In the Argentine version of *Ferdydurke* the Spanish language is forced up almost to rupture, contorted and artificial; it looks like a language of the future.[9]

Those Spanish-speaking scholars and writers who discuss Gombrowicz's "Spanish" works tend to make the language the focus of their attention, highlighting its originality and innovative character. Unable to compare the Spanish texts to the Polish versions, their statements lack a reflection on the content of those translations, which were done during the years Gombrowicz lived in Argentina.

Regarding *Ferdydurke*'s process of translation, it is possible to find a fair amount of information in Gombrowicz's own explanations of his work as they appear in his *Diary 1953–1956*, as well as in the "Preface for the Spanish edition" and in the "Notes about the translation" which precede the first Argentine edition of the novel (1947). This now legendary translation is, in fact, a second version of the novel, this time written in Spanish. Gombrowicz himself stated that it "only from afar resembles the original text."[10] To prove this it is enough to peruse the numerous and significant differences that exist between the Polish original work and the so-called Spanish translation. The key point that supports the claim that it is a second version of the same work is the fact that in the Spanish text Gombrowicz rewrote almost all of Chapter 4 (Preface to "The Child Runs Deep in Filidor"). From that moment onwards, Gombrowicz demanded that the new version of that chapter be used in all future editions of *Ferdydurke*, both Polish and foreign.

In contrast to *Ferdydurke*, we know very little about Gombrowicz's Spanish translation of his drama *Ślub* (*El casamiento*), published in Buenos Aires in 1948. In the case of *El casamiento* the process of translation was less spectacular than that of *Ferdydurke*. Fewer people participated in it, and in fact in the "Preface" to its Argentine edition Gombrowicz attributes the authorship of the Spanish translation to his friend Alejandro Rússovich.[11] Nevertheless, according to Rússovich, the Spanish translation of *El casamiento* was the result of a close collaboration with the author since Rússovich did not know Polish. Admittedly he knew a lot *about* the original language of *El casamiento*. Even at a very advanced age, he remembered that the translation of *El casamiento* was an attempt to recreate the music, the melody and the rhythm of the original

work rather than translating its contents.[12] Rússovich, who also participated in the collective translation of *Ferdydurke,* claimed that in both
cases Gombrowicz did not translate but "created anew" his works.[13]
In a brief note on the process of the Spanish translation, Gombrowicz,
in turn, refers the reader to the "Preface for the Spanish edition" and
the "Notes about the translation" of *Ferdydurke.* Talking about *El
casamiento,* Gombrowicz claims:

> Regarding this work it may be said what was already said about
> *Ferdydurke*'s translation: It was about trying to find an equivalent
> of a Polish language which was at times distorted, always rather
> arbitrary, and very far from any academic norm.[14]

The Argentine *El casamiento* was published in Buenos Aires by a music
publisher and went completely unnoticed. It fell into oblivion to such an
extent that rather than taking advantage of the author's translation, the
prestigious publisher Barral Editores of Barcelona published in 1973 a
new Spanish translation based on the French version. Incidentally, this
translation contains many mistakes, to begin with, its very title which
is rendered as *El matrimonio* (The Marriage). Thus, like *Ferdydurke,*
which was first published in Spanish in its author's version[15] and later
translated into Spanish directly from the Polish language,[16] in the case
of *Ślub* (*The Wedding*) there are also two very different Spanish versions.
   The following reflections on the possibility of different interpretations of *The Wedding* according to the Polish (*Ślub*) or the Argentine
(*El casamiento*) version originated by comparing the two Spanish translations, that is to say, the first Spanish translation done by Gombrowicz himself (which we will call the "Argentine version") and which,
according to Gombrowicz's intention, was called *El casamiento* (*The
Wedding*), with the second Spanish translation, which was based on the
French translation and erroneously entitled *El matrimonio* (*The Marriage*).[17] Furthermore, the realization that the two Spanish translations
are quite different brought me to the question of comparing the Polish
Ślub and the Argentine *El casamiento.* Nevertheless, before proceeding
to analyze the differences between these two versions it would be appropriate to explain briefly the peculiarity of this drama which allows for
two different interpretations.
   Inspired by Shakespearian and Calderonian dramas, as well as by
Romantic Polish drama, *El casamiento* is about the problems of the individual confronting the order of the world and that of history. Gombrowicz summarizes the content as follows:

> Enrique — the drama's protagonist — in his dream elevates his fa-
> ther to the dignity of king. He does this so that his father will bestow
> marriage upon him. However, later on, Enrique declares himself

king and wants to bestow marriage upon himself.... But at the decisive moment he breaks down, falls under the weight of his actions,
which, being different from himself, exceed him.[18]

The protagonist, Henryk, participates in the drama of the dissolution
of the old world, which was based on authority and transcendent sanction. Henryk rebels against all axiological systems and attempts to impose his own order. However, very soon, Henryk finds out that instead
of the old order an "interhuman church" is emerging, where all values,
norms, and even the sacred are created "between" individuals. Accordingly, his acts would not be exactly his but born in the sphere of the
"in betweenness," and they will become alien to the intentions of their
material author.

In my detailed comparison of the Argentine version to the Polish original I will use the names of the characters as they appear in the Polish
text. However, in the quotations taken from the Argentine version of
this drama, I will use the names as they appear in the Spanish text,
where Enrique corresponds to Henryk, Pepe to Władzio, and María to
Mania in the original Polish version. This analysis leads us to discover
important differences in the sphere of language, which would be logical, but also in the very structure of the text. In the Argentine version,
there are fragments that, compared with the Polish version, have been
deleted, substantially changed, or added. The text of the Argentine version is preceded by two paratexts written by the author: the "Prefacio"
("Preface") and the "Comentario" ("Commentary"), followed by "In-
dicaciones para los actores y el regisseur" ("Instructions for Actors and
Director") as well as thirty long footnotes. The "Commentary" partially coincides with the text entitled "Idea dramatu" which Gombrowicz put before the Polish edition. The footnotes, however, only appear
in the edition for a foreign reader or audience. We might suspect that,
not totally convinced by his Spanish version, the writer decided to "clarify" certain ideas contained in the drama, not only through a precise
dramatic form but also through discursive forms. This may be deduced
from a commentary by Rússovich: "The footnotes enrich the text with
a first interpretation. We shouldn't forget that they were written after
finishing the Spanish version."[19]

It is necessary to admit that if *Ślub* is a difficult work in Polish, in
Spanish it is from time to time almost unintelligible or at least confusing.
That is due to Gombrowicz's intention to force the Spanish language
to behave as if it were Polish. Often he translates literally into Spanish
words and expressions from the Polish original that even in Polish might
appear forced within certain contexts. However, in the Polish original
text they produce particular associations in the mind of the audience
since those words and expressions refer to a socio-cultural reality shared
by all Polish people. However, translated into such a remote language as

is Spanish with respect to Polish, those words and expressions appear as suspended in a void, without reference to any known phenomenon or meaning. Regarding Gombrowicz's decision to keep in the translation even those "mistakes full of meaning," Rússovich claims:

> We used to work on the translation of *El casamiento*. Every evening at the Café Rex, a place I detested, dulled by the smoke of the cigars and shivering with cold every time somebody would open the large windows of the coffeehouse, yawning, I would look up ravenously the appropriate word to express in Spanish what he was saying in French, Polish or in his ineffable Spanish, with precision, directly, wrongly, using a sovereign style, confident, strewn with mistakes full of meaning, which I would try to preserve.[20]

Similarly, in a text entitled "On translation" ("Sobre la traducción"), which is included in the 2010 edition of *El casamiento*, Rússovich, the co-translator, wrote:

> In a certain way this translation overrode the original text by transporting it into a language that has nothing to do with Polish. But at the same time it was about retaining the sense, the rhythm, the sonority and even the deformations of the Slavic language. In the final analysis, the result was a new text, a true rewriting, with the additions that Gombrowicz made himself led by the music and the peculiar spirit of the Spanish language.[21]

Because this is a second version of the drama, I shall focus on the structural differences between these two versions, which might suggest different interpretations in each case.[22] Thus, in Act II, in the culminating scene where Henryk betrays the Father-King and, induced by the Drunkard-Ambassador, carries out the coup d'etat, Gombrowicz added twelve pages that are absent in the Polish version. These added pages allow the audience, among other things, to identify more accurately the place and time of the action, particularly by mentioning a military mobilization of the neighboring power toward "the Polish border." Furthermore, in Footnote 19 (which is also missing in the Polish version), Gombrowicz refers to the drunkard as "the ambassador of Hitler."[23] But let us focus on the content of this added fragment.

After a conventional exchange of courtesy between the Father-King and the Drunkard-Ambassador, expressing their two neighboring states' spirit of peaceful coexistence, and the latter's statement that "my government has the best willingness to collaborate,"[24] the Chancellor, who was listening to the conversation, announces, "We have just so happened to have received the news that you are mobilizing along the Polish border (*The Chancellor hands the Father the telegram*)."[25] Furthermore, in the aforementioned Footnote 19, Gombrowicz wrote, "The Ambassador becomes Hitler's Ambassador and the King weakens again."[26] It must be mentioned here that the King had previously shown signs of his weakening authority. Thus, not being able to get rid of the Drunkard-Ambassador's presence, the King belittled his authority when requesting the Chancellor to scratch his itchy body. This raised concerns in the mother, who asked the King whether he was cold and such a concern, as we know from reading *Polish Memories,* is humiliating and denigrating for the object of that concern. However, after hearing the news about the mobilization of the foreign armed forces along the Polish border, the Father-King falls into a state of total weakness, which he attempts to conceal with assertions of strength: "Even if the news were true, we have already taken our precautions."[27] This fragment written for the Argentine reader sounds exceptionally familiar to Polish ears. Imperial proclamations such as "Our troups are invincible" or "Our army is invincible" seem to be drawn from Polish political speeches produced before September 1939.[28]

The fact that Gombrowicz directs the Argentine reader's attention to the Polish-German conflict seems to be an attempt to bring the European problems closer to people who were experiencing a very different political reality at that moment. But, at the same time, it appears that the author was trying to make his readers aware of the dangers of a tyranny posed by a mediocre individual who society catapulted to power and "inflated with illusions of grandeur." Perhaps situating the action of Act II in Poland at the very place where the greatest crime of history began may be interpreted as a way of helping the non-European reader understand the idea of the drama. That is, the danger posed by a mediocre and tyrannical individual worshipped by the masses—although this danger is not restricted to Europe but is universal. On the other hand, this warning may also be read as an allusion to Juan Domingo Perón's rise to power, who at that moment was acclaimed by the masses in Argentina as a "providential man."

Although Gombrowicz's literature is very far from dealing with current politics, the author is particularly sensitive to certain phenomena of his time. He commented on this on repeated occasions. Accordingly, when he says that *El casamiento* is a metaphor of "the transition of a world based on divine authority, divine and paternal authority, to another world, where Enrique's own will must become the divine, creative will ... like the will of Hitler or Stalin," Gombrowicz is not rejecting the interpretation of *El casamiento* as an "external drama."[29] Thus, in the article "Jaki jest sens *Ślubu?*"[30] ("What is the sense of *The Wedding?*"), Gombrowicz endorses Goldman's claim that *El casamiento*, written in 1947, is a work "closely related to the bloody history of those years."[31] Furthermore, he asserts that when he wrote it he was thinking more of Hitler than of Stalin but that, in any case, the drama's central issue is dictatorship. It is important to mention here that, in his *Diaries,* directed to the Polish reader, Gombrowicz had in principle nothing against the historical perspective proposed by Goldman, but he was much more critical of Goldman's interpretation in general.[32]

Leaving historical references aside, this second version of *El casamiento,* in my opinion, fits better into the category of "external drama" than the original Polish version. Granted, in both versions the dream is central and Henryk/Enrique verbalizes his condition of dreaming in each.[33] At a certain moment, he even says, "Be careful ....Don't tire me too much or I shall wake up ... and you will all disappear...."[34] Moreover, in both versions, within this dream we are facing an imaginary world governed by the oppositions "inwardness-outwardness," "identity-split identity."[35] It seems, however, that, in the Argentine version, written shortly after the Polish one, the author arranged the emphasis and proportions of those oppositions in a different way, although in both of them Gombrowicz led the protagonist to the same end. But he did it through different paths as if the Spanish language imposed on him a different way to solve the drama, more appropriate for people who are more immersed in the "interhuman" (external) world. Thus, in two key moments in *El casamiento* (when Enrique commits treason against his Father and the moment of Pepe's subordination to Enrique's will), Gombrowicz constructed, in the Argentine version, the relationship between the protagonists of the drama in a different way. Let us focus briefly on the moment of Enrique's treason.

In Act II of the original Polish version, instigated by the Drunkard-Ambassador to betray his Father, Henryk recites a monologue by means of which he convinces himself that he was right, that it is imperative to abolish the established authorities and replace them with his own authority.

> Oh, God! What God? Oh, Father! What Father? It was I who
> made them what they are. By virtue of my bounty! By virtue of
> my will! Why should I kneel down before them? Why not
> kneel down before myself, myself, myself, the sole source of
> my law?...
> ... It is I who create kings!
> It is I who should be King!
> I am supreme! There is nothing higher than me!
> I am God! ...[36]

Right after Henryk's monologue, the Father pronounces a discourse that begins by expressing his firm belief that his son would be incapable of betraying him and ends with the discovery of Henryk's betrayal. Immediately afterwards Henryk ascends to ultimate power and commands that the Father and the Drunkard-Ambassador be arrested.

In the Argentine version, the process experienced by Enrique from the conversation between Enrique and the Drunkard-Ambassador, who induces the former to treachery, to the moment treachery materializes is much longer and psychologically more complex than in the Polish version. To begin with, in the Argentine version, the Drunkard-Ambassador exerts much more pressure on Enrique to act against the King, assuring him, first, full support in the attack on the King. "Pounce on him...! We will follow you! Pounce on him!,"[37] the Drunkard-Ambassador urges Enrique. Furthermore, after noticing Enrique's hesitation the Drunkard-Ambassador threatens Enrique that if he turns back and does not attack the King "we will pounce on you ... traitor...!"[38] Thus, in the Argentine version, Enrique resists assuming the role of a traitor. The Argentine version lacks all the monologue of the Polish version from where I extracted the fragment quoted earlier.

Moreover, as opposed to the Polish version, in the Argentine translation Enrique begins to subordinate Pepe under his will at a much earlier moment. In the original Polish, this motive (the subordination of Władzio to Henryk's will) does not appear until Act III, when Henryk discovers that he is jealous of his friend. In sum, it seems that, in the Polish version, the subordination of Władzio demanded by Henryk is motivated by personal revenge. Instead, in the Argentine version Enrique's demand of Pepe's subordination appears rather as if it were a not yet totally conscious preparation on Enrique's part to exert absolute, dictatorial power.

Henryk orders Władzio to pounce on the Drunkard-Ambassador who prompts him to betray his Father-King. In the Argentinean version, in the fragment I will quote next, when Enrique demands Pepe's subordination, it appears clearly formulated as one of the main ideas of Gombrowicz's philosophy, namely, that all that is human is actually interhuman. Accordingly, human acts are not individual but arise between human beings. Thus, if a human being gives the commands and the other obeys, not only is everything possible but responsibility also disappears. And this is the mechanism that produces tyrants.

> Enrique
> I can't myself pounce upon him since
> That's not correct.... However you
> Can...due to my command... I'm commanding you then:
> If he pounces on the king my father, you pounce
> On him ... Can you do that?
>
> Pepe (Loudly, resolutely)
> If you command me I can do everything
> Very simple! You command me,
> I obey. Between the two of us
> Everything can be done.

Enrique (Loudly, resolutely)
If you obey, I can do everything
Nothing simpler than that! I command,
You obey. Between the two of us
Everything can be done.[39]

In this way, Pepe arrests the Drunkard-Ambassador in the presence of the King due to Enrique's command. For a long time, Enrique is not totally convinced of the need to overthrow the King in order to obtain his goal of receiving from the monarch's hands the purifying marriage to María. Accordingly, before making the decision to overthrow the King, Enrique tries to persuade him to grant him marriage. But the Kingman is no longer able to keep up with the dignity of the Sovereign-King. Horrified by his own greatness resulting from the subordination of the other people to his power, he wants to abdicate.

The question arises as to why the betrayal comes naturally to Henryk in the Polish version, while, in the Spanish version, it takes Gombrowicz twelve pages of a subtle psychological play between Enrique, Pepe, and the Drunkard-Ambassador to make it possible? Comparing the two versions—*Ślub* and *El casamiento*—the feeling arises that, in the Polish version, the betrayal is the result of the inner drama of Henryk, who has to abolish the old order because he lost his faith in it, finding no justification to keep it. Instead, the Argentine version strengthens the effect of the betrayal as the result of the interaction among the characters involved in the drama (even when those characters may be the product of Enrique's subconscious). Betrayal is created "among them" in a more evident fashion than in the Polish version. In other words, the main difference between the two versions seems to lie in the fact that in the Argentine version the "interhuman factor" appears more intensified than in the original Polish version. It appears as if the author added new elements to the Argentine version to make the "drama of Form" more easily accessible to the Spanish-speaking audience. Thus, for example, in Act III, there is the sound of certain external voices who claim that Enrique is jealous due to an alleged relation between Pepe and María. In the Polish original, in contrast, that jealously appears as the result of Henryk's internal experience, imagining that everybody in the world sees his fiancée in relation to Władzio. To put it slightly differently, in the Argentine version, the "outside world" dictates Enrique's suspicion that he has to be jealous because the others believe that he is so.

The end of the drama is also solved in different ways in each version. In the Polish version, when the Drunkard-Ambassador discovers Władzio's corpse, he expresses his surprise and asks who the author of the crime is:

Drunkard-Ambassador (shocked)
A corpse!/
Stitched by knives, I shit on…
Who did away with him?[40]

And he receives from Henryk a univocal response along with the full admission of guilt:

> A guest (to Henryk)
> Sire!
> He killed himself with a knife a moment ago!
>
> Drunkard-Ambassador
> He killed himself?
> Why did he kill himself?
>
> Henryk
> On my orders.[41]

In the Argentine version, neither the Drunkard-Ambassador nor the people surrounding Enrique have the faintest doubt that Pepe died by his own hand.

> Chambelan
> He killed himself!
>
> The Drunkard-Ambassador (astonished)
> Corpse!
> With the knife he....[42]

To this, Enrique responds, "Now I can get married."[43] Thus, in the Argentine version there is no confession of guilt. The guilt was diluted because it was never expressed. The crime did itself, it was born among men. This allows Enrique to recite with full conviction the very well-known words about his own innocence, which also appear in the Polish version: "I am innocent/I declare I am innocent as a child. I did nothing. I don't know anything./Here nobody is responsible for anything!/Responsibility doesn't exist!"[44] That's why for Enrique to submit to the collective coercion that assigns him the blame is tantamount to accepting the external world's victory.

El casamiento may be perceived as a kind of duel between Enrique's inner world, which distorts the external world, and the external world, which imposes itself on Enrique and at the same time distorts him. Comparing the Polish and Argentine versions of the drama in terms of the struggle between both forces (the inward and the outward), there is a feeling that in the Polish version the inner force predominates, while the external force predominates in the Argentine version. Indeed, Polish scholars who interpreted the Polish original tend to agree that Gombrowicz's Polish drama should be interpreted as an "inner drama" rather than an "external" one for the simple reason that, according to them, *Ślub* does not attempt to explain twentieth-century European history. Rather, in the view of the same critics, *Ślub* is the representation of a dream: namely, a kind of cultural subconscious whose products are the individuals. In the view of Jan Błoński, shared by Jerzy Jarzębski, *Ślub* is the personal drama of Henryk, who creates, in his interior world, the enemies with whom he will have to deal. Accordingly, Henryk's struggle is a struggle against his own inner conflicts, his psychological complexes, his crisis of conscience, and his perversions.[45] It may be objected, however, that even when the struggle takes place in the interior world of the protagonist, that interiority is a product of the external world and the "interhuman" play that determines all that is human.

Czesław Miłosz understood and expressed with superlative precision the relation between the internal and the external worlds in Gombrowicz's drama. He asserted:

> Of all his Works, Gombrowicz thought most highly of *The Marriage*. In this new version of *Hamlet* everything happens in a dream and, what is more "inside a mind" that a dream? Henry is conscious the entire time that he is sleeping, but his consciousness is powerless, it can prevent nothing, Henry partakes in the action or rather he is acted upon others and whatever is to happen happens. The awareness that whatever I do is nonsense, although I cannot do anything else, because I'm coerced into it by the interhuman reality in which I have found myself (what is worse, which lives in my head)—that is the very essence of the twentieth century Split, common to every day life in a technological Civilization, to participation in mass movements, and to the establishment of terror.[46]

My interpretation is that within the context of the Split between inwardness and exteriority, by placing greater emphasis on the interhuman play within the protagonist's process of distortion, the Argentine version of *El casamiento* seems to gravitate more toward the "external drama" than the original Polish text.

Notes

1 This essay was translated by Silvia G. Dapía. The research was carried out in "The translation in the Catalan literary field since the end of the Franco regime (1976–2000): studies of reception and literary language" (Ref. FFI2014-54915-P), Pompeu Fabra University, Barcelona, principal investigators Dr. Enric Gallén Miret and Dr. Marcel Ortín Rull. The project has been funded by the Ministry of Economy, Industry and Competitiveness of Spain.

2 Referring to the Argentine translation of *Ferdydurke*, Piglia said:

> "Gombrowicz in fact rewrote *Ferdydurke*.... Gombrowicz's Argentine *Ferdydurke* is one of the most original texts of our literature.... In the Argentine version of *Ferdydurke* the Spanish is forced almost to rupture, strained and artificial; it looks like a language of the future."
> Piglia, "La novela."

3 On Argentine authors' perceptions of Gombrowicz's works, see Suchanow, *Argentyńskie*, 244; Terradas, "Recepción."

4 On Ferrater's introduction of Gombrowicz's work to the Peninsular Spanish audience, see Stasiakiewicz, "Gombrowicz in Spain."

5 In his *Memorias*, Barral wrote about Ferrater's trajectory as an editor and his fascination with Gombrowicz's works. In 1966, Ferrater first supported Gombrowicz's nomination for the award *Premio Internacional de Literatura* for his novel *Pornografía*, the first of his novels published in Spain in the Spanish language. This novel appeared in 1968 under the title *La seducción*, translated into Spanish by Ferrater. See Barral, *Memorias*, 545. In the same year, his novel *Ferdydurke* appeared in Catalan. The Catalonian translation was based on the "Argentine version," and this was expressly authorized by Gombrowicz. It was done by Ramon Folch i Camarasa and published by Ediciones 62.

6 Ferrater, *Presencia*, 192.

7 Ibid., 194.

8 Piglia, "polaca," 76.

9 Piglia, "polaca," 78.

10 Gombrowicz, *Ferdydurke* (Argos), 13.

11 Gombrowicz, *El casamiento* (EAM), 6.

12 The typescript of the Spanish translation of *El casamiento* is in the Gombrowicz Museum at Wsola, Poland. In addition to some handwritten corrections of the vocabulary done by Gombrowicz or Rússovich, what meets the eye are marginal annotations written by the author, indicating fragments that have to sound like a verse. The graphical layout of the text, which corresponds to the form of the verse, is often marked by hand.

13 Rússovich, "El otro."

14 Gombrowicz, *El casamiento*, 4.

15 The Spanish version of *Ferdydurke* done "by the autor, who was assisted by the 'Translation Committee,'" as we read on the page of the copyright to the first Argentine edition (Argos), was re-edited by Editorial Sudamericana (Buenos Aires, 1964) and later published on two occasions in Spain by Edhasa (Barcelona, 1984) and Seix Barral (Barcelona, 2002).

16 Translation by Rubió and Sławomirski (2005).

17 The French word "mariage" has two meanings. In one it refers to the marriage as an institution; in the other it refers to the ceremony, the nuptial rite. The Spanish word "matrimonio" refers only to the institution and not the ceremony. Thus, in the body of the second Spanish translation, the translator uses the word "boda" ("wedding") several times instead of "matrimonio." Accordingly, the title *El matrimonio* definitely misconstrues the main point of the drama which, as Gombrowicz claims, is principally a drama of the Form. This idea is summarized in a phrase contained in the *Comentario* which precedes the Argentine translation: "Form is created between men and the latter are contingent upon to the former." Gombrowicz, *El casamiento* (EAM), 7. The marriage's ceremony is the form or convention that will bring back to the protagonist and his fiancée the purity that supposedly belongs to bride and groom. Thus, the drama is not about the institution but about the ceremony and the dilemma regarding the one who should administer it.

18 Gombrowicz, *El casamiento* (EAM), 7.

19 Rússovich, *Palabras*, 237.

20 Ibid., 226.

21 Rússovich, "Sobre," in Gombrowicz, *El casamiento* (El cuenco), 5–6.

22 In this essay I will use the first Spanish edition of *El casamiento*, that of 1948.
23 Gombrowicz, *El casamiento*, 75.
24 "Mi gobierno tiene la mejor voluntad de colaboración."
25 Gombrowicz, *El casamiento*, 75: "Justamente hemos recibido la noticia que Ustedes se movilizan en la frontera polaca (entrega al Padre el telegrama)."
26 Ibid., 11: "el Embajador se vuelve Embajador de Hitler y de nuevo el Rey se debilita."
27 Ibid., 75: "Aunque esa noticia fuese cierta, nosotros hemos tomado nuestras precauciones."
28 Ibid. "nuestras tropas son invencibles"; "nuestra armada es invencible."
29 Gombrowicz, *Testament*, 109.
30 Gombrowicz, "Jaki jest." He was responding to Lucien Goldman's article entitled "La critique n'a rien compris," *France–Observateur*, June 2, 1964.
31 Gombrowicz, "Jaki jest," 519–20.
32 Gombrowicz, *Diary* (Vallee), 670.
33 The use of the dream as motivation may be interpreted as Gombrowicz's winking at literary tradition. After all, the dream as resource has been used in literature since immemorial times as justification for all that in a literary work appears strange, irrational, and unexpected. However, the case of *El casamiento* is more complex because even when it is clear that what happens in the drama is the protagonist's dream, it is nevertheless an "interactive" dream. Thus, as Gombrowicz states in the "Preface" to its Argentine version: "Henry resembles rather an artist than a person who is in a deep sleep. Everything is incessantly 'created' here, Enrique creates the dream and the dream creates Enrique." Gombrowicz, *El casamiento*, 8. As Michał Głowiński observed, the dream in this drama constitutes a problem and it is the subject of continuous questions, doubts, and reflections. Głowiński, "Komentarze," 133–34. Henryk, the protagonist, wonders on diverse occasions whether he is really dreaming or he has gone crazy. However, when the Drunkard (a cartoonish alter ego of Henryk) accuses him of madness, Henryk takes hold of the idea of being dreaming.
34 Gombrowicz, *El casamiento*, 59: "Cuidado conmigo.... Porque si me cansan demasiado, me despertaré... y vosotros desapareceréis...." Polish version from Gombrowicz, *Dramaty*, VI, 148: "Ostrożnie ze mną.... Bo jeśli zanadto mnie zmęczycie, to ja zbudzę się ... i wszyscy znikniecie...."
35 Zaleski, "Ślub," 616.
36 Original Polish from Gombrowicz, *Dramaty*, VI, 165:

> Bóg! Jaki Bóg? Ojciec! Jaki Ojciec? Ja sam ich sobie ustanowiłem. Oni
> z łaski mojej, z mojej woli! Po cóż klękać przed nimi? Dlaczego nie
> klęknąć przed sobą, sobą, sobą, jedynym źródłem prawa mojego? ...
> ... Ja stwarzam królów!
> Ja powinieniem być królem!
> Jestem Najwyższy! Nic wyższego ode mnie!
> Ja jestem Bogiem!

37 Gombrowicz, *El casamiento*, 76: "¡Échate sobre él...! ¡Nosotros te seguimos! ¡Échate!"
38 "Entonces nosotros nos echaremos sobre ti ... traidor...." Ibid.
39 Enrique:

> Yo mismo no puedo echarme sobre él, puesto
> Que no está bien.... Tú sin embargo

Puedes ... por mi orden.... Te ordeno pues:
Si él se echa sobre el rey mi padre, tú te echas
Sobre él... ¿Puedes hacerlo?

Pepe (en voz alta, con frescura):
Si me ordenas todo lo puedo
¡Muy fácil! Tú me das la orden
Yo cumplo. Entre los dos
Se puede hacer todo.

Enrique (en voz alta, con frescura):
Si me obedeces, yo puedo todo.
¡Qué más fácil! Yo ordeno,
Tú cumples. Entre los dos
Se puede hacer todo.

Ibid., 77.

40

Pijak (zdziwiony):
Trup!
Nożem sztachnięty psiakre...
Kto go sztachnął?

Gombrowicz, *Dramaty*, VI, 220.

41

Jeden z gości (*do Henryka*):
Panie!
Nożem on siebie przed chwilą
Zabił!

Pijak:
Zabił sam siebie? Po co zabił?

Henryk:
Z mojego rozkazu.

Gombrowicz, *Dramaty*, VI, 220.

42

Chambelán:
¡Se mató!
El Borracho (asombrado):
¡Cadáver!/Con el cuchillo se...

Gombrowicz, *El casamiento*, 186.

43 "Ahora ya puedo casarme." Gombrowicz, *El casamiento*, 132.
44 Gombrowicz, *El casamiento*, 134:

"Soy inocente/Declaro que soy inocente como un niño, no hice nada,
no sé nada./¡Aquí nadie de nada es responsable!/¡La responsabilidad no
existe!" In the Polish version: "Jestem niewinny. Oświadczam, że jestem
niewinny, jak dziecko, ja nic nie zrobiłem, o niczym nie wiem/Tu nikt za
nic nie jest odpowiedzialny!/Odpowiedzialności w ogóle nie ma!"

Gombrowicz, *Dramaty*, VI, 223.

45 Jarzębski, "Pytania," 101–15; Jarzębski, "Literatura polska," 248–49.
46 Vallee, "Who is Gombrowicz?", xviii.

5 "Intermolecular Mockery and Derision, an Inbred Superlaugh"

On English Translations of Gombrowicz's *Ferdydurke* and Their Plural Original

Magdalena Heydel

Beth Holmgren has written about the problems American readers have had with Witold Gombrowicz.[1] Praised as one of the most important artists and thinkers of late modernity, compared to Joyce and Proust, Gombrowicz proves to be not only difficult to read, but perhaps some might believe not quite worth the effort since his writing is too idiosyncratic and convoluted. This feeling, together with the oft heard mantra of untranslatability chanted invariably whenever his unique style and language use are mentioned, has placed Gombrowicz in a gray zone, a limbo for the great but unread, acknowledged but unknown. Holmgren explains this situation by the duality inherent in the American literary establishment, with its ever-widening gap between academia and intellectuals, on the one hand, and the general reader at large, on the other hand. The former—a relatively narrow group of more courageous comparatists, Slavic literature scholars, and Polish émigré writer-professors—create the lofty image of the writer and must expend considerable effort to promote the circulation of his works.

Sadly, says Holmgren, in spite of these attempts, the position of Gombrowicz in American humanities reflects the marginal position of the study of literature from less well-known languages in general. Gombrowicz is thus read, taught, and analyzed behind the doors of Slavic departments as an exotic specimen of an exotic branch of modernism, and if he ever escaped that enclosure, it was only to showcase the intricacies of the politics and history of the region.[2] This is not necessarily relevant to the interest of non-specialist American readers and hardly makes it into the circle of masterworks of international modernist literature.[3] The reception of Gombrowicz in America, claims Krystyna Lipińska-Iłłakowicz, sheds light on the stereotype of the Eastern European writer who, as a rule, is an obscure, strange figure, whose works are concentrated on politics, the language complex and untranslatable.[4] Hence, there is a general feeling that their work is irrelevant to the American reader.

The positioning of Gombrowicz within English language literary culture resulted from various factors, but undoubtedly the first of these was translation. The story of the early renditions of his work into foreign languages, coupled with his personal story, exposes mechanisms of marginalization at work. It also reveals much about both the institutional and linguistic progress of Gombrowicz's international career. This radically Polish author, whose work is read in his native culture as a great and painful (if humorous) struggle with the notion of Polishness, as well as a creative re-working of the Polish language together with its class-bound tradition, reaches the international audience through a complex series of rewritings. This influenced not just its linguistic and stylistic form but also its potential meaning. The author himself expended a considerable effort to create his literary acceptance.[5] Translations were the main instrument of this work, as is clear from his letters collected under the title *Walka o sławę* (Struggle for Fame).[6]

I would like to claim that it is the history of the early creation and reception of Gombrowicz's work, more than the difficulty of the original, which influenced his position in international literature. In what follows, I will briefly look at the history of *Ferdydurke*'s early international creation and reception in Argentina and in France. Then, I will describe the first translation of the novel into English, Erich Mosbacher's 1961 work, which was replaced by Danuta Borchardt's new version in 2000. Subsequently, I will give several examples of the differences between the two translations to illustrate how the history of their creation shaped their respective artistic qualities and how it placed them within the receiving cultural system. I argue that without taking the historical dimension into account, any strong critical claims as to the quality of the versions fail to help us understand the presence of Gombrowicz's novel on the international literary scene.

The Making of Original 2

Beginning with the outbreak of the war in September 1939, Gombrowicz lived in Argentina where he remained for twenty-four years. The place to which he emigrated was both accidental and deliberate at the same time. According to different sources, the writer was either trapped in South America or chose to stay there in order to avoid war in Europe, or both.[7] Whichever is correct, his relocation put him into a radically isolated position.

Gombrowicz did not know Spanish and had practically no literary or professional contacts in Buenos Aires. To make matters worse, he very soon managed to antagonize the local Polish circle with his famous 1940 lecture in Teatro del Pueblo, which was perceived as a violent attack on Poland and all things Polish.[8] Czesław Miłosz, after a difficult period spent in France in the early 1950s, settled in the U.S. and became a university professor in the mainstream of world literary culture. Conversely, Gombrowicz, in spite of his efforts to gain recognition for the genius he considered himself to be, was located not only outside his native milieu, marginal as it was, but also outside international literary circles. The Spanish translation of *Ferdydurke* appeared in Buenos Aires in 1947, but the writer had to wait another six years until François Bondy noticed it in France and published parts of it in French in his journal *Preuves*. It was not until 1959 that the whole novel appeared in French. The first English version, based on the French and German renditions, came out in 1961.

In 1947, in his "Letter to the Ferdydurkists," a short, tongue-in-cheek text published in the Polish literary magazine *Nowiny Literackie* (Literary News), Gombrowicz says:

> Do not lose hope. Be warmed with the news that very soon the proud flagship of *Ferdydurke* will be launched onto the waters of Spanish seas (twenty-six people were toiling over the translation of this holy and immaculate book) and then, I believe, it will visit French and English shores, firing all its cannons straight into the gaping mugs of the good old silly natives.[9]

In his unmistakable style and using equally unmistakable colonial imagery, Gombrowicz voices his ambition to gain a shocking international renown and sees translations as the vehicles (or vessels) to carry on this project.

Two filters were at work between the original and this translation—the author attempting to express his eccentric creation in a language in which he was a novice and the editing/re-writing/re-imagining by a group of native Spanish-speakers from Cuba and Argentina with no knowledge of the source language, culture, and reality. The group of translators, one can imagine, had to negotiate between languages: Polish, unknown to them and Spanish, only marginally known to Gombrowicz.

On the linguistic and stylistic levels, the relationship of the final outcome of this two-stage translation procedure to the original Polish text is necessarily highly problematic and defies a simple comparative analysis by juxtaposing the original and the translation, if for the simple reason that the status of the original itself seems to be uncertain. The 1937 book published in Poland seems to be a pre-text for a Polish-French-Spanish inter-lingual creation which came into being during the translation sessions at Café Rex. The original is present in the process in the form of authorial accounts, a momentary and elusive creation without a stable written form.

The "translation committee" did a wonderful job in many respects. They also marked the beginning of a new period in Gombrowicz's life; but to treat the textual effect of their efforts as a neutral product of a regular translation process is a mistake—one that has been made quite often and has powerfully influenced the reception of the translations. Seen in such a perspective, *Ferdydurke* becomes an independent, innovatory work of international literature in Spanish, its immediate links with the Polish original text and incomprehensible contexts necessarily shifted to the background.

In spite of the complex way it came into being, this version was to become a source text not just for new interpretations but also for further renditions into other languages. It secured for itself the status of self-translation, as the author took part in its creation, which has given it a privileged position as far as the prestige and authority of the text is concerned. The authorial "imprimatur," bestowed on the Spanish translation, further influenced the history of *Ferdydurke*'s translations into other languages. It is the Café Rex version that they referred to, not the 1937 Warsaw publication; in light of his correspondence, Gombrowicz's position in the transactions was not only that of the author of the original, but to a large extent a negotiator between translators and publishers.

The Making of Original 3

Gombrowicz started working on the French translation in May 1956 while still in Argentina. He collaborated with Roland Martin, a French journalist and writer who knew no Polish and based his work to a large extent on the Spanish rendition as well as his conversations with the author.[10] "Conquering Paris"[11] was for Gombrowicz, who was brought up in the French-centered culture of pre-war Poland and a speaker of French, the utmost ambition. Late in 1957, he sent the text to Konstanty Jeleński, a Paris-based Polish intellectual and literary critic who was taking care of the French end of the business. Jeleński wrote an introduction and the translation was published in October 1958 under the penname of "Brone." This edition, re-published in 1967 before it was replaced with George Sedir's 1973 translation from the Polish,[12] became yet another authorial version—a "third original."

During the long and painful process of editing the French translation, based on the Spanish text, and getting it published, Gombrowicz corresponded extensively with Jeleński. The letters reveal not only his anxiety as to the outcome of the whole enterprise but also a deep uncertainty about the quality of the foreign version. He clearly did not trust neither his own judgment as to the choices made nor the suggestions on the part of the publisher's editor. He sought Jeleński's help with difficult or dubious passages in the translation; yet when the latter gave his opinion and made suggestions, Gombrowicz usually disagreed and demanded that Martin's version be maintained, arguing that as his name was going to be mentioned as a translator he would take the responsibility. The letters show how much Gombrowicz was dependent on agents for translation. In one of the letters, he wrote:

> I must confess I am very much concerned about those translation corrections. … the thing is those translation nuances are a fiendishly subjective matter and my experience has taught me no one is to be trusted here. I am afraid you will introduce changes my translator here is going to object to and that discussions and arguments will follow….[13]

In the case of his collaboration with Martin, the team was not as large as in the case of the Café Rex project. Moreover, Gombrowicz knew the language of translation fairly well, so this rendition was definitely less experimental. Still, as was the case of the Café Rex version, a closer look into the history of Brone's translation and the role the author played in it leads to the conclusion that comparing the French text with the Polish 1937 edition in search for equivalence or fidelity is a methodological mistake that ignores the conditions of its creation. The fact that Brone's rendition was replaced with another translation, directly from the Polish, might be seen as a confirmation that it was inadequate on that level, but it does not change the impact the first translation had on Gombrowicz's international career.[14] It was Brone's version, together with the 1960 German translation from the Polish by Walter Tiel—another rendition whose quality was in doubt[15]—that in their turn became the bases for the first rendition of *Ferdydurke* in English.

"In the area of English, I'm as thick as a plank"

Gombrowicz spoke no English, had a rather limited knowledge of both British and American cultural life, and had few contacts. His letters show deep uncertainty as to managing his reputation in that language.[16] His U.S. correspondent, the Polish émigré Józef Wittlin, in his letters to Gombrowicz presented American culture as a purely business-oriented, ruthless, and intellectually unsophisticated environment.[17] The troubles Gombrowicz experienced in his attempts to find a publisher seem to prove this correct. Most of his letters to Alfred Knopf, Richard Seaver of Grove Press, *The Atlantic Monthly*, Simon and Shuster, and Viking resulted only in refusals.

The Gombrowicz archive in the Bienecke Library includes his correspondence with the editors as well as copies of editorial reports from the years 1963–1964 when Gombrowicz was trying to publish his novel *Pornografia*.[18] Some of them also include remarks on *Ferdydurke* (already published) and in general judge his writing as obscure, puzzling, not well formed, heavy, and perverse. The overall view of Gombrowicz's writing was that it might be brilliant, but was unsuitable for American readers who are not interested in intellectual play. These opinions were already being voiced after 1961 when Eric Mosbacher's translation of *Ferdydurke* was published in New York by Harcourt Brace Jovanovic and in England with MacGibbon and Kee.

The book sold no more than one thousand copies.[19] This made American publishers reluctant to undertake the risk of publishing his further work. Still, the growing fame of the author in Europe, where during the 1960s he was gradually becoming an influential intellectual, helped his books on the American market. Mosbacher's version was re-published in 1964 by Grover Press, for more than thirty years serving as the standard translation. This happened in spite of the fact—often stressed by critics, especially those in Poland—that it was definitely not the equivalent of the original on both the linguistic and stylistic levels. Unfortunately, as opposed to the cases discussed earlier, there are hardly any sources pertaining to how Mosbacher's translation was made since the author did not take part in the process.

In the year 2000, 63 years after the original book saw the light of day and 39 years after the first English translation appeared via Spanish, French, and German, Yale University Press published a new English rendition of *Ferdydurke*. This time it was made directly from the original Polish by Danuta Borchardt, a Polish immigrant who left her homeland at the age of 11 and thereafter lived in English-speaking countries.

The Language as a Character

Ferdydurke, while certainly not "untranslatable," is a difficult and complex object of translation. It combines the factual difficulty—there is no denying that pre-war Poland and its social structure serve as a framework for what the novel does—with the linguistic intricacy. Gombrowicz's language is creative, not re-creative, hence the distortions, repetitions, de-regulations, and shocks, both in the discourse of the characters and the narrator.[20] Any word is a settled form, enclosing and reducing one with its constraints; so, implies Gombrowicz, the obligation of the creative artist is to break the constraints. He mixes idioms and dialects and condenses their characteristic features. He also introduces his own inventions, uses nouns as verbs or adjectives, and introduces solecisms and other distorted grammatical constructions. These release the element of parody[21] to allow the language stick out its tongue at us.

The stylistic form and special use of language in *Ferdydurke* cannot be taken at face value. It stems from the deep layers of Polish tradition and in the process turns this tradition inside out. Jerzy Jarzębski notes that it is a mistake to see Gombrowicz simply as a master of the grotesque and paradox who deconstructs the old-fashioned forms. Gombrowicz, writes the critic,

> refers to the legacy of national literature, his blasphemies are rooted in the current flowing from the Sarmatian baroque and nineteenth

century apologies of the familial. That is why when he blasphemed, he cut his readers to the quick, because he reached to the areas of the soul where every Pole keeps their 'holy of the holy': a complex of myths which has educated and informed them.[22]

The parodistic effect is produced on the level of the story and the thick net of intertextual links to Polish culture.[23] But for translators, who work into cultures distant from the Polish domestic contexts, language matters the most. The novel is a feast of linguistic excess with its characteristic nervousness, obsessive repetitions, and multiplications, as if the narrator was incessantly on the panicky lookout for a more apt way of making himself understood and catching the elusive quality of human life he is after. Jarzębski writes that Gombrowicz's language is "consciously opaque, which is to say it is not a pane of glass to see the world through but becomes a character in the novel in its own right."[24] It is not a language of representation but condensation and distortion. The linguistic features are kneaded into symbols of inter-human relations. The effect is both sur-real and hyper-real. By destabilizing communicative situations, Gombrowicz gets into their core. By masking them with playful language, he actually uncovers his universal discovery concerning the human world.

Gombrowicz did not author any treatises on social philosophy, his literary work though, thanks to its language, may be to a large extent read as a reflection on inter-human and social relations.[25] The concept of the "inter-human church,"[26] the communicative and social space that defines us, is made of words. This means much more than just an eccentric literary style, a predilection to play on words and images rather than ideas and concepts, an inclination to comedy and satire rather than meditation and reflection. A project to "translate" Gombrowicz's writing into a language of social philosophy would miss the point—it is the creativity of the language that guarantees the creativity of the thought.

The How, Not the What

One of the American editors who rejected Gombrowicz's *Pornografia* in the 1960s claimed, "I don't think Gombrowicz will ever have the appreciative audience in America that he does in France, because it's the How, not the What of his book that is important."[27] If the "How" fails to get through in translation, the novel misses its point. "One realizes and admires Gombrowicz's sensitiveness and subtlety, but would like to know what he is being sensitive to and subtle about," D. J. Enright famously remarked in his 1967 *New York Review of Books* essay on Alistair Hamilton's translation of *Pornografia* and Eric Mosbacher's *Ferdydurke*.

The critic expands much effort to fit Gombrowicz into the framework of modernist writing and uses various contexts to understand his allegedly artistically wonderful and politically relevant writing. *Ferdydurke*, he says, at least has some funny bits in it: "Perhaps it doesn't make much more sense than *Pornografia*, but it certainly provides more amusement." And he adds, "I doubt whether without knowing of the book's strange and sad publishing history and its suppression in Poland one would have spotted its supposed (and prophetic) political relevance, though one perceives and appreciates its timeless and unlocalized mockery."[28]

Ferdydurke is much more than a social satire or a critique of pre-war Polish society and its institutions. It speaks against the accepted models of interactive relations that reflect the interpersonal hierarchies and inter-human power struggles. Thanks to its language—at the same time rooted in a particular tradition and overcoming it from within—in addition to all the fun and comedy and the bitter commentary on Polishness, it offers a merciless vision of the human being in the incessant process of impossible self-definition in the world of mugs. As the novel's translator says, it pokes fun at "destructive elements in human relationships" and pupas: "gentle, insidious, but definite infantilizing and humiliation."[29] "But most important," says the narrator in Borchardt's translation, "there was something at my heels at all times, something that I would call a sense of inner, intermolecular mockery and derision, an inbred super-laugh of my bodily parts and the analogous parts of my spirit, all running wild."[30] The language of the novel "all running wild" gets us to its philosophical core.

"To Approach Gombrowicz with Humility and the Reader with Audacity"

Borchardt's translation appeared not long after Gombrowicz's death and outside of his personal struggle to be recognized, but also after there had been more than thirty years of scholarly and literary reception of his work. As opposed to Mosbacher, who translated an unknown work of an unknown writer whose original language was too exotic to be known, Borchardt worked with a modern classic from the language of two recent Nobel Prize winners, Czesław Miłosz and Wisława Szymborska. All of her translations of Gombrowicz's novels have enjoyed considerable critical success. *Ferdydurke* (Yale, 2000) brought her the National Translation Award. She received a grant from the National Endowment for the Arts to translate *Cosmos* (Yale, 2005). Then followed *Pornografia* (Grove, 2009), for which she won the Found in Translation Award. In 2014, her rendition of *Trans-Atlantyk* appeared from Yale University Press.

The differences between the two translations of *Ferdydurke* are manifold. They have different source texts. They were done in different epochs, forty years apart. The status of Gombrowicz on the international literary scene had largely changed. They were done by translators whose professional, linguistic, and cultural competences were different. Interestingly though, Borchardt is a psychiatrist by profession, and Mosbacher, who was a journalist, is best known for his Ignazio Silone renditions, but he also translated Sigmund Freud and Sandor Ferenczi's work.

In his translation, Mosbacher generally reproduced the features of the French version by Brone, but he failed to include whole passages. For example, the so-called "pre-existentialist" fragment of the opening monologue where the sense of anxiety and fear is stressed by allusions to Kierkegaard and Schopenhauer and the obsessive multiplications that also set up the style of the narration. His version of this scene is not much more than a matter of fact relation of the uneasy awakening of the character and an explanation for the morning fear: Johnny had a bad dream about a "regression" to the age of 15.

Borchardt, on the other hand, is careful to reproduce the absurdly alliterative, enumerative, and synonymic syntax of Joey's initial monologue. The passage missing in the previous translation in her version reads:

> It was the dread of nonexistence, the terror of extinction, it was the angst of nonlife, the fear of unreality, a biological scream of all my cells in the face of an inner disintegration when all would be blown to pieces and scattered to the winds. It was the fear of unseemly pettiness and mediocrity, the fright of distraction, panic of fragmentation, the dread of rape from within and of rape that was threatening me from without ....[31]

Before we even learn about the dream and the "reversal in time," the anxiety of the character builds on us thanks to the way the translator makes language work. But together with the anxiety what is produced is a feeling of mockery: is this really and earnestly a description of metaphysical angst? Perhaps the author of these convoluted sentences is not as traumatized as he wants us to believe? Or does he by any chance sound a little bit tongue in cheek here?

Mosbacher, with his omissions, goes for the serious and the philosophical. This also may be the heritage of his French source text. As early as page 2 of his preface to Brone's translation, Konstanty Jeleński mentions Sartre's *L'Etre et Neant* and suggests that some sentences from Sartre's work are, as he says, "abstract formulation of certain themes central to Gombrowicz."[32] He also speaks of the writer's "philosophical and psychological intuition," of Blanchot and Barthes, and of psychoanalysis, with Marxism and behaviorism as context for its interpretation.[33] This erudite reading seems to support the idea that for the American audience the novel was too sophisticated and complex.

Borchardt goes for the rhythmical, the hasty, the excessive, the absurd, and the inside-out quality of the language without losing the philosophical content in the process. She gets—and gives back—the jazz of it. This effect is also clear in the final words of the novel. In the original, the couplet is surprising but sounds pretty childish, as if uttered by one of the infantile pupils of professor Piórkowski's school. In fact, it is a semi-quotation from absurd school couplets: "Koniec i bomba/A kto czytał ten trąba!" [literally: The end and a bomb/who has read it is a trumpet]. To my ear, the English version seems funnier and with its syncopated rhythm more interesting: "It's the end, what gas,/And who's read it is an ass!"[34] Mosbacher's version again cuts the phrase out.

Interestingly, Mosbacher's version has not one word for "pupa." Depending on the situation, there is "pretty little backside,"[35] "backsidick-ins,"[36] "super-bum,"[37] or "arch-bum."[38] The Polish "gęba" ["mug"] in Mosbacher's is just the neutral "face," that is absolutely misleading. In the French version, there are two words: "gueule" and "cucul." Jeleński again comments that they serve as a foundation for Gombrowicz's "anthropomorphic style" which makes the philosophical concepts acute and even obscene.[39] Still, in the Gombrowicz-Jeleński correspondence, there is a controversy about the multiplication of French equivalents of "pupa." The author supported Brone in thinking that many words rather than one help introduce some more anarchy into the text. Jeleński was against this solution, arguing that the novel's central concepts lose their "official vocabulary"; the special terms dissolve into the narrative.

Mosbacher does not on the whole give too much attention to special Gombro-terms—for example, "chłopię," an old-fashioned word suggesting immaturity and innocence because of its neuter grammatical gender which he uses for young people, or "chłopak," situated on the other extreme of the scale, being straightforward, maybe even lower class. In Mosbacher, these go unremarked as simply boy or adolescent, while Borchardt experiments successfully with "lad"/"kiddo" vs. "guy."

Borchardt chooses "mug" for gęba and "pupa" (pronounced, as she says in her comment: "poopa") for "pupa." The latter word needs commentary. The translator says "it means the buttocks, behind, bum, tush, rump, but none of these (nor any other I considered) adequately conveys the sense in which Gombro uses 'pupa' in the text."[40] This list shows the meticulousness with which the translator considered her decisions and the problems that might arise because her knowledge of Polish was "too good." The phrase "dać/dostać po pupie" (literally: give/get on the pupa—spank someone's behind/get a spank on one's behind), for any native speaker of Polish, is intimate and humorous, bringing back childhood memories, at the same time traumatic and tender (with all the psychoanalytic context involved). The choice of non-translation might seem an evasive solution here but, interestingly, the reasons behind it were different. Borchardt said in an interview:

> When *Ferdydurke* was to be published, Jonathan Brent, the then editor of Yale University Press, asked Susan Sontag to write a foreword. ... she objected to "tush." She had reservations about its Yiddish derivation, and she didn't think it would work for

English-speaking readers. Jonathan Brent sided with her. It was also his suggestion to keep the Polish *pupa*. I went along with that. He said we use *ruble*, so why not have *pupa*? But I would like to change that. I still yearn for the "tush" and the verb "to tush," and feel that Susan Sontag has "tushed" me. But I have heard since then that the readers' opinion was mixed. Some people rather liked *pupa*.[41]

It remains to be seen whether the pupa will remain with us for good or not.

Neutralizations in Mosbacher's version are present also on the level of proper names, many of which in Polish are meaningful, funny, and/or mocking. Proper names in Mosbacher are often changed for no clear reason. Gałkiewicz, the pupil who opposes the literature teacher in the famous scene, is called Kotecki; Zosia, who appears in the final part of the novel, with her name taken from the national epic *Pan Tadeusz*, and is forced into the "pupa" of naïve romantic innocence and the mug of an abducted fiancé, is rechristened to the foreign-sounding Isabel.

Borchardt makes the proper names work for her. An example: one of the characters at school is called Miętus. Mosbacher was happy with just a change in spelling to "Mientus" to make the word readable but not necessarily suggestive. Borchardt chooses Kneadus, a name based on the verb "to knead." This choice frees it from the Polish association with "mięta" (mint—one of the meanings of the noun "miętus" is mint candy) and introduces one with "miętosić" (to crumple, crunch, and knead). This word brings with it a possible allusion to adolescent sexual behavior (the meaning is close to "grope" and carries an allusion to masturbation) but also to a process of distorting, deforming, and turning something into a shapeless mass. Kneadus, as we know, will later be the center of the human heap, shapelessly emerging in the glorious final scene at the manor house.

Earlier his name is re-used in Borchardt's title of Chapter 3, which is a combination of an English idiom and an inventive translation from the Polish. It reads, "Caught with His Pants Down and Further Kneading" ("Przyłapanie i dalsze miętoszenie"). There are no actual pants down in this chapter, but the feeling of indecency during the Latin lesson and the surreal fight, in which Joey is forcefully engaged, are expressed not only in the story, but also in the linguistic choices of the translator. Mosbacher's version of this title simply reads, "The Duel" which turns it away from the associations with some shameful adolescent behavior toward a fully grown-up honorable ritual.

One of the interesting changes the new translation introduces is that the novel frees itself to a large extent from the immediate Polish context: "More than sixty years after *Ferdydurke* was written," writes Susan Sontag, "little remains from the specifically Polish targets of Gombrowicz's scorn. These have vanished together with the Poland in which he was reared and came of age."[42] Her interpretation is prospective rather than retrospective and does not inquire about the historical contexts of the original. Rather, she is interested in how this text works here and now, when most of the opinions against which Gombrowicz fought are still valid points of contention. She calls *Ferdydurke* one of the few novels that could be called Nietzschean and definitely the only comic novel of this sort. "It is," writes Sontag, "a project of unmasking, of *exposing*, with a merry satyr-dance of dualisms: mature versus immature, wholes versus parts, clothed versus naked, heterosexuality versus homosexuality, complete versus incomplete."[43] Even if *Ferdydurke* cannot really offend any more, it still seems "extravagant, brilliant, disturbing, brave, funny … wonderful...."[44]

In her introduction, Sontag finally corrects the notorious mistake repeated on the cover of all editions of Mosbacher's translation. "Ferdydurke" is not the name of a character in the novel, but it is an absurd word that means nothing. Sontag sees in the language of the novel the signs of the author's insolence and his drive toward contradicting any given order. What is very interesting from the perspective of translation analysis, she underlines the lightness and a "dancing" quality of this prose. Although, in her short essay, she does not comment much on the language of Borchardt's translation, the sense that the narration is jocular and infused with charming insolence rather than the difficult and obscure Eastern European moods is a new tone in the novel's reception and illustrates the difference between the two versions.

Borchardt translated from the Polish original. Mosbacher did not. She knows the language and its literature in an intimate, native way; he did not. Mosbacher was commissioned to translate the novel. His knowledge of the author must have been limited, especially in that he had no access to his other works. Borchardt, as she herself admits in interviews, read *Ferdydurke* as a young person and was deeply impressed with the use of language,[45] as she was later when, as a budding writer herself, she read *Pornografia*.[46] Gombrowicz's work had a personal appeal to her and it seems he is one of her main literary fascinations, not just a writer to translate. Any comparison of the texts of these translations must take these conditions and aspects of the translators' habitus into account.

There are also other aspects. Mosbacher translated into his native tongue. Borchardt's position as a translator from her native language into her acquired one was a challenge, but she managed to turn it into an asset. She worked with native speaker Thom Lane (her husband at that time) who reviewed her draft versions and assessed her particular decisions. This must have assisted her in solving various difficulties, but it also made it clear that there was a distance between her and the language of translation.[47] As she reminisced in the "Translator's Note," her partner would remark, "We don't say it this way,"[48] which made her realize acutely that Gombrowicz's language is equally problematic in Polish and that her task was to devise a special style in English which would do justice to this unique linguistic quality. This realization helped her create a space of freedom: she might not have access to the author to ask him what he meant—as the Café Rex translation committee and

Roland Martin did back in the 1940s and 1950s—but, on the other hand, there was no authorial power over her work. Neither Gombrowicz's authority nor his demands influenced her choices and interpretations. She was in charge of the text and responsible for it.

Her own estrangement from the English language (slight as it was) made her attentive to Gombrowicz's estrangement from the Polish. "It's pure Gombrowicz," as she wrote, that was her final court of appeal in the debates over translation problems. "Clearly," she said in her note, "I was dealing with yet another language: Gombrowicz's Polish"[49] and adds, "Had I not worked as a psychiatrist with English speaking schizophrenics who invent their own languages I may not have felt comfortable 'neologizing' English in such crucial words and phrases...."[50]

If Borchardt's circumstances, a collaboration with a sensitive native speaker and her medical training (a qualification rather unusual for a translator of literature), helped her loosen the constraints of English, it is striking how important also was the self-assurance with which she used English. For all her inventiveness in creating equivalents for Gombrowicz's linguistic irregularities, it is hard to disregard the other side of Borchardt's translation: the fantastic freedom and great proficiency with which she engages the colloquial and slang elements of contemporary American English.

"I had to put all my sense of conventional prose aside and be open to the unexpected," she explained in an interview.[51] This attitude allowed the translator to achieve a level of freedom from both the constraints of the original and the obligations to the target language. She is expert both in Polish and in English but, as a migrant, not completely at home in either of these languages. This is one of the best definitions of translator: she is a double agent and uses this position to its fullest.

Translation and Authority

What is striking in the international history of Gombrowicz's "flagship" is that for many years the original Polish novel has been largely absent from the scene. The "original original" was there only as far as the author was concerned, but the translators basically worked with no unmediated access to it. They could neither read it for the story and the cultural background with its specificity and the philosophical content, nor appreciate the inventiveness of the language, its mockery, the way it builds up levels of irony or experience the message included in the very linguistic set-up of the narration. What the translators worked with was an authorial interpretation in the form of a draft translation into a foreign language or his comments and explanations, given either in the form of letters or conversations. The Polish version was unattainable and thus irrelevant, while the two "secondary originals," Spanish and French, both holding the author's imprimatur and thus enjoying the status of the novel's proxies, took central position.

Self-translations and other forms of authorial engagement in the process of foreign language version production hardly ever ensure a higher degree of "fidelity" or "equivalence," understood as the maximum proximity between the target and source texts.[52] Just the opposite, it tends to become a "new original."[53] The author is allowed more freedom in producing a foreign language version than any regular translator could ever be. Spanish and French *Ferdydurkes* are not self-translations but "authorized translations." The author does not actually translate but grants his authority to someone else's work,[54] thus investing the resulting text with the authorial power. Such "authorisation" helps the translation to gain recognition as well as serving as a strong explanation of any deviations from the original text. It may become an excuse for production of neutralized, impoverished, and uncreative versions or, alternately, an invitation for creative work, opening up the original to the possibilities offered by the language of translation.

In the case of *Ferdydurke*'s first translations, critics have pointed out to impoverishments—simplifications, omissions, inconsistence, and stylistic neutralization—while creative input on the part of the translators usually goes unnoticed. Additionally, what is being stressed in a highly critical tone is the fact that the English translation was not made directly from the Polish, a practice deemed "unacceptable" and "a scandal."[55] This proves that the authorization of the second and third original was too weak. Still, a majority of the critical analyses come from Polish scholars, hence the radical view on the value of the original and its untranslatability.[56] In the case of *Ferdydurke*, untranslatability has become a stereotype which is being challenged in any discussion of the novel in translation.[57] What is even more important, these translations have been successful in bringing Gombrowicz considerable recognition in the cultures of their respective languages and preparing the ground for the new versions translated from the Polish.

The fact that the new translations were made and published both in French and English only strengthens the success of their predecessors in contributing, along with literary scholarship and criticism, to Gombrowicz's international position. Still, it is a paradox that only after the author's death, when his own self-promoting and self-translating efforts were over, did the translators actually start working with the original Polish text and not the hybrid authorial versions to produce successful works of European Modernist literature.

Notes

1 Holmgren, "Gombrowicz," 331–44.
2 Holmgren, "Gombrowicz," 337.
3 Longinović, *Borderline Culture*.
4 Lipińska-Iłłakowicz, "Gombrowicz i Ameryka," 62–78.
5 Lefevere, *Translation*.

6 Gombrowicz, *Walka*.
7 Suchanow, *Ja, geniusz*, I, 375–86.
8 Ibid., 409–18.
9 Gombrowicz, *List*, 269. Heydel translation.
10 Gombrowicz, *List*, 10.
11 Gombrowicz, *Walka*, II, 10.
12 Laurent, "Język Gombrowicza," 21–36.
13 Gombrowicz, *Walka*, II, 15. Heydel translation.
14 Tomaszewski, "Trans-Atlantyk," 178.
15 See Dzikowska, "Koń by się uśmiał," 85–102.
16 Gombrowicz, *Walka*, II, 117.
17 Ibid., I, 24.
18 Lipińska-Iłłakowicz, "Gombrowicz."
19 Ibid., 67.
20 Ziomek, "Solecyzmy," 221–38; Bartoszyński, "Kosmos," 282–331.
21 Margański, "Józio," 7–21; Thompson, *Gombrowicz*, 117–24.
22 Jarzębski, "Gombrowicz: ucieczka," 21.
23 Gombrowicz, *Testament*, 29–49.
24 Jarzębski, "Gombrowicz," 21.
25 Nowak, *Gombrowicz*, 19.
26 Łapiński, *Gombrowicza świat*.
27 Lipińska-Iłłakowicz, *Gombrowicz*, 71.
28 Enright, "Dancing the Polka."
29 Borchardt, "Translator's Note" in Gombrowicz, *Ferdydurke*, xix.
30 *Ferdydurke* (Borchardt), 1–2.
31 *Ferdydurke* (Borchardt), 1.
32 Jeleński, "Gombrowicz," 8. Heydel translation.
33 Jeleński, "Gombrowicz," 9.
34 *Ferdydurke* (Borchardt), 281.
35 Gombrowicz, *Ferdydurke* (Mosbacher), 40.
36 Ibid., 41.
37 Ibid., 266.
38 Ibid., 272.
39 Jeleński, "Gombrowicz," 9.
40 Gombrowicz, *Ferdydurke* (Borchardt), xix.
41 Tul'si Bhambry, interview with Borchardt, no date, www.asymptotejournal.com/interview/an-interview-with-danuta-borchardt/ (accessed May 26, 2018).
42 Sontag, "Foreword" in Gombrowicz, *Ferdydurke*, xiv.
43 Ibid., xx.
44 Ibid., xv.
45 Bhambry, interview.
46 Sykora, "Translating Gombrowicz."
47 Bhambry, interview.
48 Gombrowicz, *Ferdydurke* (Borhardt), xviii.
49 Ibid.
50 Ibid.
51 Bhambry, interview.
52 Toury, *Descriptive*, 75.
53 Cordingley, *Self-Translation*, 9.
54 Hermans, *Tongues*, 18–25.
55 Jarniewicz, "Frazes," 191.
56 Pym and Turk, "Translatability," 273–76.
57 Heydel, "Angielskie," 103–15.

6   Translating the Secret

Olaf Kühl

One of the possible concepts to describe the life of Witold Gombrowicz is "Secret." Since the publication of his intimate personal notes as *Kronos*, and with the addition of Klementyna Suchanow's impressive biography,[1] we know that Gombrowicz's life had both bright and dark aspects, it's day and night sides. After his discussions in cafés, after his public readings that grew increased in Paris and Berlin, he dove into "darkness"—in a metaphorical sense. He went on a hunt for male partners on the streets and in the parks, he followed waiters and sailors, men from the lower social strata. The significant attribute of this darkness was its *invisibility*. Gombrowicz himself described his Argentine years, his final coming out as a homosexual, by using the concept of "darkness." He claims, "I say that from the first, I fell in love with the catastrophe that I hated, that, after all, also ruined me. My nature told me to greet it as an opportunity to join with inferiority in *darkness (ciemności)*."[2]

But the Secret—or the language of the Secret—is not only a possible key to Gombrowicz's biography; it is also a *formula* to describe his language and thinking. The notion of the Secret as a hermeneutic key need not be applied to his texts from outside—this is how Gombrowicz himself referred to it in his early stories (*Bacacay* and others). In the short story "The Memoirs of Stefan Czarniecki" ("Pamiętnik Stefana Czarnieckiego"), the title character proudly announces that he is in possession of a "secret language," and what is more, that he is a Secret himself: "'I am a secret, too!' I said. 'I own my own language of the secret.'" Unsuccessfully, he tries to convince his fiancée to pronounce the words of this *secret language*: "ciam - bam - biu, minu - mniu, ba - bi, ba - be - no – zar."[3]

Another example appears in the short story "The Events on the Banbury" ("Zdarzenia na brygu Banbury") where the narrator mentions a "word on S," whose meaning he would prefer not to know (and naturally is not disclosing to the reader): "The line of the mainspar is unnecessarily turning into the letter S. S is the first letter of a word I thought up but which I would have preferred not to know."[4]

In "A Premeditated Crime" ("Zbrodnia z premedytacją") the son of the departed confesses under the pressure of the investigator, but he does not confess the strangling of his father, his confessing comes in a cryptic, ambiguous way. He says, "I went for a drive" ("pojechałem").[5] It is the investigator who forces this uttering to mean "I killed my father." The Polish phrase "jazda na całego" (at full speed) in the original adds the connotation of temporary insanity, so that "pojechałem" can be taken by the investigator as the confession of murder. The whole story is about ambiguity and the polysemy of words and behaviors. "Pojechałem" does not become a word in Gombrowicz's "secret dictionary," but in the microcosm of this story the mechanics of how such meanings are born can be demonstrated very well. Gombrowicz charges words with non-canonical meaning, thereby privatizing them and incorporating them into a dictionary of his own, a "secret language." Words manipulated in this way from then on possess an additional, latent connotation or meaning.

As in "A Premeditated Crime," the ambiguity of expressions and behaviors determines the plot and the heroes, so ambiguity—or polysemy—is a central notion in Gombrowicz's universe. Its effects reach far beyond the realm of semantics. Ambiguity is charged with a strong erotic component. One of the most productive fields to explore the effects of ambiguity is the semantics of Ontology or Being.

The Ambiguity of Being

To fully understand the meaning of ambiguity, it is first helpful to have a look at the opposite, the connotations of monosemy found in Gombrowicz. In the semantic polysemic view, one word has multiple meanings that are separately stored, while the right meaning is activated when it has to be activated. As opposed to this, the monosemic view claims that a word has one core meaning and, when the core meaning is used in a specific context, then other possible meanings may be derived from it. It may be argued that semantic monosemy has its physical complement in the singularity of the object, its separateness. In this respect, as early as the first textual version of *Ferdydurke*, we can see physical singularity and visibility as something which is infringing upon lust and desire. In one of the first scenes in the novel, when Józio is in front of the mirror, we can see an insistence of the singularity of the object; in this case, body parts. Józio's narcissism is heavily impeded by the fact that each of his body parts is so visible, so expressive, and recognizable: "The minute details, the clarity and precision of the outline... all too clear.... Because that's the way I am. Strange indeed, like Mme Pompadour. And unpredictable. But why? An ephemeron."[6] However, as soon as he denies that the mirror image is his own, nothing is left; he no longer exists. The narrator claims:

> I continued to move toward him, and, unable to stop the sweep of my outstretched hand, I struck him in the face. Off with you! Off! *No, this is not me at all! This is something randomly thrust upon me, something alien, an intrusion,* a compromise between the inner and

outer world, it's not my body at all! He groaned and – with a leap – he vanished. I was left alone but actually not alone — how could I be alone *when I wasn't even there, I had no sense of being there*, and not a single thought, gesture, action, or word, in fact nothing seemed to be mine, but rather it was as if it had all been settled somewhere outside myself, decided for me — because in reality I was quite different![7]

As opposed to this, in an early version of *Ferdydurke* the scene unfolds in a totally different way. In that version, Józio is not alienated by the mirror images, which cast shame on him. Instead, he overcomes the feeling of shame and is rewarded by a lustful euphory, an ecstasy of being:

> The distinguishing marks that were previously a source of disgrace and indecency, now, after being reinvigorated by the radiance of vision became absolute, given unarguably once and for all, like the beard of God the Father. Wrinkles and flaws...and what to an outsider could seem a pathetic symptom of weakness and death, gazed with power and independence of life. Even more, it was life itself, the life that until now I sought everywhere, but not within myself. ... thus I do not have to fear, or be *ashamed*. I may *exist*. I, I, Oh ecstasy.[8]

Here we have a decisive, early and very expressive example of Gombrowicz using a word but attaching to it his own specific meaning. In the dictionary, the word "to exist" ("istnieć") has no antonyms that connote "being afraid" or "being ashamed." By confronting the verb "to exist" with "to fear" or "to be ashamed," Gombrowicz charges the word with a very specific meaning of lust or euphory. But parallel with this *euphoric* meaning, there will always exist a *dysphoric* value. This can be illustrated by Gombrowicz's use of the verb "to be" ("być") in the following quotation:" I *am too much*.... I can't want because I am too much. ... I am made, finished, *delineated*... I am and I am so much that this casts me beyond the limits of nature."[9]

In standard semantics, this is a binary question: to be or not to be. Either you are, or you are not. However, in Gombrowicz's work, there is an oscillation or wavering between euphoric and dysphoric meanings, in this particular case, of the verb "to be." This oscillation is not necessarily connected to Gombrowicz's own age and, consequently, the period of his work. Thus, some pages after this dysphoric use of the verb to be in the *Diary*, you can find, in the same text, expressions which refer to the same euphoric experience of being as in the early version of *Ferdydurke*: "a stronger, more real *existence*. I am alone. That is why I exist more."[10] Because dysphoric and euphoric meanings of the same verb "to be" can be found some pages apart, Gombrowicz's explanation, that the growing stiffness of his form is connected to advancing age, should be dispelled as a rationalization in the Freudian sense.

The dysphoric meaning of "being" which Gombrowicz sometimes refers to as a "Procrustean bed" is intimately connected with the notion of *Form*, one of the central concepts in Gombrowicz's philosophical universe. This kind of "being" is characterized by a feeling of being narrowed, by passively growing stiff. We must omit here all the theoretical attempts to discuss the psychological and philosophical background of the form (that is, Lacan's "shell of alienated identity").

> Because, during my lifetime, I have created for myself a special sensibility towards Form and, quite frankly, the fact of having five fingers on one hand scares me. Why five? Why not 327,584,598,208,854? And why not all these quantities at the same time? And why fingers? For me nothing is more fantastic than to *be* here, now, and be *as I am*, defined, concrete, and not someone else. And I fear Form as if it were a wild animal![11]

For the rest of his life, Gombrowicz's writing and his characters wavered between these two poles: euphory about the possibilities of his own existence and dysphory or fear of being defined, shaped, and delineated (by others, by nature). In the novel *Pornografia*, we find a description of the horror of being defined that is astonishingly similar, including even single words, with the early scene in *Ferdydurke*: "a horrible intensification of the *concrete* nature of things, we were in the cosmos, yet we were like something terrifyingly *known, defined in every detail*."[12] "Concrete" and "defined" (or "delineated," as "określony" is sometimes translated into English) are the keywords of this imagery, suggesting the "trap" in the "Procrustean bed" of uniformity or conformity.

Euphoric and dysphoric experience of being can be expressed in an identical grammatical and lexical surface so that only the context will determine the actual meaning. This bestows on the translator great responsibility. In this case—as seldom occurs with this very sophisticated translator—Danuta Borchardt's translation of the Polish "dane" as "known" seems to miss the philosophical context. It is not that man is *known* to himself, but that he is *given* (by somebody or something else—for instance, God or nature—the "old whore," Gombrowicz says in *Pornografia*).[13] The previous translator of *Pornografia*, Alastair Hamilton, instead translates this as "definite."[14]

The Connection of Being with Erotics

The dualism of *Being* in terms of value and connotation has far reaching consequences that are closely connected to Gombrowicz's erotics (at this point meaning not his personal erotics, but those inherent in his writing and his characters). The dysphoric being—the delineated, definite form, the "terrifyingly given" one—means unambiguity. And *unambiguity* is something which is killing erotic lust. As demonstrated earlier, this had already been applied to the narcissistic self-love of the young boy, and it also applies to the homosexual desire of his later years.

As soon as social conventions force the relinquishing of ambiguity, lust begins dying. Such is the experience of the hero of the short story "Adventures" (Przygody). After his internal consent to marrying his fiancée, after relinquishing his deviations (*zboczenia)* and returning to normal—heterosexual—love, desire is dead. Consequently, everything is what it is: "a birch tree was a birch tree, a pine—a pine, a willow—a willow."[15] Monosemy has come to reign again. The only thing left is to try to escape again, to search for new adventures with the white negro.

Throughout Gombrowicz's oeuvre, the authorization of heterosexual partnership has the consequence that somebody wants to kill somebody—in most cases the victim is the woman who expects to be loved. You can find this in Józio's thoughts about killing Zuta in *Ferdydurke* and in Witold's dreams about hanging Lena in *Cosmos*. And then at the end of the play *Ivona, Princess of Burgundia*, the main heroine is also killed.

Challenges for the Translator

As long as Gombrowicz's deviated semantics in his own language remain latent, it can be transferred without difficulty from Polish into another natural language. Problems begin when the deviations become visible within the grammatical surface. Then the translator has to solve a problem, and he has to make decisions about meaning. This is when what I called "the language of secret" becomes visible. This is the case, for example, when sheer existence is being adverbially determined. Compare the way in which Borchardt and Hamilton translate the same passage:

- "because Fryderyk… was indeed here, next to me. And he was immensely silent."[16]
- "because Frederick… was there, next to me. And he was curiously silent."[17]

In these extracts, Gombrowicz is building an intensification of the presence of "był" ("was"), repeating and amassing the word and its compound (for instance, "przebywałem był") several times. He starts this game in the second sentence of the novel: "At the time – the year was 1943 – I was living in what was once Poland and what was once Warsaw, at the rock-bottom of an accomplished fact."[18] Danuta Borchardt is doing the best she can to rescue these recurring emphases on "was," but if you speak out loud the original compound "przebywałem był w byłej Polsce," you can hear the intensification through repetition which is lost in the English version (I was living in what was once Poland).

After this introduction, and in this context, "was ... silent" cannot be read any more in the sense of "he was sitting still" (being an execution of the order "bądź cicho!," for instance, meaning "be still!"). It is not Fryderyk sitting still here, it is his sheer existence being immensely silent.[19] Similarly, in another example, Borchardt builds an intensification of the presence of "był" ("was") by repetition. She writes, "but at the same time here he was ... and somehow here he was."[20] By contrast, the previous translator opted for softening this reiteration by changing the word: "he was there! ... but he remained there."[21]

Deviation is also present with the *comparison* of a normally uncomparable ontologic state or process such as "being." Gombrowicz uses the Polish "jestem bardziej" ("I am more"). Vallee renders this as "Not talent, reason, or moral values determine hierarchy, but this most of all: a stronger, more real existence. I am alone. That is why *I exist more*."[22] You can see in the change of the verb an indication of the difficulties the translator had with this formulation. She tried to soften the deviation by replacing "am" with "exist," whereas the original has "am" ("jestem") in both cases. The Polish original read word-by-word is "I am alone. That is why I am more." By using "exist more" the translator can avoid a misreading of "I am more" as "I am a more important person" or some similar connotation.[23]

This is the euphoric variant, referring to the very first emphasis on "existing" in the early version of *Ferdydurke* (see earlier). But in the *Diary*, there appears also the dysphoric version:

> And even though I could still do something unpredictable for myself, I no longer want to. I can't want because I am too much. Amid this indelineation, changeability, fluidity, under the ungraspable sky, I am made, finished, delineated ... I am and *I am so much* that this casts me beyond the limits of nature.[24]

Incidentally, in Goethe's *Italian Journey*, we find a description of shells breeding, where he describes their ontological quality with very similar notions: "What a beautiful, marvellous thing is everything living. How real, and how *being*!"[25] The Polish translation instinctively tries to eliminate the deviation of the word "being" and replaces it by the adjective "concrete": "Jakże zdumiewający i doskonały jest żywy organizm! (...) Jakiż jest autentyczny i *konkretny*!"[26] Here, we recognize another favorite word which Gombrowicz uses in the context of his latently uploaded ontology— "konkretny." When analyzing such fragments, the systemic difference between the German and Polish languages should be taken into account. In Polish you can say "I am here" by simply saying "Jestem" ("I am"). In German, the language of Hegel and Heidegger, "Ich bin" without an adverb denotes the pure ontological fact of being. Moreover, these observations are not confined only to a special group of lexemes. The quality of Being can be signalized not only by a verb, but also by an adjective like "real": "and Fryderyk was perhaps more *real* than the grass."[27]

Fakt

A very prominent noun in this context is "fakt" (fact). It appears in the early version of *Ferdydurke*: "'O, ty, kochanko, ojczyzno, ty *fakcie!*'"[28] During its journey through that literary work, the word *fakt* takes different meanings and one, you could say, remembers them. As in the case of "being" and its synonyms, "fakt" can also assume different connotations on the scale from euphoric to dysphoric. Typically Gombrowicz transfers the abstract notion to a meta-abstract or once again a nearly concrete position, so it can take on physical qualities: "at the rock-bottom of an accomplished fact."[29] In the later novel *Cosmos*, this transfer verges on a grotesque shift from concrete to abstract: "And yet this FACT was hanging, a hanging fact, a Ludwik-like fact was hanging, hitting one on the head."[30] As in other cases, the previous translator did not follow the text as closely as Danuta Borchardt and tried to soften the deviation, saying, "Nevertheless here it was, this fact, this hanging fact, the fact of Louis hanged, an enormous, brutal, heavy, aggressive fact."[31]

In the same way as the dead Ludwik is transferred into the abstract notion of the factuality of death, so is also the case in the *Diary* with the ordeal of the Jews: "What forces of life brought out this terrifying *fact* – no one knows. They who are this fact, who constitute it, let them not delude themselves even for a moment that they will be able to get themselves out of these chasms onto an even plain."[32]

Darkness

Earlier we mentioned the word "darkness" ("ciemność") as belonging to the class of the lexemes suggesting ambiguity, polysemy, etc. Not by chance does this word play a prominent role throughout Gombrowicz's works. And it is not only the physical darkness, as the author emphasizes, for instance, in *Cosmos*: "*Darkness!* I needed it! Darkness was vital to me as an extension of the night during which I had be banging into Lena!"[33] "These beginnings of mine in Argentina today look like total *darkness*, concealing within its womb a tragicomical *quid pro quo*."[34] Thus, the semantic range of *darkness* reaches from a simple designation of lack of light to the lack of education, primitiveness, and simple mindedness, and on to the connotations of homosexual love. The latter can be easily explained because the erotic object in Gombrowicz is the "inferior" male member of society; for example, a sailor or a villain. Thus, we can find many examples of this range of meaning in Gombrowicz's works. Just to mention one more: "the boy's inferiority and his *darkness*, together with his country origin, made him behave like an automaton."[35] Again we see Alastair Hamilton trying to soften the enigmatic context by displaying the semantic constituents of the word *ciemność:* "but the inferiority of the boy and his *peasant stupidity* were impenetrable."[36]

Nevertheless, not even in this last case, where "darkness" connotates most of Gombrowicz's idiosyncrasies, would the translator be forced to engage into a deeper understanding of the real—and latent—meaning of the word. He could simply transfer it from the Polish "ciemność" into the English "darkness." But as soon as the "secret" meaning of the word becomes manifest enough to disturb the grammatical surface structure and make the whole pronouncement unclear (Gombrowicz's "ambiguity"), the translator is forced to become an analyst and interpreter of the original: "Vaclav... watched the chief *made dark* by the boy, the boy – by the chief."[37] Again, Hamilton's solution is poetic and creative, but it does not allow the reader to identify the prominence of the leitmotif of "darkness" as it is in the original: "Albert ... watched the leader *clouded* by the boy, the boy by the leader."[38] But where does the ambiguity originate here?

The ambiguity of this fragment originates not only from the semantics of the word "dark," but also from the instrumental case "chłopcem," (the boy). The Slavic instrumental case possesses a wide range of semantic possibilities. Therefore, it is the favorite case of poets like Julian Przybosz and writers like Bruno Schulz. With the help of the instrumental, they can transform the usual image of reality into something quite astounding and new. Unfortunately, in languages like German and English, in which this case is missing, the translator has to narrow the semantic richness of such propositions. In the German translation by Renate Schmidgall, we find a similar solution as in the English translation: "er sah zu, wie sich der Anführer durch den Jungen *verdunkelte* – der Junge durch den Anführer" (literally: he watched how the leader *darkened* by the boy—the boy by the leader).[39] But what does this mean? The leader was made dark by the boy? Does he change his color? Is he blushing, for instance? An additional complication derives from the possibility of "boy" and "leader" denoting abstract roles, as can often be observed in Gombrowicz. In *Ferdydurke*, we find sentences like:

- "Pimko stary, który [...] profesorem przyniewalał" ("old Pimko, who... was... coercing her with his professorship").[40]
- "chciał przynajmniej Norwidem zaważyć w jej życiu" ("he was going to use Norwid so that he could play a prominent part in her life").[41]

Taking into account Gombrowicz's idiosyncratic, "secret" meaning of "darkness" as outlined at the beginning of this essay, this passage may be interpreted as saying that a very specific, erotic relationship is developing between the leader and the boy—the relationship between the "inferior" young villain and the "higher" commanding—and often elder—man.

Of course, Gombrowicz is not stating this clearly. But he is expressing it through his "secret language." Therefore, on its passage from early *Bacacay* and *Ferdydurke* to the later *Cosmos*, the word "darkness" is accumulating typical Gombrowiczian meanings that are deviating from the standard lexicon. Moreover, with every actualization of the word, these latent layers of meaning become stronger. This diachronic semantic technique (or as Soviet formalist Viktor Shklovskyi called, "prijom") is sometimes extended to other lexemes not connected to the semantic field of the Erotics of Being. I will discuss only one example: the verb *Załatwić się*.

In *Pornografia* we read, "They stood back from here and left her alone so she could *deal with* her dying."[42] In Hamilton's version, "They all seemed to have withdrawn from her, leaving her *to die* alone."[43] We could find at least five different meanings of the polish verb "załatwić się," here translated as "deal with." To be sure, I am referring to the language of Witold Gombrowicz, not the standard dictionary. Thus, in Gombrowicz's "Secret Language," "załatwić się" may mean:

1. to pee or to defecate: "Rabelais ... intended nothing at all because he wrote the way a child *pees* against a tree, in order to relieve himself."[44]
2. to die: "we wanted father, we wanted father—to take care of it by himself!"[45]
3. to get sexual satisfaction: "You go the brothel, where you *got to be done* without love."[46]
4. to onanize:

   • "shoving them in, savoring, chewing, and swallowing, it took a long time for him *to be done* with each morsel.... He gratified himself by eating. He masturbated by eating, which was rather tiresome."[47]
   • "we are here for the sole reason of his *doing his business* in our presence... with his own... self-gratifying... gratify yourself... We waited for him to be done."[48] The previous translator, Eric Mosbacher, was more definite, yet: "we were here for the sole purpose of enabling him to *obtain his satisfaction* in our presence. 'One is what one is.' We waited for him to finish."[49]

5. to commit suicide: "[an insect] committing suicide.... But why did he come to my cabin to do it? Could he not have managed in the crack?"[50]

Why is it so important—and at the same time almost impossible—to maintain one and the same lexeme for "załatwić się" in every context as Gombrowicz did? Martin Buber and Franz Rosenzweig called this the "Leitwortstil" or "konkordante Übersetzung," when they undertook the task of a new translation of the Old Testament. *Leitwortstil* means to maintain the identity of a word in each of its appearances—may it even be in other chapters, other books of the Testament—so that the inter-connections and mutual influence and repercussions between them can be realized. This is important, because Gombrowicz deliberately used new contexts to contaminate a word with new, deviate semantics. This is his way of saying something without clearly stating it. The fragment of *Banbury* quoted earlier continues as follows: "On land, too, one some-times sees dogs or horses, but there's more discretion, and no one will crawl out specially to someone else just to show them."[51]

As we can see, here "załatwić się" is charged with the meaning "com-mit suicide," on the one hand, and "defecate," on the other hand (be-cause dogs and horses do not commit suicide). The author contaminates one meaning with the other. The *tertium comparationis* of all possible meanings of "załatwić się" is probably the shame. The surrounding peo-ple in *Pornografia* watch Amelia dying with the same feeling of dis-comfort and shame as they watch Leon masturbating in *Cosmos*. The same applies to "A Premeditated Crime": "out of fear, out of *shame* … everyone was locked in their room."[52] Shame is what at the end puts the investigator in "A Premeditated Crime" on the trail of the son—his shame originates from his feelings for his other, not from being guilty. But in the plot of this story, it is interpreted as proof of guilt. This is how semantic shifts in Gombrowicz's language and leads us to the psycho-logical reasons underlying his characters and their world—a question which would draw us too far away.

Conclusion

If *ambiguity* is so fundamental for the poetics of Gombrowicz, as we have postulated earlier, then it becomes clear why his literature must be in constant conflict with every kind of monosemantic world view, with every sort of ideology, every attempt to define once and forever Good and Evil. Inherent to his writing, there is a queerness independent even of his personal homosexuality or that of his characters. This queerness is a constant provocation. In the 1950s and 1960s, it was undermining and attacking the simple-minded ideology of real socialism. It was for this reason that Polish officials attacked him so furiously when he stayed in West Berlin with the Ford stipend. And to be sure, Gombrowicz is the best antidote today against the nationalistic propaganda that is growing stronger and stronger in today's Poland. It is no wonder that he was re-moved from the obligatory lecture list in Polish schools.

On the other hand, Gombrowicz would have been fascinated by people like Jarosław Kaczyński. He was fond of duels. To convince yourself of this, only think about the three quarrelling gentlemen in *Trans-Atlantyk* or the two professors—the analytic and the synthetic—fighting each other in *Ferdydurke*. Genotypes survive over centuries and generations. Independent of the specific ideologies, the phenotype dominating the ruling party of Polish politics today (2018) is very similar to Gombrowicz's antecedent, the socialist functionaries of the 1950s and 1960s, who were totally convinced they possessed the truth.

The best thing to survive our difficult times should be to fuel oneself with the reading of Witold Gombrowicz. In a time where fake-news and all kind of propaganda are trying to make us unsure about who we are and if we as individuals are really so important, his teaching about the importance of BEING, even if you are alone and even if You are not sure WHO you really are, is the best medicine against any seduction of those who in the end intend nothing else than to dominate us.

Notes

1 Suchanow, *Ja, geniusz.*
2 Gombrowicz, *Diary*, 160.
3 Author's translation. Gombrowicz, *Opowiadania*, IX, 32: "Ja też jestem zagadką!—rzekłem.—Ja też mam własny *język tajemnicy.*"
4 Author's translation. Gombrowicz, *Opowiadania*, IX, 131: "linia grot-rei niepotrzebnie skręca się w literę S. Na literę S zaczyna się jedno słowo, które sam wymyśliłem, a którego wolałbym nie znać."
5 Author's translation of "pojechałem." Gombrowicz, *Opowiadania*, IX, 64.
6 Gombrowicz, *Ferdydurke* (Borchardt), 13; Gombrowicz, *Ferdydurke. Dzieła*, I, 19: "Sprecyzowany—wyraźny w konturze i drobiazgowo określony, szczegółowy... zbyt wyraźny. (...) A więc taki byłem. Dziwny, doprawdy, jak pani de Pompadour. I przypadkowy. Dlaczego taki, a nie inny?"
7 Gombrowicz, *Ferdydurke* (Borchardt), 13–14. Gombrowicz, *Ferdydurke, Dzieła*, I, 19:

> ruszyłem na niego - i nie mogąc już powstrzymać wyciągniętej ręki trzasnąłem w twarz pełnym zamachem. Precz ! Precz ! *Nie, to wcale nie ja !* To *coś przypadkowego, coś obcego, narzuconego,* jakiś kompromis pomiędzy światem zewnętrznym a wewnętrznym, to wcale nie moje ciało! Jęknął i znikł - dał susa. A ja zostałem sam, a właściwie nie sam - *gdyż nie było mnie, nie czułem, abym był,* i każda myśl, każdy odruch, czyn, słowo, wszystko wydawało się nie moje, lecz jakby gdzieś ustalone poza mną, zrobione dla mnie - a ja właściwie jestem inny!

8 Special thanks to Grażyna Kozaczka for the translation of the original Polish quotation:

> Oznaki *szczególne,* poprzednio źródło hańby i nieprzyzwoitości, teraz, ożywione blaskiem wzroku, stały się czemś *danem raz na zawsze* i nie znoszącem sprzeciwu, absolutnem jak broda Boga Ojca. I zmarszczki i skazy... i to co komuś zewnątrz mogło się wydać godne pożałowania, jako objawy słabości czy śmierci, spozierało z potęgą i niezależnością życia, więcej, było życiem samem, tem życiem, którego dotąd szukałem wszędzie, a tylko nie w sobie. ... a więc nie potrzebuję *bać się*, ani *wstydzić*, mogę *istnieć*, ja, ja, o rozkoszy!
> Gombrowicz, "Wstęp," *Ferdydurke* (Bolecki and Jarzębski), II, 282.

9 Gombrowicz, *Diary*, 211. Gombrowicz, *Dziennik*, VI, 225: "*zanadto jestem.* Pośród tej nieokreśloności, zmienności, płynności, pod niebem nieuchwytnym jestem, już zrobiony, wykończony, *określony*... jestem i jestem tak bardzo, że to mnie wyrzuca poza obręb natury."

10 Gombrowicz, *Diary*, 259. Gombrowicz, *Dziennik*, VI, 273: "silniejsze, bardziej rzeczywiste *istnienie*. Jestem sam. Dlatego *bardziej jestem.*"

11 Gombrowicz, *Testament*, 148–49. Gombrowicz, *Testament. Rozmowy*, 137:

> Gdyż w ciągu mojego życia wyrobiłem sobie szczególną wrażliwość na Formę i ja naprawdę lękam się tego, że mam pięć palców u ręki. Dlaczego pięć? Dlaczego nie 328584598208854? A dlaczego nie wszystkie ilości naraz? I dlaczego w ogóle palec? Nic dla mnie bardziej fantastycznego, jak że tu i teraz jestem jaki jestem, określony, konkretny, taki akurat, a nie inny. I boję się jej, Formy, jak dzikiego zwierza!

12 Gombrowicz, *Pornografia* (Borchardt), 21. Gombrowicz, *Pornografia*, *Dzieła*, III, 22: "straszne wzmożenie konkretności, byliśmy w kosmosie, ale byliśmy jak coś przerażająco danego, określonego we wszystkich szczegółach."

13 Gombrowicz, *Pornografia* (Borchardt), 153; Gombrowicz, *Pornografia* (Hamilton), 36. Gombrowicz, *Pornogafia*, 114: "Trzeba znać starą k... Wie pan o kim myślę? Ona tj. Natura."

14 Gombrowicz, *Pornografia* (Hamilton), 27.

15 Gombrowicz, *Bacacay*, 135. Gombrowicz, *Opowiadania*, IX, 116: "brzoza była brzozą, sosna - sosną, wierzba – wierzbą."

16 Gombrowicz, *Pornografia* (Borchardt), 9. Gombrowicz, *Pornografia*, 14: "bo Fryderyk ... wszak *był* tu, obok mnie. I *był* niezmiernie *cicho*."

17 Gombrowicz, *Pornografia* (Hamilton), 18.

18 Gombrowicz, *Pornography* (Borchardt), 3. Gombrowicz, *Pornografia*, 9: "Wówczas, a było to w 1943-im, przebywałem był w byłej Polsce i w byłej Warszawie, na samym dnie faktu dokonanego."

19 The German translation "Er war ungemein still" is an almost indiscernible form of the normal idiom "he was still." *Pornographie* (Tiel and Schmidgall).

20 Gombrowicz, *Pornography* (Borchardt), 8. Gombrowicz, *Pornografia*, 12: "ale jednocześnie był ... i byłjakośodrębnie, a nieubłaganie. ... on byłw tym ścisku i był."

21 Gombrowicz, *Pornografia* (Hamilton), 16–17.

22 Gombrowicz, *Diary*, 259. Gombrowicz, *Dziennik*, VI, 273: "silniejsze, bardziej rzeczywiste istnienie. *Jestem* sam. Dlatego *bardziej jestem.*'"

23 In my German translation, I left "am" in both cases but decided to put the "bin" in quotation marks to underline its special, emphasized semantic loading: "Ich bin allein. Und 'bin' deshalb mehr." Gombrowicz, *Tagebuch*, 354.

24 Gombrowicz, *Diary*, 211. Gombrowicz, *Dziennik*, VI, 225: "Pośród tej nieokreśloności, zmienności, płynności, pod niebem nieuchwytnym jestem, już zrobiony, wykończony, *określony... jestem i jestem tak bardzo*, że to mnie wyrzuca poza obręb natury."

25 Letter, Oct. 9, 1786 from Goethe, *Goethes Sämmtliche*, X, 70. Author's translation.

26 Goethe, *Podróż*, 83.

27 Gombrowicz, *Pornography* (Borchardt), 14. Gombrowicz, *Pornografia*, 17: "Fryderyk był teraz prawdziwszy od trawy." Compare with Hamilton's translation: "Frederick now seemed more real than the grass." Gombrowicz, *Pornografia* (Hamilton), 22.

28 Gombrowicz, "Ferdydurke" (*Skamander*), 266–67.

29 Gombrowicz, *Pornografia* (Borchardt), 3. Gombrowicz, *Pornografia*, 9: "na samym dnie faktu dokonanego." Compare with Hamilton: "at the depths of the *fait accompli*." *Pornografia* (Hamilton), 13.

30 Gombrowicz, *Cosmos* (Borchardt), 176. Gombrowicz, *Kosmos*, IV, 148: "A jednak ten FAKT wisiał, wiszący fakt, fakt ludwikowaty wiszący, w łeb

walący, wielki, ciężki, zwisający, coś w rodzaju byka plątającego się luzem, olbrzymi fakt na sośnie i z butami...."

31 Gombrowicz, *Cosmos and Pornografia*, 155.

32 Gombrowicz, *Diary*, 99. Gombrowicz, *Dziennik*, IV, 107: "Jakie moce życia wywołały ten *fakt* straszliwy, nie wiadomo — ci, którzy są nim, którzy go stanowią, niech ani na chwilę się nie łudzą."

33 Gombrowicz, *Cosmos* (Borchardt), 85. Gombrowicz, *Kosmos*, 75: "*Ciemność!* Potrzebowałem jej! Była mi konieczna jako przedłużenie nocy." Compare with Mosbacher: "Darkness. I needed it myself, to prolong the night during which I had battered at Lena's door." Gombrowicz, *Cosmos* (Mosbacher), 80.

34 Gombrowicz, *Diary*, 418. Gombrowicz, *Dziennik*, VII, 145: "Te początki moje w Argentynie wyglądają mi dzisiaj jak *ciemność*, kryjąca w swym łonie tragikomiczne qui pro quo."

35 Gombrowicz, *Pornografia* (Borchardt), 126. Gombrowicz, *Pornografia*, 95: "ale niższość chłopca i jego *ciemność*, wraz z jego wiejskością, były jak automat i powtarzał wciąż to samo."

36 Gombrowicz, *Pornografia* (Hamilton), 114.

37 Gombrowicz, *Pornografia* (Borchardt), 182. Gombrowicz, *Pornografia*, 135: "patrzył on, jak wódz *ciemnieje* chłopcem, chłopiec – wodzem."

38 Gombrowicz, *Pornografia* (Hamilton), 159.

39 Gombrowicz, *Pornographie* (Tiel and Schmidgall), III, 158.

40 Gombrowicz, *Ferdydurke. Dzieła*, I, 166. English translation: *Ferdydurke* (Borchardt), 164.

41 Gombrowicz, *Ferdydurke. Dzieła*, I, 165. English translation: Gombrowicz, *Ferdydurke* (Borchardt), 163.

42 Gombrowicz, *Pornografia* (Borchardt), 101. Gombrowicz, *Pornografia*, 78: "pozostawili ją, aby *załatwiła się ze swoim konaniem.*"

43 Gombrowicz, *Pornografia* (Hamilton), 92.

44 Gombrowicz, *Diary*, 34. Gombrowicz, *Dziennik 1953–1956*, VI, 78: "Rabelais ... w ogóle nic nie zamierzał ponieważ pisał, jak dziecko *załatwia się* pod krzakiem, aby sobie ulżyć."

45 Gombrowicz, *Bacacay*, 71. Gombrowicz, *Opowiadania*, IX, 63: "chcieliśmy, żeby ojciec - żeby ojciec - sam się z tym załatwił!"

46 Author's translation. Gombrowicz, *Opowiadania*, IX, 155: "idziesz do burdelu, gdzie bez miłości *się załatwiasz.*"

47 Gombrowicz, *Cosmos* (Borchardt), 161. Gombrowicz, *Kosmos*, 137: "wsuwanie, smakowanie, przeżuwanie, przełykanie, trwało długo zanim w ustach *załatwił się* z kąskiem. Rzecz niezwykła, milczał, i chyba dlatego mało kto się odzywał przy stole, zajadano. Jedząc zaspokajał się. Onanizował się jedząc, co było dosyć męczące."

48 Gombrowicz, *Cosmos* (Borchardt), 187. Gombrowicz, *Kosmos*, 158: "my jesteśmy tu po to tylko, żeby on *się* przy nas *załatwił...* z tym swoim... wsobnym... swój do swego... Czekaliśmy aż skończy."

49 Gombrowicz, *Cosmos and Pornografia*, 165.

50 Gombrowicz, *Bacacay*, 165. Gombrowicz, *Opowiadania*, IX, 141: "robak ... popełniając samobójstwo. Ale dlaczego wybrał się z tym do mnie? Czy nie mógł załatwić się w szparze?"

51 Gombrowicz, *Bacacay*, 166. Gombrowicz, *Opowiadania*, IX, 141: "Na lądzie też widuje się czasem psy albo konie, ale przecież jest większa dyskrecja i nikt nie będzie wyłaził specjalnie do kogoś, żeby mu pokazać."

52 Ibid., 71. Gombrowicz, *Opowiadania*, IX, 63: "wszyscy pozamykali się na klucz z podświadomego strachu i wstydu przed śmiercią, której zbliżanie się przeczuwali."

Part II

Cartography of Affect in Gombrowicz's Works

7 "Indomitable Boredom Above the Entire World"

Gombrowicz (and Other Polish Writers) on Existential Predicament[1]

Michał Paweł Markowski

Metaphysics of a Two-Headed Calf[2]

The French invented *ennui*[3] long before the revolution of modernity, but they connected it almost exclusively with an eternal human condition and the language of the heart.[4] Pascal dialectically connected boredom with the need for distraction: the human being is bored and thus seeks entertainment beyond herself, to drown out the nothingness of her existence. Up to the mid-nineteenth century, boredom (the symptoms of which were difficult to distinguish from other severe illnesses of the soul—melancholy, depression, spleen) was almost universally considered as (1) an ailment characteristic of the human condition; and (2) an illness from which only outstandingly sensitive individuals suffered.[5] Only from the middle of the nineteenth century, when boredom started to leave aristocratic salons and threaten almost everyone, irrespective of social status, was it radically detached from both these conditions. Boredom began to be understood as a specifically modern predicament and one that went beyond the particular individual, although it was not universal.

It has to be emphasized that boredom became the primary distinguishing feature of a specific socio-cultural formation (modernity), and in connection with this took on a particular character, hitherto unknown. This character does not result from a human condition that is beyond time, but from the transformation that social life has undergone, starting from the middle of the nineteenth century. As a result of the vast social changes connected with industrialization, the mechanization and automatization of labor,[6] urbanization, and the secularization of the individual's life, the individual ceases to perceive her existence as a whole that belongs to her, and she starts to have a fundamental difficulty with self-definition. "Today I really don't know who I am," says the protagonist of one of the plays of Stanisław Ignacy Witkiewicz, Edgar Wałpor, who earlier was "groaning with indecision." "Boredom and suffering—a vicious circle, endless and self-contained and closed in upon itself forever."[7]

In Witkiewicz's play, *Szewcy* (Shoemakers), Scurvy says the same as Edgar, but with a minor change: "I suffer more because I haven't had any idea who I am ever since I gained political power."[8] Witkiewicz, like any other Modernist theoretician and practitioner of boredom, thus reasons: the boredom that makes self-definition impossible is not only at the point of exit in an individual's life but also at the end of accession. No symbolic social mechanism (here, political power) invalidates boredom, nor does it provide an answer to the question who one is. This condition occurs because boredom ceases to be the result of the illness that individuals suffer from and becomes an ontological condition of reality itself in all its historical manifestations. The alienation, of which Marx wrote that it deprives the worker of control over the work she does,[9] is a sign that is characteristic of modern boredom, although this alienation, social in its manifestations, has its beginning in ontological experience. It means that Modernity is an epoch that, for the first time, established a social grounds for ontology (as it is customary to argue following Durkheim), but also for the first time attempted to explain the structure of social life employing the language of ontology. Until now, those two languages had belonged to entirely different spheres of experience. Modernity brought them into collision. Gombrowicz and Schulz, as we shall see, took the more metaphysical (ontological) side of this debate. Witkiewicz—the most pessimistic of all—installed himself on the impossible grounds of the social apocalypse.

Mourning for the Absent Subject

In this article, I am attempting three things: one is related to Witold Gombrowicz, another to the history of Polish literature, and yet another is my theoretical contribution to the understanding of boredom as the subjective condition. First, I am trying to delineate the contours of Gombrowicz's comprehension of boredom as—here is my main point—this understanding sets up the foundations for his entire work.[10] Next, I am arguing that this position was barely possible to develop without multiple references to other Polish writers—Bruno Schulz and Stanisław Ignacy Witkiewicz—whose concerted literary effort was an original Modernist context for young Gombrowicz to launch his literary career.[11] And finally, in my more theoretical part, I am trying to suggest that boredom, as an existential experience, consists of radical de-subjectification, and more precisely in the impossibility of constructing a "strong" subject. Each of the Polish writers I am mentioning here attempted in a different way to show that the confrontation of the I with its emptiness and with the void of the world makes it impossible to create a distance between the I and the world, a distance without which no autonomous subject, and therefore no clear cognition, is possible to achieve.

Martin Heidegger, whose importance for the Modern understanding of affectivity cannot be overstated, tried to show that boredom, alongside anxiety,[12] is one of the most basic existential frames of mind whereby a human being not so much knows reality, but opens herself up to it and stays in it. Polish Modern writers I am going to quote here to build the context for Gombrowicz's early work show that although Heidegger's analyses touching the liquidation of meaning in the experience of boredom are accurate, they may lack any positive content.[13] It is because the Modernity in which boredom reaches epidemic levels is not salvation for the human being, but rather a curse. At the same time, however, this ontological language does not obscure the most important motif in the modern discourse of boredom. Thus, the impossibility of constructing the subject does have not only an epistemological meaning (the world cannot be transformed into a meaningful, i.e., intellectually graspable totality) but also a social one. Erecting the subject is the only available means of avoiding the confrontation of the I with its emptiness, and at the same time of symbolically (and, thus, supra-individual) grounding one's existence.

As Émile Tardieu wrote in his treatise on boredom in 1903, the one way to deal with boredom is to "give oneself to a duty, devote oneself to an ideal."[14] This language is close to Freud's considerations on mourning and melancholy.[15] The subject, withdrawing her emotional investment from the place vacated by the absent object of love, has to change its object, which may be a concrete person or an idea, to work through mourning and not get bogged down in melancholy. In this sense, boredom appears as mourning, which has not been worked through. This is how both Gombrowicz and Schulz formulate it. But since the subject's existence depends on a symbolic mechanism that works properly in a given society, modern boredom can also be understood as grief, which has not been worked through, for a social catastrophe (which Wikiewicz was proving). As Elizabeth Goodstein says, "in boredom, the disappearance of experience is manifested in ... alienation from one's doing and being: it is a quotidian crisis of subjectivity."[16] In this article, I am showing that this "quotidian crisis of subjectivity" was very acutely problematized by Gombrowicz and two other Polish writers: Bruno Schulz and Stanisław I. Witkiewicz.

The Muddle Gets Worse

In the Sunday issue of *Czas*, on February 27, 1938, the reader could read on a note entitled "Marzec w Zakopanem" (March in Zakopane).

> In March in the Tatras, there is always the most lovely weather, and perfect snow conditions make it possible for many groups of skiers fully to enjoy winter sports. A stay in Zakopane in March is also enjoyable because it involves only minimal costs.

However, three pages later there is something quite different on the subject of a stay in Zakopane. For, "driven by an inconsolable existential momentum," Gombrowicz came to Zakopane. Gombrowicz traveled to Zakopane frequently; neither his work as a court intern nor his work as a writer prevented him, and his health required repeated periods of recuperation.[17] His stays in Zakopane were scarcely filled with fascinating adventures, but the *feuilleton* from his visit to the Tatras has a specific, philosophical character.

> If you leave out the apparatus, if you leave out the skiing, cards, bottles, and your more or less smooth moves on the dance floor – enormous boredom arises, and a terrible awkwardness. People here pull and drag each other, like those candies they call twists. ... And all that dragging becomes a drag. ... The time infects the bones, and everything somehow limps along. ... Hey, it wasn't that way once. People are losing their dash.[18]

This feuilleton is a mini-treatise on boredom. Gombrowicz is amusing here, but at the same time very serious. Boredom is not a phenomenon connected with the individual, nor is it a psychological phenomenon; it has a social character instead. It arises as a result of a reduction of "apparatus," or, in other words, of the attributes of social intercourse. Sociability masks boredom manifested by an acute sense of time, which is not an "inner" experience,[19] but a bodily one. All that dragging around becomes a drag, and time starts to pass more slowly.

But not only time is at stake here. "I settled in the mountains. I fell into dreaminess (rozmarzenie), slovenliness (rozmamłanie), and idleness (rozwałkonienie)."[20] Of course, Gombrowicz does not link these three words by chance, for he wishes to show—through the prefix roz-[21]—the condition of a world given over to boredom. The world is "rozmamłany" (made slovenly) because it has lost clear outlines. "It is something muddy, unclear, and doubtful; I don't myself know what or how...."[22] "Generally it's cloudy and difficult to discern anything."[23] This effacing of the outlines of things brings further complications.

> Gulping the soup immediately gets mixed up in the confused and dissolute atmosphere here with the drawing of a sleigh by horses – and horses get mixed up with cows, of which there aren't any – and cows again get mixed up with veal with beans and potatoes – after which that whole dish, which you stuff yourself on, gets mixed up with you, and in the end you don't know yourself if the veal goes into you or if you stuff yourself into the veal. And finally, you can't distinguish between your flesh and the flesh you eat, or the flesh consumed by others, and even in general – the flesh of others.[24]

For a humorous feuilleton, this has a lot of non-feuilletonist thoughts. The muddle that Gombrowicz speaks of does not come from excess (an excess of gestures, figures, movement, events),[25] but from the opposite. We are not dealing with ambiguity, the cause of which would be an excessive production of meanings, but with a leakage of meaning caused by the effacing of the outlines of reality, or also, as the previous quotation indicates, an effacing of borders not only between I and what is not I, but even between particular sectors of the world. In boredom, reality becomes blurred, loses clarity and obviousness, and the human being has nothing to hold onto to stand on firm ground, for firm ground, a foundation on which a strong subject might stand, no more exists. Boredom liquidates the social adhesion of the subject and also exposes her bodily—fleshy—foundation. The clash of de-subjectified flesh with the dense matter of time, which has also lost its subjective roots, is the effect of the operations of boredom according to Gombrowicz.

Depravation

In autumn 1937, Gombrowicz published *Ferdydurke*. In the critical first chapter, sensationally entitled "Porwanie" (Abduction), the main subject is immaturity, which the writer chooses in spite of the demands of a "mature," and therefore "official," culture ("I spun my themes from more lowly quarters and filled my narrative with legs, frogs, with material that was immature and fermenting").[26] The subject is also the dependency on the judgments of others: "It's as if you were being born inside a thousand souls that are too tight-fitting for comfort!"[27] At one point, the writer's double turns up, whose otherness the narrator cannot abide, because it makes him aware of the complete deformation of his being, a deformation produced by "cultural aunties." "Oh, to create my own form! To turn outward! To express myself! Let me conceive my own shape, let no one do it for me!"[28] And, indeed, from Gombrowicz's desire to liberate himself from the transforming judgments of others, there emerges a new form: *Ferdydurke* itself.

Gombrowicz had long been trying to produce a final draft of the novel. He wrote several preliminary stories, but he published an essential excerpt in the July issue of the journal *Skamander* in 1935, under the title "Ferdydurke." The theme of immaturity is absent here, or at least not in such an extended form as in the final version. There are no "cultural aunties," nor is there the whole well of Gombrowicz's obsession of a person's shaping through the judgments of other people. The matter is simpler but at the same time somewhat more complicated. The narrator is not an author who does not know what to do with his literary career, but is rather a man who is conscious of the irreversible loss of youth, and does not know what to do with himself since no one "misses" him.

> For what indeed was I? A fright, as dull as a billiard table, full-time or contract employee, who had run out of the gas of youth – I bored

myself and others; from time to time I went to chance parties and played bridge, but there was no life in all that.[29]

The situation is similar to that in the final version, but not entirely. Here, there is no violence of foreign judgment, but only an overwhelming emptiness, a lack of life, in other words, overwhelming boredom. Here, we encounter a situation that is the reverse of that described in the Zakopane feuilleton. There, boredom appeared as an effect of "removing the apparatus." Here, boredom is an original existential situation, the inconveniences of which can only be combated by "adding apparatus," that is, more social props.

For this reason, all the repertoire of adhesive social institutions is mentioned: social service, the Fatherland, humanity. None of these, however, is sufficient but all of a sudden, the double appears; in this case, however, in a reverse manner to that in the final version. The double gets revealed as "life itself,"[30] which the narrator sought everywhere in his inner world, but could not find within himself. Unfortunately, not knowing what to do with this obscene and immediately revealed life, the narrator spits in the apparition's face.

> The apparition groaned and vanished. And I remained alone, but rather not alone, but with a feeling of overwhelming emptiness, as if life had escaped from me, and not seeing anything before me, only a vain and futile existence, inevitably ending in death, I dozed a little.[31]

After a brief nap, the narrator wakes up, "horribly exposed spiritually, shaky and uncertain."[32] He asks himself "who he is" and discovers that maybe "simply – he is and nothing more."

> But that phrase "I am," with no additions, a fact bare and terrible, filled me with terror. It seemed that there was nothing more difficult than to be, nothing more and nothing else, only oneself. In that word, there was contained a terrible nakedness.[33]

And here, as in the final version, there begins the "turning himself" outwards, toward various social relations, which permit the protagonist to forget about the naked experience and live his life as if nothing happened. But we know that if anything happened to him, it was nothing(ness).

Ontological Nakedness

It is time to formulate my thesis. The discovery of the naked facticity of existence intensifies the experience of original boredom, from which the narrator of the first version of the novel attempts to escape. "I bored myself and others," he says, identifying boredom with lack of life. However, when life as such appears, unmediated by nothing else and by no one else, the narrator cannot bear it and escapes into sleep, to discover finally after waking up that he is in no state to endure the existential nakedness. This radical nakedness is shown to be boredom itself, which is not the absence of something (absence of employment, absence of entertainment, absence of social relations), but an autonomous experience, not a dialectical one, and one that altogether ruins the dialectic. Boredom is a revelation of existence as such, unmediated by any social adhesive. The nakedness of which Gombrowicz writes is an ontological nakedness, from before the making of inter-personal relations, from before the assembling of "additions" and "apparatuses," whereby the subject is established as an element of a more extensive relation. If we accept that subjectivity is always relational because it is ever set in reference to the world, from which it wishes to separate itself, then boredom, however, as Gombrowicz says frequently, is a non-relational experience, without any props, and from this equation there comes a reasonably obvious result. Boredom, thus, makes the constitution of subjectivity impossible insofar as subjectivity is always involved in the mundane relations with the world and with others. When the I is in itself and for itself, clothed in the nothingness that would not belong to it, when the I is immediately given to itself and unmediated by anything that belongs to the world, or is a simple negation of its immediacy, then there is no place for the constitution of the subject. The subject is only the effect of an intense reaction to the immediate experience (impossible to bear) of the world, a world that manifests itself in the I without any symbolic veil. It is because of this immediate ontological apocalypse that the world Gombrowicz described in his Zakopane feuilleton loses clarity, turns into an incomprehensible mess, and finally gets transformed into the fog, in which there is no way to distinguish anything from anything else. Boredom is not a psychological problem, nor is it a social one: it is ontological through and through, and it exposes the impossibility of establishing the subject as a consequence of the lack of any mediation—social, ethical, cognitive, and aesthetic.

Before the Subject

In a lecture entitled *Was ist Metaphysik?* given on April 24, 1929, at the University of Freiburg, Heidegger linked boredom with metaphysics in the following way:

> No matter how fragmented our everyday existence may appear to be, however, it always deals with beings in a unity of the "whole," if only in a shadowy way. Even and precisely when we are not busy with

things or ourselves, this "as a whole" comes over us—for example, in authentic boredom. Such boredom is still distant when it is only this book or that play, that business or this idleness, that drags on and on. It irrupts when "one is bored." Profound boredom, drifting here and there in the abysses of our existence like a muffling fog, removes all things and human beings and oneself along with them into a remarkable indifference. This boredom manifests beings as a whole.[34]

Heidegger is the first twentieth-century philosopher who devotes very much attention to boredom, understood as a fundamental way in which humans relate to the world.[35] Above all, as we have seen, he distinguishes the boredom evoked by something boring from boredom as a fundamental "state of existence," in which manifest "beings as a whole." This deeper, metaphysical boredom is ambiguous. On the one hand, it shows us beings as a whole, which means that we cease to pay attention to particular beings, to individual things, to individual people. On the other hand, this revelation does not sharpen our cognition, but blurs it, because boredom is a "silent fog" that levels the differences in our world.

Since differences are leveled, since the world is deprived of meaning and is reduced to "beings as a whole," this means that boredom lifts the human being out of subjectified intercourse with things and other subjects, and forces the de-subjectified I to encounter its naked and blurred core. In this sense, the human being, as a result of fundamental boredom, which sweeps from her world previously established meanings, confronts herself. That is why Heidegger says that boredom is one of the fundamental attunements. A just appreciation of boredom, of course, means that the human being who is seized by this, so to speak, radical eradication of discriminations, should treat boredom as purification from life's oppression and as an opportunity to renew her existence. The examples that I cite, however, indicate how difficult it is to achieve that renewal through boredom.

As a result of its eradication of discriminations, boredom empties our experience on two levels—that of meaning and of time. Since the fog of boredom embraces all, nothing can have meaning (because meaning arises via the reference of things to the world and the subject), but also since under the fog of boredom all differences die, time, too, ceases to flow and starts to weigh. In *A Philosophy of Boredom* Lars Svendsen describes this, thereby commenting on Heidegger's musings.

> Dasein stiffens in everydayness – and in the world. Boredom is to reveal this stiffness. In boredom one is caught in a vortex of immanence, where Dasein is no longer genuinely ec-static, i.e., transcending. Boredom is reminiscent of eternity, where there is no transcendence. Time collapses, implodes, into a vast, empty present. Time is usually transparent – we do not take any notice of it – and

it does not appear as a something. But in our confrontation with a nothing in boredom, where time is not filled with anything that can occupy our attention, we experience time as time.[36]

In his *Cahiers*, Emil Cioran describes the same experience.

> That attack of boredom that I experienced as a five-year-old (1916), one afternoon, which I will never forget, was the first and the real awakening of my consciousness. From that afternoon dates my birth as a conscious being. What was I before? A being and nothing else. My I began from that split and revelation that mark the double nature of boredom indeed. Suddenly I felt the presence of nothingness in my blood, in my bones, in my breath, and in everything that surrounded me. I was as empty as the objects. There was no heaven and no earth, only an enormous extent of time, mummified time.[37]

The original experience of boredom for all three writers, Gombrowicz, Heidegger, and Cioran, is the birth of "self," of *Dasein* or *Moi*. "Without boredom," writes Cioran, "I would not have an identity. ... Boredom is an encounter with one's self – through a perception of one's nothingness."[38] Of course, this encounter with one's self, shown most clearly by Gombrowicz in the confrontation of his protagonist with his double, has most unwanted consequences.

On the High Seas

In the spring of 1930, one Zantman, whose situation "on the European continent was becoming more disagreeable and indistinct with every day," boards by mistake a ship sailing to Valparaiso, and immediately falls into the embrace of boredom.[39] First, literally: "I rendered to the sea all that I had to render, and I groaned, void as an empty bottle."[40] Later the passenger, physically devastated, begins to share his boring existence with the whole crew. "It seemed boredom was making itself felt rather strongly," writes Zantman in his notebook, and this observation becomes the main thread of Gombrowicz's entire story.

> When I climbed up to the bridge, Clarke said:
> "Boredom, sir. Sea boredom."
> "Hm," I replied.
> "Not a pleasant thing, boredom. Eh? Not pleasant. Things are boring. It's not clear what."[41]
> "I expect it's boring for you on board, Thompson," I said benevolently.
> "I'll say it's boring," groaned Thompson. "It's hard to stand it, sir."[42]

Of course, circumstances compel the situation, but we would be solving the problem of boredom in this story too quickly if we reduced boredom simply to a lack of occupation on board ship. It would be easy to concur that "On this sh ... brig nothing happens from morning to evening,"[43] and that the captain has to think up tasks for the crew, because otherwise, they would "drop dead from boredom."[44] However, the situation is more serious than that. The boredom that rules the ship is not simple boredom, the result of a lack of activities, but it is rather fundamental boredom, which liquidates differences and ultimately sucks all meanings from the world. In this sense, it appears close to stupidity.[45]

At one moment, in a situation of monstrous tension that results from the fact that the sailors, unaccustomed to confront their nothingness, stop putting up with the void now surging all around them, Zantman, in reaction to the captain's announcement that he will implacably suppress a mutiny on board, notes down in his log: "What foolishness! At such a moment! Why was it that foolishness wouldn't leave me alone for even a second? A terrible weariness flowed over me like olive oil."[46]

I would like to draw attention to two matters. The first is that olive oil here replaces the Heideggerian fog, and instead of enveloping the horizon, it washes over our protagonist, whereby not only do "the borders of dreams become blurred"[47] but also, above all, "a blurring of the difference between things, and also between good and evil"[48] takes place. Now we can see why stupidity turns out to be so close to boredom. Stupidity is not ignorance, impeded cognition, or faulty thinking. Stupidity is a state prior to the constitution of the rational subject, who begins to exist at the moment of her introduction into the world of fundamental discriminations: I-the world, good-bad, true-false. This pre-subjective situation becomes clear at the end of the story when the protagonist hides away in his cabin and refuses to come out on deck because he is afraid of mutinying—he imagines—sailors. After several days, looking out through the window, he begins to note a radical change in the landscape—"garish willow-green colors," "a satiety of light," and "richness of decoration"[49]—which, however, produces no enthusiasm in him. The ending is critical here.

> No, I do not wish to know. I do not wish to know, and I have no desire whatsoever for hot weather or glamour and luxury. And I would prefer not to go out on deck for fear of seeing something ... something that previously had been obscure, hidden, and unspoken, now parading in all its brazenness amid peacock feathers and the hot glare. Because from the beginning everything was mine, and I, I was just like everything—the exterior is a mirror in which the inside can be observed![50]

Varied are the ways to interpret this ending. It is convincing to see here the principal protagonist's insanity, which reading gets confirmed in the light of what I have hitherto said of boredom. Zantman does not wish to know not only of what is happening on the ship, but he also denies himself any knowledge at all that would separate his I from reality. In this sense, he chooses stupidity over knowledge. He does not wish to see what hitherto was turbid and shrouded by the fog of obfuscation, because he does not believe in the distance between the inside and the outside. If he declares that from the beginning "everything was mine," this does not mean that it appeared as such from the moment of his erroneous embarkation on board the Banbury, that everything that then happened was the result of the delirious imagination of a character assailed by seasickness (for such a reading is also possible). In my interpretation, Zantman cannot go beyond a confrontation with his emptiness, the symbolic equivalent of which is the boredom that dominates everywhere. Unable to escape from the paralyzing grasp of boredom, Zantman falls into insanity, because insanity (like stupidity and like boredom) is the result of unmediated intercourse with his self.

Loneliness

"I've been sitting here for years feeling bored,"[51] says the narrator of "Samotność" (Loneliness), one of Schulz's most important, but also certainly shortest, stories. "The world has become boring" and "Today emptiness and inertia breathe on me from the landscape," Schulz writes to a close acquaintance.[52] He defines boredom in a modern manner: it is "undifferentiated monotony" or "uneventful monotony."[53] Time ceases to flow; nothing can occur. Boredom eliminates a differentiated and continuously differentiating existence, replacing it with being in itself, the unmediated reference of the I to its self. In this sense, boredom is also the liquidation of the subject, which cannot liberate itself from its self through the negation of it.[54]

This process is most clearly shown in the story "Samotność," very peculiar even by Schulz's standards because it is the only monolog we find in his work in which no other character other than the narrator appears. From the juxtaposition of the two quotations with which I began this part, we can see that one could read this monolog autobiographically. We should not reject this hypothesis out of hand.[55] Schulz, at least from 1934, suffered from "chronic depression"[56] which he frequently called boredom. In a letter he confesses:

> Now I feel the terrible emptiness and nothingness of life. I can do nothing; I cannot pick up any book because it sickens and bores me terribly. ... I do not recognize myself. I who was always full of issues, problems, always excited by the most varied ideas, now I trudge along empty, without a thought, and lethargic, and I have

the impression that this is the end of everything. For months I haven't written; I'm incapable of writing even the shortest of articles. ... I feel that everything is not just a consequence of my affairs of the heart, but that I have entered some new phase of life, the dominant note of which is a great and principled disappointment – the nothingness of life.[57]

Two months later, Schulz writes in a letter to the same correspondent:

For four weeks I was in the country round Turka, almost entirely on my own. I took no consolation from this loneliness, and I rid myself of the illusion, an old one and rooted in me, that I am created for solitude. Perhaps once I was; today emptiness and inertia breathe on me from the landscape; I can no longer feed myself at the table of the Lord. It is inelegant always to complain and not manly, but I must say that something has gone wrong in me. Do you still find anything in the world that is truly beautiful and captivating; are you still capable of enthusiasm? It seems to me that the world has become boring.[58]

It is time to return to *Loneliness*. The narrator, let us recall, declares, "I have been sitting here for years feeling bored."[59] Here, or in other words in his childhood room. "And so I do live on nothing in this dead room."[60] I, or in other words "a lonely posthumous child,"[61] "a pensioner."[62] In Schulz's work the figure of the pensioner should be taken literally, as someone who has been thrown out of service, worn out, beyond the ambition of an active life.[63] Schulz's pensioner, when he looks in the mirror, does not see himself *en face*, but always at an angle, from the side; his gaze and the gaze of his double never intersect with each other. "When I move, he moves too, but turned halfway to the back, as if he is not aware of me, as if he has gone beyond many mirrors and can no longer return."[64] The room in which the narrator sits and cannot see himself in the mirror is walled up, but the protagonist knows that he could get out of this room if he could only imagine an exit. "There is no room so walled up that it cannot be opened with such a trusted door if only one has enough strength to insinuate it."[65] The point is that neither Schulz's narrator nor Schulz himself had such strength of insinuation. Schulz's double, differently from Gombrowicz's double, who reveals to the narrator of *Ferdydurke* his unbearable nakedness, is a reflection of indifference, or undifferentiation, which seizes the person who looks in the mirror. The double "does not know" anything about his original, which can only mean that it is coming unstuck from the narrator, eluding a dialectical union in which there resides a chance of constructing a subject that is conscious of itself. Instead of the subject, we have—almost as in Kafka[66]—an immobile, "immortal mouse,"[67] from which the narrator distances himself, "returning slowly to reason,"[68] but not to the extent to establish himself in the position of the subject. From the mouse, he jumps to his double, which cannot look at him and turns his gaze away. Schulz's narrator is, thus, suspended between two inhuman orders—between the animal to which he compares himself, and the reflection in the mirror that turns away from him. There is no space for him in a purely human order because all ties with the world have been torn. He does not lose his reflection, but the contact with it, which is proof of complete de-subjectification, in other words, the loss of speculative abilities. When such competencies are extinguished, the world ceases to mean anything, because it can only carry meanings for the subject.

This moment of flaccid de-subjectification, characteristic for Schulz's work, can be seen in the story "Wiosna" (Spring). In this long story, the youthful narrator is cruelly bored with his peers ("they were days to be grown into, days full of waiting, pallid from boredom and impatience")[69] up to the moment when one of the boys shows his friends a stamp album and "the flaming beauty of the world" gets revealed.[70] This moment of ecstatic fascination with stamps from foreign lands creates a breach in the closed world of boredom. Up to this moment, the world has gone on "without definition"[71] that one expected "from time."[72] Now when the world is bursting with different colors, with meanings sent from another universe, boredom must relax its grip. Boredom and time are mutually exclusive, just as essence excludes existence, nakedness clothes, and loneliness a social life. Boredom eliminates time as a horizon, against which everything takes on sense, but becomes unbearable when time replaces the world.

The Mystery Has Gone to the Dogs

Witkiewicz's novel *Pożegnanie jesieni* (*Farewell to Autumn*) begins with the reflections of the protagonist Anatazy Bazakbal on the subject of the "transcendental exitlessness of the situation, and the insolubility of the problems connected with it." It also deals with the "incommensurability of internal states and material facts" or, to put it simply, the incoherence of life and thought. One of his first reflections is as follows:

> However, at the very bottom of existence, at its very basis, there is some hellish nonsense, and it is boring nonsense. But this boredom is a result of modern times. Once all was grand and powerful, and now, the mystery has gone to the dogs, and there are fewer and fewer people who know this. Until at the end a homogenous greyness covers everything for many, many years before the extinguishing of the sun.[73]

Bazakbal says what Witkacy, the biggest pessimist in modern Polish or even European culture, thinks. His reasoning is as follows.[74] Humanity, as a consequence of modernization and democracy, has reached the moment in which the metaphysical feeling of the "Mystery of Existence" has been irrevocably lost. Religion has lost all meaning; into its place has come art, but that had to surrender to the aggressive mechanization of life, lack of real ideas, and superficiality. "Everything took place ostensibly: this more than anything else summed up the epoch."[75] As a consequence of the general disappearance of metaphysical feelings, culture, deprived of any transcendental sanction, degenerates into perversion, which becomes the only accessible artistic experience. But even perversion is not able to veil the emptiness of basic experience that floods over reality. "His skin ached from the indomitable boredom above the entire world."[76] Witkiewicz was not only diagnosing, after Spengler and others, the fall of the Western culture but also tried to show that the social catastrophe, the political effects of which could be observed in the aggressive growth of totalitarian regimes, had their roots in the metaphysical situation of the individual. As opposed to many critics, for whom the individual's spiritual life became impossible because of the intervention of mass culture, Witkiewicz was emphasizing that the crisis of civilization was the consequence of a radical loss of ground on the part of the individual. In *Insatiability*, the protagonist Genezyp Kapen experiences this loss of ground thus:

> And all the while he positively knew that he knew nothing: neither the person he would become nor who he was in essence. Before him yawned the hole, bottomless, narrow, inhospitable. The world, as though suddenly swept away, disappeared under his feet. He hung suspended over some abyss.[77]

It is not the technically shaped culture that rapes the innocent individual, as many critics have suggested in defense of the individual against the mass, the city, and the machine, but rather the individual discovers in himself an indelible lack, which he subsequently recognizes, to his horror, in social reality. In this sense, Witkiewicz establishes a continuity between two dimensions of existence: individual experience and the social network of relations. From boredom discovered in oneself, there is no escape in any social constructions, because the essence of social relations is founded on even greater boredom. To put it differently, Witkiewicz knows that the history of Western culture is a history of gradual decline, a vanishing of metaphysical feelings, but he also knows that the individual is defined not by fullness, but only by emptiness. When he declares that everything was "hollowed out, gutted; a void reverberating like a dried-out gourd,"[78] that empty "everything" means both dimensions of human existence: the inner and the outer life, both of which loss their sharp antithetical status.[79]

Without Any Tricks

Gombrowicz tried to find an exit from the confrontation with pure existence, which reveals itself once "the apparatus" gets removed, Schulz dramatically searched for the opportunity to escape from the double that turned away from him, and Witkiewicz knew perfectly well that no liberating transition between esse and socius was possible, because the boredom reigned everywhere. Existence, in general, was something monstrous in its core and no social ideas and fictions that come from them could help. In his analyses of boredom, Heidegger wished to show a deeper, more authentic level of existence than that imposed by a contemporary culture that had led it to the level of superficial journalism. Witkiewicz did not believe that such a deep level of authentic confrontation with oneself is possible to attain. He rather believed in it as a metaphysical postulate, but all the examples he provided in novels and plays prove the impossibility of standing face to face with oneself. For this reason, every protagonist in his texts must suffer defeat, the cause of which turns out to be despair.

There is no escape from internal boredom since on the outside all is subordinated to it. "The formidable task of catapulting the ego into infinity—unaided by art, science, religion, philosophy, or any other tricks,"[80] which Genezyp Kapen attempted toward the end of his life, came to nothing. At a certain moment, he felt how a great wave of boredom swept over him, but he knew perfectly well that it had not come from the world deprived of its metaphysics in which it was his lot to live, but that it was transmitted "by some metaphysical power station housed inside this creature."[81] Witkiewicz without any doubt was the ontologist of boredom, and he perfectly knew that its destructive operation touched equally both the I and the whole world.[82] It is, nevertheless, necessary to say what boredom is as the foundation of existence (individual and social). In *Insatiability*, describing the thoughts of the protagonist as to who his fiancée is, Witkiewicz writes, "A certain boredom, the price of every perfection, was inescapable. Perfection breeds suspicion; at times it can conceal an absolute negativity: empty form."[83] At times? When one is reading Witkacy's novels and dramas, one cannot resist the impression that the ontological hollowness, described in all dimensions, from an individual feeling of emptiness to the perception of a lack of meaning in the world, is identical with the nothingness that does not constitute a deficiency, but rather an autonomous entity. In this sense, Witkacy is a radical (because ontological) nihilist. Boredom identified with emptiness defines the manner of the world's existence and is not only a psychological feeling on the part of the protagonist or a lack of occupation, a liberation from which might be art, religion, or politics.

Understood ontologically, boredom makes it impossible to get beyond oneself, beyond the immediately experienced I toward the subject and, thus too, toward the social world. It appears that, from boredom understood in that manner, there is no way to escape other than to fall into depression (Schulz) or to take one's life (Witkiewicz). Early Gombrowicz shared this pessimistic view of reality, and his disbelief in the overcoming of metaphysical boredom was invincible. Whether he continued to think so in the years of his Argentinian and Parisian exile after the war, the answer to this question must for a while remain in suspension.

Notes

1 A different version of this article appeared in *Tekstualia* 2014.
2 This unusual heading alludes to the play by Stanisław I. Witkiewicz (1921) of the same title.
3 A feeling of listlessness, boredom, tedium, lethargy, and weariness.
4 See Markowski, *Anatomia ciekawości*. On boredom, see Spacks, *Boredom*; Goodstein, *Experience*; Toohey, *Boredom*.
5 Benjamin, *Arcades*, 101–19; Goodstein, passim.
6 Benjamin cites a sentence from Friedrich Engels: "The wearisome routine of endless drudgery, in which the same mechanical process is ever repeated, is like the torture of Sisyphus; the burden of toil, like a rock, is ever falling back upon the worn-out drudge." Engels, *Condition*, 186. This is also Witkiewicz's understanding when he points to "the scientific organization of labor," or Taylorism, as one of the primary sources of the individual's alienation. Witkiewicz, *Insatiability*, 19.
7 Witkiewicz, "Water Hen" in his *Madman*, 46.
8 Witkiewicz, *Mother*.
9 Marx, *Economic*, 77.
10 See Markowski, "Ręka," 215–52.
11 See Markowski, *Polska*.
12 Heidegger, *Metaphysics*; on anxiety Heidegger, *Being and Time*, 178–84.
13 Heidegger, *Contributions*, 123.
14 Tardieu, *L'Ennui*, 290.
15 Freud, "Mourning," 4, 152–70.
16 Goodstein, 10.
17 Gombrowicz, *Memoirs*, 169, on Zakopane, 169–77.
18 Gombrowicz, "Niedole zakopiańskie," *Czas*, No. 57, Feb. 27, 1938, 8.
19 Husserl, *Vorlesungen*; Mann, *Zauberberg*.
20 Gombrowicz, "Niedole," 8.
21 I have written extensively on the fundamental meaning of the prefix "roz-" (in English roughly "dis") in Bruno Schulz's work in *Powszechna*.
22 Gombrowicz, "Niedole," 8. Substantially more radical in this regard is *Diariusz wiejski*, inserted in *Diary* from 1954. See *Diary*, 131–32.
23 Gombrowicz, "Niedole," 9.
24 Ibid.
25 See Markowski, *Czarny nurt*.
26 Gombrowicz, *Ferdydurke* (Borchardt), 4.
27 Ibid., 7.
28 Ibid., 14.
29 Gombrowicz, "Fragmenty," 278.
30 Gombrowicz, "Fragmenty," 281.
31 Ibid., 282–83.
32 Ibid., 283.

33 Ibid.
34 Heidegger, *Pathmarks*, 87.
35 Heidegger calls it "a silent fog in the abysses of Dasein." Heidegger, *Metaphysics*, 77.
36 Svendsen, *Philosophy*, 127.
37 Cioran, *Cahiers*, 768.
38 Ibid.
39 Gombrowicz, *Bacacay* (Johnston), 142.
40 Ibid., 143.
41 Ibid., 158.
42 Ibid., 168.
43 Ibid., 160.
44 Ibid., 157.
45 See *Czarny nurt*, especially in Part III: "Popłoch i wymiot."
46 Gombrowicz, *Bacacay*, 187.
47 Ibid., 188.
48 Ibid., 189.
49 Ibid., 192.
50 Ibid., 193.
51 Schulz, *Collected*, 231.
52 Letter to Zenon Waśniewski, Drohobycz, Aug. 4, 1937, in Schulz, *Księga*, 86.
53 Schulz, *Collected*, 206. Both definitions come from "Dodo" and refer to the life of the eponymous protagonist, which was like "an entirely straight, monotonous highway without events or surprises."
54 The confrontation of the I with its own emptiness, which defines Modern boredom, was perhaps best summed up by Pessoa in the 1930s. "It's not only the emptiness of things and living beings that troubles the soul afflicted by tedium, it's also the emptiness of something besides things and beings—the emptiness of the very soul that feels this vacuum, that feels itself to be that vacuum, and that within this vacuum is nauseated and repelled by its own self." Pessoa, *Disquiet*, 316.
55 In the first printing, this text is entitled "O sobie" (Of Myself). Schulz adopted the final version of the title only when sending *Sanatorium pod Klepsydrą* to print.
56 Schulz letter to A. Pleśniewicz, Nov. 29, 1936. See Schulz, *Księga*, 115.
57 Schulz, *Księga*, 85.
58 Ibid., 86.
59 Schulz, *Collected*, 231.
60 Ibid.
61 Ibid.
62 Ibid.
63 "Loneliness" is one of the poles of Schulz's pensioner diptych. The second is the story "Emeryt" (The Pensioner), in which the protagonist, a retired official, experiences a regression and enrolls in primary school, where he recovers his vigor and finds himself at the center of attention, after which he lets himself be blown away by the wind. I favor reading this final scene as a metaphor of ecstasy's transporting the pensioner from the boredom of everyday existence.
64 Schulz, *Collected*, 232.
65 Ibid.
66 See Kafka, "Josephine, die Sängerin."
67 Schulz, *Collected*, 232.
68 Ibid.
69 Ibid., 108.

70 Ibid., 110.
71 Ibid., 108.
72 Ibid., 109.
73 Witkiewicz, "Pożegnanie," in *Dzieła zebrane*, II, 14–15.
74 Wikiewicz most fully set out his catastrophic vision in *Nowe formy w malarstwie i wynikające stąd nieporozumienia*, written after his return from Russia in 1918 and published a year later.
75 Witkiewicz, *Insatiability*, 20.
76 Ibid., 64.
77 Ibid., 72.
78 Ibid., 475.
79 The best image of this historical-ontological boredom is the board with the inscription "Boredom" that appears God knows from where or by whose agency on the stage in Witkacy's last play *Shoemakers*. After a while, it disappears and is replaced by a second board with the inscription "Even worse boredom."
80 Witkiewicz, *Insatiability*, 482.
81 Ibid., 480.
82 In my *Polska literatura* (339–68), I present a more extensive (and slightly different) analysis of Witkiewicz's struggles with boredom, on a private and an intellectual-literary level. See also my essay "Facemaker" in Potocka, *Witkacy*.
83 Witkiewicz, *Insatiability*, 457.

8 Becoming Gombrowicz

On the Way of Trans-Subjectivity and Trans-Modernity

Piotr Seweryn Rosół

From the very beginning, Gombrowicz struggled to overcome the limitations imposed on modern subjectivity, placing himself and his work "between": between superiority and inferiority, maturity and immaturity, delight and disgust, the North and the South (which meant more than between city and village), countries and continents, styles and genres. This was interpreted as only a kind of desperate escape from obvious identities and definitions such as heterosexual/homosexual, man, Pole, landlord, emigrant, writer, etc., or, on the other hand, the strategy of an "incomprehensible artist" who does not want to belong to any groups, trends, or schools.[1]

In fact, his game had a much higher stake. The visible transgression of modern dualities (body-mind, depth-surface, speech-writing, other-same, passive-active, private-public, etc.) was only the first step to the rejection of modern values — such as post-Cartesian rationalism, sovereign and self-aware subject, the idea of progress, rational and colonial civilization, vanguard, emancipation, disenchantment—and to the appreciation of those which modernity rejected as non-modern and consequently stigmatized as abnormal or pathological. Obviously, it was not a simple choice of categories that were seriously marginalized (for instance, immaturity as opposed to maturity), but a subtle movement of deconstruction discovering hidden moments of resistance. Thus, it was not a revolution, a post-Nietzschean "revaluation of all values," but the constant introduction of what was considered to be pathological into the area of normality. Gombrowicz knew that modern dualities were not created to describe reality—according to their own assumptions, objectively and neutrally—but to impose a clear and legible hierarchy separating the norm from the unacceptable and thus in every otherness creating their own enemy. Modernity, striving at any price for disenchantment and demythologization, demanding elimination of everything that was pre-rational, in fact turned out to be a "para-religion or anthropocentric cult based on the infinite power of man as an individual."[2] Since one of the main objects of his writing was "to cut a path through Unreality to Reality,"[3] he had first to overthrow modern myths based on the central position of the subject.

Although since the 1960s, the field of pathology has undoubtedly diminished and the field of otherness enlarged, making it possible to reveal the excluded subjects, Gombrowicz's own history had not developed in the rhythm of this change. In other words, the otherness brought into prominence in his work has no actual political dimension, remaining the private voice of the excluded individual that does not support any post-Foucauldian counter-narrative. As he said, "But I never wrote one word about something other than myself — I do not feel authorized to do so."[4] Indeed, it is not difficult to find in Gombrowicz's work characters or individuals whose most important topic is the creation of themselves. It is, however, much harder to find a path that leads from privacy to community, from *oikos* to *polis*, and thus from pathology to norm. This was the path followed by those who interpreted Gombrowicz. Each interpreter, of course, has the right to a generalization that explains the author's intent and each writer has the right to defend his work against this form of instrumental use.

When Gombrowicz returned to Europe in 1963 to "conquer Europe" and "met" his last "double," Jean Genet, it coincided with an extremely colorful decade of great discoveries in the French humanities, especially in literary theory. This was the time of revolution, which fairly quickly penetrated the old Sorbonne and inaugurated the time of the *"demons of theory,"*[5] which in May 1968 took political power on the streets of Paris. The highest form of this intellectual, and in consequence political, movement ("post-structuralism") exceeds the traditional hermeneutic model of interpretation which, in the eyes of Roland Barthes, Michel Foucault, and Jacques Derrida, seemed now a violent imposition of allegedly exhaustive and credible explanations.[6] The response to such an instrumental and institutional interpretation model was supposed to be a new kind of personal and creative reading whose purpose was seeking otherness instead of identity.[7]

Gombrowicz fits into this anti-modern anti-theory paradigm[8] when he strongly rejects any possibility of identification with general terms which deprive him of singularity and builds his own independent dictionary in opposition to the dominant one. Second, he deconstructs the division of mind and body, intelligence and sensuality, naturalness and artificiality, particularity and universality, and individuality and generality. These, along with Youth, Immaturity, and Inferiority, are not just a reverse of modern values, but are trans-modern categories. They claim a proper place facing Western modernity but are never specifically defined.

In this perspective, Gombrowicz's work can be divided, I propose, into two parts. First, Gombrowicz's heroes make numerous attempts to fit in some way into various norms defined by modernity: social, national, existential, sexual, cultural, and symbolic. Second, they already know that these attempts do not bring the desired effects, and therefore, they try to transfigure all existing Forms, abandoning all dualities. This is the path of modern subjectivity that seeks liberation from what has been formed. The moment of transition comes in *Trans-Atlantyk*: abandonment of modern Europe in crisis means a final journey into the unknown. Suspension of discredited Forms opens the way for formlessness or immaturity. This liberation can be seen in all his works published before the war, but only this personal and universal disaster made it possible for him to cross the previously impassable boundaries.

The Impurified Double

The process of immaturity is already apparent in *Memoirs of a Time of Immaturity* (*Pamiętnika z okresu dojrzewania*). The first scene of the first short story "Lawyer Kraykowski's Dancer" ("Tancerz mecenasa Kraykowskiego") begins with the conflict between maturity and immaturity, order and disorder, and Europe and the "nation of Zulus,"[9] and therefore between modern people and those who have not yet achieved modernity and are condemned to eternal resentment. On one side, there is poverty, dirt, and illness (the epileptic dancer), and, on the other side, wealth, purity, and health embodied in the life of a lawyer. This symbolizes the disintegration of the modern project, already present at the very beginning in the dualistic notion of *modernité* in Baudelaire's "La chambre double" and other poems in *Paris Spleen*. As a noun, "double" means twin, dual, or twofold, but can also mean a duplicate, copy or a second self. The dancer begins a series of "doubles" in Gombrowicz's writing that are placed in the dialectic of the master and the slave, attracting and repelling his proper economy of desire.

Performing this duality in numerous instances of imitation and submissiveness reveals a deep interdependence between both worlds. The lawyer will be forever a hostage of the dancer and the dancer will be the unwanted, disgusting side of the lawyer. In spite of all, disgust remains as a repressed truth of "pure" modernity. Impurity cannot be fully subordinated by the law. In this combination of extreme opposites, we can recognize not only the abject present in modernity as an unappreciated double, but also something more important – the abject of modernity itself, which loses the ability to maintain the division and as a result is no longer what it initially appeared.

According to Bruno Latour, "we have never been modern" when we realize that the "purification" was never complete because it was always dependent on mediation or "hybridization."[10] Gombrowicz, like Latour, seems to acknowledge that "differentiation" is central to modernity's self-image and shows constantly moments in which what should be divided is actually confused, especially our careful distinctions between nature and society, between human and animal, that are only a matter of faith. Alongside the purifying practice that defines modernity, there exists another seemingly contrary one that mixes everything, thus undermining the constitution of modernity. Since "we have never been modern" but living in the world of hybrids, Gombrowicz appears to suggest, we are not just non-modern, as Latour contends, we are trans-modern.

We find the first presage of crossing this duality, a movement proper for the second part of his writing, in the short story "The Memoirs of Stefan Czarniecki" ("Pamiętnik Stefana Czarnieckiego"). The tension between incomprehensible oppression and unconscious subversion— present at home, school, and the army—constructs the dramaturgy of the disgusting other's fate in the symbolic Polish imaginary. Being "a colorless rat, a neutral rat,"[11] who does not understand national and cultural codes leads to "an upstart—or better, a moral bankrupt."[12] The connection of what should not be connected, "the spirit" and "the nose," makes a Jewish mother and her son transform into the abject,[13] neither subject nor object. Repulsion becomes the most violent emotion still, like purification, supporting the taboos of modern civilization. In the reinstatement of the abject to the representation, we find indeed the first scene of trans-subjectivity and the first moment of trans-modernity.

As Winfried Menninghaus has proven:

> Eighteenth century's foundation of modern aesthetics can be described negatively as a foundation based on prohibition of what is disgusting. The "aesthetic" is the field of a particular "pleasure" whose absolute other is disgust: so runs its briefest, its only undisputed, yet wholly forgotten basic definition. Nevertheless, a careful reading of the "classic" aesthetic theory reveals unexpectedly complicated relations between "disgust" and aesthetic "pleasure." The most surprising discovery may be this one: like a sweet that is all too sweet, the beautiful is in danger — from the first and by its very nature — of turning out to be *in itself* something disgusting. This applies precisely to the extent that beauty's "purity" is *not* contaminated and supplemented by something that is not (only) beautiful. The absolute other of the aesthetic thus returns as the inmost tendency of the beautiful.[14]

While many theoreticians of taste were essentially looking for a way to defend beauty, Gombrowicz (in this regard Baudelaire's follower) exceeds the boundaries of taste, not to strengthen them, but to reveal the inevitable and lasting presence of disgust in modern life itself. So if, for Mendelssohn, Lessing, Herder, or even Kant, there is no beauty without aversion and there is no aversion without beauty, for Gombrowicz, as for Baudelaire and many early and late modern writers and philosophers (especially Friedrich Nietzsche, Walter Benjamin, Georges Bataille, Jean-Paul Sartre, and Jean Genet), beauty itself is repulsive and what is repulsive is beautiful. That is why we can put his work within a rich tradition of *tremendum et fascinans* (probably most clearly expressed by Bataille).[15] Every "double" in the world of Gombrowicz is a shameful object of desire because shame is imposed by the relation of power-knowledge which sets the norm. This is not only abnormal in the space of discourse, monstrous in the field of representation and seductive in the area of desire, but also disgusting, therefore desirable.

In 1963, on board of the *Federico Costa*, Gombrowicz returned to Europe after spending twenty-four years in Argentina and prepared for his meeting with himself and his last "double," Genet. Then the unexpected: "I walk ... suddenly I look, something is lying on one of the deck planks, something small. A human eye ... – Did somebody lose it or was it poked out?"[16] The scene is really *uncanny* (in the Freudian sense) because it is dangerous, fantastic, and at the same time familiar, previously seen somewhere. This passage is almost exactly quoted from "The Events on the Banbury" ("Zdarzenia na brygu Banbury").[17] This short story was organized around constant and futile attempts of self-purification, in a literal, physiological sense, and, more importantly, in a moral and philosophical sense as well. This scene pushes the subject into continuous vomiting that is more than a consequence of seasickness, thus approximating him to what is real (and Real in the Lacanian sense).

"The eye," says Tomasz Swoboda in *Historie oka* (Stories of the Eye),

> is a part of the human body and at the same time inhuman as if it were not ours, because it concentrates and reflects what is external (...) is also the most animal, beside the genitals, part of our body.[18]

"It's a flimsily attached organ," added the narrator of "The Events on the Banbury," "a sphere inserted into a socket in a person, nothing more."[19] Nothing more, and so much, because the gesture of "eye-opening" hides the desire to open the body to things that have so far slipped away, and consequently reveal the intent of overturning a clear division between what is beautiful (and pure) and what is disgusting (and impurified). It signifies the return of what was excluded by the representation and concealed in the constitution of modernity.

Martin Jay, discussing the history of visual phenomena in the French philosophical and literary discourse, comes to the paradoxical conclusion that, from René Descartes to Jean-François Lyotard, this discourse, on the one hand, was undoubtedly based on *ocularcentrism*. However, on the other hand, this ocularcentrism was challenged by, for example, Jean-Paul Sartre, Jacques Lacan, Michel Foucault, Roland Barthes, Jacques Derrida, or even Maurice Merleau-Ponty and especially in Georges Bataille.[20] Much the same takes place in Gombrowicz's short story in which the traditional concept of the eye as a source of rationality is at the same time shaken and maintained; elevated to the level of evidence and yet also discredited. In this way, the fight against ocularcentrism turns out to be a trans-modern fight against the exclusion of the abject from the field of representation.

Gombrowicz, before the imagined meeting with Genet in whose writing "he found everything he didn't dare to write himself,"[21] found himself close to Genet despite the never expressed union of beauty with repulsion, and his own hidden homosexuality. Thus, he is confronting his own abjection, trying in vain to purify himself. The "double," beginning with *Memoirs From the Time of Immaturity*, gave shelter, the ability to hide, to escape into the figure of the unspoken (among them the most important examples are Zantman, Lawyer Kraykowski's Dancer, Stefan Czarniecki, Johnnie, Mientus, Frederick, and finally Leo). In the imaginary encounter with Genet described in his *Diary*, Gombrowicz takes on extraordinary autonomy and risks revealing himself from the very beginning:

> Imagine! How embarrassing! That homosexual attached himself to me, kept following me, I go somewhere with acquaintances and there he is on the corner, somewhere, under a lamppost, beckoning or something ... sending me signals! Just as if we were out of the same mold! Shame! And also – the possibility of blackmail![22]

Sadomasochism

Both of these early short stories – "Lawyer Kraykowski's Dancer" and "The Memoirs of Stefan Czarniecki" – seem emblematic of the sadomasochistic dialectic of Superiority-Inferiority, Master-Slave, Mature-Immature, and Teacher-Disciple, in which Gombrowicz's writing develops. The dancer, a double of lawyer Kraykowski, the insane, the epileptic, the man of resentment, a slave imitating the gestures of his imagined master, a masochist enjoying the adoration of his idol. He follows him, identifies with his story, waits on the corner and looks, and when the lawyer beats him with a cane, he receives it "in a state of grace and beatitude."[23] "I was happy. I received it into myself like a communion, and I closed my eyes. In silence I merely bent over and offered my back."[24] He is faithful to the end, but in that fidelity he gives his master a try, exposing his weaknesses.

Stefan Czarniecki tries vainly to follow the same path of complete subordination to modern cultural norms until the very end when he announces he will impose on others his singularity and his will. First, Gombrowicz reverses the classical *Bildungsroman* presenting the formation of a "man without qualities" unable to understand and accept social roles, and then shows that such experience finally gives rise to a strong need of transgression. "But what would happen if I were to acquire my own mystery and impose it on your world...?,"[25] Stefan wonders. He states further:

> I wander around the world, sailing across that abyss of inexplicable idiosyncrasies, and wherever I see some mysterious emotion, whether it is virtue or family, faith or fatherland, I always have to commit some villainy. This is my mystery, which for my part I impose upon the great enigma of being.[26]

This clear declaration of independence performed against arbitrary rights and obligations is also Gombrowicz's promise of writing "a book, my book, a book resembling myself, identical with myself, born of myself, a book which was to be the supreme affirmation of myself in the face of everything and everybody."[27]

Gombrowicz's world is a world of constant *agon* (of bodies, desires, texts) and a constant imitation – desire of another desire (following Hegel/Kojève),[28] which leads to what René Girard calls the mimetic mechanism.[29] Gombrowicz shows the profound master's dependence on the slave in the historical and existential dimension: Superior enamored of Inferior, and in this way looking for recognition of his superiority. On the other hand, by casting his hero as slave he is on the path from resentment to betrayal; he exposes the weakness of the master but never takes his place. The struggle for recognition ("I" gain identity only through recognition of others) in Gombrowicz's writing is also found in his *Diary*, a "fight for eminence," imposition of self – his own desire inscribed in text.

The dialectic of master and slave connects Gombrowicz's eroticism with trans-subjectivity and trans-modernity finding in sadism and masochism, as Gilles Deleuze desires, two different strategies for overthrowing the Law. The masochist is a humorist, *logicien des conséquences,* while the sadist is an ironist, *logicien des principes.*[30] The first accepts the consequences of the Law, apparently submits to them, but in the meticulous fulfillment of orders he also finds, beside the forbidden pleasure, an opportunity to deny his unjustifiable claims. The second, aware of the fact that every law is usurpation and mystification, transcends it in the name of a higher necessity to which the law finally turns out to be a secondary force. He creates a new, alternative "principle of principles," turns minority language into the dominant one, and reverses existing categories and values.

In this sense, before the war Gombrowicz seems to be a passive masochist exploring the possibilities of discourse, first obedient to social norms but in the end betraying them. After the war, he became an active sadist. With the Immature clearly striking the Mature, "son-land" opposes "fatherland." The precursor of this change of strategy is included in the fate of Stefan Czarniecki who, exactly after the war, abandoned his obedience to the norms in favor of finally accepting his otherness. This is how in *Memoirs From the Time of Immaturity*, *Ivona, Princess of Burgundia*, and *Ferdydurke* successive modern Forms are ridiculed, which opens the field to their radical transgressing, especially in *Diaries*, *Trans-Atlantyk*, and *Pornografia*.

Becoming the Other

The famous *incipit* of his *Diary* seems to be the manifesto of a strong and stable identity – from Monday to Thursday the only subject of writing is Me. However, this multiplied Me at the same time stabilizes, enhances, and blurs identity. It is as if he were saying I cannot be myself without being constantly someone else. It is not about pointing to "someone else," but reaching the final abolition of the distinction between "self" and "other." Self-becoming Other does not mean that it constantly changes masks, but that the essence of writing for Gombrowicz exceeds the subject which is nothing more than a fiction. In the *Diary*, he repeatedly returns to the source of the subject as something subordinated and produced by discourse, thereby exposing the mechanism of violence.

This constant movement of breaking identities finally turns out to be the source of his writing. Gilles Deleuze recognized this process in Gombrowicz but did not pay him much attention when he created his theory of becoming:

> To write is certainly not to impose a form (of expression) on the matter of lived experience. Literature rather moves in the direction of the ill-formed or the incomplete, as Gombrowicz said as well as practiced. Writing is a question of becoming, always incomplete, always in the midst of being formed, and goes beyond the matter of any livable or lived experience. It is a process, that is, a passage of Life that traverses both the livable and the lived. Writing is inseparable from becoming: in writing one becomes-woman, becomes-animal or vegetable, becomes-molecule to the point of becoming imperceptible.... Becoming does not move in the other direction and one does not become Man, insofar as man presents himself as a dominant form of expression that claims to impose itself on all matter, whereas woman, animal, or molecule always has a component of flight that escapes its own formalization.... To become is not to attain a form (identification, imitation, Mimesis) but to find the zone of proximity, indiscernibility, or indifferentiation.[31]

"I am not just a writer but Gombrowicz!"[32] he says in *Trans-Atlantyk*, but the only value he believes is not Gombrowicz himself as a human being, personality or subjectivity, but "Gombrowicz" as a project in permanent construction and transformation. That is why "becoming Gombrowicz" is the real purpose of his life and writing, which requires becoming boy, non-European, minoritarian until imperceptible. If the paradigm of modernity is based on the construction of the excluded Other, all of Gombrowicz's themes of desire lead to an attitude deeply anti-modern.[33] That is why he places himself on the side of what is excluded and stigmatized, but does not support the emancipation of groups omitted by history and does not create emancipatory, insurrectional counter-stories focused on a fight for justice and a new identity politics.[34] When he talks about the painful experience of exclusion he is never the political voice of the excluded. The goal is to see value in what modernity has rejected and not in the equivalence of various Others. Becoming Gombrowicz does not imply that what was excluded becomes hegemonic. Rather, it means to go beyond whatever is dominant, taking alternative directions.

"I'm going to make a bet," writes Anne Guérin, "that everyone who goes to visit Witold Gombrowicz will come away from him not the same as he came in…. It starts innocently from grammatical ambiguity." The question "who are you?" posed to Gombrowicz makes no sense to him, because it undermines the very notion of the only, indivisible "I." "I am an incarnation of someone named Gombrowicz," he says, "like an actor, I play for you a fiction of myself."[35] He cannot be grasped, understood, and entirely interpreted. He is like his writing with which he is in unity. When caught, he reveals his elusiveness. Gaining a concrete meaning, he stops meaning anything until he has become quite ordinary, boring, and completely indifferent. That is why he does not want us to think of him as a homosexual, emigrant, Pole … not even as a writer. Who is he? "I'm absolutely nothing; I'm an artist. And that's too much said. I'm Gombrowicz. But it's too much. I am who I am."[36] He repeatedly emphasizes the private, personal, and intimate nature of his work: "I'm a private man. I make private literature, and even in a sense, confidential literature."[37] "I am writing from the perspective of a 'single man.'"[38] "My style of writing – private, personal."[39] So: I am who I am and what I write is nothing more than what it is, because the whole of my literature, like *Trans-Atlantyk*, "has no topic other than the story it tells."[40] Tautology in a strange way combines here with the multiplicity of parallel worlds which cannot be identified in any way.

By staging the moments of resistance and subversion or treacherous obedience, Gombrowicz confirms the irrevocable presence of the Law. This means not only that the transgression, as Bataille explains it, is not at all an annihilation of the injunction, but on the contrary, in this crossing movement at the same time it restores the Law, but also that Gombrowicz, like Genet, a writer of transgression and margins,[41] cannot be a writer of emancipatory otherness. Becoming Gombrowicz is to reach areas that cannot be either repressed or represented.

Otherness presupposes the recognition of the Law and it is possible in the world of equality, diversity, and tolerance, in the world of accepted anomalies. Gombrowicz's world, on the contrary, is formed in the face of an absolute hierarchy clearly separating the normal from the pathological and never forgetting it. So instead of striking the dominant discourse and creating once again another counter-discourse, he steadily defends singularity: "the task before serious art is quite different. Serious art will either remain what it has been for centuries – the voice of the individual, the medium of man in the singular – or it will perish."[42]

Paradoxically, however, this pursuit of absolute individualism must reach degenerated, rejected figures – non-European, non-modern, minoritarian — and finally transgress all forms of subjectivity until its dispersal in *Kosmos* and *Kronos* among things and events deprived of meaning. Exceeding the interpretation means building an archive of idiocy,[43] trans-human, and imperceptible. It is not only about getting away from yourself, scattering the subject in attempts to cross the border of anthropocentrism, not only the famous look of one cow or other numerous elements of bestiary, not only love identifying with a boy, but creating an alternative archive of bodies and things without history.

Conclusion

Gombrowicz never became "Gombrowicz" as he wanted. At the end of his life, he had a clear awareness that by escaping from further forms he had become a Form of Gombrowicz and his greatest dream – becoming constantly the other – after all, had to remain unfulfilled. So, it is time to give up that interpretation in favor of creative reading, to recreate the way he went and to follow it to the end, until disappearance and silence.

Notes

1 He used to say he was the first structuralist or existentialist. Even if it was not only a tactic calculated on the "conquest of Paris," the priority did not mean a simple affiliation.
2 Dobrowolski, *Sztuka*, 82.
3 Gombrowicz, *Testament*, 31.
4 Author's translation. *Trans-Atlantyk, Dzieła* (Błoński), 7.
5 Compagnon, *Le démon*.
6 Burzyńska, *Dekonstrukcja*.
7 Attridge, *Singularity*, 79–93.
8 Burzyńska, *Anty-teoria*.
9 Gombrowicz, *Bacacay*, 4.
10 Latour, *We Have*, 10–11.
11 Gombrowicz, *Bacacay*, 34.
12 Ibid., 17.
13 For the abject see Kristeva, *Powers of Horror*.
14 Menninghaus, *Disgust*, 7.

15 Bataille, "Attraction" in Hollier, *Le Collège*, 120–68.
16 Gombrowicz, *Diary*, 590.
17 Gombrowicz, *Bacacay*, 173.
18 Swoboda, *Historie oka*, 8.
19 Gombrowicz, *Bacacay*, 174.
20 Jay, *Downcast Eyes*, 211–63.
21 Gombrowicz, *Gombrowicz w Europie*, 129.
22 Gombrowicz, *Diary*, 621.
23 Gombrowicz, *Bacacay*, 11.
24 Ibid.
25 Ibid., 33.
26 Ibid., 34.
27 *Ferdydurke* (Mosbacher), 20–21.
28 Kojève, *Reading of Hegel*.
29 Girard, *Evolution*.
30 Sade and Masoch represent the two main attempts at a radical subversion of the law; Deleuze, *Présentation*, 75.
31 Deleuze, *Essays*, 1.
32 Gombrowicz, *Trans-Atlantyk* (French and Karsov), 13.
33 Compagnon, *Antimodernes*.
34 Domańska, *Historie*.
35 Author's translation. Gombrowicz, *Varia 3*, 65.
36 Author's translation. Ibid., 83.
37 Author's translation. Ibid., 20.
38 Author's translation. Ibid., 27.
39 Author's translation. Ibid., 38.
40 Author's translation. Gombrowicz, *Trans-Atlantyk*, *Dzieła*, 7.
41 Delaperrière, "Marginalność," 471–83.
42 Gombrowicz, *Diary*, 22.
43 I am using the term "idiotic" as understood by the French philosopher Clément Rosset. Rosset points out that, in its original sense, the term "idiotic" has to do with singularity and uniqueness. Rosset, *Le réel*.

9 What Really Happened Aboard the Banbury? Reading Gombrowicz with Eve Kosofsky Sedgwick

Błażej Warkocki

If we read the penultimate short story ("Five Minutes before Sleeping") from Gombrowicz's debut volume *Memoirs from a Time of Immaturity* (1933) as an account of an anxiety-laden dream interpreted along the lines of the Freudian principle that a "dream is a fulfillment of life," we quickly arrive at the conclusion that it tells of the desire to become a great Polish writer.[1] However, this "Polishness" must have been a limiting form for Gombrowicz. That is why it seems that the most appropriate role model for the young Gombrowicz would have been the well-known writer of nautical fiction. At that time, there was only one artist who seems to have transcended the condition of a semi-peripheral Polish writer (to use Immanuel Wallerstein's term); one who went beyond the symbolic economy where the main reward is becoming the national bard, worshiped, and tormented by a leprous tribe in love with death—Poles. That is why the young Gombrowicz would not have looked to such writers as Adam Mickiewicz, Juliusz Słowacki, or Henryk Sienkiewicz as role models, all mentioned in a parodic fashion by Stefan Czarniecki in the short-story "The Brief Memoir of Jakub Czarniecki" ("Krótkim pamiętniku Jakuba Czarnieckiego"). An artist who, at least seemingly, transcends this condition is a writer who had to exert great effort to break through Polish syntax[2] and convert to a foreign (hegemonic and "colonial") language, becoming its master and esteemed classic writer. This implicitly "strong poet" to which one could refer, in accordance with the male, homosocial model as presented by Harold Bloom[3] is, of course, Joseph Conrad. Only he could be the proper role model for the young artist, especially if we turn our attention to how much Gombrowicz breaches, for the sake of polemic, the identification of the (male) reader with the "male" theme.

The significance of Joseph Conrad and his work for early twentieth-century Polish literature is undeniable. This is attested by Gombrowicz's critical review of "The Statue of Man Upon the Statue of the World."[4] However, for Gombrowicz, the author of "The Events on the Banbury," a subversive, almost parodist, take on the nautical theme, another aspect of Conrad's writing could have been particularly significant, namely, the category of masculinity, which is here so basic that it is almost transparent and unnoticeable. Richard Ruppel in "Joseph Conrad and the Ghost of Oscar Wilde" notices that

> Few readers of Joseph Conrad would disagree that he was far more interested in the relationships among men than in the relationships between men and women, and he explored the homosocial continuum as fully as he could considering that he was under extraordinary restraints.[5]

Conrad wrote at a particular time in history, a transitory period in the development of the definition of homo/heterosexuality. Beginning in 1885 male homosexuality was in England defined as a subcategory of sodomy, penalized under the Labouchere Amendment which refers to "acts of gross indecency between men," an amendment which laid the legal framework for Oscar Wilde's arrest a decade later. At this time, Conrad was beginning his belated writing career in England, though due to financial constraints he resided outside London. At that time, as Ruppel writes:

> On the one side were the Wildean aesthetes who despised the bourgeoisie, and on the other was the bourgeois majority who despised and feared Wilde's followers. Conrad courted ostracism if he supported the former, but courted mediocrity and philistinism if he remained with the latter. So, as usual, he took refuge in indirection, in subtlety, and in irony.[6]

And this is one of the reasons why artistic exploration of relations among men, a central theme in Conrad's work, was threatened by the restraints haunted by Oscar Wilde's ghost. This is something that would have great significance for the young Gombrowicz.

The last story from Gombrowicz's *Bacacay* originally bore the title "The Events on the Banbury: The Aura of the Spirit of F. Zantman." The subtitle, containing the German anagram of the word "dancer,"[7] which appears to be a discrete allusion to the first story of the collection, "Lawyer Kraykowski's Dancer," was removed by the author from the postwar edition from 1957. However, the original title also triggers certain disorientation on account of the name of the ship the main character used to set off from Europe, the *Banbury*. Zdzisław Łapiński[8] reminds us that this intertextual reference was deciphered by Henryk Markiewicz. This mysterious word is a key character in Oscar Wilde's last comedy, written and staged before his trial, *The Importance of Being Earnest*, and covertly signifies a double life.[9] This tension between Wilde and Conrad seems to be an important cognitive horizon and frame for interpreting Gombrowicz's earlier work.

Eve Kosofsky Sedgwick did not write about Conrad. However, she did devote a large study to another author who also had spent many years at sea and wrote classic nautical fiction. This author is Herman Melville, whose last novella, *Billy Budd, Sailor* from 1891, is considered a masterpiece. Though Sedgwick's work is based on "a deconstructive procedure of isolating links in a web of interconnected binaries,"[10] it is, above all, a study that strongly historicizes the analyzed material. This is significant insofar as the second half of the nineteenth century, and certainly its two last decades, saw a culmination of problems connected with defining "the modern homosexual identity and the modern problematics of sexual orientation."[11] Changes in legislation clearly reflect this, as in this period anti-homosexual laws appear in Europe. Of particular significance in this regard, also in Poland under the partitions, was the unification of Germany under Prussian leadership, which resulted in the formation of the German Empire in 1871. The same year, "homosexual crime" was penalized in the whole Reich. Meanwhile, as historian James Steakly notices, the approximate amount of homosexuals in Germany begins to rise drastically, and, by being recorded, "documents the end of homosexual invisibility."[12] And this is one of the reasons why European literature from the turn of the century, that is, in a formulaic simplification from Wilde to Proust, seems so intent on characterizing this new "human species" to use Michel Foucault's category.

Sedgwick undertakes an acutely historical close reading of two literary texts from almost exactly the same period in history under the common title, "Some Binarisms." There, she examines Melville's previously mentioned *Billy Budd* and then approaches Wilde's *Portrait of Dorian Gray* (1890). This juxtaposition is valid because it "unglues" the two classic novels from identity labels ("masculine" and "homosexual," respectively). After all, both novels are very similar in their general story line. In both cases, we are dealing with a relationship between three men, where one, the titular Billy Budd in Melville and Dorian Gray in Wilde, has exactly the same key characteristic, namely, they are remarkably attractive (Billy is called Handsome Sailor). As a result of conflicts between these three male protagonists, in both cases, the attractive character dies.

It is Sedgwick who notices that Herman Melville's *Billy Budd* clearly features a homosexual character. His name is John Claggart and he is presented as essentially different from the other shipmates. What is particularly noticeable are the many adjectives used to describe this character; their semantic field is determined by otherness, abnormality, mysteriousness, and depravation (some of these words had a medical connotation by the end of the century). Claggart freely and without psychological basis despises the Handsome Sailor, which should be read in the familiar context of persecutory paranoia, that is, in the convention where it is difficult to differentiate persecution from desire, as they create a knot of conflicted affects, with which, in Gombrowicz's story, the white black man and the first-person narrator from "Five Minutes Before Sleeping" are clearly linked. Melville builds his ethical sanctions on the basis of a semantic field of what is natural and what is *contra naturam*, which constitutes the old building blocks of nineteenth-century debates regarding the definition of homosexuality.

This historical perspective is important but also because it presents this text as a battlefield and document tracing the beginning of the modern definition of homosexuality. It, therefore, poses the question about the essence of male homosexuality, a question that will return in various forms throughout the course of the twentieth century. Though Claggart is regarded as depraved, due to his homosexuality (or disenfranchised on account of his homophobia, as these phenomena are sometimes very similar), his desires can legitimately be called homosexual. How do the desires of the other shipmates appear in relation to the Handsome Sailor? We quickly notice that the third protagonist, the mighty and just ruler of life and death aboard the ship, Captain Vera, nicknamed Starry, also looks at the body of the young attractive sailor with a large degree of pleasure. And not only he. We learn from the text that Billy Budd's physical appearance evokes delight in all his shipmates, even makes them into better people and helps them become one big loving family. How then do we differentiate one from another, natural desire from unnatural, natural gazes from unnatural, in a period when the male gaze on the beauty of a male body is clearly no longer marked by the kind of epistemological innocence characterizing the ecstatic descriptions of the beauty of *Apollo Belvedere*'s torso found in Johann Joachim Winckelmann's classic *History of Ancient Art*[13] from 1764. One possible answer is offered by the definition of the essence of homosexuality.

This is why Sedgwick presents Melville's work as a game between an essentialist and a constructivist understanding of homo/heterosexuality, or in other words, between minoritizing and universalizing understandings of their definitions. The paranoid Claggart accuses (let us remember in the epistemological sense "it takes one to know one") Billy Budd, whose cognitive innocence borders on stupidity, of the most serious crime aboard a ship, namely, conspiracy and mutiny. Then, Captain Vere (with the text granting him the widest possible vantage point) confronts these two men. He sits Billy across from Claggart and issues two conflicting commands ("Say something! Defend yourself" and "Easy, boy," with the second accompanied by a hug). Shocked by the accusation, Billy is unable to utter a single word, and then with one blow kills Claggart. Vere, praised for his fairness, arranged a confrontation out of which none of the parties escaped with their lives. Claggart dies from the inflicted wound, and Billy, as his killer and potential conspirator, is tried, convicted, and then hanged. The death sentence is delivered to Billy by Captain Vere, which is connected to a gesture of the largest intimacy between men in this text, a hug. Billy Budd dies, declaring just before his execution: "Long live Captain Vere!" From one of the endings, we learn the mystery of his death has for a long time preoccupied the sailors, as there was a lack of "mechanical spasm in the muscular system,"[14] that is, the absence of an erection, which according to nineteenth-century beliefs every hanged man was supposed to have. From another ending, we learn that many years later on his own deathbed Captain Vere muttered Billy's name, the Handsome Sailor, who he had condemned to death. This is how in a broad summary this story about the relations between three men aboard the *Bellipotent* concludes. If, therefore, following Sedgwick, we read this text as a "game between a minoritizing and universalizing definition of homo/heterosexuality,"[15] Claggart's death, the man thanks to whom the minority definition made its appearance (as it is he who is *contra naturam*), simultaneously allows for the epistemological innocence in the relationship between Captain Vere and Billy Budd.

The most forbidden word on the *Bellipotent* (as well as aboard the *Banbury*), one which is surrounded by an aura of mystery and transgression, is mutiny. Panic at the possibility of a mutiny forces the court, with the captain at its head, to condemn Billy to death. Conspiracy and mutiny can lead to the destruction of the community based on male hierarchy, where discipline is often indistinguishable from terror. In Melville's novels, therefore, we can find a developed socio-political discourse on the topic of mutiny (rebellion). This is not surprising given that mutiny on a ship has two aspects: one could say a minoritizing and universalizing. On the one hand, this is a question of disturbing the male, or perhaps masculine, hierarchy on board the ship: mutiny means death for the mutineers, some men have the power of life and death over others. On the other hand, munity on a ship is a synecdoche of political rebellion that alters the entire political system. The clearest example of this is the almost legendary (due to it having been adapted culturally many times), but nonetheless real mutiny on the *Bounty* that took place in 1789. It is here that it should be noted, as Jerzy Franczak[16] reminds us, the word "Banbury" is a kind of pun, as it phonetically brings to mind the name "Bounty," which could have significance given that almost nothing in Gombrowicz's *Bacacay* is coincidental, as an aura of paranoia consistently develops. In April of 1789 aboard a ship belonging to the Royal Navy, a mutiny broke out when a part of the crew forced the captain along with eighteen loyal shipmates to leave the *Bounty* in a ship's boat. The mutineers then began their search for the paradise islands in the south of the Pacific Ocean. The year 1789 is significant. From the perspective of the British monarchy, this mutiny is a possible sign, a warning, a synecdoche of a rebellion which will symbolically begin in July of the same year with the storming of the Bastille, known to history as the French Revolution. Every rebellion in the Royal Navy was a possible harbinger of what had happened on the continent, a potential revolution destroying the feudalistic order. The mutiny on the ship is, therefore, on the one hand, a disturbance of a male/male disciplinary system within a "small" male community or also, in a larger sense, a subversion of broader socio-political bonds, which are fantasmatically supported by bonds between men.

Let us return to Melville's novel. Sedgwick notices there a particular "open secret," a tacit, though always present and euphemistic, potential propensity of every man to rebel.[17] Even when Captain Vere issues orders regarding Billy Buddy, "the word *mutiny* was not named."[18] The taboo word was not uttered. It is, therefore, not surprising that Sedgwick, in observing the mutual relationships of these three men on the backdrop of other male bonds and men's desires toward other men, which are increasingly surrounded by panic, builds a distinct analogy, or rather discerns a kind of irreducible double entendre between rebellion and homosexuality. The most basic question which Sedgwick asks of this classic literary text about male relationships on the sea, read in the context of nineteenth century debates about the definition of homoheterosexuality, is as follows: "Is men's desire for other men the great preservative of the masculinist hierarchies of Western culture, or is it among the most potent of the threats against them?"[19] At the turn of the century the answer to this question can take two directions.[20] That is why the analysis of this text becomes even more interesting, as this text uses the issue of mutiny to arrive at the question about the essence of male desire for other men, and thus ultimately at the question of essentialism versus constructivism.

This way *Billy Budd* leads us to the widest interpretational frame of "The Events on the Banbury," and perhaps of many later texts by Gombrowicz. This has to do with certain fundamental epistemological uncertainty, which can be formulated with the help of Sedgwick's question: "What are the operations necessary to deploy male-male desire as the glue rather than as the solvent of a hierarchical male disciplinary order?"[21] Or: why is this desire so often the most potent solvent and not glue? When posing this type of question, one has to be very careful, something that Sedgwick emphasizes on many occasions, not to place "homosexuals" in the role of scapegoats, which happened all too often in classic psychoanalytical discourse where the "blame" of various obsessive and paranoid behaviors was placed on concealed homosexuality and never on homophobia as in the example of Schreber's disease analyzed by Freud.[22] However, the question of the male hierarchical order is also a question of power, and thus of patriarchy. Is it possible to notice some continuity in "men supporting the interests of other men" (the shortest and most simplified definition of patriarchy) and "men loving men" (the shortest and most simplified definition of homosexuality)?[23] Does the radical discontinuity that exists today between male homosocial relations and male homosexual relations mean that this is how it has been and must be? Is homophobia, and especially homophobia aimed at men by other men indispensable for the patriarchal system? The times of ancient Greece as described in Kenneth Dover's *Greek Homosexuality*[24] indicates that it is not necessarily so: male/male sexual relations were unproblematically inscribed into the Greek patriarchy.[25] How did this look at the beginning of the twentieth century in the mind of the young artist, Witold Gombrowicz? Can male desire directed toward other men be the glue binding the male hierarchical order? Or is it a necessary and the strongest solvent, murderous in its consequences? And thus the best form of rebellion. How in this context should we understand homosexual identity? And what exactly is rebellion for Gombrowicz?

✽   ✽   ✽   ✽   ✽

"The Events on the Banbury" is the longest story in the debut volume and, at the same time, the most boring. Boredom is an aesthetic category; in a way it is the topic of the story and also the unintended effect on the reader. Nautical fiction, even if only stylizing itself as popular fiction, should, nevertheless, contain colorful "adventures" (as in "Five Minutes Before Sleep"). However, nothing like this happens. The plot unfolds gradually, as if unable to develop, as if it were more "internal" than "external." German Ritz[26] mentions this phenomenon in relation to "tacit homosexuality." In the context of "The Events on the Banbury" Tomasz Kaliściak writes: "Homosexuality in Gombrowicz's story, much like in other narratives from this period, exists as a secret, which cannot be disclosed or spoken aloud. Gombrowicz here makes use of paralipsis, suggesting meanings which cannot be expressed *expressis verbis*."[27] It is difficult to disagree with this diagnosis, but it is easy to notice a paradox. If Mr. Zantman, a camouflaged dancer, is a potential homosexual, he should be happy with the fact that he found himself on a male ship bearing a Wildean name. This, however, is not so. Quite the opposite. Mr. Zantman exhibits states that are increasingly anxious and escapist.

It is also worth noticing the uncertain ontological state of the events that had taken place aboard the *Banbury*. On the one hand, we receive a description of events on board the ship concerning the many and not always logical interactions between Mr. Zantman and the crew; on the other hand, the fantastic element infiltrates the represented world, from outside of the brig: fish, birds, whale, scorpion. Such a construction of the represented world makes the reader uncertain whether the reality perceived by the character has an objective ontological status or whether it is more of a projection (the titular "aura") of his mind; whether it is "external" or "internal" (to refer to the distinction often repeated in "A Premeditated Crime"), especially in the context of the title, "aura of the mind," and the sentence from the last paragraph of the story and volume: "Because from the beginning everything was mine, and I, I was just like everything."[28] There is no clear delineation here, reality and projections clearly overlap.

This type of narration can of course be explained, if we refer once again to the analysis of Schreber's case, where paranoia depends on the play of projections. On a related note, Sedgwick claims that what in her earlier literary analyses happened *between men* now at the beginning of the twentieth century takes place *within a man*. It is also worth remembering that her analyses, exemplified by paranoidal gothic, are not focused on proving that some character (or author) was a homosexual but on capturing the effects resulting from the "double bind" of modern masculinity, that is, the necessity of close and intimate male/male relationships and at the same time their prohibition as potentially or factually homosexual. It is precisely this situation that takes place aboard the *Banbury* accompanied by the ever-present and looming threat of violence.

On this basis it is necessary to formulate, or rather develop and potentially modify Tomasz Kaliściak's analysis found in *Statek odmieńców* (*Ship of Queers*). This interpretation changes the paradigm of how this story is to be read. Kliściak wrote:

> Homosexual panic,[29] which is a motor for various behavior, directed the script of events with a literary flair. I would like to notice, therefore, that 'The Events on the Banbury' are a product of this panic.[30]

Indeed, the last story from *Memoirs from a Time of Immaturity* is a story about homosexual panic, and is even perhaps written under the sway of homosexual panic. I would like to take Kaliściak's thesis as a point of departure for my own analysis, even more so because it is an important and precise, historically and theoretically, Sedgwickian concept.

Let us return to the story. Mr. Zantman, as a result of his incident with Dick the sailor, begins to suspect "askew identity" in himself. *Banbury* is en route to South America, and its passenger begins to notice rats.

> In this manner several days passed, in the course of which I explored the ship. It was an old vessel, seriously gnawed by rats, huge numbers of which had bred below—in places the hull was completely eaten away, while the stern, as if out of spite, was filled with rat droppings. All in all it was reminiscent of the old Spanish frigates. The excess of rats I found far from delightful—these rodents have disagreeable habits; their fat tails are so long, the pointed tips so far away, that they lose their sense of the tail's being connected with the rest of their body, as a consequence of which they are continuously prey to

the ghastly illusion that they are dragging behind them a tasty piece of meat which is quite foreign to them and just right for devouring. This makes them very nervous. Sometimes they sink their teeth into their own tail, writhing with a squeal, as if mad with craving and in terrible pain. The arrangement of the rigging and the disposition of the tackle, like the design of the port side of the ship, entirely failed to meet with my approval—and when I saw the shape, dimensions, and hue of the ventilation pipes, I returned to my cabin with signs of great dissatisfaction and remained there till evening.[31]

This strange sight, where the description of rats mixes with the description of the ship, appears puzzling at first, but, at the same time, it steers us in various directions. First, it guides us intertextually in the direction of Freud and his "Notes Upon a Case of Obsessional Neurosis." There is also a striking similarity between these texts, as if planned consciously, now even more clearly than in "The Memoirs of Stefan Czarniecki." I am referring to the opening scene in Freud's description of the case which developed into the formulation of obsessive compulsive disorder and constituted the point of departure for a developed analysis of its causes that was described in the subchapter "The Great Obsessive Fear" and was the direct cause of the patient coming to Freud's office. The situation takes place on the sea and the source of the panic is the captain who, similarly to Clarke in Gombrowicz, was characterized by exceptional cruelty. He was known to threaten his subordinates with a particular punishment. "Are you perhaps thinking of impalement?"[32] asked Freud.

> 'No, not that; ... the criminal was tied up,' he expressed himself so indistinctly that I could not immediately guess in which position – ' a pot was turned upside down on his buttocks ... some rats were put into it ... and they ...' – he had again got up, and was showing every sign of horror and resistance – '... bored their way in...' – Into his anus, I helped him out.[33]

The sea, the ship, the cruel captain, the obsession with cleanliness and rats (irritable in Gombrowicz's story): a similarity undoubtedly exists, though I would not consider them a key for interpreting "The Events on the Banbury." It would be more beneficial to outline a potentially intertextual context, with three tropes clearly emerging. First, the rats on the *Banbury* can be clearly related to anxiety. And this would be a distinctly male anxiety, anal. It is in this function that it appears for Freud; however, this anxiety, though male, is not connected to castration. Taking this Freudian reference further with its contemporary reconceptualization should allow us to think differently about the male body, in a less symbolically phallic way, as if after an "anal turn," which, as Krystyna

Kłosińska writes, "constitutes a significant attempt to reformulate the symbolic of the male body."[34] This is particularly striking in relation to Melville's story, where phallic symbolism is clearly displayed (through the publicly discussed topic of erections).

Second, we should bear in mind that the "rat" from *Bacacay* serves as a kind of identification. In "The Events on the Banbury," Mr. Zantman was referred to as "a land rat," which was meant to distinguish him from the other men on the ship as he is the only "land rat" there. [35] It is worth remembering that Stefan Czarniecki also called himself a land rat, a "colorless"[36] one at that, which was to remind him of his mixed provenance and was a kind of negative, or at least ambivalent, identification.

Third, this suggestive image of a crazed rat, which desires his own tail, takes us in another, though complementary, direction. A rat desires himself and suffers, desires in an auto-erotic and at the same homoerotic way. He desires "the same," which in Greek means, as we know, homo. Perhaps the image of a rat desiring itself is the best Gombrowiczian figure of paradoxes and inconsistencies, something that Sedgwick included in the concept of "homosocial desire."

There is a lot of "the same" aboard the *Banbury*—in the form of the exclusively male sailors who form among themselves various relations, structured according to a strict professional and class hierarchy. However, some of these relations, from today's perspective, can appear strange or "suspect." Kaliściak in the introduction to his article refers to postcards from the beginning of the twentieth century presenting sailors dancing with themselves (and these naval postcards are also referenced in the story).[37] Postcards with such pictures were officially distributed, proving that such male closeness was normative, though today such closeness is impossible without transgressing the everyday order. There are many examples of this imagery, and especially ample visual material can be found in Polish prewar film, which was analyzed in this context by Sebastian Jagielski.[38] So what happened in the twentieth century? In short, homophobia began to institutionalize itself ever more clearly, thereby internalizing itself in male bodies, which has an influence on the distribution of closeness between men. In other words, homophobia plays an increasingly large role as a force structuring the relations between men. Let us add that this applies to all men, not just the minority.

For the sake of clarity, let us emphasize that sailors dancing with one another are not "covert" or "latent" homosexuals, though such an interpretation might emerge from today's commonsensical or perhaps paranoid suspicions founded on psychoanalysis, among other things. That is why male/male dance could have been an apologia of masculinity and today the same dance would be seen as its parody. The male homosocial continuum is regulated by institutionalized homophobia to such a degree that accusing someone of homosexuality can incite in men a state bordering on panic. This is something Eve Kosofsky Sedgwick describes as "homosexual panic," which, it should be emphasized, can affect both homosexual and non-homosexual men.

Let us return to Gombrowicz's story. It would seem that Mr. Zantman, an encrypted dancer with a "defective queer identity," having found himself on a ship with only men, should be happy and fulfilled in what would appear to be a potentially erotically charged heaven. In other words, we could assume that the *Banbury* is for him a kind of *locus amoenus*. And this is the direction most interpretations take, toward a coded possibility of homosexuality in the story.[39] For example, Janusz Margański, in an inspiring book, *Gombrowicz wieczny debiutant*, (*Gombrowicz: A Perennial Debutant*) noticed that in one of the final scenes with an androgynous fish, containing a man, a woman, and a "little priest," there is reference to *Song of Songs*. He notices that this gesture

> underscores the stakes of the literary game carried out by the author. This gesture is meant to guarantee the meaning of homosexual desire which overtakes the crew of the *Banbury*, and which the monologuing narrator attempts to hide from himself.[40]

However, it is difficult on this basis to understand *why* the whole crew of this ship is overwhelmed by homosexual desire and also *why* this situation leads the queer, Mr. Zantman, to *hide* himself and his desire. Should it not be the opposite?

To develop the main thesis of this interpretation, it must be pointed out that "The Events on the Banbury" is not a homoerotic narrative demanding a "homosexual allegoresis" or the identification of the encoded homosexual signs of desire; it is not a story about the crew being possessed by homosexual desire to which everyone succumbs. In this sense, the Banbury is not "a ship of queers." To a larger degree, it is a ship of "normalsów" ("straight")[41] where we find an increasingly frightened queer. Frightened to the brink of paranoia, which exposes the mechanisms of homophobia. The key in the form of a paranoid intrigue is already given in "A Premeditated Crime." This situation incites in the character a type of homosexual panic and results in him completely hiding himself in the closet, and in our case in a private cabin.

In order to correctly understand this thesis, it is necessary to recall Sedgwick's concept of "male homosexual panic," a concept that structurally supplements the concept of "male homosocial desire." Historical interpretations concerning changes in the relations between men have led to a hypothesis that homophobia does not only have power over a certain minority population but also over the relations between all men, and in that sense it has power over men identifying themselves with homosexuality as well as, and perhaps to a greater extent, with men identifying themselves with anti-homosexuality. An important historical hypothesis found in *Between Men* states that changes in the system of economic, social, and gender relations in the eighteenth century, which sometimes we call the beginning of modernity, resulted in susceptibility to the blackmail of Western maleness through the "leverage" of homophobia.[42] Normative or even sanctified relations between men can, especially on the outside, which is especially noticeable at the beginning of the twentieth century, resemble that from which we should cut ourselves off, because this unnamable is a contradiction to masculinity. In this context perhaps, Sedgwick's definition will be more understandable: "So-called 'homosexual panic' is the most private, psychologized [state] in which many nineteenth century western men experience their vulnerability to the social pressure of homophobic blackmail."[43]

This concept of homosexual panic provides a support structure for Gombrowicz's story. Aboard the ship, relations between men are governed by violence: cutting, pricking each other with pins, gouging out eyes, which also entails physical distance between male bodies. In the center of this environment we find the queer, Mr. Zantman, an accidental passenger, whose "sock was hanging" and who feels increasingly intimidated. It is, therefore, not surprising that he is afraid to the brink of panic. The unnamable content of this fear is betrayed by his paranoid projection: Mr. Zantman will accuse every sailor on the ship of mutiny, illicit intimacy of male bodies, a *homosexual* conspiracy. Next, he will hide in his private cabin, observing from afar the situation—notice the general similarity to "A Premeditated Crime," where a paranoid judge makes baseless accusations against a young man of patricide and then hides in a closet. The content of this projection not only betrays its causes but it also unveils the whole frame of a network of problematic issues. Similarly, the young Gombrowicz in his story intuitively builds a laboratory of male homosocial behavior, where the key, structuralizing role is played by homophobia. Even the male on male violence against eyes, which the sailors on the Banbury at one point begin to gouge out, can be understood in terms of Sedgwick's concepts and not, for example, in Freudian terms as a male attitude toward the most sensitive and private part of the body which may trigger panic. It can cause homosexual panic, which will lead to accusatory paranoid projections.

It is worth turning our attention at this point to the characteristic images of anxiety. This is anxiety, not fear, entailing a kind of paralyzing dread, whose source, cause, and place of attack are unidentifiable. The main metaphor for this anxiety is a jungle and other fantastic, mainly animalistic, phenomena. This image most strongly appears at the very end of the first part of the story. Let us recall this superb passage:

> It's as if I'm in a dark forest, where the bizarre shapes of the trees, the plumage and calls of the birds entice and amuse with a curious

masquerade, but from the depths of the woods there comes the distant roar of a lion, the thunder of the buffalo and the creeping step of the jaguar.[44]

A stylistically similar image appears in the second part, just before the accusatory projection: "I'm like a sheep among wolves, like an ass in the lions' den."[45] In the third part in the form of a story about a huge spider web which wanted to eat the little spider the following appears: "how black and motionless she was, sitting there astraddle and waiting hypnotically. Like Mene, Tekel, Peres; and how he begged her not to devour him."[46] In the same stylistic diction and type of representations appears in the fourth part, the shortest describing the world "after hiding," in the form of disturbing "peacock feathers and the hot glare."[47] This semantic web representing anxiety through the metaphor of a jungle is all the more interesting as it in a Freudian *uncanny* manner resembles a similar metaphor appearing in the later and semi-biographical story by Henry James, *Beast in the Jungle*, which Sedgwick interpreted through the concept of "homosexual panic," titling her study "Beast in the Closet."

Let us return to Gombrowicz's story, as what is most clearly shown, as it changes along with the development of the plot, is the spatial distance and quality of relations between men. Earlier the male bodies were far removed from one another, exemplified most aptly by the mutual "ciachanie," pricking each other with pins and gouging of eyes, it is later, in the third part, this completely changes.

> At that moment I heard, behind me and somewhat to the left, the distinct sound of a juicy kiss. I looked around, thinking it was a sail flapping—no one was there—but a moment later the same sound reached me with even greater clarity. A kiss? A kiss on the ship? How on earth could that be, since there were no women? ... Since there were no women, there could also be no kisses—and therefore I ought not to have heard something that did not exist. If, on the other hand, there really was a conspiracy, retreat was the appropriate course of action.[48]

Therefore, the distance between male bodies has been reduced, and it is this that is construed as a conspiracy. At the same time, the atmosphere becomes more sexual. Tommy, the young cabin boy with a "tender, high-pitched" voice begins to seduce other sailors and also Mr. Zantman who, unlike everyone else, is horrified by this. In the end it seems that the violently charged distance between male bodies completely bursts, as Mr. Zantman timidly reports:

> "Now then, captain," I added, leaning on the rail, "there on the deck there are not a few but a great number of sailors—it seems

even that all the sailors are together; they're whispering, embracing one another and heading this way—excuse me, I think I'll go back to my cabin."[49]

Mr. Zantman construes this reduction of distance between male bodies, seen as sexualization, as a conspiracy, as a potential mutiny from which he must hide.

The paranoia hypothesis endows this text with unity. Accordingly, the whole third part, this homosexual conspiracy, should be read as a projection of a frightened subject, his "aura of the mind." The legitimacy for this reading is evidenced by other narrations utilizing the paranoid gothic convention, especially "A Premeditated Crime," which unfold according to a similar logic, from paranoid accusations of murder to "hiding." In a key moment an even similar metaphor of a sickly imagination as an aggressive dog will return.[50] This protagonist accuses the sailors of illicit homosexual relations and then hides in his private cabin, waiting for the consequences of his accusation.

Gombrowicz's story resonates with Melville's *Billy Budd* as per Sedgwick's interpretation. Of course, there are also differences. Melville's narration is cast in third person, whereas Gombrowicz's is in first person. Nonetheless, a claim could be made that Claggart, the paranoid third-person narrator possessed by a "mania of an evil nature" who on a male ship accuses Billy Budd of conspiracy, is reflected in "askew" identity of the paranoid first-person Mr. Zantman, who likewise on a male ship, accuses all the men of a homosexual conspiracy. It is as if, by way of this first-person narration, Claggart was given voice. At the same time, in this story what is homosocial cannot be easily distinguished from what is homosexual. There is always the threat that the exterior eye will place one below the other ("from now on I won't be able to look without embarrassment at two sailors, or even at one sailor. I'll have to turn my head away)."[51] This way the young Gombrowicz perfectly, though in his own way, grasps this particular inconsistency of modern masculinity. However, this "homosexual conspiracy" does not have an anti-patriarchal dimension. Though homosexuality is here the biggest threat to the hierarchical masculinist order, rebellion is not aimed at "men supporting their own interests." Sexualizing relations between men is more of a symbol of constructive anarchy and the battle between "young" (men) against the "old." Women find themselves beyond the horizon, literarily and metaphorically.

The story ends with the forth and shortest part, a tale about hiding. Mr. Zantman sits "four days" in his cabin without anyone visiting him. The *Banbury* deviated off course toward paradisiacal islands, full of the singing of hummingbirds and parrots, heralding a "(speaking frankly) impending and amazing adventure." The mutineers seem to be triumphant. However, if we assume that in "The Events on the Banbury," as in a gothic novel, "homophobia appears ... thematically in the form of paranoid intrigue,"[52] we will better understand the necessary return to an almost compulsive hiding in a cabin. This is the way that not only the last story of the volume but also *Bacacay* concludes. The last paragraph provides a clear and vivid image of hiding. By summarizing the effects of paranoid intrigue and evoking the dialectics of inner and outer as building blocks for the subjective "I," Gombrowicz provided a condensed depiction of the epistemology of hiding, epistemology of the closet:

> No, I do not wish to know. I do not wish to know and I have no desire whatsoever for hot weather or glamour and luxury. And I would prefer not to go out on deck for fear of seeing something ... something that previously had been obscure, hidden, and unspoken, now parading in all its brazenness amid peacock feathers and the hot glare. Because from the beginning everything was mine, and I, I was just like everything—the exterior is a mirror in which the inside can be observed![53]

Notes

1 See Warkocki, *Pamiętnik afektów.*
2 See Gasyna, *Polish.*
3 Bloom, *Anxiety.*
4 Gombrowicz, "Statue of Man," 272–73, 277.
5 Ruppel, "Ghost of Oscar Wilde," 19.
6 Ibid., 19.
7 Grimstad, "Co się zdarzyło," 61. He refers to the anagram Zant-man — Tanz-man. The morpheme "Zant" creates the anagram of the German Tanz (dance).
8 Łapiński, *Przypisy*, I, 251.
9 "I may mention that I have always suspected you of being a confirmed and secret Bunburyist; and I am quite sure of it now. ... Besides, now that I know you to be a confirmed Bunburyist I naturally want to talk to you about Bunbury. I want to tell you the rules." Wilde, *Being Earnest.*
10 Sedgwick, *Epistemology*, 132.
11 Ibid., 91.
12 Ibid., 133.
13 Winckelmann, *Ancient Art.*
14 Melville, *Budd*, 124.
15 Sedgwick, *Epistemology*, 127.
16 Franczak, *Poszukiwanie*, 279.
17 Sedgwick, *Epistemology*, 101.
18 Ibid.
19 Ibid., 93.
20 A good example of a conceptualization in which the male/male sexuality can become a social "glue" is to be found in Männerbunde theories. The concept of "manliness" becomes one of the most important problems and causes of an internal division of the prewar German homosexual emancipation

movement. See: Oosterhuis and the chapter "Manliness and Homosexuality" in Mosse, *Nationalism*, 23–47.

21 Sedgwick, *Epistemology*, 94.
22 Warkocki, *Homo niewiadomo*, 20–24.
23 Sedgwick, *Between Men*.
24 Dover, *Homoseksualizm*.
25 For analysis of Dover's *Greek Sexuality*, see Sedgwick, "Męskie pragnienie," *Krytyka Polityczna*, 178–80.
26 "The male description of the world (identification of it) does not approach its limit in homosexual speech; it loses itself and likes to find signifiers (it is metonymic speech)." Ritz, *Nić*, 59.
27 Kaliściak, "Statek odmieńców," 344–45.
28 Gombrowicz, *Bacacay*, 193.
29 "Homosexual panic" was originally coined by psychiatrist Edward J. Kempf in 1920 for a condition of "panic due to the pressure of uncontrollable perverse sexual cravings." Kempf, "Psychopathology, 477–515.
30 Kaliściak, 344.
31 Gombrowicz, *Bacacay*, 146–47.
32 Freud, "Uwagi," 32.
33 Ibid., 32. Italics in original.
34 Kłosińska, *Feministyczna*, 645. "Anal turn" already has a considerable bibliography. Sedgwick often returns to the issue of anality, especially when writing about James. See Sedgwick, "Anality" in her *Weather in Proust*.
35 Bill Johnston translates "szczurem lądowym" ("land rat") as "landlubber" in Gombrowicz, "Banbury," 159.
36 Gombrowicz, *Bacacay*, 34.
37 Kaliściak, 344.
38 Jagielski, *Maskarady*.
39 Franczak, *Poszukiwanie*, 279.
40 Margański, *Gombrowicz wieczny debiutant*, 56.
41 See Goffman, *Piętno*.
42 Sedgwick, *Between*, 89.
43 Ibid. Sedgwick returns to this definition (developing the concept) in her essay "The Beast in the Closet. James and the Writing of Homosexual Panic" in *Epistemology of the Closet*, especially 182–95.
44 Gombrowicz, *Bacacay*, 163.
45 Ibid., 174.
46 Ibid., 189.
47 Ibid., 193.
48 Ibid., 186.
49 Ibid., 190.
50 "Imagination, like a vicious dog let off the leash, was baring its teeth, growling low and lurking in recesses." Ibid., 185.
51 Ibid., 187.
52 Sedgwick, *Between*, 92.
53 Gombrowicz, *Bacacay*, 193.

10 Affect and Youth
Reading Gombrowicz with Deleuze

Daniel Pratt

"Form" has been understood as the primary concept of Gombrowicz's oeuvre since he published *Ferdydurke* in 1937.[1] "Form belongs to the most often used and most universal concepts in [Gombrowicz's] creative output," claims Jerzy Jarzębski in his article on the term[2] which has lent itself to structuralist, post-structuralist, psychoanalytic, and gender analyses, placing Gombrowicz at the crossroads of a multitude of theoretical outlooks.[3] To be a Gombrowicz scholar means, to a greater or lesser degree, to deal with his term and the present author is no different.[4]

What has been less examined, and less understood, is what is *not* Form. Gombrowicz is rather unclear on this subject himself, as he applies a litany of terms in opposition to Form: immaturity, *pupa*, youth, *synczyzna*, etc. In his most straightforward and traditionally philosophical work, *A Kind of Testament*, Gombrowicz admits:

> this Immaturity is still much more important to me than Form, but I haven't said too much about it in this book because it isn't easy to discuss it and I would rather people looked for it in the live matter of my artistic work.[5]

In one section of his *Diary*, Gombrowicz even states "No other world needs youth as much as Gombrowicz's world."[6] In the contemporary structuralist/post-structuralist theoretical mindset, Form presents critics and theorists with excellent source material, whereas youth, or immaturity—no less important to Gombrowicz himself—has been underdeveloped as a term.

One problem for understanding Gombrowicz's notion of youth has been its position in the "live matter" of his novels. In his review of Gombrowicz's first novel, one that Gombrowicz himself commends in his *Diary* for capturing the spirit of *Ferdydurke*, Schulz observes:

> Our immaturity (and perhaps at bottom our vitality) is tied in a thousand knots, braided with a thousand atavisms to a second-rate suit of forms, to a second-class culture. While under the cover of official forms we honor higher, sublimated values, our real life plays

itself out secretly and without higher sanctions in that dirty realm, and the emotional energies located in it are a hundred times more powerful than those the thin layer of officialdom dispenses.[7]

Schulz applauds Gombrowicz for noticing the "emotional energies" that play out below the surface of the world.[8] Youth functions within these emotional energies, which can only be experienced through a body. When the narrator of *Ferdydurke* meets Zuta the modern schoolgirl, it is her "powerful presence"—that is, her very corporeality—that upsets both him and Professor Pimko.[9] Unlike Form which exists in abstraction, and perhaps needs abstraction itself, youth cannot be separated from an embodiment.

These emotional energies can be understood as similar to Deleuzian affects. Deleuze calls affects a connection that can "weaken us in so far as they diminish our power to act and decompose our relationships" or "make us stronger in so far as they increase our power and make us enter into a more vast or superior individual."[10] Youth, like affect, affects one's potential, changing the possibilities of action, thereby undermining Formal structures. Affect is pre-ideological, pre-conscious, working like Gombrowicz's youth "under the cover of official forms," playing "out secretly and without higher sanctions in that dirty realm."[11]

If youth represents something akin to Deleuze's term affect, however, it is a decidedly ambivalent antagonist to Form. Gombrowicz most fully develops his term youth in *Pornografia*, in which, according to Hanjo Berressem, youth "is used to heat up and thus soften, the hard, crystalline, and repulsive world of adults," thereby destroying mature Forms.[12] Berressem, like most critics, finds youth to be a positive antidote to the "repulsive world" of adults and Form. However, youth also possesses the power to kill and destroy. The murderous finale of the novel shows how youth is, at least, a double-edged sword, wielded with bloody consequences. Far from the playful conception of youth in *Ferdydurke*, youth in *Pornografia* destroys not only established forms of maturity, but also mature and immature bodies. On the one hand, youth retains the power to reinvigorate Formal structures, but in *Pornografia* Gombrowicz displays youth's destructive power in all of its horror.

Youth and Eroticization

Before continuing, I must admit I have, thus far, avoided discussing youth in Gombrowicz because of his problematic depictions of young people. Gombrowicz consistently eroticizes and objectifies young people; they are shown as objects of desire without subjectivity or agency. In *Transatlantyk*, for example, Ignacy is the object of desire for Gonzalo, and also in a reverse-Oedipal way for Ignacy's father, but Ignacy never says a single word throughout the entire work. Ignacy never chooses for himself nor exerts his own agency. His character remains merely the object of desire for both Gonzalo and, in another sense, his father. Portraying someone as an eroticized object would be fairly normal, if still troubling, but the emphasis on Ignacy's youth complicates the issue. Ignacy's one defining feature is that he's a young man, not yet of age to make his own decisions. Admitting to Ignacy's youth turns Gonzalo into a sexual predator attempting to prey on an immature boy.

In one scene, Gombrowicz the narrator finds him alone, asleep, and naked, showing Ignacy as a purely eroticized object.[13] Witold runs from the idea of murdering Tomasz the father and finds that

> on a bed by the wall Ignacy a-lying is, naked as a Newborn babe, by sleep overcome and naught, sleeping, breathing. Upon seeing him I was struck dumb, since seemingly as a decent youth he slept. But whilst he sleeps, within him Knavery and—ah, God a Knave he is, naught else, Knave, Knave, capable of any Knavery, and were he given free rein he would become a Knave like to those Knaves![14]

If this scene happened once in a larger context, then it would be troubling but perhaps trivial, but Gombrowicz repeats the scene. In the second, switching positions from Gonzalo to Tomasz, Witold exclaims, "he lies naked as his Mother bore him and breathes. Ergo he lies and sleeps, and breathes. Oh, how Innocent! Oh, how sweetly sleeping he is. How calmly his Chest swells up! Oh, what Beauty, what Health!"[15] In both scenes, Ignacy is objectified, and Witold projects his own understanding onto the boy, dubbing him either a knave or innocent.

This lack or, at least, the minimization of subjectivity in young people provides a troubling view of the relationship between youth and maturity. These scenes could be understood as describing a reality in which young people are dehumanized on a regular basis, in which their agency is diminished or ignored, and they are forced to follow the desires of their elders. However, we would expect a critique of this kind of structural issue if that were the case. Instead, there is a tacit admission that the objectification of young people is not only normal but acceptable. Even though in his *Diaries*, Gombrowicz claims that he "dared to admire youth irrespective of its sex" and to take "it out from under the domain of Eros," enough erotic content remains to make these scenes disturbing.[16]

One reason I ignored the troublesome topic of youth in Gombrowicz was due to his place in queer criticism and his role in the Polish canon. Because the accusation of pederasty, and/or the conflation of pederasty with homosexuality, remains a common justification for homophobia both in Poland and elsewhere, it is all too easy for critics of Gombrowicz to dismiss his work because of his sexuality or his erotic depictions. I have no intention of undermining the excellent and important work that has been done using queer theory to discuss Gombrowicz and Gombrowicz's role in bringing homosexuality and queer sexuality into the Polish canon. I also do not mean to use this discussion to make claims about Gombrowicz's sexuality or make any accusations of pederasty. The scene is troubling regardless of gender: the issue here is that a powerful, older person has the potential for sexual control over an objectified young person who is not given any agency in the novel.

I may be more sensitive to this scene because of contemporary discussions of sex, power, and agency. Being a scholar in the twenty-first century, when we are beginning to address sexual predators and the systems that support them thanks to the #MeToo movement[17] among others, makes the scene all the more troubling. Ignacy is a de-subjectivized erotic object, making him yet another in a long line of such figures. We can criticize Gonzalo as a predator: he's the older man, with power, and Ignacy has no agency in the book. The scene described earlier is so troubling because of the possibility of violence to the sleeping, naked youth, even if Gombrowicz the narrator has expressed no sexual interest in Ignacy. I do not want to ignore this scene, because this lets Gombrowicz off the hook for eroticizing a passive youth.

However, I believe that the discomfort the scene causes is part of the point. The choice between *filistria* and *patria* offered in *Trans-Atlantyk* is a choice between sexual assault on a young man and sending him to war potentially "for death or maim."[18] The abstract choice between the un-Formed character of Gonzalo and the stifling patriotism of Tomasz would not carry the same weight as when we consider the same choice with a young person's life, body, and future involved. Involving Ignacy as a youth, presumably innocent, without a say in his future, increases the stakes of our choice. With this in mind, I think it is worth discussing Gombrowicz's construction of youth. I do not intend to absolve Gombrowicz of his erotic objectification in doing so, since he does objectify Ignacy. But there are other elements to Gombrowicz's understanding of youth beyond erotic objectification.

Gombrowicz does seem aware of the dangerous territory he is wading into in discussing youth the way he does. In *Pornografia*, Witold, the narrator, says that he feels "a little awkward talking about this—and also at some point," he continues, he will "have to explain why he's putting the words (boy) and (girl) in parentheses."[19] In a typical Gombrowiczian fashion, he never does. If Witold claims that the discussion of youth makes him feel awkward, then Gombrowicz is pointing directly at the issue.

Gombrowicz's Youth

Although youth and immaturity figure into Gombrowicz's work from his earliest collection *Memoirs from the Time of Immaturity* (later *Bacacay*, 1933), he deals with youth most concretely in *Pornografia* and in his *Diary* from the time he wrote and published the book (roughly 1955–1958). *Pornografia* has been discussed the least of any of Gombrowicz's novels, with the exception of *Possessed*, and it has usually been discussed as one element in his entire oeuvre.[20] Youth as a term from *Pornografia* has yet to be thoroughly analyzed, even though it marks a departure from his earlier understanding of youth, moving from the adult defining the immature in *Ferdydurke* to the youth defining the old in *Pornografia*.

Ferdydurke begins with Professor Pimko's infantilizing Joey, setting off the absurd sequence of events of the novel. The power structures of *Ferdydurke* revolve around the older defining the younger, thus limiting their agency. In *Pornografia*, however, youth creates the central tension of the story. Witold, the narrator, discovers the "striking and reciprocal sex appeal" of two young people, Henia and Karol.[21] Witold along with his friend Fryderyk try to match the two together in an elaborate game, while the two youths have "not even noticed it: it is drowned, we might say, in their youthful incapacity for fulfilment."[22] After several attempts at getting the two to take erotic notice of each other, Witold and Fryderyk lure Henia and Karol into a triple murder, consecrating their relationship with blood.

The young person in Gombrowicz is someone between childhood and maturity, an adolescent around 16. Zuta of *Ferdydurke* is 16, Henia and Karol are as well, and Ignacy of *Trans-Atlantyk* is presumably the same age, although his age is never explicitly mentioned. Gombrowicz distinguishes between youth and childhood, writing "Childhood being something that is less related to youth, is however infinitely less drastic; that is why it is easier for a mature man to be childish rather than youthful."[23] This distinction shows that Gombrowicz emphasizes the mutability of youth, since pubescence is a time of drastic changings, being on the cusp of adulthood, strung between childhood and maturity.

Youth for Gombrowicz is not merely an attribute of a person, but rather a type of becoming, a potentiality, a driving, relational, force. Youth affects the world around; it

> makes the feeble, inferior, helpless being, who needs protection, appeal to the stronger. The mature man does not need to seduce; he is powerful, he dominates, he governs. Charm and beauty are the arms of the woman, the adolescent, the child.[24]

Youth creates a reaction in the older, mature person; because young people are socially, culturally, intellectually, and physically inferior to an adult, they must create an affect in order to protect themselves from the adult onslaught.

Here we see Gombrowicz's understanding of human relationships through forces and power. Every interaction contains forces and struggles between the people involved, akin to Nietzsche's will to power, or at least to Gilles Deleuze's treatment thereof. Deleuze claims that will to power can be understood as a dynamism of forces, in which "the relationship between forces in each case is determined to the extent that each force is *affected* by other, inferior or superior, forces."[25] Deleuze's interpretation of Nietzsche resonates strongly with Gombrowicz's description of Youth and its interactions with maturity. Both Deleuze and Gombrowicz shared Nietzsche as an influence, and they created surprisingly similar post-structuralist readings of the philosopher.

Gombrowicz and Deleuze

Other scholars have used Deleuze to understand Gombrowicz, most notably Michael Goddard's *Gombrowicz, Polish Modernism, and the Subversion of Form* and to a lesser extent Berressem's *Lines of Desire*, but these interpretations have mostly figured into the traditional methodology of reading literature through theory, art through a philosophical outlook.[26] Both works take Gombrowicz's oeuvre mostly in order of publication and apply post-structuralist theory to each successive work. *Lines of Desire* offers a fascinating Lacanian interpretation, but it gives Gombrowicz's own philosophical ideas short shrift, privileging Lacan and Deleuze and Guattari's theories, and to a certain degree it ignores the literary value of Gombrowicz's work. Goddard offers an intricate reading of Gombrowicz through Deleuze's philosophy, but the methodology of the work relies on this traditional form of reading literature through philosophy or theory. I am not interested in delving into such an interpretation here, however, partially since it has been done, but also because Gombrowicz clearly meant more to Deleuze than another author to analyze.

Deleuze peppers his texts with references to Gombrowicz, often without any footnotes that would allow a reader unfamiliar with Gombrowicz's work access to the ideas.[27] Being an avid reader, it is no wonder that Deleuze would read Gombrowicz, especially in the 1960s when Gombrowicz burst on the Parisian scene with the publication of his novels, plays, and official diaries in French. However, Deleuze for the most part refers to canonical works in French and world literature (such as Lewis Carrol, Proust, Kafka, Robbe-Grillet, etc.), so his references to Gombrowicz seem out of place if his audience would be less familiar with the Pole's work.[28] This is not to say that Gombrowicz is not deserving of greater fame or is even a peer of those other authors of world literature, but rather that if Deleuze wants to explain his thought by referring to works that belong to a common French/world canon, then his references to Gombrowicz show a deep respect for the Polish author's work more than merely using Gombrowicz for clarification.

In emphasizing these references to Gombrowicz, I am not suggesting that Gombrowicz had an oversized influence on Deleuze (nor that he did not); I do not want to make any claim about influence at all. Tracing the influence of one writer on another creates many philological problems, especially moving from one discipline to another. It is not clear to me that such an influence can ever be decisively stated, unless Deleuze had said outright that Gombrowicz had influenced him in a major way, if then. Rather, I want to point to a resonance between the two writers, as when two strings tuned to the same pitch resonate when just one is plucked. I gave this chapter the subtitle of reading Gombrowicz with Deleuze because I wanted to emphasize the "with" as opposed to a "through;" I will not explain Gombrowicz through Deleuze nor explain Deleuze through Gombrowicz, but rather concentrate on how the two can be read together and how the resonance between both authors creates a harmonic chord.

In other words, Gombrowicz and Deleuze were working on affect and youth in different methodologies simultaneously, Deleuze in philosophy and Gombrowicz in literature. Through their respective readings of Nietzsche, they both arrived at surprisingly similar takes on the role of affect or youth, attempting to reinscribe the body into their respective outlooks. In reading the two together, we gain a philosophical structuring of the term affect, as well as concrete examples of youth/affect in its positive and negative lights.

Youth/Affect

Deleuze's construction of affect when discussing Nietzsche's concept of will to power resonates strongly with Gombrowicz's intersection of youth and maturity. Maturity, the bearer of Form, seems to be the stronger element initially in Gombrowicz. Professor Pimko infantilizes Joey in *Ferdydurke*, limiting his ability to act in the world. Youth is de-subjectivized in *Trans-Atlantyk*, but it has become the battleground for the opposing forces of *patria* and *filistria*. In *Pornografia*, however, Gombrowicz switches the normal order, and "makes old age dependent on youth, superiority dependent on inferiority."[29] He further added that "the adult be subordinated to the Younger."[30] This shift demonstrates a change in Gombrowicz's understanding of the forces at work in youth, similar to Deleuze's concept of affect.

For Deleuze, affect is first and foremost a sensation, located among bodies affecting the way we understand the world. In writing on Spinoza, so foundational for Deleuze's philosophy, Deleuze analyzes the relationship between appetite, mind, and affect. He writes,

> appetite is nothing else but the effort by which each thing strives to persevere in its being, each body in extension, each mind or each

idea in thought (*conatus*). But because this effort prompts us to act differently according to the objects encountered, we should say that it is, at every moment, determined by the affections that come from the objects. *These determinative affections are necessarily the cause of consciousness of the conatus.*[31]

As a body, we sense the world around us, and that sensation leads to how we situate ourselves in any surrounding.

Gombrowicz explicitly connects the desires of the body, corporeality itself, with youth. *Pornografia* was meant to "get at certain antinomies of the soul *through the body*."[32] Witold in *Pornografia* continually remarks on the presence of other bodies. In his meeting with Fryderyk, he comments,

> I had Fryderyk right in front of me, two other heads separating us, his head was close, close by, and I could see it—he was silent and riding on—while the presence of alien, brazen bodies, crawling and pressing on us, only deepened my tête-à-tête with him ... without a word....[33]

The physical presence of Fryderyk, as well as the influence of the other bodies around him, creates a non-verbal, but nevertheless intimate conversation between the two heroes. The ellipses in the text further emphasize the corporeal aspect of the story by omitting the verbal.

Young bodies affect the most in the novel. At mass, Witold sees "part of a cheek and the nape of a neck ... it belonged to someone standing in front of us, in the crowd a few steps away ... Oh, I almost chocked! It was ... (a boy) (a boy)."[34] Witold reacts to the youthfulness of Karol, and the presence of Karol's corporeality stuns Witold. As soon as he sees Henia's neck, it "took hold" of Witold "so strongly," and the two together completely "carry [him] away (*porwał*)."[35] Gombrowicz uses this visceral verb to convey how strongly the youth have affected him, gripping him and capturing him. Youth affects Witold, demonstrating the connection of affect to youth. Witold was affected by the presence of Fryderyk from the beginning, but youth has truly captivated and affected him.

For Gombrowicz, adults act on young with the potentiality of violence. In his *Diary*, Gombrowicz writes that men

> agree to adore youth only insofar as it is accessible to them, only insofar as they can possess it so that a youth contained in their own shape, youth with which they could not join, was, in some incomprehensible way, hostile.[36]

On the one hand, Gombrowicz "could see manifestations of kindliness, and even tenderness, of the Older for the Younger all the time," but at the same time "certain facts were evident which meant just the opposite: cruelty."[37] The mature relationship to the young, for Gombrowicz, means possession or cruelty. If youth is no longer accessible for a mature person, that person will turn to forming the younger into his or her own image or to cruel punishment.

Simultaneously, the young desire to be mature, to be formed, to move beyond the middle stage of adolescence into the confirmed position of the adult. This desire puts the fates of the young into the hands of the older. When Siemian the Underground leader comes to the estate, Karol, "our (young) Karol" was

> thrown into an intense, willing obedience and eager readiness by the newcomer's presence—and, consumed with loyalty, his wits sharpened, suddenly he found himself close to death, a guerilla, a soldier, a conspirator about whose hands and shoulders roamed a murderous yet quiet power, who was at Siemian's beck and call like a dog, obediently adroit technically skillful.[38]

The presence of Siemian has transformed, affected, Karol and turned him into an *obedient* soldier. Karol's "willing obedience" demonstrates this desire to be adult, to be formed by the adult world.

These conflicting desires create a destructive dynamic between the adults and the young. Because Karol and Henia are not yet Formed, they become the battleground for the adults, like Ignacy in *Trans-Atlantyk*. The adults need the young people to assert their adultness, since through their control of the young their position is increased. Henia's parents want her to marry Vaclav, an older man with a good income and estate, pushing her into premature maturity. Witold and Fryderyk, on the other hand, attempt to keep Henia young with a relationship to Karol in their pursuit of voyeuristic titillation. Both the parents and the pair Witold and Fryderyk commit to a violent interaction with youth, since the parents desire to destroy the youth of their daughter by marrying her, and Witold and Fryderyk push her toward their own violent ends.

On the one hand, the desire to be adult gives additional power to the mature, but if youth is understood as the ability to be affected in Deleuzian terminology, then the young have more potential to act than the mature. As he was beginning *Pornografia*, Gombrowicz wrote in his *Diary* that he "demanded that 'the adult be subordinated to the Younger,'" that despite the cruelty of the older, "perhaps the Adult was repressing the Younger so that he would not fall to his knees before him?"[39] For Gombrowicz, youth can affect the older, but the real power of the youth lies in its ability to be affected.

The Power of Youth

For Gombrowicz, youth and maturity need each other and represent two diverging desires. He claims that

> man has two ideals, divinity and youth. He wants to be perfect, immortal, omnipotent. He wants to be God. And he wants to be in full bloom, fresh and pink, always to remain in the ascendant phase of his life—he wants to be young.[40]

To put this in Deleuzean terms, people desire to be affecting, in the all power position of God, and affected in the young, ascendant phase of life.

For Deleuze, the will to power is not merely manifested in one's ability to affect, but also in one's ability to be affected. The more someone can be affected, the more power can be used. In other words, "the more ways a body could be affected the more force it had."[41] Power is manifested "as the capacity for being affected," because "the will to power is always determined at the same time as it determines, qualified at the same time as it qualifies."[42] The will to power is a doubled structure of power, where not only does the power to affect increase one's abilities, but also the power to be affected, to be reactive to the world around.

The youthful power to be affected shows itself in Karol and Henia's ability to kill. When the older characters decide that they must kill Siemian, none of them can do it. "We, the adults," Gombrowicz writes, "weighed down by our awareness and our seriousness, know what death is. But someone light will accomplish it lightly—and we entrust this murder to the boy."[43] The older can give the order to kill, but the murder has to be completed by the younger, who do not yet know what killing means. Because Karol has not developed into an adult yet, he can act beyond the capabilities of those that have already matured. Karol retains the potentialities of becoming that the mature have abandoned.

Despite the power the youths have on Witold and the rest of the adults, they remain innocent in their eyes. Karol had already fought in the underground to some extent but left, according to Hipolit, because of "some mischief...eee, it was really stupid, he stole something, took a shot at someone, a colleague, or his commander."[44] Hipolit downplays whatever happened, even if it was shooting a commanding officer. Such disobedience would normally carry a weighty punishment, but due to Karol's youth he remains unpunished. "Did he merely shoot, or shoot dead?," Witold wonders, "If he had shot dead, one could find him not guilty by reason of his being of an age that erases everything."[45] Because of his age, Karol remains innocent even if he has already killed.

Karol remains innocent because his youth prevents him from being entirely one thing or another, prevents him from being Formed in Gombrowiczian terminology. Karol,

> Torn between child and man (which made him at the same time innocently naïve and relentlessly experienced), he was, nevertheless, neither one nor the other, he was a third possibility, namely, he was youth, inwardly violent, harsh youth that was handing him over to cruelty, to brute force and obedience, condemning him to slavery and humiliation.[46]

Karol represents the un-Formed potential between childhood and adulthood. He is not entirely one or the either, but in the state of becoming between the two.

Gombrowicz has created an ambivalent structure with youth and maturity, where the mature have more control and power, but they lack the ability and "lightness" to complete certain actions. Siemian himself ages from when he was working in the Underground to when he leaves due to his fear of dying; he has transformed from a young, successful soldier to an impotent older man. The mature desire completeness, but they lack the ability to complete actions, whereas the younger even when they complete an action leave everything incomplete by nature. This leaves the story, despite its absolute completion with regard to the three deaths, ending "in unfulfillment."[47]

Both Deleuze and Gombrowicz wrote about affect and youth, respectively, in a time of revolutionary foment. Although Gombrowicz wrote *Pornografia* during the *Revolución Libertadora* of 1955–1958, he returned to this idea in his *A Kind of Testament* of 1967, remarking on how "we are now witnessing a revolt of youth," both in the East and in the West.[48] Deleuze wrote on Nietzsche's will to power in 1963 and continued through the student protests of May 1968. For both Gombrowicz and Deleuze, the revolutions did not live up to their potential, despite being placed in the hands of youth.[49] In the end, those revolutions like *Pornografia* end in unfulfillment.

Notes

1 Schulz, "Ferdydurke" (Coates), 25.
2 Jarzębski, "Pojęcie," 313. Author's translation.
3 See Goddard, *Gombrowicz*; Jarzębski, "Pojęcie." In terms of gender analysis, see Szczuka, "Gombrowicz," 145, in Ritz, et al., *Nowa świadomość*.
4 Pratt, "Narrative and Form," 7–20.
5 Gombrowicz, *Testament*, 173.
6 Gombrowicz, *Diary*, 391.
7 Schulz, "Ferdydurke," 49–56, 51. Author's translation.
8 Gombrowicz, *Diary*, 290.

9 Gombrowicz, *Ferdydurke* (Borchardt), 105. *Ferdydurke, Dzieła*, I, 110.
10 Deleuze, *Dialogues*, 60.
11 Schulz, "Ferdydurke," 51.
12 Berressem, *Lines of Desire*, 150.
13 When Gombrowicz uses his own name for the narrator, I will use Witold to distinguish the narrator from the author Gombrowicz.
14 Gombrowicz, *Trans-Atlantyk* (French and Karsov), 93–94.
15 Ibid., 114.
16 Gombrowicz, *Diary*, 173.
17 The #MeToo movement is a movement against sexual harassment and sexual assault. #MeToo spread in October 2017 as a hashtag used on social media in an attempt to demonstrate the widespread prevalence of sexual assault and harassment, especially in the workplace. It followed soon after the sexual misconduct allegations against Harvey Weinstein, an American former film producer who founded the entertainment company Miramax.
18 Gombrowicz, *Trans-Atlantyk* (French and Karsov), 89.
19 Gombrowicz, *Pornografia* (Borchardt), 24. Further citations to *Pornografia* in English will be in the text.
20 Notable exceptions are Michał Głowiński's articles and Juszczyk's "Apetyt na starość" in Jarzębski, *Witold Gombrowicz nasz współczesny*, 316–27.
21 Gombrowicz, *Testament*, 141.
22 Ibid.
23 Gombrowicz, *Diary*, 164–65.
24 Gombrowicz, *Testament*, 137.
25 Deleuze, *Nietzsche*, 62.
26 Goddard, *Gombrowicz*; Berressem, *Desire*.
27 For example, *Cosmos* shows up several times in *The Logic of Sense*, sometimes with a direct reference to Gombrowicz, sometimes not.
28 Although Gombrowicz did enjoy a certain amount of popularity in France in the 1960s, especially among intellectuals, I doubt knowledge of Gombrowicz equaled that of Carrol, Proust, Kafka, etc.
29 Gombrowicz, *Diary*, 164.
30 Ibid.
31 Deleuze, *Spinoza*, 21.
32 Gombrowicz, *Diary*, 487.
33 Gombrowicz, *Pornografia* (Borchardt), 7.
34 Ibid., 23.
35 Ibid., 24–25.
36 Gombrowicz, *Diary*, 176.
37 Ibid.
38 Gombrowicz, *Pornografia* (Borchardt), 129–30.
39 Gombrowicz, *Diary*, 164, 177.
40 Gombrowicz, *Testament*, 139.
41 Deleuze, *Nietzsche*, 62.
42 Ibid.
43 Gombrowicz, *Testament*, 142.
44 Gombrowicz, *Pornografia* (Borchardt), 29.
45 Ibid., 29–30.
46 Ibid., 31.
47 Gombrowicz, *Testament*, 142.
48 Ibid., 143.
49 See Deleuze and Guattari, "May '68" in *Two Regimes*, 233–36; Gombrowicz, *Testament*, 143–46.

11 "The Quieter the Louder Indeed"

Silence and the Space of Literature in *Trans-Atlantyk*

Tul'si (Tuesday) Bhambry

"An exceptional opportunity! The moment everyone has dreamed of!"[1] This is how Gombrowicz characterizes the condition of the exile writer in 1952. His attitude towards émigré literature is decidedly positive. Deprived of the security of the homeland, but also freed of its restrictions, the writer experiences the thrill of unlimited freedom: "All bonds burst. One can be more of oneself. ...one can move toward the future in a more ruthless way."[2] Nevertheless, although exile should result in creativity, Gombrowicz continues, Polish writers have failed to produce outstanding works after the war. Even the most remarkable individuals who ought to "roar like lions"[3] have hardly made themselves heard in exile. "Why don't they,"[4] he asks. "Why has the voice of these people faded abroad?"[5] Here, Gombrowicz establishes a crucial paradox: "They do not roar because, first of all, they are too free. Art demands style, order, discipline."[6]

These reflections are part of Gombrowicz's polemic with the Romanian exile writer E. M. Cioran, whose essay "Avantages de l'exil" he translated for *Kultura*. His commentary[7] begins by contesting the very notion of the "exile writer," a label that unhelpfully groups together artists of every caliber. Great writers, he argues, always find themselves in the position of exiles, even within the borders of their homeland. Art is by definition a lonely pursuit that alienates the artist from society, so the condition of exile should be familiar to any writer of merit. Actual exile serves to distinguish the genuine artist from the amateur whose success at home was only made possible by the artificial mechanisms supporting domestic literary production. Those whose careers are destroyed by emigration never had a chance to become "authentic writers" in the first place. To the remaining few, expatriation "should constitute an incredible stimulus."[8]

An excess of freedom, however, can threaten the émigré writer's development. Removed from the critical apparatus at home, he is prone to slide off into "anarchy," which is more detrimental than the obvious lack of practical support or the absence of a readership. What is more, those writers who fail the test of emigration may end up subscribing to the patriotic cause, hoping to regain the homeland where they had enjoyed success. This leads to a vicious circle: "He does not know how to be a writer without a homeland – but, in order to regain his homeland, he has to stop being a writer, at least a serious writer."[9]

In the final section, Gombrowicz compares the expatriate writer to a bankrupt count who realizes that his salon manners are of no use where there is no salon. Such writers will be in danger of letting their circumstances push them into "'democratic' shallowness, into a kindly ordinariness or into a crude 'realism' and sometimes it condemns them to isolation."[10] Exile writers, he insists, ought to find a way "to feel like aristocrats once again (in the deeper sense of the word)."[11] He concludes by pointing out how the challenges of writing in emigration relate to the intrinsic challenges of literature: "We have to produce that portion of freedom, boldness, ruthlessness, and even, I would say, irresponsibility, without which creation is impossible."[12]

Katarzyna Jerzak compared the essays by Cioran and Gombrowicz. She argues that both writers redefine the opposition between the twin modernist topoi "the nostalgia for the lost sense of belonging" and "the glorification of homelessness."[13] Despite his contentiousness, Jerzak suggests, Gombrowicz concurs with Cioran that exile offers no substitute for the discipline of style. She also demonstrates that Gombrowicz's translation, uncredited at his own behest, attenuates Cioran's positive representation of exile. For instance, he renders the French title "Avantages de l'exil" as "Dogodności i niedogodności wygnania" ("Advantages and Disadvantages of Exile"). According to Jerzak, Gombrowicz's manipulations have

> done Cioran a great disservice in the eyes of the Polish readers. Cioran's text is a celebration of exile, but ever since the title's mistranslation, and Gombrowicz's polemical response, Cioran's supposed pessimism in face of exile has been juxtaposed to Gombrowicz's verve and optimism.[14]

Gombrowicz's model of exilic authorship rejects Mickiewicz's Romantic notion of the selfless bard who places his gift at the service of the nation.[15] As Jerzak indicates, he also made sure, in a manner that was less than honorable, to distance himself from contemporary exile writers' representations of their shared predicament.[16]

Gombrowicz's polemic with Cioran signals how his model of authorship had evolved since he left Poland. There is a shift in his view of the artist's relationship with the audience. The narrators of his first novel *Ferdydurke* (1937) dismissed idealizing notions of high art in favor of popular writers' more pragmatic strategies. Gombrowicz put their ideas into practice in his second novel, *Opętani* (*Possessed*), which caters to all sorts of lowbrow tastes at once, fulfilling Gombrowicz's dream of making some quick cash with a novel for the masses.[17] But it is not as much a potboiler as an experiment with producing compelling rubbish or kitsch.

Although it appeared under a pseudonym, it enacts the theory of author-ship proposed in *Ferdydurke* and represents the culmination of Gom-browicz's early experiments with pragmatic attitudes towards literature.

It is striking that before the war, when he was an upcoming artist from a privileged family, Gombrowicz ostentatiously courted the public, while in Argentina, where he lived in the most precarious circumstances, he refused to cater to popular tastes and proclaimed that art was an aim in itself and demanded sacrifices:

> It is very painful not to have readers and very unpleasant not to be able to publish one's works. It certainly is not sweet being un-known, highly unpleasant to see oneself deprived of the aid of that mechanism that pushes one to the top, that creates publicity and or-ganizes fame, but art is loaded with elements of loneliness and self-sufficiency, it finds its satisfaction and sense of purpose in itself.[18]

In Argentina, Gombrowicz celebrates the image of the solitary writer who remains indifferent toward readers' expectations – the exact image he had previously ridiculed. This ironic twist can be seen as a response to the cultural context of postwar Poland, in particular the resurgent popularity of patriotic literature and the dominant status of Socialist Realism. Instead of a desire to please the masses, be they "patriotic" or "proletarian," he now declares his commitment to the loftiest and most "aristocratic" ideals of artistic integrity.

But Gombrowicz's postwar works are not free of contradictions. While his autobiographical works idealize the independent artist, *Trans-Atlantyk* tells the story of the émigré writer who lets himself be co-opted into a pa-triotic agenda. The anti-hero Witold – for the sake of clarity I will use "Gombrowicz" to refer to the author and "Witold" to refer to the fictional character – has a healthy instinct for self-preservation: he dodges the draft and then accepts a lucrative offer to represent Poland as the national au-thor. His decision to enlist as the "Great Polish Author" is not honorable but compromising: "And why look a gift horse in the mouth!"[19] What is more, as futile as the transubstantiation of "sh.t" into "Bread and Wine"[20] is—of institutional support into inspired verbal performance—it fails to take place and Witold is vanquished by the "Gran Escritor." It is hardly surprising that a scandal ensued when excerpts of the novel appeared in *Kultura* in 1951. After its complete publication in Paris (1953) and War-saw (1957), *Trans-Atlantyk* was mostly read as a straightforward repre-sentation of Gombrowicz's biography and ideological convictions, and critics were quick to accuse him of treason and moral aberration.[21] Mi-chael Goddard suggests that "for Gombrowicz, exile necessitated taking up a confrontational position in order to bring himself into existence for a second time in an even more virulent manner than he had done with *Ferdydurke*."[22] But Gombrowicz, impolitic though he was, anticipated that most readers would have little understanding for his seemingly anti-Polish diatribes, and he attempted to guide his audience toward what he considered the "correct" interpretation of his work. Marian Bielecki observes that Gombrowicz wrote more prefaces to *Trans-Atlantyk* than to any other of his works.[23] Gombrowicz also asked the respected émigré writer Józef Wittlin to contribute an endorsement of *Trans-Atlantyk* to *Kultura*. Wittlin obliged, stressing that "a great deal of courage is required for a Pole to admit, in Poland's most tragic hour, to his own cowardice," and therefore "respect is due to the protagonist of *Trans-Atlantyk*, who publicly confesses his lack of reverence" for Polish sanctums.[24]

Artistic courage, integrity and self-gratification are key to the public image Gombrowicz forged for himself in the postwar years. In his diary of 1960, he addresses the difficulties he endured owing to his defiant attitude. He emphasizes his marginality and uprootedness with almost masochistic relish:

> Today I awakened in the delight of not knowing what a literary award is, that I do not know official honors, the caresses of the public or critics, that I am not one of "ours," that I entered literature by force – arrogant and sneering. I am the self-made man of literature! Many moan and groan that they had difficult beginnings. But I made my debut three times (once before the war, in Poland; once in Argentina; and once in Polish in emigration) and none of these debuts spared me one ounce of humiliation.[25]

Gombrowicz's rhetoric of disregard for pragmatism and prudence, which simultaneously reproduces and subverts the traditional messianic model of the author's self-sacrifice, also appears in *Testament*. He insists that he had no hope for the immediate success of *Trans-Atlantyk*, and that the writing process was fueled by sheer desire for self-expression and the joy of reckless creativity:

> [*Trans-Atlantyk*] was such a folly, from every point of view! To think that I wrote something like that, just when I was isolated on the American continent, without a penny, deserted by God and men! In my position it was important to write something quickly which could be translated and published in foreign languages. Or, if I wanted to write something for the Poles, something which didn't injure their national pride. And I dared – the very height of irresponsibility! – to fabricate a novel which was inaccessible to foreigners because of its linguistic difficulties and which was a deliberate provocation of the Polish émigrés, the only readership on which I could rely!
>
> That is what happens in the hour of defeat. One writes, in spite of everything, for one's own pleasure. What a luxury I permitted myself in my misery![26]

Insisting on the disinterested pleasure of the creative act Gombrowicz doubtless intended to bolster his public image of radical independence. In fact, it is surprising that he makes so little of his refusal to accept any official appointments with the government of the People's Republic of Poland.[27]

A sense of irresponsibility and pleasure underlies the extravagant style and dynamic plot of *Trans-Atlantyk*. But the novel is more than a product or enactment of Gombrowicz's devotion to artistic independence and self-gratification. On the contrary, it also addresses the importance of limiting freedom and self-indulgence. In the following section, I will offer an allegorical reading of the character constellation, focusing on the way Gombrowicz foregrounds the role of silence in the creative process – a theme that anticipates his postulate that "art demands style, order, discipline."[28]

An Allegorical Reading of the Character Constellation

DE ROUX: How would you describe the plot of *Trans-Atlantyk?*
GOMBROWICZ: For me plots are never very important, they are only a pretext.[29]

This dialogue opens the chapter on *Trans-Atlantyk* in *Testament*. Gombrowicz relegates the storyline to a secondary position, but if the plot is a mere pretext, a guise, a ploy, then what is the novel really about? Gombrowicz gives us no hint, at least not explicitly. One clue emerges from the etymology of the word "pretext." Derived from the Latin *praetextum*, "disguise," and *praetexere*, "to weave in front," it involves the notion of two layers: the *pre*text is immediately apparent, while the true (sub)text remains concealed. Both imply the same thing: the text. Trying to uncover the text beneath the pretext of the plot, therefore, my focus will be on the novel's self-referentiality. Indeed, the plot already indicates Gombrowicz's preoccupation with authorship. His fictional alter ego tells the story of his struggle for recognition as an artist among the conservative Polish community of Buenos Aires. The narrator carries the author's name, and several real-life literary figures, Gombrowicz's friends and acquaintances, appear in cameo roles that present models of exile and authorship that contrast with Witold's.[30]

Gombrowicz's fictional interview with de Roux continues with a synopsis that is remarkably detailed, given the alleged irrelevance of the plot:

> In an archaic prose, as though it were set in the distant past, I tell how, just before the war, I landed in the Argentine, how war broke out when I was there.

I, Gombrowicz, make the acquaintance of a puto (a queer) who is in love with a young Pole, and circumstances make me arbiter of the situation: I can throw the young man into the queer's arms or make him stay with his father, a very honorable, dignified and old-fashioned Polish major.

To throw him into the puto's arms is to deliver him up to vice, to set him adrift, to push him into the abyss of freedom, into limitless abnormality.

To wrench him away from the queer and make him return to his father is to keep him within the confines of the honest Polish tradition.

What to choose? Fidelity to the past...or the freedom to create oneself as one will? Nail him to the old form...or let him loose and may he do what he likes! Let him create himself!

In the novel the dilemma leads up to a general burst of laughter, which sweeps away the dilemma.[31]

It is striking to what extent Gombrowicz dwells on the narrator's dilemma in this plot summary, and to what extent the dichotomy father vs. "puto" echoes the concept of Form vs. Anti-Form that Gombrowicz reiterates across his oeuvre.[32] What is more, the binary structure highlighted in this plot summary brings to mind Gombrowicz's dialectical concept of authorship as a reconciliation of control and creativity, a concept that underlies his self-definition as "a disciplined anarchist."[33] In *Trans-Atlantyk*, the father easily stands for tradition, discipline and control while the puto embodies spontaneity, "anarchy," and the freedom of self-creation.

In Gombrowicz's summary of *Trans-Atlantyk*, another hint to suggest that the character constellation often contains a self-reflective layer can be found in the exclamation "let him create himself" or "niech sam się stwarza." Gombrowicz echoes Gonzalo's assertion that Ignacy should be free to make his own choices, but the elision of the pronoun "on" (him) in the imperative, standard in Polish, introduces an ambiguity about the grammatical subject: the sentence could also be translated as "let *it* create *it*self." This subtle reference to *artistic* self-creation resonates with Gombrowicz's notion of a literary work's self-engendering power, a theme that appears across his output.[34] There is no evidence, however, to suggest that Ignacy is an allegory of the emerging text, and so his relevance to Gombrowicz's concept of authorship still remains to be assessed.[35]

Among the four main characters in *Trans-Atlantyk* – Witold, Gonzalo, Major Kobrzycki, and Ignacy – the first three clearly enact the dialectics of Gombrowicz's model of authorship. Gonzalo and Major Kobrzycki play the opposing roles of creativity and control. The narrator Witold, carrying the author's name and torn between originality and tradition, is a recognizable embodiment of the writer plagued by the need to negotiate these opposing forces. The role of the fourth character, Ignacy, is less straightforward. The boy exerts an irresistible attraction on both Gonzalo and Witold; he generates the antagonism that drives the plot, and he sets in motion the novel's finale, a carnivalesque synthesis of the opposing forces. Despite his central position, however, Ignacy remains almost entirely speechless. His silence, read allegorically, disrupts the binary of Form and Anti-Form, control and creativity, and adds a new dimension to Gombrowicz's model of authorship.

To my knowledge, Stefan Chwin is the only critic to have mentioned Ignacy's silence. "Throughout the novel," he writes, "Ignacy does not even utter a single word – but does physical beauty need to speak at all? He speaks through a graceful promise of delight."[36] This statement is not quite accurate, as Gombrowicz does in fact show Ignacy to be possessed of language. When Gonzalo mentions that his mules cannot be mounted, Ignacy declares, "I will try."[37] This one utterance remains unanswered. Ignacy's words are completely inconsequential; at best, they indicate his remoteness from the realm of language. Ignacy and Horacjo fall off the mules and burst out laughing. It is this laughter that carries weight, not Ignacy's speech. Later Witold hears his laughter again and is enchanted by it: "the Son before me and his fresh *Voice*, brisk laughter, movements, the whole Body's Blitheness, sprightliness!"[38] This laughter, here as well as during the finale, remains non-verbal, a signifier without a signified.[39]

The function of Ignacy's speechlessness can best be understood in the context of other silences in *Trans-Atlantyk*. The first moment of silence occurs during the verbal duel between Witold and the "Gran Escritor" at the beginning of the novel. Witold, appointed as the token genius of the Polish nation, is set up to compete with the Argentinian maestro. He ends up defeated and in his humiliation he realizes that he is speechless: "I was left with no words for I had lost my tongue! And the scoundrel, he had made me mute so that I had no Words, as what is mine is not Mine, apparently Stolen!"[40]

In exile, it seems, Witold has no voice, since verbal prowess and prestige are owned entirely by the local poet laureate. Michał Paweł Markowski reads this scene as one of symbolic castration.[41] I would juxtapose the narrator's silencing, his *mut(e)ilation*, with the deliberate quietness that characterizes the "Gran Escritor": "That voice of his he quietened constantly but, the quieter the louder indeed, as other, having quietened themselves, all the more intently did listen (though they listen not)."[42] This scene presents silence simultaneously as a threat to authorship and as an attribute of the great writer. After this duel of wits the "Gran Escritor" disappears from the novel, but the themes of silence and authorship assume a central position.

Somewhat later in the narrative, Major Tomasz Kobrzycki is shown to control his environment in a similarly authoritative manner. During a brawl Gonzalo throws a beer glass at Kobrzycki, but the old major remains motionless and silent while blood dribbles from a cut on his forehead. His dignified attitude quiets the rowdy company: "From Tomasz's silent drops all became silent and Tomasz looks at us and we at Tomasz; and the fifth Drop dribbles."[43] Witold is impressed with the way the major and the "Gran Escritor" command respect through their masterful use of silence.

Witold also experiences silence as a conveyor of erotic tension. Wandering through Gonzalo's palace at night, he keeps stumbling over servant boys sleeping on the floor. He spits on the ground in disgust, but his spittle hits one of the boys in the face: "Indeed there a Boy, darkish, quite Large, a-lying was, whom I, not willfully, did bespit and down his ear the Spittle was dripping. Naught he says, only at me gazes."[44] Just as the major silently allows his blood to trickle down his face, so too the servant boy passively lets Witold's spit dribble down his ear. The verb "ściekać" (to drip) is used in both cases.[45] And yet, while the old man's stoicism appears brave and honorable to Witold, the servant boy's impassivity strikes him as a provocation. Outraged, he spits at him again and again. His contemptuous speech intensifies the erotic undertone until the scene comes to evoke a sadistic scenario. Witold eventually becomes aware of the incident's latent homoeroticism: "perchance he thinks that I so for my Pleasure, for my Delight?"[46] At this thought, he panics and flees into a random bedroom, where (echoing Freud's account of his "uncanny" return to the prostitutes' quarter in an Italian town) he finds himself, once again, facing the sleeping, naked Ignacy. Throughout *Trans-Atlantyk* Witold's silent encounters with Ignacy and the servant boys connote a loss of control and a threat to the narrator's sense of self.[47]

Silence takes on yet another layer of meaning in the episode of the "Chevaliers of the Spur." The recruits are imprisoned in a cellar whose doors are left open. They sit in deathlike silence, fearing torture if they draw attention to themselves: "no one says a word, ... breath they nigh seal."[48] The narrator, too, is perfectly quiet: "as a Corpse speak naught, breathe not, sit."[49] The atmosphere is tense and oppressive: "Ergo perchance three or four hours we Sat in this way, one next to another, with no movement, with no sound, and something there Amongst Us was growing, growing."[50] Although most of the Chevaliers have been coerced to join the Order, there is no escape, since every movement is severely punished and the failure to discipline an insubordinate fellow is sanctionable by even greater violence. Dehumanized by this terror, the Chevaliers spend their days in silence: "from morn till eve we Sit and keep Silence, speak little."[51] At night, however, they whisper meaningless syllables:

> Evermore then sonorous, raucous nightly Natterings and there one squirms, Wriggles, another "Chuli, buli" whispers, or "klumka, klumka," and from that Speech my hair stood on end and my heart grew faint as if I in the circles of Hell abided.[52]

In this episode, silence is used to present the Polish community as a dystopian fantasy of surveillance, restriction, and loss of meaningful expression.

These passages indicate that while *Trans-Atlantyk* is rife with representations of silence, its role eludes classification. On the surface, silence connotes a range of phenomena: the minor author's domination by the established author; artistic and moral authority; overwhelming, unspeakable desire; and finally, fear and the crushing of individual expression. On a subtextual, allegorical level, meanwhile, silence pervades *Trans-Atlantyk* in the portrayal of Ignacy, who finally initiates the novel's explosive and noisy finale.[53] Let us have a closer look at Witold's relationship with Ignacy.

Witold's attitude toward Ignacy is characterized by ambiguity. On the one hand, he clings to the traditional value system in which the son must be subjected to the father's will, but, on the other hand, he is seduced by Gonzalo's revolutionary vision of "synczyzna." Witold's contradictory feelings are expressed in his tendency to lose control of his walking: whenever his walking becomes automatic, he finds himself drifting towards Ignacy. Thrice he enters the boy's bedroom:

> the Going itself directs me towards the Son; and so of a sudden I to the Son go (and that Going of mine has become slow, shy). The Son, the Son, to the Son, to the Son![54]
>
> Ergo I walk and Walk. Yet when I so Walk 'twas as if my walking began to go somewhere and to lead me somewhere (although I myself know not where)...and in some place there Ignacy sleeping lies...then that Walk of mine walks and walks and walks and there Ignacy....[55]

The third time, Witold does not enter Ignacy's room involuntarily. "Then to the Son I resolved to go. Oh Son, Son, Son! To him I will go, him once more by Night I will see and perchance within some feeling I will feel... perchance his freshness will refresh me...."[56] However, Witold is uncertain of the purpose of his visit: "now myself know not whether I as a talebearer of Gonzalo's go or of Tomasz's...and perchance I Go on behalf of the Chevaliers of the Spur that youth to murder...."[57] Witold repeatedly finds himself standing in front of the naked boy, but his fascination is never carried to its erotic conclusion. The sleeping Ignacy's silence apparently prevents Witold from ever letting himself go completely.

On one occasion, Witold comments on the fact that when he walks, even if he has an aim in mind, he will end up going astray: "Thus you Go but you Stray, and you resolve, plan but you Stray, and seemingly according to your will you contrive but you Stray, Stray, and you speak, Do but in a Wood, at Night, you stray, stray...."[58]

The references to composition, language, and intentionality in this passage suggest an allegorical interpretation of Witold's automatic walking. His metanarrative comments appear to have slipped in, as if he had deviated unintentionally from his subject (his account of *walking*) and ended up betraying his fascination with *language*. His tendency to stray in his walking appears to be bound up with his susceptibility to drift off, in his storytelling, into a preoccupation with language. Both appear to defy his (authorial) control, and both appear to lead to an encounter with silence, as Witold faces the silent sleeping Ignacy, while his text becomes self-aware and leads him to confront the limits of language. Writing, Gombrowicz suggests, has a tendency to concern itself with writing; language is intrinsically self-reflexive.

The Central Role of Silence

The central role of silence links Gombrowicz's model of authorship to Maurice Blanchot's philosophical reflections on the dilemmas of writing. In *L'espace littéraire* (1955), Blanchot addresses the necessity to complement the sheer urge to write by embracing silence. To write literature, Blanchot asserts, is not to pursue self-expression, but to renounce it. It is to become the echo of an inner voice that speaks automatically, without beginning or end. This voice does not belong to individual subjectivity, nor does it express some "universal" or communal truth. In order to give expression to this never-ending flow of inspiration, and to give it a coherent form, the writer must interrupt this flow: "To write is to make oneself the echo of what cannot cease speaking – and since it cannot, in order to become its echo I have, in a way, to silence it."[59] By imposing silence, his own *authorial* silence, on this incessant "giant murmuring" of inspiration, the writer retains control and authority, and asserts his individual "tone." "The tone is not the writer's voice, but the intimacy of the silence he imposes upon the word. This implies that the silence is still his – what remains of him in the discretion that sets him aside."[60]

Blanchot argues that the writer cannot affirm his authorial identity through language. Language only expresses that interminable being ("l'être") which is removed from the writer's "I," whereas the space of authorial self-expression is the silence that the writer imposes on the flow of language.

Blanchot proposes a visual image to elucidate the duality at the heart of literary creativity: the hand that writes incessantly, that will not let go of the pen, must be stilled by the hand of mastery. The writer's authority and individuality reside in the hand that silences the flow of writing:

> The writer's mastery is not in the hand that writes, the "sick" hand that never lets the pencil go—that can't let it go [...]. Mastery always

characterizes the other hand, the one that doesn't write and is capable of intervening at the right moment to seize the pencil and put it aside. Thus mastery consists in the power to stop writing, to interrupt what is being written, thereby restoring to the present instant its rights, its decisive trenchancy.[61]

There is a crucial ambiguity in Blanchot's view of authorship as a "silencing" of the incessant murmur of language. On the one hand, the writer maintains the authoritative though silent affirmation of the effaced "I" by renouncing his individual subjectivity; he breaks the bond between himself and language: "This silence has its source in the effacement toward which the writer is drawn."[62] But, on the other hand, this silence expresses his authority: "it is the resource of his mastery, the right of intervention which the hand that doesn't write retains – the part of the writer which can always say no...."[63]

Blanchot's paradoxical notion of renouncing and asserting one's ego, of relinquishing self-expression in order to impose on the text the unique quality of one's own silence, illuminates Gombrowicz's view of authorship as developed allegorically in *Trans-Atlantyk*. The father, Major Kobrzycki, stands for form, literary tradition, and authorial control; Gonzalo, the puto, represents free-flowing, formless inspiration and unrestrained creativity; Ignacy embodies a cluster of notions centered on the fascination of silence. To reconcile the opposing duo of creativity and control (Gonzalo and Kobrzycki), Witold must confront the potentially explosive force of the silent Ignacy. He must surrender to the passive boy's magnetic pull, and let himself go (walk or wander) toward him, without ever giving in completely, without arriving, touching, or "coming." Witold is overwhelmed with erotic tension and at the same time he fears this eroticism; he is just as affected by Ignacy's peaceful silence (his sleeping body) as he is affected by the contagious noise of his laughter (his ecstatic body).

For Gombrowicz, to write, especially to write in exile, is to experience the full impact of two contradictory desires: to remain part of a tradition and to launch oneself into the unknown. Ignacy's figure allows him to explore the libidinal dimension of silence. By confronting silence – without, however, being seduced by it – the author, in Gombrowicz's view, allows the work to emerge on its own terms and at the same time restrains its free development. So far there is an overlap between Gombrowicz and Blanchot. But in the allegorical representation of writing in *Trans-Atlantyk*, the author does not need to *impose* silence on the work, as Blanchot suggests: Witold does not try to appropriate the kind of silence with which the "Gran Escritor" and Kobrzycki command the crowd. Silence is not merely a means of exerting control, nor can it become, in itself, an expression of creativity (the servant boys are entirely passive; the Chevaliers of the Spur are paralyzed with fear and sit around in deadly silence). In order to enter the space of composition, Witold, the author in the story, needs to find the silent space where creativity and control intersect.

The Genesis of *Trans-Atlantyk*

Gombrowicz gives a fairly detailed account of the genesis of *Trans-Atlantyk* in his diary of 1957. He begins by reminding his readers of the tension between his person and his work, and the mutual influence between his life and his writing:

> The history of my becoming is the history of my constant adjustment to my literary works – which always surprised me by being born in an unpredictable way, as if not of me…. To a certain degree my books are a result of my life – but my life was formed in greater measure from them and with them.[64]

He goes on to describe the inspiration that led to the creation of *Trans-Atlantyk*. One night, walking the streets of Buenos Aires he entertained himself by weaving a story about his adventures in emigration. Gombrowicz insists that this was before he had even considered writing an autobiographical novel. As he went along, a certain style, unusual but artistically promising, impressed itself upon him:

> Once when returning from Caballito at night, I began to amuse myself by composing reminiscences from my first days in Buenos Aires on the model of some sort of Grand Guignol, and, at the same time, by dint of the past, I felt anachronistic, draped in an antique style, entangled in some sort of almost ancient scleroticism – and this gave me so much joy that I immediately commenced writing something that was to have been an antiquated memoir from that time.[65]

This playful creativity brings Gombrowicz such joy that he begins to work seriously on the emerging project, transposing it from a mental improvisation to a written text. Again he emphasizes the work's force of self-creation and its defiance of authorial intention:

> But naturally – and as always – the commenced work began to slip away from me and began writing itself: what I had conceived as a chronicle of my first undertakings after landing had transformed itself somehow … into a strange novel about Poles, with a "puto," a duel, and even a sleigh chase…. After a little more than a year, I noticed that I was the author of [*Trans-Atlantyk*].[66]

Setting the moment of inspiration in the streets of Buenos Aires at night, Gombrowicz recalls his fictional narrator Witold walking and talking to himself: "Thus you Go but you Stray, and you resolve, plan but you Stray, and seemingly according to your will you contrive but you Stray, Stray, and you speak, Do but in a Wood, at Night, you stray, stray...."[67]

The coincidence of walking and writing that occurs in Gombrowicz's autobiographical text as well as in his fictional narrator's (interior) monologue connects the author and his alter ego and highlights the autorepresentational aspect of the motif of walking in the novel.

It is also remarkable that in the diary Gombrowicz portrays the writing of *Trans-Atlantyk* in relatively cheerful terms. His accounts of the composition of his first novel *Ferdydurke*, by contrast, frequently focus on his struggle against the text's self-creation:

> when I started *Ferdydurke*, I wanted to write no more than a biting satire.... But my words were soon whirled away in a violent dance, they took the bit between their teeth and galloped towards a grotesque lunacy with such speed that I had to rewrite the first part of the book in order to give it the same grotesque intensity.[68]

Gombrowicz never uses the image of a resigned compromise with reference to *Trans-Atlantyk*. Its creation is presented as a happy realization after the fact, as if he never needed either to control its wild creativity or to worry about finding the creative power in himself. Gombrowicz's accounts of composition rarely exude such contentment and optimism.[69]

As Jerzy Giedroyc recalls, more subscriptions to *Kultura* were cancelled in protest against *Trans-Atlantyk* than in reaction to any politically controversial article.[70] Stanisław Barańczak, meanwhile, remembers the enthusiasm with which Poland's cultural elite received the novel in 1957.[71] Gombrowicz, strangely, showed himself disappointed by the impact of *Trans-Atlantyk*: "People ignored it. It was too bizarre to be taken seriously. The dynamite passed unnoticed."[72] Perhaps, after a decade of virtual non-existence as a writer, he had hoped to re-enter the literary scene with an even greater bang, a "bam, boom, boom, bam Boom!" to quote the closing words of Carolyn French and Nina Karsov's translation of the novel's closing words.[73] He never explicitly addressed his encounter with silence in the decade after his emigration. But by thematizing the to-and-fro movement between walking and writing, writing and silence, silence and laughter, he posits *Trans-Atlantyk* as a self-conscious coda to his second debut – his debut as an exile writer — and claims his territory roaring like a lion.

Notes

1 Gombrowicz, *Diary*, 50; italics in the original.
2 Ibid.

3 Ibid.
4 Ibid.
5 Ibid.
6 Ibid.
7 Gombrowicz, commentary, *Kultura*, 6 (1952). Quote from the version of Gombrowicz's commentary published in the *Diary* of 1953, Gombrowicz, *Dziennik*, VII (Błoński), 64–68 and Gombrowicz, *Diary*, 48–52.
8 Gombrowicz, *Diary*, 50.
9 Ibid., 50–51.
10 Ibid., 51.
11 Ibid.
12 Ibid., 51–52.
13 Jerzak, "Defamation in Exile," 178.
14 Jerzak, 203 note 1.
15 On Gombrowicz's engagement with the Polish Romantic tradition see, Holmgren, "*Wieszcz* Tradition," 556–70; Phillips, "Polish Complex," 28–46; Kraszewski, 213–32.
16 On representations of exile by Gombrowicz, Cioran, and Czesław Miłosz see Karpinski, 131–38.
17 Gombrowicz discusses three early attempts to write popular fiction in *Memories* (Johnston), 45–46.
18 Gombrowicz, *Diary*, 48.
19 Gombrowicz, *Trans-Atlantyk* (French and Karsov), 28.
20 Ibid.
21 Gasyna, 144–45.
22 Goddard, 88.
23 Bielecki, *Interpretacja*, 205.
24 Wittlin, "Apologia," 89.
25 Gombrowicz, *Diary*, 460–61.
26 Gombrowicz, *Testament*, 106, translation modified.
27 On Gombrowicz's rejection of a post as cultural attaché for Communist Poland's Argentinian embassy, see Suchanow, *Argentyńskie przygody*, 83–95.
28 Gombrowicz, *Diary*, 50.
29 Gombrowicz, *Testament*, 106.
30 Czesław Straszewicz is mentioned as Witold's fellow traveler. Straszewicz did cross the Atlantic with Gombrowicz, but returned to fight for Poland. There is no consensus on who might have inspired the "Gran Escritor." Jorge Luis Borges, with whom Gombrowicz had a notoriously problematic relationship, is cited most frequently, but Ricardo Piglia suggests other possible models, such as Eduardo Maella or Manuel Mujica Láinez. See Piglia, "¿Existe?" 13. According to Rússovich, the queer Gonzalo was modeled on the Cuban writer Virgilio Piñera. Rússovich, "Russovich," 12.
31 Gombrowicz, *Testament*, 106–7, translation modified.
32 Van der Meer discusses this antithetical system in *Trans-Atlantyk*. See his *Form vs. Anti-Form*, 76.
33 Gombrowicz, *Diary*, 672.
34 Gombrowicz, *Ferdydurke* (Borchardt) 72–73; *Ferdydurke* (Bolecki), 67; Gombrowicz, *Testament*, 51; Gombrowicz, *Dziennik*, X (Błoński), 42; Gombrowicz, *Diary*, 97; Gombrowicz, *Dziennik*, VII (Błoński), 125–26.
35 Gasyna analyzes the metonymic functions of several characters in *Trans-Atlantyk* in Gasyna, 148–53.
36 Chwin, afterword to Gombrowicz, *Trans-Atlantyk* (2004), 145.
37 Gombrowicz, *Trans-Atlantyk* (French and Karsov), 96.
38 Ibid., 110.

39 Ignacy has an almost speechless predecessor in the heroine of Gombrowicz's play *Iwona, księżniczka Burgunda* (*Ivona, Princess of Burgundia*), published in 1938. Iwona is an unattractive commoner whom the Prince marries in protest against conventions of desire. The royals perceive her silence as subversive and assassinate her. Ignacy's speechlessness, unlike Iwona's, is not thematized in the fictional universe and cannot be accounted for in psychological terms, however broadly defined. Ignacy's silence is abstract, which heightens its allegorical significance. On Iwona's silence, see Żółkoś, *Ciało mówiące*, 13–24.

40 Gombrowicz, *Trans-Atlantyk* (French and Karsov), 39.

41 Markowski, *Czarny*, 31.

42 Gombrowicz, *Trans-Atlantyk* (French and Karsov), 38–39. Translation modified to render Gombrowicz's use of capital letters.

43 Ibid., 56.

44 Ibid., 93.

45 Ibid.

46 Ibid.

47 I agree with José Quiroga who argues that the stylized language of *Trans-Atlantyk* enacts a tension between control and loss of control—a tension that is symptomatic of Gombrowicz's play with silence as a code of homosexuality. See Quiroga, *Tropics of Desire*, 137.

48 Gombrowicz, *Trans-Atlantyk* (French and Karsov), 100.

49 Ibid.

50 Ibid.

51 Ibid., 104.

52 Ibid., 105.

53 For a Bakhtinian reading of the finale see Ziarek, "Scar," 224.

54 Gombrowicz, *Trans-Atlantyk* (French and Karsov), 75.

55 Ibid., 92–3. Olaf Kühl suggests about the passage quoted here that grammatical nominalization renders Witold's "walking" more "independent," allowing it to become the agent that "pushes" Witold, "where he himself would never have dared to go." See Kühl, *Stilistik*, 72–73.

56 Gombrowicz, *Trans-Atlantyk* (French and Karsov), 113.

57 Ibid.

58 Ibid., 72.

59 Blanchot, *Space*, 27.

60 Ibid.

61 Ibid., 24.

62 Ibid., 27.

63 Ibid.

64 Gombrowicz, *Diary*, 295.

65 Ibid., translation modified.

66 Ibid., 296.

67 Gombrowicz, *Trans-Atlantyk* (French and Karsov), 72.

68 Gombrowicz, *Testament*, 50.

69 After *Trans-Atlantyk* the role of authorial control reappeared in a new guise: in his later works, Gombrowicz used discipline and control not to tame the flow of the writing, but in an effort to approach the source of creativity.

70 See Giedroyc, *Autobiografia*, 163–64.

71 Gombrowicz, *Trans-Atlantyk* (French and Karsov), ix.

72 Gombrowicz, *Testament*, 106.

73 Gombrowicz, *Trans-Atlantyk* (French and Karsov), 122.

12 The Anatomy of Feeling in Gombrowicz's "A Premeditated Crime" ("Zbrodnia z premedytacją")

Silvia G. Dapía

Introduction

In the works of contemporary artists such as the Hungarian (living in Brazil) Peter Pál Pelbart or the Dutch Aernout Mik, we repeatedly encounter characters who are not defined as distinct, autonomous individuals but as members of a group, suggesting the existence of an affective operation that acts upon them. Accordingly, in one of Pál Pelbart's performances, we come across wool that comes out of an actor and at the same time "creates a web across the group."[1] Referring to this performance, Pál Pelbart points out the existence of "one material or one flow or one intensity," which "crosses the field" and establishes a relationship among those diverse figures.[2] It soon becomes clear to the audience that the wool does not allude to "an individual kind of code" but to "material spanning across the group and probably even further," establishing affective and bodily interconnections between the characters.[3] Moreover, these bodily interconnections force the audience to reframe its notion of the individual in non-solipsistic terms. It is certainly difficult to conceive the individual in Pál Pelbart's work as an autonomous, sovereign self. On the contrary, his performances usually encourage alternative modes of thinking about the subject, emphasizing the complex interdependencies that exist between individuals. As Pál Pelbart asserts:

> the limits are not clear and the 'space between' becomes more important than individual people. It allows a kind of elasticity. It is a way of feeling and being collective, without becoming a compact unity, but rather through a game of proximities and distances, deindividuations and individuations, in a very sensorial way because it is not an intellectual decision: it's through affective and bodily connections.[4]

Similarly, as Ralph Rugoff points out, in Aernout Mik's videos, the artist's camera regards his characters "all with a leveling gaze that diminishes and blurs their differences, leaving us to consider the collective identity of those who, under different conditions, might appear as discrete individuals."[5] Moreover, in some of his videos, as the camera "travels from body parts to objects and objects to other objects or when people assume each other's compulsive movements and emotions," these aesthetic strategies, as Mik explains, suggest "an action of contamination or spreading out that becomes an independent force."[6] I believe the reader of this article would find it particularly interesting to learn—as its author did—that Mik declared being deeply inspired by Gombrowicz in his own aesthetic. Mik explained:

> There's this beautiful scene that Gombrowicz describes in his diary, where he's in the tram and looking at the neck of someone standing in front of him. Then he realizes that he has been looking at the neck for just a bit too long. At that moment he is somehow trapped. The neck becomes something in itself. It separates itself from the body, connects with other necks and takes him on a road that he can't stop. Through his accidental gaze, the neck is in a way dismembered. It becomes something that, even if he wants to avoid it, he's already reacting to and is therefore dependent upon. That is a powerful thing, this independent force that connects things, that defines what's taking place and pulls you in its own direction.[7]

It is precisely this "contamination" or transmission of affect as it operates in Gombrowicz's work that constitutes the subject of this article. It is thus my goal to explore the affective, bodily connections, and the complex ways in which the characters of Gombrowicz's story, as embodied beings, negotiate their subjectivity. Or, to say it in Pál Pelbart's words, the "game of proximities and distances, deindividuations and individuations" that operates in Gombrowicz's story by means of "affective and bodily connections." Therefore, I shall focus on Gombrowicz's characters as *affected* subjects, paying particular attention to their encounters and the way in which they are *affected* by the forces generated in those very encounters. But first of all, I believe a brief clarification of how I use the terms "affect," "feeling," and "emotion," is in order.

Interest in "affect" has grown considerably in the last decades in the humanities. To signal this increasing interest critics have coined the expression "affect turn." The "affect turn" implies a shift away from research based on discourse to focusing instead on embodiment, encounters between bodies, processes, becoming, the virtual and potential. Affect theory, however, comes under diverse forms. There is, for example, a phenomenological strand that is concerned with how individual bodies come into contact (Sianne Ngai,[8] Lauren Berlant,[9] Sara Ahmed[10]). There is also a line of research that draws mainly upon neuroscience and biology (Silvan Tomkins,[11] Eve Kosofsky Sedgwick,[12] Antonio Damasio[13]). Last but not least there is an important line of affect scholarship that takes an ontological approach to affect (Gilles Deleuze,[14] Brian Massumi,[15] Eve Kosofsky Sedgwick). But what is "affect"? Disregarding the particular emphasis of these diverse lines of research, most affect theorists would probably agree that affect is not a "personal feeling" but "an ability to affect and be affected."[16] Thus, at any encounter between bodies, each of those bodies impinges upon (affects) the other, and, at the same time, each responds to the other. Affect theorists conceptualize this impact or influence as "intensity." For Brian Massumi, for example, affect is "a pre-personal intensity" and it corresponds "to the passage from one experiential state of the body to another and implying an augmentation or diminution in that body's capacity to act."[17] By using the expression "pre-personal," Massumi indicates that for him affect is always prior to and/or outside of consciousness, a non-conscious moment of unstructured potential. As Margaret Wetherell rightly claims, an assumption underlying the thought of many affect theorists, including Massumi, is "that humans first encounter the world bodily and then secondarily discursively."[18] In this sense, as Linda M. G. Zerilli points out, "affect theory may be read as another chapter" in the debate about "conceptual and nonconceptual modes of orientation to the world."[19]

Affect theorists usually distinguish between "affect" and "emotion." Thus, as we suggested, Massumi, for example, restricts the use of the term "affect" to refer to unconscious "intensity" that eludes representation, applying it *only* to bodily phenomena that operate below the threshold of conscious recognition.[20] Moreover, while he reserves the term "affect" for unconscious bodily experiences, he applies the term "emotion" to its conceptual or "sociolinguistic fixing."[21] In other words, for Massumi, the term "emotion" indicates the moment affect is framed in linguistic terms. Thus, as Wetherell claims, Massumi seems to assume a process by which affect is "tamed, turned into something people can recognize, talk about to each other and communicate as 'domesticated' emotion."[22] As opposed to Massumi and this ontological line of research, for some recent critics,[23] however, affect cannot be separated from discourse, conceptualization or emotion. These critics believe that we cannot focus only on "some constructed moment of initial impingement, and ignore the meaning making contexts and histories that so decisively shape the encounters between bodies and events."[24]

In this essay, rather than engaging with the distinction between pre-reflective affect and culturally circumscribed emotion, I prefer to think of affect and emotion as operating on a fluid line of continuity and I will often use these terms interchangeably. In this respect, I am following Susanne Langer, a true precursor of the "affective turn," whose work has unfortunately not yet received the attention it deserves from affect critics. For Langer, feeling is nothing other than a "phase," a "mode of appearance," of the body under certain conditions. To put it slightly differently: there is no additional entity—feeling—that is added to the body; there is simply the body and feeling is just a "phase of a physiological process."[25] Langer explains how feeling works by conceiving it as analogous to an iron bar:

> When iron is heated to a critical degree it becomes red; yet its redness is not a new entity which must have gone somewhere else when it is no longer in the iron. It was a phase of the iron itself, at high temperature.[26]

Thus, as with the redness of the iron, feeling emerges as a quality of the body under certain conditions. She claims: "One may say that some activities, especially nervous ones, above a certain (probably fluctuating) limen of intensity, enter into 'psychical phase.' This is the phase of being felt."[27] Moreover, feelings are known immediately and corporeally, but they lack symbolic or conceptual form. For this reason, they are frequently unnoticed or quickly forgotten. Langer claims:

> The real patterns of feeling—how a small fright, or "startle," terminates, how the tensions of boredom increase or give way to self-entertainment, how daydreaming weaves in and out of realistic thought, how the feeling of a place, a time of day, an ordinary situation is built up—these felt events, which compose the fabric of mental life, usually pass unobserved, unrecorded and therefore essentially unknown to the average person. It may seem strange that the most immediate experiences in our lives should be the least recognized, but there is a reason for this apparent paradox, and the reason is precisely their immediacy. They pass unrecorded because they are known without any symbolic mediation and therefore without conceptual form.[28]

Feelings are already intentional, already meaningful[29] – albeit that their complete meaning only gets realized in their conjunctions with the signs, symbols, discourses, words, or any conceptual form that they permeate. A focus on feeling therefore avoids the problems of intentionality associated with certain restricted conceptions of affect and thus permits a more thorough and nuanced analysis of the felt or affective dimensions of human interaction. For this reason, I conceive here affects and emotions as analogous to Langer's conceptualization of feeling, including both the bodily aspects generally described as embodied or affective and those usually categorized as mental or cognitive.

Due to Gombrowicz's notion of Form, critics have paid attention to those controlling social norms and human interactions that shape us and normalize us. Less attention has been paid, however, to his use of affect intensities and emotions (feelings) to accomplish this process. Because "attending to emotions," as Sara Ahmed claims, "might show us how all actions are reactions,"[30] I shall read Gombrowicz within an affective framework. Thus, I intend to focus on embodiment, take the entanglement of bodies as the unit of analysis, pay attention at the circulation of affect and its crystallizations as emotions. It is precisely this emphasis on affect and emotions (feelings) that, I argue, broadens Gombrowicz's notion of social interaction and Form, not limiting it to language or discourse but, on the contrary, expanding it to affective dimensions understood as non-separated from meaning (in the sense of Susanne Langer).

"A Premeditated Crime"

"A Premeditated Crime" ("Zbrodnia z premedytacją") revolves around an investigating magistrate who arrives at the manor of a landed gentleman named Ignacy K. in order to help him with a property-related business and finds out that the gentleman in questioned died the night before his arrival. The story is told from the perspective of the magistrate, who not only gives us some "background" information about the trip but registers in detail his feelings, emotions, and the circulation of affect that accompany his encounters with the different members of the landed family. Thus, through the voice of the magistrate, we learn how in preparation for his trip, he sent his client a telegram letting him know the day and time of his arrival and asking him to send a carriage to pick him up at the railway station. However, to his dismay, he found out upon his arrival that no carriage was sent. As a consequence of this, not only was he forced to hire an uncomfortable, small wagon to go to the landed gentleman's manor but to shiver during four hours "bumping across the fields by night."[31] To make matters worse, when he finally arrived at Ignacy K.'s country manor and knocked at the door, he was attacked by the dogs. Moreover, when a young man, who turned out to be the son of the landed gentleman, lastly opened the door, he simply dismissed the magistrate "with God's blessing."[32]

From the beginning of the story, Gombrowicz succeeds in showing affects and emotions, which become visible, almost palpable, as they emerge in the characters' encounters. Gombrowicz has the reader discern those affects not only in the characters' words but also in the description of their tones, gestures, and bodies. Thus, for example, in his encounter with the son, the magistrate's annoyance at his bizarre reception becomes tangible in the harsh tone, not devoid of sarcasm, with which the magistrate "apologizes" for not having arrived earlier. If he "wasn't able to get here sooner," the magistrate claims, "it's because no horses were sent to" the station.[33] His annoyance becomes "stuck" to his body and cannot be separated from it. Similarly, in his first encounter with the landed gentleman's daughter, his annoyance turns into disgust when he is introduced to her and she extends to him a sweaty hand. Thus, in this first encounter with the daughter, the magistrate mentions several bodily details (her indifference, untidiness), being the dominant trait in his presentation of this character the sweatiness of her hands. He claims, "the hand she gave me was perspiring—who gives a man a perspiring hand? — and the femininity itself, despite a charming little face, seemed somehow, how shall I put it, perspirational and indifferent, devoid of reaction, unkempt, and disheveled."[34] Thus, like Julia Kristeva's flows that challenge the clean and proper body,[35] the sweatiness of the daughter's hands triggers the magistrate's disgust and a self-conscious sense of the borders of his own body, impeding the converging of his body with something that is not him. It is as if the sweatiness of the daughter's hands, by establishing the "frontier" between their bodies, reinforces his non-belongingness to the social world of the gentry family.

Throughout the story, a sense of borders between the magistrate's body and those of the members of the landed family is repeatedly emphasized and linked with a mixture of disgust and irritation. In the landed family's bodies, the magistrate discerns what we may call a gentry class "affective style," a combination of arrogance and contempt that irritates him. The magistrate identifies first this "affective style" in the son's distinct and solemn tone when he affirmatively responds to the magistrate question whether his father was at home. His answer sounds to the magistrate's ears as if he had said, "The King, my Father, is at home!"[36] Similarly, when the mother becomes part of this affectif,[37] the same gentry class "affective style" impinges upon the magistrate again and makes him perceive her as a "dethroned queen."[38] As the mother joins them, the "atmospheric" affect becomes especially intense, "more artificial and oppressive."[39] Thus, like the first encounters with the son and the daughter, the first encounter with the mother is clearly dysphoric or negative. Moreover, like the daughter's sweaty hands, the mother's ice-cold hands produce on the magistrate's body the same self-conscious sense of the borders of his own body, underlining his separateness from the gentry family's social world.

Throughout those bodily encounters the magistrate displays a very permeable, porous self, and senses "forces" that though many times he cannot pinpoint, fix or conceptualize, pull him in their own directions. He rapidly starts to perceive himself through the affective reactions of the landed family's bodies, alternatively seeing himself as the cause of their offense, fear, pity, and shame. He claims:

> What was this? It looked truly bizarre—as if they were offended by me, or were afraid of me, or they felt sorry for me, or they were [ashamed of] me.... Planted in their armchairs, they avoided my gaze, nor did they look at each other; they bore my company with the greatest discomfort—it seemed that they preoccupied exclusively with themselves, and the whole time they were worried only that I may say something to insult them. In the end it began to irritate me. What were they afraid of? What was it about me? What sort of reception was this, aristocratic, timid, proud?[40]

The magistrate's fear of offending or shaming the landed family may be interpreted as part of an affective mechanism that, on the one hand, encourages submissiveness to the Forms supported by the landed gentry's social world. However, on the other hand, this same fear of offending or shaming the landed family also produces in the magistrate's body a resistance to his own compliance. In this sense, it comes as no surprise that the magistrate reacts to this dysphoric, negative emotion with irritation ("In the end it began to irritate me,"[41] he claims. Irritation does not, of course, solve the magistrate's dissatisfaction with his situation in the landed manor. Rather it serves, in Sianne Ngai's sense, as an index of the magistrate's material social condition of subordination vis-à-vis the landed family.[42] Indeed, this scene works as a very condensed vignette of those affects that operate at the limit between affective consciousness and material social conditions.[43]

Along with disgust and irritation, embarrassment, too, "sticks" to the magistrate's body, becoming another crucial motor in much of the magistrate's interaction with the family. The magistrate sometimes oscillates between shame and embarrassment. However, that does not mean that these two feelings or emotions do not differ along important dimensions. Martha Nussbaum points out the differential features of embarrassment. Thus, as opposed to shame, embarrassment, in Nussbaum's view, is "momentary, temporary and inconsequential," while shame lasts longer and is more serious.[44] The magistrate's embarrassment is elicited in different circumstances. Thus, for example, he feels embarrassed or, as he says, "ever more vulgar, foolish, and uncomfortable," as the result of the affect circulating among them during dinner.[45] Furthermore, after the mother tells him that her husband passed away the night before, the magistrate feels embarrassed because he failed to offer his condolences to the mother right away. The magistrate claims:

> It was so unexpected that to begin with I was completely put out of countenance. In my confusion I rose from my chair and mumbled something indistinctly along the lines of: "I'm terribly sorry ... I'm very... I'm sorry."— I fell silent, but they did not respond whatsoever, for this was still too little for them.[46]

What is most striking about this scene is the enumeration of bodily gestures and details that the magistrate registers as contributing to the emergence of his embarrassment or painful consciousness of not complying with established social practices. He asserts:

> I looked at them: all three of them were waiting. They were modest and grave, but—they were waiting, with stern, reserved faces and pursed lips; they were waiting stiffly...with lowered eyes and unmoving faces, their clothes untidy, he unshaven, the women with

disheveled hair, their fingernails dirty—they all stood without saying anything....they were waiting, immersed in their suffering. They
were waiting without looking—Antoni was drumming his fingers
lightly on the tabletop, Cecylia was embarrassedly picking at the
hem of her dirty gown, and their mother stood motionless, as if
turned to stone, with that stern, unyielding matronly expression.[47]

Furthermore, the memory of those situations in which he felt embarrassed keeps the magistrate in permanent tension. For example, the
embarrassment he felt when he was having dinner and learns that the
father passed away is reenacted by the narrator every time he remembers
the episode.[48] Indeed embarrassment is a dysphoric, negative emotion,
which the magistrate wants to avoid. Thus, in an attempt to avoid it, he
tries to adhere, almost in an obsessive manner, to those social norms he
is expected to follow but was not. Accordingly, with excessive humility,
he repeatedly kisses the mother's hands and kneels down with his head
bowed in front of the deceased. His humility shows that he sees himself
as representing a lower social status and lack of worth in comparison
with the landed family.[49] Thus, if humiliation involves being forced into
a degrading or ridiculed position by some kind of powerful force,[50] the
magistrate expresses this feeling of powerlessness by highlighting the
mother's and son's role in this dysphoric feeling ("[t]hey (the mother and
the son) made a fool of" him).[51]

Moreover, it appears that the magistrate is not really aware of what he
was doing as he repeatedly kisses the mother's hands and kneels down
with his head bowed in front of the deceased. He claims: "On your
knees! — 'What is it,' I thought slowly to myself. 'Who staged all this?...
Could I be acting a part? Where did this artificiality, this affectation
come from in me — I'm usually completely different — have they *infected*
me?"[52] As Martha Nussbaum points out, embarrassment involves an audience in front of which we are performing awkwardly.[53] In this sense it
is significant that Gombrowicz's narrator establishes connection between
embarrassment and performance.[54] The narrator claims:

> "What is it—ever since I arrived, everything in me has been coming
> out artificially and pretentiously, as if it were being performed by a
> third-rate actor. I've completely lost myself in this house—I'm acting
> up almost terribly. Hmm," I murmured, and once again not without
> a certain theatrical pose (as if I were already sucked into the game
> and I could no longer return to normality).[55]

Thus, if embarrassment implies that one perceives oneself as being cast
in a role in front of an audience, this is masterfully described by Gombrowicz as the magistrate perceives himself acting "artificially and pre-
tentiously" ("sztucznie i pretensjonalnie") in front of the landed family,

who in this case plays the role of the audience. Moreover, he feels he has been cast in a role that he does not know how to play ("I'm acting up almost terribly;" "okropnie się zgrywam").[56] Thus, he has been "sucked into the game" of Form and is not able to destabilize those rigid norms that have captured him.[57]

To this picture, we must add the magistrate's self-centeredness and paranoia. Thus, for example, when he perceives that the son, mother, and daughter "avoided [his] gaze, nor did they look at each other" or that that they appeared to be "preoccupied exclusively with themselves,"[58] it never crosses his mind that the negative affect he is sensing may have to do with something or someone other than himself. It is true that the magistrate (along with the reader) does not know at this point that the siblings' father passed away the night before. Once we learn about their loss, however, reasons emerge to suppose that the siblings were not so much preoccupied about the magistrate's presence but experiencing emotional distress due to their tragic loss. The affect circulating among the siblings, and the depressing energies these entail, may have entered into the magistrate, who interprets them, from his self-centeredness and paranoia, as if they "were offended" by him, or "were afraid of" him, or "they felt sorry" for him, or "they were ashamed" of him.[59] Thus, he is always worriedly ruminating about how the family perceives him. He does not seem able to interpret what the members of the family say and do, arriving at false conclusions as to how they regard him. Similarly, his self-centeredness emerges when the magistrate attributes the landed family's shame to "the official nature of [his] job" instead of simply ruling that it was triggered by his presence "as an intruder" in such an intimate moment as the death of the father was.[60] Indeed, the magistrate frequently displays paranoid behaviors, [61] seeing others (the mother, particularly) as deceptive and manipulative ("That wretched woman.... How they've arranged everything so cleverly").[62] Perhaps the most emblematic image condensing his paranoid trait occurs at the beginning of the story, upon his arrival, when after finding out that there is no carriage at the station, he hires an uncomfortable, small wagon to go to the landed gentleman's manor. He comments, "I stared at the driver's back and thought—turning one's back like that! Permanently, often in secluded places, to be turned the other way and exposed to the whims of those sitting behind!"[63] Therefore, overly focused on himself, the magistrate appears to miss the mark when he tries to identify the cause of the family's shame. Moreover, shame appears as contagious and the appearance of shame in the siblings causes the narrator's shame. The narrator claims, "this [shame] of theirs embarrassed me terribly, embarrassed me, in fact, entirely disproportionately."[64]

As Spinoza asserts, affects shape what bodies can do, as "the modifications of the body by which the power of action on the body is increased or diminished."[65] In this sense, we may claim that the "power of action" on the magistrate's body will increase. In the pivotal scene that changes the distribution of "power of action" among the members of this affectifs, the narrator claims:

> When I finally found myself alone in my room, I took off my collar, and instead of placing it on the table, I hurled it to the floor and crushed it with my foot. My face was contorted and infused with blood; my fingers closed convulsively in a manner that was entirely unexpected for me. I was quite clearly in a fury. "They've made a fool of me," I whispered. "That wretched woman.... How they've arranged every-thing so cleverly. They make people pay homage to them—kiss their hands! They demand sentiments from me! Sentiments! They demand to be humored! And I—let's say, I hate that. And let's say—I hate it when they use trembling to make me kiss their hands, when they compel me to mumble prayers, to kneel, to produce false, revoltingly sentimental noises—and above all I hate tears, sighs, and droplets at the tip of noses; whereas I like cleanliness and order."[66]

This scene is important, I argue, for at least two reasons. First, it marks a turning point in the affective economy of the story. It prompts the magis-trate's decision to "activate" what he calls his "official character" ("mym charakterem urzędowym") as investigating magistrate,[67] increasing thus the "power of action" on his body. Second, it is also important because of the way Gombrowicz describes it, adding layers of details such as bodily movements (crushing his collar with his foot), facial expressions (his "face was contorted and infused with blood"), and gestures (his "fingers closed convulsively"). This, in turn, adds layers of meanings to the scene so that the reader does not see a simple discursive construction of "fury," "shame" and "humiliation" but a more complicated inter-twine of discourse and affect weaved tightly together.

His compliance with the role that has been assigned to him by the social world supported by the landed family makes him feel ashamed of his submissiveness.[68] For Eve Kosofsky Sedgwick, arguing after psycho-analyst Silvan Tomkins, shame is a uniquely productive affect, because, by forcing an individual into an awareness of herself as seen by others, it produces a sense of individuality.[69] Queer theorists in particular have taken up Sedgwick's emphasis on the transformative capacities of shame. Because of this link between shame and the production of subjectivity, shame has become a central concept in affect studies.[70] In the magis-trate's case, however, even though shame forces him into an awareness of himself as seen by the landed family, this awareness does not lead him to a transformation of his subjectivity. On the contrary, it leads him to retaliation and aggression.[71] Thus, the magistrate's shame turns into anger, directing the focus of his hostility outwardly, toward the landed family, particularly the son. In fact, he seems to feel trapped between shame understood as a feeling of lack of worth due to his submissiveness, on the one hand, and a simultaneous sense of self-aggrandizement and need of vengeance, on the other hand ("I was too ridiculed, too vengeful, and I had already ventured too far").[72]

That the "power of action" on the magistrate's body increases may be proved by the way he manipulates the son's shame. Shame is supposed to guard the boundaries of intimacy. In this sense, it is understandable that the son, like the daughter and the mother, experiences a feeling of a negative self-exposure in his encounter with the magistrate (the Other). Shame implies an experience of oneself as an object, the recognition of being an object for the Other.[73] Clearly, in the son's case, it is the encounter with the magistrate (the Other) that gives rise to his shame as an unpleasant form of self-consciousness, impinging upon him when the magistrate inquiries about his father. The son's shame does not require internalizing the Other: it requires an encounter with the Other (the magistrate) and being affected by him. Moreover, it is this very same feeling of negative self-exposure that explains the fact that the son did not tell the magistrate as soon as he met him that his father passed away the night before. It may also explain the solemn tone that the magistrate identifies in the son's voice when responding to the magistrate's question whether his father was at home. Thus, most likely the affect that the magistrate feels as a gentry-class "affective style" may have less to do with such an "affective style" than with the fact that the son was trying to deal with his father's recent death and felt ashamed at the thought of exposing his intimacy. That he was not inclined to express his feelings is clearly indicated by his embarrassment when his mother tells the magistrate about her husband's death and the fact that her hands have not stopped trembling since then. "No one is...no one will be...it makes no difference. It's embarrassing!" claims the son, who "burst out violently and suddenly turned his back and walked away."[74] Moreover, his aversion to emotions becomes evident again when the magistrate asks him about his feelings for his father. The magistrate claims:

> "Did you love your father very much?" I asked, picking up an album with views of Kraków that lay on the table.
>
> This question clearly took him by surprise. No, he was not prepared for it; he bowed his head, looked to the side, swallowed—and muttered with inexpressible constraint, almost with repugnance:
>
> "I suppose."
>
> "You suppose? That's not very much. You suppose! Only so much?"[75]

Thus, central to the judge's attempt to reverse the flow of affects to his advantage are the son's shame and ambivalent feelings for his father, which the magistrate has no difficulty perceiving. It seems reasonable to believe that the son will not reject but rather welcome ways of "reparation" for his shame. In this context, the magistrate offers him the "logic of guilt," opening up for the son a field of "reparation." Indeed, the son knows he has not committed a crime and that his condemnation as a parricide is unjust. However, the magistrate knows that, to say it with Freud's words, the son will "accept the undeserved punishment as a substitute for the punishment he deserves for his death wish against his father."[76] Indeed Freud's words when discussing the crime of parricide in Dostoevsky's *The Brothers Karamazov* may also be applied to "Premeditated Crime": "It is a matter of indifference who actually committed the crime; psychology is only concerned to know who desired it emotionally."[77] Thus, based on this Freudian knowledge, the magistrate manipulates the son's guilt.[78]

Discussing this story, Jerzy Jarzębski claims that because the narrator cannot base his narrative on "real facts" and wants to justify his role as a magistrate, he has to resort to "psychological facts."[79] This statement may be qualified. Not only does he rely on "psychological facts" but also on a different model of subjectivity. Thus, for example, when the narrator reflects on what he believes are shameful, embarrassing, and humiliating experiences at the landed gentleman's manor, Gombrowicz frames them in terms of a model of a self that rather than being self-contained emphasizes the complex affective operations that cut across the encounters between him and the members of the landed family. Accordingly, he presents the magistrate's emotions and affects as arising from those encounters and somehow "entering" into him. Thus, his shame, embarrassment, irritation, resentment, and anger are explained as the result of affective operations that cut across the members of the group. Similarly, when he pushes the son into strangling the father's corpse, affective forces generated in their interaction play an important role. To trigger the son's guilt, however, Gombrowicz does not apply the same model of subjectivity: he resorts to a traditional psychological model that conceives the human subject in solipsistic terms. To put it slightly differently: in the judge's narrative, the son's ambivalent feelings for his father appear as arising from his own psychic interiority (as opposed to emphasizing the complex bodily and affective interdependencies that exist between individuals). What is at stake here is how the idea of transmitted affects is denied for the explanation of the son's behavior toward his father, while profusely used to explain the judge's own behavior.[80]

Moreover, just as Gombrowicz operates with two models of subjectivity, he also operates with two groups of phenomena, those traditionally categorized as bodily or affective and those traditionally regarded as psychological, mental, or cognitive. More importantly, he erases the borders between them. Thus, analogous to Susanne Langer's conceptualization of feeling, Gombrowicz seems to deny the opposition between mind or reason, on the one hand, and affect, on the other hand, and treats the magistrate's intellect as a "high form of feeling."[81] It seems to me that this last statement needs an explanation.

The magistrate is not concerned with "how things really happened." Thus, rather than accepting the hypothesis that the father's cause of death was natural and confirming it by means of the "evidence" provided by the external world (that his face is swollen and livid like someone who has been asphyxiated, that there are no signs of struggle either on the body or in the room), he accepts as a working hypothesis that "the dead man was murdered." Talking to the widow, the son, and the daughter, he claims:

> Believe me, ladies and gentlemen, the physical shape of the act, the mistreated body, the disorder in the room, all the so-called evidence—these are entirely secondary details, a supplement, to be precise, to the real crime, a forensic formality, a tip of the hat by the criminal toward the authorities, nothing more. The real crime is always committed in the soul."[82]

Thus, although the magistrate is aware that "[h]owever I strained my imagination, my intuition, my logic, the neck remained a neck, and whiteness remained whiteness, with the obstinacy characteristic of lifeless objects,"[83] he pursues a totally different hypothesis and tries to justify it not by checking it against the world but by confirming that a belief coheres with other beliefs. In other words: his *intellect* imposes a plot on the "facts" so that his narrative accounts for the hypothetical murder of the father by the son. Indeed, his decision to "activate" his cerebral or "official" character as investigating magistrate, as I suggested above, marks a turning point in the affective economy of the story. This is so not only because in this way he increases the "power of action" on his body but also because this second part of the story suggests the affective side of reason, showing how the magistrate's reason interact with his affects to attain his goal: feeling too shamed and "ridiculed," he needs to rationally conceive an effective vengeance. This is what I meant earlier when I asserted that the magistrate's intellect is a "high form of feeling," in Susanne Langer's sense. Indeed, Gombrowicz's move draws attention to a material, affective dimension often toned down from accounts of the functioning of human reason. Reason and affect do not appear in this story as two separate realms. On the contrary, Gombrowicz effectively suggests the dependence of reason on affect and emotions.

In his *Diary* Gombrowicz reflects on the Eastern European conception of the subject that, in his view, radically differs from the West European understanding of the subject. Gombrowicz claims: "In spite of everything, the West lives with a vision of isolated man and absolute values. We, on the other hand, begin to see the formula: man plus man, man multiplied by man...." He also clarifies that this conception should "in no way be connected with any kind of collectivism," which, following Martin Buber, he defines "as a function of the masses but really subordinates it to such abstractions as social class, state, nation, and race." He claims further:

> It will be on the corpses of these worldviews that the third vision of man will be born: man in relation to another man, a concrete man, I in relation to you and him.... Man through man. Man in relation to man. Man created by man. Man strengthened by man [...] To us, sons of the East, the problem of individual conscience is beginning to melt in....[84]

Certainly, Gombrowicz is suggesting in this story a new conception of the self and a strong potential resonance with affect/emotion (Langer's feeling).

Notes

1 Pál Pelbart and Egert, "Sharing Distance," 242.
2 Ibid.
3 Ibid.
4 Ibid., 243.
5 Rugoff, "Man of the Crowd," 76.
6 Maerkle, "Mik."
7 Ibid.
8 Ngai, Ugly Feelings.
9 Berlant, Cruel Optimism.
10 Ahmed, "Affective Economies," 117–39; Ahmed, *Cultural*.
11 Sedgwick & Frank, eds., *Shame and Its Sisters*; Tomkins, *Exploring Affect*.
12 Sedgwick, Touching Feeling.
13 Damasio, *Feeling*; Damasio, *Looking*.
14 Deleuze and Guattari, *Plateaus*; Deleuze, *Essays Critical*.
15 Massumi. "Autonomy of Affect," 23–45.
16 Deleuze and Guattari, *A Thousand Plateaus*, xvi.
17 Ibid., xvi.
18 Wetherell, 355.
19 Zerilli, 262.
20 Massumi. "Autonomy of Affect," 27.
21 Ibid., 28.
22 Wetherell, 354. Ruth Leys clarifies this phenomenon in the following terms: "There is a gap between the subject's affect and its cognition or appraisal of the affective situation or object, such that cognition or thinking comes 'too late' for reasons, intentions, beliefs, and meanings to play the role in action and behavior usually accorded to them. The result is that action and behavior are held to be determined by affective dispositions that are independent of consciousness and the mind's control." (Leys, 443)
23 Papoulias and Callard, "Biology's Gift," 29–56; Leys, 434–72; Wetherell, 354; Zerilli, 262.
24 Wetherell, 355.
25 Langer, *Mind*, I, 23.

26 Ibid., 21.
27 Ibid., 22.
28 Ibid., 57.
29 As John Cromby asserts, feelings provide "directions" that "resist some interpretations and promote others." A feeling of pleasure, for example, as Cromby claims, is not a feeling of anxiety. Hence, meaning is never only linguistic. Cromby, *Feeling Bodies*.
30 Ahmed, *Cultural*, 4.
31 Gombrowicz, *Bacacay*, 35.
32 Ibid., 36.
33 Ibid.
34 Ibid., 37.
35 Kristeva, 71.
36 Gombrowicz, *Bacacay*, 38.
37 We use here the term "affectif" as defined by Robert Seyfert as "the entirety of all heterogeneous bodies involved in the emergence of an affect"– "an assemblage of heterogeneous elements...[including] the nature of the connection that can exist between these...elements." Seyfert, "Beyond Personal," 33.
38 Gombrowicz, *Bacacay*, 38.
39 Ibid., 39.
40 Ibid., 37–38.
41 Ibid., 38.
42 Ngai, 3.
43 Ibid., 353–54.
44 Nussbaum, *Hiding from Humanity*, 204–5.
45 Gombrowicz, *Bacacay*, 39.
46 Ibid., 40.
47 Ibid.
48 The magistrate claims: "I was so ashamed all of a sudden that even today I blush at the thought of that embarrassment." Ibid., 42.
49 In his recalling of the rituals the family had his perform, the magistrate shows some "family resemblance" with Dostoyevsky's "mouse-man" wallowing in a self-poisoning preoccupation with the past as it appears in *Notes from the Underground*. For a study of a relationship between Gombrowicz and Dostoevsky, see Spektor, "Between Mourning," 186–207.
50 Hartling and Luchetta, "Humiliation," 259–78.
51 Gombrowicz, *Bakakaj*, 38.
52 Gombrowicz, *Bacacay*, 44–45. Italics are mine.
53 Nussbaum, 205.
54 About a connection between shame and theatricality, see Stanislavski, *Creating a Role*.
55 Gombrowicz, *Bacacay*, 45.
56 This focus on appearances explains why, for many critics, embarrassment is "shallow": it is so, according to those critics, because, as opposed to shame, one does not perceive one's action as revealing anything about who one is. See Deonna et al., *Defense of Shame*, 115.
57 Michael Goddard discusses Gombrowicz's use of the image of theatre, establishing an opposition between theatre and performance. He claims: "To say that Gombrowicz's account of form is theatrical is therefore to express its dynamism as expressive of the tendency for both aesthetic and everyday performances to become captured or frozen in formal, theatrical arrangements, while its performativity would be the reverse tendency for static forms to be destabilized by unpredictable performances." Goddard, 68.

58 Gombrowicz, *Bacacay*, 37.

59 Ibid., 37–8.

60 Ibid., 41.

61 For a study of paranoia in this story within Sedgwick's framework, see Warkocki, "Zbrodnia inkorporowana," 237–58.

62 Gombrowicz, *Bacacay*, 45.

63 Ibid., 35.

64 Ibid., 41.

65 Spinoza, *Ethics*, 85.

66 Gombrowicz, *Bacacay*, 45–46.

67 Ibid., 46.

68 Reading Gombrowicz's work in a Lacanian context, Hanjo Berressem claims that the subject's shame stems from his inferiority relation to the symbolic order that has been imposed on him. The ego is ashamed of its submission under any cultural law. Berressem, 113.

69 Sedgwick, *Touching*, 35–65.

70 Recent studies of shame include Probyn, *Blush*; Deonna et al., *In Defense of Shame*; Hutchinson, *Shame and Philosophy*; and Velleman, "Genesis of Shame," 27–52.

71 The transformative capacities of shame are, in my view, absent in the magistrate's character. They do play a role in "Lawyer Kraykowski's Dancer," where shame "sharpens" the narrator's sense of individuality. See Warkocki, "What a Shame!" 185–201.

72 Gombrowicz, *Bacacay*, 52.

73 Sartre calls this my "being-for-Others," a form of self-consciousness that arises from recognizing that there are other subjects in the world who can perceive me. About the relationship between Gombrowicz and Sartre, see Karst, *Problem of the Other*; Franczak, *Rzecz o nierzeczywistości*; Gall, *Performativer Humanismus*.

74 Gombrowicz, *Bacacay*, 42.

75 Ibid., 57.

76 Freud, *Dostoyevsky*, XXI, 183.

77 Freud, *Dostoyevsky*, 189.

78 As Olaf Kühl claims, "the son of the departed confesses under the pressure of the investigator, but he does not confess the strangling of his father, his confessing comes in a cryptic, ambiguous way. He says: 'I went for a drive' ('pojechałem'). It is the investigator who forces this uttering to mean 'I killed my father.' The Polish phrase 'jazda na całego' (at full speed) in the original adds the connotation of temporary insanity, so that 'pojechałem' can be taken by the investigator as the confession of murder." Olaf Kühl "Translating the Secret."

79 Jarzębski, *Gra w Gombrowicza*, 396.

80 Something similar occurs in "Lawyer Kraykowski's Dancer," where the attorney is presented in terms of the traditional model of an autonomous self while the narrator is inscribed in an alternative model of the self that allows for in-betweenness and affect. For an interpretation of the narrator as representing an "ontologically intertwined" conception of the individual, see Paloff, *Lost in the Shadow*, 250–54.

81 Susanne Langer claims: "the wide discrepancy between reason and feeling may be unreal; it is not improbable that intellect is a high form of feeling – a specialised, intensive feeling about intuitions." Langer, 149.

82 Gombrowicz, *Bacacay*, 61.

83 Ibid., 65.

84 Gombrowicz, *Diary*, 25.

Part III
The Political Gombrowicz

13 Gombrowicz's Wild Youth

The "Ferdydurkean Individual" Fades Away

Jerzy Jarzębski

In 1937, the Rój Publishing House issued the first edition of *Ferdydurke*, evoking strong positive and negative emotions among critics and readers alike. Those with a positive attitude soon treated the novel as a treasury of quotes to interact with and to laugh at the defects of the human world. Soon after the war, Jarosław Iwaszkiewicz's daughters called themselves "Ferdydurkean fans" and worshiped "God Gombrowicz" as the patron of "true intelligence."[1] In their eyes, the creator of the "Ferdydurkean individual" was probably not very complicated, just a writer gifted with more brilliance and sharpness in his polemics, sense of absurd humor, and sense of Form than other people possessed, a Form that Gombrowicz could break and destroy with parody and put together again. His concept of the individual was, however, marked with something disturbing from the start. In *Wspomnienia polskie* (Polish Memories), Gombrowicz revealed a characteristic that he shared with his entire generation. Like other Poles early in the century, he was already freed from the nineteenth-century stylistics of patriotic stereotypes. As Gombrowicz wrote, "their sensitivity protected itself with cynicism, and they preferred making jokes to making speeches."[2]

Kazimierz Wyka pointed to the need for mockery which, together with tragedy, was to give birth to a true, valuable realism, interestingly, giving as an example Gombrowicz's *Ferdydurke*.[3] If not for its contradiction of the Socialist-Realist standards, Gombrowicz's novel would have become popular after World War II as an uncompromising mockery of the social reality of the Second Polish Republic, exposing the followers of such or another idea as buffoons, and presenting funny juxtapositions of the ideology of modernism with anachronisms then still prevalent in Poland. By 1950, the imposition of Socialist Realism absolutely precluded this possibility. What this could have looked like is shown in *Jezioro Bodeńskie* (Lake Constance), published in 1946 by Stanisław Dygat who clearly wrote his novel under the influence of various elements of Gombrowicz's work, notably the notion of Form. Dygat even shaped some of the scenes of his novel, such as the ridiculous presentation of Poland at the end of the book, following the model of *Ferdydurke*. If, however, Dygat blames contradictions and ridicule of Poles principally on national literature,

Gombrowicz instead focuses on immature dreams that undermine the adopted or imposed Form. In both cases, this Form is tortured, although Gombrowicz makes this a more intimate and personal act whereas Dygat makes the disgrace very broad, on a social spectrum, and has it carefully planned by the protagonist. One thing is certainly common to both writers: the carnival-like loud laughter, laughter at pressures tormenting the individual, at masks deforming faces that the individual must wear.

The "Ferdydurkean individual," in this approach, is principally perceived as a grotesque figure with various ridicules imposed by society. During the "Polish October,"[4] when Socialist Realism was discredited once and for all, critics, mocked by Gombrowicz, finally viewed his protagonist as a caricature referring either to the Poles as a nation, or to the system of social education in the Second Polish Republic or in totalitarian systems. Therefore, the "Ferdydurkean individual" had a great satirical potential but was free of Gombrowicz's darkness, void, and terror; namely, all that related him to the existentialists' subjectivity and made him a cousin of Roquentin, the protagonist of Jean-Paul Sartre's *Nausea*.[5] Critics dealing with Gombrowicz's complete works claimed that *Ferdydurke* was "bright," whereas darkness characterized the writer's post-war works. A number of readers liked Gombrowicz's pre-war works which they admired for their "conquering force" or their "power of laughter," whereas the post-war works disappointed them. The latter they perceived as difficult, grim, forced, and confined by perversion intertwined with cruelty. Only recently have opinions changed on this issue[6]—although one must admit that there is some truth to the differentiation between the "bright" and "dark" side of works written in different periods of Gombrowicz's life.

When did Gombrowicz's fear really begin? If one believes *Polish Memories*, it was before World War I and the source of the fear lay in the sense of unreality. Gombrowicz refers to "the Asiatic destitution that was consuming us from below," compared to which "our entire culture was a flower pinned to a peasant's sheepskin coat." He added that

> the Poland that was born out of the First World War was a land of paralyzed people. The most vital elements were condemned to provisionality and vegetativeness. Everything was put off from one day to the next; everyone was temporizing till the world settled down, the state was consolidated, and there appeared some room for maneuver.[7]

Would that mean Gombrowicz's fear was a "local" feeling, related to the condition of the state in which he was living? Gombrowicz seems to me more sensitive to the horror being born within humanity. It may be argued that Gombrowicz expressed his fears for the first time before *Ferdydurke* in the short-story "The Brief Memoir of Jakub Czarniecki"

("Krótkim pamiętniku Jakuba Czarnieckiego") contained in the volume *Memoir from Adolescence (Pamiętnika z okresu dojrzewania)*. There, the handsome and colorful cavalry soldier Kacperski is wounded on a battlefield, losing both of his legs and having his abdomen torn, which causes him to burst into high-pitched laughter that breaks the accepted decorum. Clearly, the laughter appears as a sign that social pedagogy from the interwar period hides something from its disciples; one cannot believe in the harmony and bland aesthetics of the world it presents when the horror is just a step away. Kacperski is not, however, responsible for the world turning bloodily grotesque. He was born in the still stable and safe late nineteenth century, so the view of his own body torn into pieces goes beyond his limits of comprehension, although this would soon become part of the everyday experience of his colleagues in the trenches during World War I.

The first change in the next generation would be in the area of interpersonal relations. Gombrowicz quite quickly noticed the emergence of a totalitarian individual as a social phenomenon. In this respect, it is important to mention here that in the first version of the early chapters of *Ferdydurke*, printed in the journal *Skamander*, there is a fragment about Pietrasiński and Piekosiński, two former friends of the protagonist, one of whom became the "Führer" of some small political party, while the other became his follower.[8] The author ironically pointed to the benefits they both had: one became God, while the other became God's acolyte. The story about Pietrasiński and Piekosiński was ultimately removed from the novel, perhaps because it disrupted the work's logic and introduced an element of *ad hoc* political satire.

In the spring of 1938, Gombrowicz traveled to Italy accompanied by a third-rate writer, a certain Kozłowski who used the pen name Brochwicz. It seems that the trip across this fascist state gave Gombrowicz a real scare. First, because he rightly assumed Brochwicz was a German agent, and next because he perceived Mussolini's Italy as a country suffering from a disease of contradictions:

> that pure, pellucid Latin climate with its ancient aroma, a separate discipline unto itself, swept over me, and I soaked it in through every pore. But in that air and against that noble landscape there was also something turbid and monstrous, a specter as if from a nightmare. The newspapers carried shrill praise of the Berlin-Rome Axis, and the stench of blackmail and betrayal—for me, the conspiracy between Italy and Germany meant the betrayal of Europe—dominated the streets, Mussolini's speeches, the fascists' songs, and even the soldier games played by the brats in front of the Villa Borghese.[9]

But the scene I believe to be of major importance when tracing Gombrowicz's awareness of the emergence of a totalitarian individual occurred slightly later, during his stay in Venice. On the way, he met some airmen traveling to Venice.

> "Very well, but what if il Duce ordered you to bomb all this?" With a sweeping gesture I took in the church, the palace, the Procuratorium.
>
> "Then not one stone would be left on a stone," replied the oldest of them, who was maybe twenty-five, in his broken French. This answer didn't surprise me. It was to be expected. But I was surprised at the joy with which he spoke—his eyes shone, and he virtually proclaimed it to me; and on his friends' faces, when they found out what was being said, I also read an unconcealed satisfaction. What were they so pleased about? Was it not that they felt themselves to be creators of history? The past had become less important than the future, and it could be destroyed.
>
> That week in Venice was onerous, poisoned with some savage element that seeped into the calm of the Renaissance and the Gothic.[10]

This scene is perhaps the most relevant one in the trip because if anything really bothered Gombrowicz in Venice, it was not the Renaissance and the Gothic buildings but the people who lived among them. The protagonists of this event are young boys and there is certainly a motive of sexual attraction on the part of the writer. He wrote several times about the new style adopted by young people in 1930s in Poland, about their unprecedented sharpness, wildness, and erotic freedom. Interestingly, the wildness alluded to in *Polish Memories* in the scene from Venice is initially perceived positively by the author. In his conversation with the aviators, however, the wildness manifests itself in its full destructive power. Furthermore, Gombrowicz made it clear that such wildness was imposed on the youth by ideological leaders. The behavior of fascist youth emerges because outer forces cannot buffer them from the push and pull of wildness.[11] The aviators do not perceive this wildness as a limitation of freedom but as an opportunity to destroy the old world and build a new one according to new rules. For them, this means another step in human "evolution," where evil — be it an external factor in the form of an order or generated as a distillate of collective emotions — becomes easy to commit, "innocent," taking a nearly "positive" form since il Duce "is building a better future for Italy" and this requires no explanation of its relationship to the destructive air raid. The young aviators ready to destroy the historic town are otherwise nice boys who travel to visit their families. They speak French poorly, which is significant because France is the cradle of rational and democratic Europe, and although they apparently return to the Roman tradition, they undoubtedly treat it instrumentally, as a set of symbols deprived of true content.

Let us go back to *Ferdydurke*. Its protagonists have not yet experienced initiation into the "wild youth," or even just aggressive youth. The school boys in *Ferdydurke* would prefer to be adults than cultivate the characteristics of this new type of youth. Even those closest to the new generation, such as Zuta and Kopyrda, resemble images taken from a fashion magazine rather than some brochure encouraging young people to abandon politeness in the name of rebellion. But what about the rest of the students? Gombrowicz perceives them as deeply childish, falling for their teachers' and parents' infantilizing strategies. What about the farmhands that also appear in *Ferdydurke*? These, in turn, are entirely shaped by the anachronistic nobility manor model of social hierarchy; their rebellion at the end of the novel thus resembles some nineteenth-century peasant slaughter rather than a contemporary youth revolution. Thus, the "Ferdydurkean individual" is incapacitated by Form at all levels of social existence and deprived of sovereignty regardless of the ideals he preaches. The narrator, however, seems to suggest that he is also a victim of this system (it cannot be avoided), but at least he can tell his story in such a way as, through a particular narrative cause-effect logic, to achieve self-knowledge and some rudiments of self-determination. In this way, he can also turn over the chessboard and scatter the pawns. But what about the reader? The reader must also become a "Ferdydurkean individual"; however, if she understands the rules of the game, identifies with the author, and escapes from Form, she can also laugh at herself and her adventures. As suggested earlier, *Ferdydurke* may be regarded as a "bright" work in the sense that although it describes a world of juxtapositions between features of modernity and anachronisms, its fictional world is more or less understandable to the reader as coherent and deriving from a single traditional root. Therefore, this fictional world can be controlled intellectually and the threats it carries can be disarmed.

Gombrowicz was thirty-four years old when his perception of the world changed. If one looks for the moment of a passing "shadow" in his biography, it was perhaps during his conversation with the Italian aviators at St. Mark's Square in Venice. Or perhaps it was while observing a party of young people in a villa in the Warsaw Okęcie district ("I had never encountered anything like this initiation into fun, vodka, and extravagance").[12] The outstandingly sensitive writer immediately noticed the common denominator of these two phenomena, namely the "'militarization' of young ladies' ways." Gombrowicz asserts:

It was the style of the young people from the military schools, the style of the military life. This unruliness amongst minors, which so scandalized their elders, had at the time—at least in the closing years of the period—its own dramatic meaning: war. Its shadow lay on everything; its ominous proximity whispered that life should be enjoyed while it could be, before it was overly mixed with death.[13]

Thus, Gombrowicz's generation had no immediate connection to the youth of the 1930s, as previously signaled by the carnival laughter heard in *Ferdydurke*. Gombrowicz tried to understand the difference, to grasp the mechanisms needed to instill in these young people the cruelty of war, totalitarian ideologies, and the worship of leaders. This is largely the theme to which Gombrowicz's post-war works have been devoted. While the "Ferdydurkean individual" was at most an elderly man who, similar to the two protagonists in *Pornografia*, watches young people with fascination and tries to work with them, Gombrowicz seems to regard the young members of the new generation as if they were creatures of another race and different nature. In any case, this collision happened just once in Gombrowicz's life and had an unusual revelatory power. It disclosed to him the fundamental untranslatability of generational experiences as well as how the differences among generations bring about large-scale cultural transformations. This is a good time to take a closer look at *Opętani* (*Possessed*), a slightly underestimated novel that is usually left aside when discussing Gombrowicz's works.

Killing a Squirrel

I believe Gombrowicz knew perfectly well that he was writing *Possessed* on the eve of the war that would engage a new type of individual which was emerging in Europe at the time, what Gombrowicz referred to as "wild youth." His entire novel is an attempt to describe this new individual, which is not mentioned openly but is clear when one compares *Possessed* with Gombrowicz's later works.

> "Can you not read, young man?" asked the whey-faced passenger, adjusting his pince-nez as he spoke. "Are you ignorant of the fact that it is forbidden to lean out of the window?"
>
> The train had just left Lublin.
>
> "What's the next station, sir?" the young man wanted to know as he turned from the window.
>
> "I believe I asked you a question," huffed the busybody with the protruding eyes, spiky hair, and gold chain slung across his paunch. "Do you not think it behoves you first of all to give me an answer by stating whether or not you are aware that it is forbidden to lean out of the window of a train in motion?"
>
> "Oh, sorry," the young man muttered carelessly.[14]

This is how *Possessed* begins, with the clash between an elderly "formal individual" and a young tennis coach who does not even care to pick the quarrel. The attacker is the impossible councilor Szymczyk who likes to represent authority. He could have even succeeded here if the young man had wished to snarl something back so as to continue this everlasting dispute between "teacher" and "student." Since I became fascinated a few years ago with the motif of the "wild youth," every appearance of this social group seems significant to me. Coach Walczak seems a polite boy who willingly succumbs to the authoritarian councilor. He does not possess the fighting spirit that makes young men confront older ones, snarl back or insult them. The scene on the train quite rightly described the relation between the young and the old in interwar society. The old have an unquestionable advantage here, the advantage rooted in a long patriarchal tradition. Gombrowicz's young Poles are not "born revolutionaries," as it was once believed in Europe, but rather resemble Ignacy obeying his father in *Trans-Atlantyk* (of course, until Gonzalo instigates insubordination).

Yet, there are wicked things in *Possessed*. Maja and Leszczuk must grow up with them, find inspiration in one another, and see the "similarity" between themselves. Yet, where does this similarity reside? Its first manifestation was at the very beginning of the novel, when Walczak/ Leszczuk watches Maja sleeping on the train and notices how she is sleeping, laying in the most extraordinary, absurd posture, just like he used to do. All the other instances where this scandalous similarity appears may be accounted for in at least three different ways. First, we may read it as a signal of a feeling that is being born between them despite the class differences that were still very vivid in Polish society at the time. Leszczuk is a simple peasant boy while Maja comes from a landowner family. Although impoverished and forced to turn their manor into a pension, Maja's family is still not deprived of claims, and certainly not of the sense of superiority over people who were liberated from serfdom merely some seventy years earlier.

Second, we may suspect an intervention of "metaphysical Evil," infecting both young people and forcing them into sinful cooperation. *Possessed* is just as much a detective story as it is a *quasi*-gothic "ghost story" as Maria Janion has it. The fictional world of the gothic novel relies heavily on the interference of the supernatural, and in this fictional world, the idea of evil plays an important role. Thus, in a first approach to this novel, the reader's awareness that she is reading a gothic novel would probably incline her to take the "similarity" between the protagonists as a marking of evil. But *Possessed* does not restrict itself to a gothic story. It also clearly contains a socio-political motif and a vision of a new generation that might do terrifying things because of the dangerous split into authors of the actions and the actual doers.

Third, we may interpret it as a reflection of social processes that lead to the elimination of class differences and, as a result, to the emergence of a modern society. This new modern society is more homogenous and therefore susceptible to a totalitarian organization. The traditional class structure is replaced with a new political order and, as a consequence, society ends up divided according to membership in parties and factions.

In such a society, individuals entirely identify with their leaders' programs, agreeing to follow even the most absurd and criminal order. Gombrowicz seems to be rather ambivalent in terms of privileging any of these three possible interpretations. Furthermore, these aspects may also be seen in *Pornografia*.

Although *Pornografia* clearly derives from *Possessed*, the latter novel clarifies the genre of the earlier work. In *Pornografia*, one can no longer speak of a "Gothic novel" although there is undoubtedly some sort of "devilishness" in it which is presented as an unconscious and spontaneous force. It is under this force that noble Amelia gets involved in the struggle against a young village thief, getting impaled on a knife. Then, at the hour of her death, she prefers the atheist Fryderyk as a partner in interpersonal communication over the power of the cross as a symbol of Christianity and spiritual support. Yet the moment of utmost horror is when Witold and Fryderyk watch Karol's and Henia's feet stomping on an earthworm that writhes in agony. This makes Witold and Fryderyk speechless, while the two "wild ones" keep chattering as if there is no sin in their deed.

What are the fundamental differences between *Pornografia* and *Possessed*? One important difference is that in the world presented in *Possessed*, there is no place for Gombrowicz who had the central position in all his other novels. Indeed, there is Leszczuk, who, as a country boy in a city, we may claim represents Gombrowicz to some extent. Yet the class difference between both of them and Leszczuk's lack of education do not allow for such an identification. Maja, on the other hand, appears better suited to play the role usually played by Gombrowicz. She is, however, a woman and thus a person destined to a subordinate role in the patriarchal world of *Possessed*, or at least to have a different position in the social structure where the author situates the plot. Thus, Gombrowicz's point of view either does not exist in *Possessed* or is "blurred," divided into both protagonists. The situation is somewhat similar to *Ivona, Princess of Burgundia* (*Iwona, księżniczka Burgunda*), published a year before *Possessed*, where both Ivona and Prince Philip rebel against the inflexible Form of the court. In this play Gombrowicz had both of his *alter egos* fail: Ivona was choked by the court Form, embodied in a crucian carp, while Philip surrendered to the court Form ending in ostensible mourning. Gombrowicz seems to be paralyzed by his not fully defined being and by his double existence in the two alter egos. The Polish language has a specific word for that: "osłupiały" (stunned and petrified), which includes both the sense of helplessness and the corresponding image of immobilization, the incapacity to react.

In Gombrowicz's works, this state of stunned immobilization is generally evoked by an act of cruelty directed to a helpless and non-understanding creature, particularly an animal. Such a condition is at the same time the moment of discovering oneself as a potential victim, who tries to understand the violator, and pain, such pain perceived as a scandal of life. It may also involve discovering oneself as the perpetrator. Gombrowicz's protagonists play all those roles, but with a special function reserved for the "wild ones," who, to some extent, due to their poor self-awareness, are the ones to whom the future will belong. Indeed a particularly vivid scene of cruelty with the involvement of the "wild ones" takes place in *Possessed*

In the evening the company from Połyka goes for a night stroll in the woods. Suddenly, they notice a squirrel that Kholawitski tries to kill by shooting it with his Browning, but he misses. This is certainly to restore his masculinity, which had been put at risk by the allegation of Maja's betrayal, and perhaps is also a test of how serious the alliance established by the duke's secretary with the dark forces truly is. Walchak, who loves animals, climbs the tree to catch and save the animal. But his cuddling of the squirrel suddenly ends in an unexpected manner:

> "Could he kill this squirrel?" she wondered. "With lips like that..."
>
> Walchak, feeling her eyes on him, wanted to put down the animal and run. He was irresistibly drawn to her, to the lovely face suffused with pale moonlight, the jet-black hair, the slender hands—and at the same time he felt an overpowering desire to flee. What did she want with him now?
>
> She had drawn him away from the others. "Could you kill this squirrel" she asked him.
>
> "What—for no reason?"
>
> "If I asked you to?"
>
> "Why?"
>
> "I bet my friend that if I asked you to you'd kill it..."
>
> She was looking him straight in the eye and he heard her laugh—a nervous, frustrated, cruel laugh that for a moment exposed a row of gleaming teeth.
>
> "All right?" she murmured, as if to confirm an understanding arrived at.
>
> He echoed her laugh and, without thinking, threw the animal as hard as he could again the trunk of the tree. It gave a sharp squeal before curling painfully into a ball.
>
> Maya stood there, breathing hard, as the others came running up.
>
> "What a brutal thing to do!" protested Christine. "What happened?"
>
> "It bit me," Walchak answered vaguely.
>
> The squirrel's eyes clouded over and it lay still. They all saw it die; only Maya could not take her eyes off Walchak.
>
> "Little pest!" spat Kholawitski, turning the corpse over with his foot.

Suddenly Maya burst into tears, and before anyone could react she went rushing off into the trees. Walchak, who had been standing motionless with his arms hanging at his sides, bounded after her and disappeared in the shadows. Kholawitski, hurling himself in pursuit, tripped over a root and fell; he got smartly to his feet and ran on, taking enormous strides and shouting, "Stop! Stop!"

Walchak caught up with Maya after a long chase. Seizing her by the shoulders, he pushed her violently against a tree. Then he staggered up to her again and hurled her to the ground. She raised herself on one knee and stared at him wild-eyed, while he glared back as if seeing her for the first time.

He lifted her chin. "So that's the real you..."

She was convinced he was going to kill her as he had killed the squirrel. Now she was on the receiving end of his cruelty. She felt his fingers tighten round her neck, saw his pupils contract. So that's what you are!' she murmured, as if unable to believe her eyes.

He hit her – hard. Maya, struggling to free herself, bit his arm. Enraged, he flung her from him brutally and then leapt on her where she lay. They rolled on the mossy ground, raining blows on each other, fighting like wildcats.[15]

So here we have "wildness" called by its name. Principally, Gombrowicz excludes Kholawitski from this circle of "wildness" as he is simply evil, but the situation is too much for him because he cannot establish a relation with the young. They, in turn, behave rather strangely. Maja first pities the animal, but ultimately, wishing to reveal the alleged relationship of Walchak with the devil, makes the boy kill the vulnerable animal. Similarly, Walchak rescues the squirrel because he loves animals but easily gives in to the dark inspiration and throws it against a tree. Thus, there is no clear source of evil: there are just two individuals who create it in the "interpersonal space," not without a hint of eroticism. Knowing that this toxic relationship can destroy them, Maja and Walchak begin to openly hate one another. Hence, their panicked escape from the site ended with the entirely wild fight between them.

Walchak does not kill a fairy-tale dragon, but a weak, vulnerable animal that everyone except for demon Kholawitski wishes to save. And the salvation, apparently pursued previously against the will of the secretary, requires unusual swiftness and courage from Walchak, but is socially profitable, having the effect of his easily achieved general acceptance because of the rescue. Thus, the slogan "one must protect delicate animals against the aggression of brutes" leaves the dark side of the relation between Maja and Walchak unclarified. The author must have had in mind the helpless, although slightly ironic question posed by the main protagonist of the short story "The Brief Memoir of Jakub Czarniecki" ("Krótkim pamiętniku Jakuba Czarnieckiego") regarding the reason why our care and sensitivity should be addressed at swallows and not, for example, frogs. It is more difficult to imagine a willingness to help a battered bat because such willingness would have to accommodate acceptance of a dark animal many people find repulsive. Yet such a feeling, with all its ambivalence, would perhaps help the young protagonists to more easily identify their dark desires and communicate. In opposition to this, the sentiment for the squirrel was quite useless from this point of view because it was clearly positive. But these two young people decided to violate this emotional stereotype and direct their aggression against the little squirrel. This scene reveals the dramatic situation of the "wild generation." These young people already know that the new social situation destines them to cooperate with one another, but they are desperate and cannot communicate and build some common project. They are actually destined to become criminals, as this provides the strongest bond and proves to be the most effective way to communicate. In the totalitarian versions, language will be provided to the "wild ones" by the ideology imposed by the system. Followers of Hitler or Stalin did not dare to blink at even the most repulsive element of the program announced by their regimes, as if it were sanctified by their "leader."

In the "Warsaw" part of the novel, Gombrowicz chooses very characteristic social places and areas of activity for his protagonists. For Maja, he chooses paid services to businessmen and diplomats as a "dame de compagnie" (escort), which did not seem to be prostitution but could easily be transformed into it, and clearly damaged the maiden's reputation. Walchak was to deal with sports, particularly tennis, which was becoming more democratic at the time. But Walchak made his career owing to a peculiar trick of reducing racket string tension, which was *foul* play. Sport and facilitated social life are symbols of the new era, but symbols that allow critical assessment and are perceived as new customs destructive of traditional order and morality.

As can be easily seen from reading *Kronos* and other testimonies, Gombrowicz was certainly not a moralist, he functioned at the margin of the "wild youth" circles presented in his literary works and memoirs. At the same time, he was acutely sensitive to his contemporary world. He thus very painfully felt the difference that separated him from the generation of the "wild ones," although he could still afford blasphemy against the traditional order. Hence, probably, his peculiar position in *Possessed*: partly inside, partly outside of the story. The protagonists of *Possessed* thus surrender, denouncing their possession and giving in, rather unexpectedly, to the calming interpretation of the events. We would like to ask what happened to the worrying signs of "wildness," how do we explain blackening lips, convulsions of a towel, and so on. But the formula of the popular gothic genre prevails in *Possessed*, where all mysteries seem to be rather carelessly explained as who would scare the poor cooks with metaphysical Evil.

What Was Gombrowicz Talking about at Teatro del Pueblo?

On August 28, 1940, Gombrowicz, invited by Director Leónidas Barletta, delivered a lecture at Buenos Aires' Teatro del Pueblo entitled "Doświadczenia i problemy Europy najmniej znanej" (Experiences and Problems of the Least Known Europe). Prior to the lecture, the speaker was interviewed by *Kurier Polski*,[16] a Polish newspaper based in Argentina. The moment when the lecture was to be delivered, two months after the surrender of France and the Nazi army entering Paris, is so important that the writer's message to the Argentinians inevitably gained significance. The more so because the lecture caused a scandal among the Poles in Argentina and resulted in the long-term ostracism Gombrowicz faced in Polish circles abroad.[17] What happened at the theatre hall on Corrientes Street? Gombrowicz gave a rather playful account, pointing out that he appeared at the lecture with a "girl from ballet circles" with a deep neckline, who occupied a theatre box that was reserved for him. It was only the emotional reaction of local Poles that made him aware something unexpected had happened. Namely, representatives of the Ukrainian and Jewish minorities used the lecture to attack Poland. His compatriots' call to him to "do something" found him completely incapable of responding: his poor Spanish did not allow him to engage in a linguistic battle against the locals. Something must have happened in the lecture to prompt the attackers to dare to speak out, to associate the content of the lecture with their aggressive approach to the Poles. What was it then that Gombrowicz spoke about to the Argentinians? Let us have a look at the interview:

> I have decided ... to talk about what has recently been formed and fermented in the Polish psyche, and generally in the psyche of the nations of Eastern Europe, lying between Bolshevism and Hitlerism. I have decided to speak sincerely because, notwithstanding the elementary duty to be sincere, the public is far too well informed, so any artificial embellishment of reality could not cause anything but disgust. I would like to point out that our recent culture is a very positive, dynamic phenomenon, making way towards new political forms, and such difficulties are a fertilizing factor. I have already given a number of lectures on Polish issues in the artistic circles here, and I'm convinced that the most discrediting thing concerning Poland in the eyes of the Argentinians is the belief that we are an anachronistic, backward nation, living in the past, and deprived of originality. It seems to me that the audience at Teatro del Pueblo deserves the discussion of a specific problem, but from the point of view of Polish culture. I have chosen the

theme of transformations and ferments of our psyche under the so-called "cultural regression" of recent times which is developing at high pace due to the war. These issues are rather difficult to grasp because they have not yet manifested in the official art and literature, but it seems to me that they open great perspectives for the future. I do not share the opinion of the pessimists who claim that "nothing has recently happened" in Poland; to the contrary, I think that the Poles had never experienced such a fertile period, that revolutionized so much the very nature of man, as recently. Only someone very superficial, who measures the spiritual life of a country by the number of books produced or concerts played, or finally the "level," can fail to appreciate the great tremors, experiences, and adventures we have been through in the last two decades.[18]

"Great tremors, experiences, adventures"? What can this be about? Certainly, the interwar period was not a time for the Poles to calmly lick their wounds after the end of World War I. Immediately after the surrender of Germany and the breakup of the Habsburg Empire, Poland had to defend its regained independence in the war against Soviet Russia. Gombrowicz, sixteen years old at the time, personally felt the public pressure to join the fight. Even youngsters like him were expected to register for the draft even if it meant falsifying their date of birth. In fact, the future writer perfectly understood he would not stand up to this war adventure, so he did not endeavor to be drafted, but he nevertheless experienced the draft psychologically.

Therefore, Gombrowicz, who had stood against traditional Polish patriotism since the early interwar period, would be speaking to the Argentinians about what he regarded as being modern in Poland — something that was dangerous because it was somewhat close to the foundation of social education in totalitarian systems. In Poland, at the time, there was the general belief in values related to patriotism and Catholic traditions, which Gombrowicz did not share. At the Teatro del Pueblo it seems that by rejecting various versions of an alleged Polish anachronism, Gombrowicz was trying to create a transition from that alleged anachronism to what was essentially modern in Poland. Although the model he chose revealed itself as something extremely dangerous, it was a new model of the individual, developed by the totalitarian systems that dominated contemporary Europe. According to this new model, the individual was capable of any crime and barbarism in the name of obedience to the leader and "collective truths." Many years after World War II, in West Berlin, Gombrowicz would say that the Germans who mercilessly murdered "enemies" and "sub-human" creatures were not monsters at all: the crime was the product of the community, not of individuals.[19]

In 1947, Gombrowicz wrote a preface for the Argentinian edition of *Ferdydurke*. He wrote:

> The protagonist of *Ferdydurke*, first infantilized by the dreaded Pimko, gets tangled into the process of mutual immaturity, a great, secret pleasure of humanity, its most sweet entertainment, and also its most terrible pain. What type of psychology does this process lead to? The characters from *Ferdydurke* have no ideals or gods, but only "immature myths," which may be defined as ideals adjusted to the level of the deepest, authentic reality of a human being (the myth of a farmhand, school-girl, aunt, etc.). They do not do what they really want, they do not feel according to their own nature; to the contrary, most of their feelings and acts are imposed on them. They keep pushing one another into attitudes, situations, feelings, or thoughts that are not what they themselves want, and only later adjust psychologically to what they happened to do, searching *ex post facto* for some justification and explanation ... always under the threat of the absurd and anarchy. Their two most characteristic features include, firstly, the fact that the complex web of mature forms of culture is just a pretext for them to establish relations among one another—and to enjoy and excite each other—and to keep each other tuned to their painful, immature games. The main thing for them is to dance; no matter what they dance. Secondly, they keep creating form, but never achieve it. They have no beliefs, ideals, convictions, skills, feelings; they simply fabricate them according to their needs and situational requirements. At every moment, they together create their own personalities—one creates another. ... Similar to someone fearing one's own nudity, we catch any clothing we can reach, even the most grotesque, and thus is this world created, made of clumsiness, insufficiency, frivolousness, and lack of responsibility, a world of subculture, of outdated, unsuccessful, deviated and impure forms, where our deepest lives take place.[20]

Let us point out that Gombrowicz's awareness in 1947 clearly differs from his awareness in 1937 when the first Polish edition of *Ferdydurke* appeared. After the end of World War II, the writer does not focus as much on the struggle against Form and the many repeated ineffective gestures of taking off masks, but on the fact that the contemporary world increasingly becomes a product of social masses that are sick with chronic immaturity, which causes them to create monster-like forms.

A decade later, in the 1950s, Gombrowicz would start working on his drama *Historia* (*History*) where the peculiar devilishness of contemporary history would involve complete incapacitation of individuals forcibly subjected to the voice of the community. And, interestingly, this enslavement would also refer to monarchs from the period just before

World War I, the monarchs who are also encouraged by Witold to take off their shoes (namely, to liberate themselves from the dictate of state mythology that forced them to defend the honor of the empire at all cost) but to no avail. Yet they at least refer to some tradition, usually of long standing. Mussolini, Stalin, or Hitler, as political *nouveau riches*, would have to construct such tradition from pieces of various national, historical, or even biological myths circulating in society, bouncing ideological slogans with their followers like tennis balls to create a certain mythological (un)reality with immense persuasive power. According to Gombrowicz, however, it would be a collective product and, regardless of the genius the acolytes ascribed to their Leader, it would be hard to say who actually produced it and who is to blame for the crimes of totalitarian systems.

The comment about grotesque costumes we are stuck in is, in turn, an introduction to the extended images of costume madness to be found almost twenty years later in *Operetta* (*Operetka*). There is nothing strange about it. He was writing *Operetta* for over a decade, it changed and matured, while in the first sketches from the 1950s it was not as much a play about the madness of history as in the final version, but rather a story about people becoming old and the peculiar relation between the old and the young. The earlier protagonists wish to erotically possess the young and control them at the same time, while the latter seem strangely comfortable with the situation because they have no distinct identity without it. Albertynka (Albertine) and Albert from *Operetta I*, dominated by the "old," are somehow remotely similar to the Italian aviators ready to bomb their heritage in the name of Mussolini and their own innocently criminal youth. It is not surprising that, in the background of this drama, the old world begins to rot and break down, which will only actually happen in the final version of the play.[21]

Seen from the point of view of Gombrowicz's experiences with the youth from the 1930s or from the standpoint of his reflections about the fall of the former world where they grew up, Gombrowicz's works seem surprisingly uniform. They appear devoted to the crisis of European culture as it emerged from the peculiar alienation that occurred between the brave plans to destroy the political and social system prior to the war and the social means launched by the reformers and destroyers to make their dreams come true. Fanatic youth raised in organizations operating within totalitarian regimes had a special role to play in this process. Gombrowicz described something similar in the scene about the shoemaker Pietrasiński and his follower, Piekosiński, which, as we commented earlier, was ultimately removed from the first edition of *Ferdydurke*.[22] Yet the effects of this true "wildness" that was growing in the 1930s, which Gombrowicz wrote about in *Polish Memories*,[23] were also visible in Poland, paradoxically giving it a modern, although terrifying trait in the context of approaching war, as it announced the inevitable cataclysm. While fighting against the image of anachronist and unpredictable Poles attacking tanks with cavalry lances, as mainly popularized by the Germans, Gombrowicz wanted to make them more modern in the eyes of the Argentinians, but without referring to the model of a new, pragmatic American civilization so popular in the inter-war Poland.[24] Its typical hero was a young engineer. In Gombrowicz's works, engineers (Młodziak in *Ferdydurke,* Ludwik in *Cosmos*), due to their mental limitations, are funny and helpless when faced with dark mysteries of human spirit and events from the social *theatrum*, which are beyond them.

As I have shown earlier, the modernity of Polish (and also European) youth was defined by Gombrowicz paradoxically through a regressive concept, "wildness." He needed this to explain the outstanding irratio-nality of war and the cruelty of a general slaughter that can be under-stood rather by reference to some atavistic properties of human nature than by reference to an intellect shaped according to the ideals of mod-ernism. The error of such a civilization seems to lie not as much in some aberrations of policy or ideology, as in the generation of some extremely dangerous Forms of interpersonal relations and interdependencies that permit actions deprived of the sense of personal responsibility for the individual's own actions. This responsibility is diluted in a certain col-lective (ir)responsibility that accepts every crime in the almost religious worship of the "leaders" who are given the completely uncontrolled right to decide about the shape of the entire world.[25]

The interview announcing Gombrowicz's lecture does not seem to particularly reveal the topic of the war in the text delivered at Teatro del Pueblo. Perhaps the author considered this topic as too overdone at the time. Yet everything he wrote later bears the traces of reflection over the war and the new Forms of power and social organization. The war and occupation play an important role in *The Marriage* and *Pornografia* as well as, in a different way, in *Operetta*. One can thus also believe that the lecture was somehow filled with these problems. This is confirmed by the fact that Gombrowicz was to speak of spiritual transformations of young people and the moral revolution. Significantly for our interpre-tation, in his *Diary 1953–1956* he also referred to a lecture delivered in the house of Antonio Berni, which apparently may be regarded as a precursor to the lecture at Teatro del Pueblo: "I described how the wave of barbarism that had crashed over Central and Eastern Europe could be used to revise the foundations of our culture."[26]

It has long been known that the erotic is closely linked to issues of politics and power; that the family structure, which is always an attempt to temper and institutionalize the erotic, has much in com-mon with the structure and order of the entire society. It thus comes as no surprise that those works by Gombrowicz written after the war always oscillate around the erotic and the family drama. It is so in

The Marriage, Trans-Atlantyk, Pornografia, Cosmos, History, and *Operetta*. As an equally important catalyst for the plot, these novels include the motif of the youth becoming "wild," or giving in to external control, which, in part, helps to justify the brutality of the actions in which they take part. This motif is also a way to describe the mysteries related to the implementation of drastic plans of events that came to reality in an unclear manner "among people." This explains, for example, how, inspired by Henryk, Władzio commits suicide in *The Marriage* and how the plot of *Trans-Atlantyk* nearly ends in a bloody manner. It also explains the bloody final of *Pornografia* as well as the death of Ludwik in *Cosmos*. Similarly, *History* and *Operetta* end with a disaster caused by history itself. Each of these plots produces a bloody end point in an eccentric manner, following a logic other than the traditional one, the logic of a world that has gotten rid of regulations until then in force. New rules appear in *The Marriage* through the evolution of power that mimics the processes occurring in the political history of the twentieth century.

In *Trans-Atlantyk*, the struggle between "Sonland" and Fatherland leads to a double crime, a struggle which, generally speaking, means replacing traditional values with an erotic fascination with youth. In *Pornografia* and *Cosmos*, the key event is the breakdown of the traditional Church and the replacement of the worship of God with the fascination of one individual with another. Hence, the drastic vision in *Cosmos* of breaking into a village church and destroying the majesty of the Holy Mass; the scene in *Pornografia* mentioned earlier between Fryderyk and dying Amelia who, barely touching the cross with her gaze, looks instead at him; or Leon's "black mass." *History* and *Operetta* similarly liberate themselves from the traditional order of power and the erotic with a new system of interpersonal relations emerging in its place. All these works may be interpreted according to the omnipresent phenomenon of social transformations. One thing appears obvious: all these drastic social transformations were announced in Gombrowicz's texts written in the 1940s and it may be reasonable to suspect that they derive from ideas discussed by Gombrowicz in his lecture at the Teatro del Pueblo.

Perceived as the creation of "wild youth," the world after World War II, as presented by Gombrowicz, looks slightly different from the way readers previously judged it. Let us take *Trans-Atlantyk* for example. Gombrowicz appears here as an apologist of "Sonland," a state that implies liberation from the concerns of the elderly, linked to sexual freedom and relaxed identity, whether sexual or national. Yet Gonzalo, who is to inspire this new (im)morality, is just as much the guru for these somewhat "wild" boys in the "estancia" as its creation and partly also its prisoner. Moreover, the patriotic terror that inspires the actions of Tomasz, who has decided to sacrifice his son for his Fatherland at the end of the novel, is not at all bloodier than Ignacy's boom-bam, with the difference being that the murder as performed by the "wild" and young boys is to be regarded as light and deprived of the intensity of horror surrounding Tomasz's plans to kill his son.

In his post-war works Gombrowicz seems to be fascinated with easy murder, committed without any dark atmosphere surrounding it or any announcements. As commented earlier, this is the way Ignacy is supposed to murder his father, Tomasz, in *Trans-Atlantyk*. This is also the way Władzio dies in *The Marriage*, a murder which is intellectually committed by Henryk but actually carried out by the hands of the victim, Władzio himself, while Henryk proclaims his own "innocence," although at the same time he subjects himself to the punishment for murder. The "innocence" of criminals in Gombrowicz's works has been very interestingly discussed by Stefan Chwin, who indicates that when referring to Hitler's crimes Gombrowicz understands them as emerging from an empowered "interpersonality."[27] Chwin also pointed out that, in Gombrowicz's view, it was not only Hitler's young acolytes who thought this way, sustaining him and making him the leader of the nation, but the German youth of the 1960s used to think in a similar manner. Disgusted with their own politeness and their role of "rational producers," this youth silently dreamt of the "repulsive beauty" of the SS officers because they were "fascinated with the Nazi 'beauty' of the vivid life of their parents' generation."[28] We thus still revolve around a conception of crime as a collective product of a "wild youth." In a sense, this "wildness" is represented by the Drunkard in *The Marriage*. Is it just by chance that in the preserved copy of the Spanish translation of *The Marriage*, with Gombrowicz's annotations on the margins, the author refers to the Drunkard as "Hitler's ambassador"? And who is the Drunkard to Henryk? He is his *alter ego*, his hidden "I." Furthermore, Gombrowicz himself pointed out the similarity between Henryk and Hitler or Stalin in the scenes of the drama where Henryk enacts an extremely authoritarian model of power. Henryk and Władzio unknowingly enter into a master-slave relationship similar to the one described satirically by Gombrowicz in the scene with Pietrasiński and Piekosiński. Those two, however, were just foolish; the protagonists of *The Marriage* really implement totalitarian subjection: actual blood is shed and the readers stop laughing.

Let us again imagine Gombrowicz in Buenos Aires from the beginning of the war. It seems to him that he has understood something from the ongoing events that perhaps he, an almost unknown outsider from across the Atlantic, can say something important to the people of the New World about the plague infecting the minds of the Europeans. He thus speaks of the Polish experience but he treats this experience as something universal; attempting to get liberated from a purely national perspective, he refers to the transformations of human nature that predict the war and the new societies' evolution toward dangerous, although fascinating wildness. But, the room is full of his compatriots and their sworn enemies belonging to national minorities who were mistreated by the pre-war Polish authorities. Nobody understands anything from his lecture ("Youngsters are wild? And where is the success of pre-war education?").[29] At the same time, the disputants wish to find a pretext to state their particular truths and pretentions, which history has just managed to render void.[30] But who would understand that! At the hall of Teatro del Pueblo, the dispute is still going on between the Baron, Pyckal, and Ciumkała, while from above, on behalf of the Nation, judgments are made by the offended members of the Polish Legation and their entourage. This noise effectively covered the reflection Gombrowicz wished to present to all of them. It, however, seems that almost everything he wrote later can be somehow related to it.

The experience of the tragic history of the twentieth century gradually led Gombrowicz to draw a schematic of the fundamental conflict that organizes contemporary societies. This conflict is in a way multifaceted. First, it is a conflict of sexes, understood not as sharpened clashes between manhood and womanhood, but rather between a society where men's and women's roles are clearly defined (which encourages development of the soldier's profession and certain customs), and one where such roles are mixed, and differences are unspecified. Second, the nature of the conflict is defined by the clash between the clearly defined national and cultural identity necessary to define a conflict, and weak identifications that remain unclear. Third, and more generally, on the one hand we have a vision of a world where all identities result from a very rigid social hierarchy, supported with a metaphysical sanction (hence the famous Dostoyevsky saying, "If there's no God, everything is permitted"). This conception clashes with a new idea of identity created through interpersonal interactions that never reaches full completion. Within this new framework identities are understood as a process that never ends because there is no rigid, pre-established structure (of values, authorities, etc.) that could decide who we are and how we are to behave. The fundamental opposition inherent in the placement of individuals into either of these two types of cultural system also has a political meaning. Today, we can easily perceive this clash in the current [2018] party policies and ideologies struggling for social support. It is the clash between those who, on the one hand, refer to "eternal divine laws," tradition, and the order of nature, and those who, on the other hand, support the freedom and sovereignty of the individual as well as negotiations as means to determine the identity of people, who are given the unalienable right to be different.

In 1940, Gombrowicz was at the verge of reflection on this issue. Soon, a time would come for him to publish articles in the Argentinian journal *Viva cien años* on Argentinian eroticism, and later *Trans-Atlantyk*.

The 1940s was also a period of intensified experiments in the area of Gombrowicz's own erotic. This seems a marginal problem, but let us remember the very significant role the writer ascribed to eroticism in human life. In this case, it was about liberation from too exactly defined gender identities, summed up in the burst of laughter ending the dispute of homo- and heterosexual eroticism at the end of *Trans-Atlantyk*. Antagonists in the novel are thus freed from the deadly conflict, yet let us remember that this was supported by the entire web of complex justifications referring to the binary clashes discussed earlier.

The laughter from *Trans-Atlantyk* is thus of annihilating and radical nature, cancelling all the binary clashes that endanger the individual's sovereignty. Gombrowicz responds with fascination, even when undermined with fear, to the "wildness" of the youth, in which, still at the time of the lecture at Teatro del Pueblo, he perceived some creative, positive potential. At the time of *Pornografia* he turned the "wild" youth into sovereign partners of the "old," tempered with excessive awareness. Those "old" are not ideologues, and the only thing they are capable of are experiments, attempts to pursue their own dreams with the hands of thoughtless doers. Yet this only happens in *Pornografia*, where, instead of work in the underground, burdened with patriotic duties and stereotypes, there is also a place for creative self-achievement through the cooperation between the young and the old, who mark death with signs other than traditional ones—the rebellious and blasphemous symbolism negotiated in joint action.

Gombrowicz did not take a stand for atheism, national apostasy, dilution of all values, or homoeroticism. He just believed that taking a stand—in the situation of a war that forced subjection to stereotypes— for affirmation of entirely different rules brings about as many threats as negating them. The rejection of masculine stereotypes of action and the military ideal of a positive protagonist is not just a fearful reaction to the threats of war. In response to the war, Gombrowicz demanded a completely different type of individual. It may be suspected that, at Teatro del Pueblo, Gombrowicz partly predicted the remedy he was to find to the horror produced by the "wild youth" serving the "leaders of the nation." Unfortunately, we shall never learn the truth.

Notes

1 Letter, Jarosław Iwaszkiewicz to Gombrowicz, May 16, 1946, in Jerzy Jarzębski, et al., *Korespondencja Witolda Gombrowicza–walka o sławę: korespondencja* (Kraków: Wydawnictwo Literackie, 1996), 126.
2 Gombrowicz, *Polish Memories*, 91.
3 Wyka, "Tragiczność," 7–29.
4 As David Brodsky explains, "politically, the phrase 'Polish October' refers to the installation of a new government in October 1956, along with the hopes this event inspired for a more liberalized regime. In cultural terms,

however, the Polish October is analogous to the 'Thaw' in the Soviet Union—but much warmer—and it includes a period of about two or three years, roughly from 1955 to 1958, during which intense debate, settling of accounts, and a reevaluation of tradition took place." See Brodsky, "Witold Gombrowicz," 459–75.

5 Relations between the first novels by Sartre and Gombrowicz have been described in Franczak, *Rzecz.*

6 On the one hand, I am thinking here about the quoted work by Franczak, while, on the other hand, about Markowski, *Czarny nurt.*

7 Gombrowicz, *Memories*, 121.

8 Gombrowicz, "Ferdydurke" (*Skamander*), 264–84.

9 Gombrowicz, *Memories*, 189.

10 Ibid., 190–91.

11 I use "outer forces of containment" in Walter Reckless's sense. In containment theory, Reckless explored why some boys reared in inner city, "high-risk" neighborhoods did not become delinquent, while others did. Reckless concluded that what differentiates one group from the other was their exposure to a variety of internal forces (frustration, hostility, and self-concept) and external forces (economic conditions, community values, and adult supervision) that push or pull them toward delinquency or toward conformity. Delinquency occurs when the outer forces cannot buffer juveniles from the pushes and pulls of delinquency. Reckless, *Crime Problem.*

12 Gombrowicz, *Memories*, 146.

13 Ibid., 147.

14 Gombrowicz, *Possessed*, 9.

15 Ibid., 90–92.

16 "Witold Gombrowicz o swoim odczycie w Teatrze del Pueblo," *Kurier Polski*, Aug. 23, 1940, 5, reprinted in Gombrowicz, *Publicystyka*, 299–302; Gombrowicz, *Dzieła*, XIII.

17 The broadest report about the circumstances of the lecture and its repercussions can be found in the chapter entitled "'Antypolska robota,' czyli odczyt w Teatro del Pueblo" in Suchanow, *Argentyńskie*, 31–46.

18 Gombrowicz, *Dzieła*, XIII, 300–301.

19 More on this issue is in the article by Chwin, "Gombrowicz, my i Niemcy," in Jarzębski, *Gombrowicz nasz współczesny.*

20 Gombrowicz, Preface to *Ferdydurke* (Argos), 9–10.

21 See Jarzębski, "Operetka," 58–66; "Rozmowa z Jerzym Jarzębskim o odnalezieniu pierwszej wersji *Operetki* Witolda Gombrowicza," interview by Zbigniew Dominiak, *Tygiel Kultury*, 2 (1996), 62–66.

22 The fragment about Pietrasiński and Piekosiński, printed in the pre-war *Skamander* journal, can be found in *Ferdydurke* (Bolecki), II, 283–87.

23 Gombrowicz, *Memories*, 147.

24 For the American model of woman, see Iłakowicz-Lipińska, "Miss America Goes Shopping."

25 Gombrowicz, *Diary*, 362, presents the issue well.

26 Ibid., 418.

27 Chwin, "Niemcy," 100–15.

28 Ibid., 107.

29 Gombrowicz, *Dzienniku 1957–1961*, 169–71. Gombrowicz wrote about the misunderstandings around the lecture in his *Diary.*

30 Polish policy on the eastern borderland ceased to be a problem since the Red Army, as it turned out, detached such lands from Poland. Regarding the situation of the Jews in Poland, it would drastically change with the Holocaust, as well as the nature of the Polish-Jewish relations.

14 "Their Astounding Strength in Overcoming Their Past…"

The Memory of Nazism in the *Berlin Diary*[1]

Andrzej Stanisław Kowalczyk

Before we start discussing the *Berlin Diary*, let us go back to the mid-1930s, when the subject of fascists or, more broadly, followers of totalitarianism, appeared for the first time in Gombrowicz's work.[2] In July of 1935 the Polish journal *Skamander* published a preliminary version of the first chapter of *Ferdydurke*, which would not be included in the final version of the novel. In this chapter, the protagonist's former classmate, Piekosiński, a shop assistant at a grocery store, pays him a visit. Piekosiński has become a member of the Society of Fighters of the Sword, which is led by Pietrasiński, a shoemaker by profession. The name of the organization, as well as the fanatical cult of the leader and a penchant for violence (threat to use "a stick"), brings to mind the National Radical Camp (Obóz Narodowo-Radykalny, ONR*)*, the Polish fascists. Piekosiński orders the protagonist to join the Society of Sword Fighters and leaves. However, the protagonist is not interested in the party's program but rather in the process in which a Form is created. He claims:

> So Piekosiński became a servant of that filthy shoemaker Pietrasiński? Well, Piekosiński serves Pietrasiński but Pietrasiński serves Piekosiński in return. And Pietrasiński serves Piekosiński rather well for the latter is in the best shape he has ever been in. He has never had that much color in his cheeks or that much fire. A completely changed human being. Certainly. But in what way do they serve each other? In the creation of heroism? Piekosiński has shown a lot of cleverness by wallowing in the dust in front of Pietrasiński. He elevated Pietrasiński to the rank of chief or God so that in due course Pietrasiński would pull him upwards by his ears. But what is the result of all this? Pietrasiński, not long ago just a shoemaker, is now God, while Piekosiński, a shop assistant, has become God's confidant.[3]

The protagonist began considering joining the Society of Fighters of the Sword for "reasons of spiritual hygiene":

> the body as the soul are in need of some training and just as one kicks a soccer ball not because of the ball itself but to strengthen

one's muscles in the guise of an innocent game and have the chance to do a bit of exercise in the open air.

So Piekosiński thought about paying "tribute to Pietrasiński not because of Pietrasiński himself, as it is clear, but to strengthen his spirit with a little exercise and fresh air."[4] Eventually, the protagonist concluded that he could pay tribute to his maid. After his homage, he and the maid formed a procession with a banner made from a handkerchief and circled the table in the room. A parody of the fascist or Nazi rituals depicts them as party members offering mutual services to each other. Piekosiński was adorned "in a wonderful steadfastness."[5] Party members created a totalitarian Form. The attitude toward fascism that both Gombrowicz's protagonist and Gombrowicz himself adopt here is that of spectators, not that of interpreters or judges. Their attention is attracted by the enticing spectacle, the participants of which are transformed from weaklings into athletes, from shop assistants at a grocery store into followers, from shoemakers into leaders. Can a Form, a necessary and inevitable phenomenon, be judged? Standing on the grounds of relativism, Gombrowicz could, but would not, appeal to supposedly immutable values. He seems to laugh at fascist rituals, but neither those rituals nor the totalitarian ideology and practices that support them are subject to moral evaluation. The protagonist of *Ferdydurke* humbled himself before the Form and paid tribute to it:

> Oh, the power of Form! Nations die because of it. It is the cause of wars. It creates something in us that is not of us. If you make light of it you'll never understand stupidity nor evil nor crime. It governs our slightest impulses. It is at the base of our collective life.[6]

Form, born among people, exceeds individual consciousness and influences every person individually. "I am like a voice in an orchestra," Gombrowicz wrote after the war, "that must tune itself to its sound," or "like a dancer for whom it is not so important exactly what is danced, the important thing is to join in the dance with others." He claims further: "I think and feel 'for' people in order to rhyme with them. I experience a warping as a consequence of this highest of necessities: tuning myself to others in Form."[7] Thus, Gombrowicz's form unites people into a community and pushes them to achieve collective goals. Therefore, it is also a force that stimulates people's political behaviors and sets in motion the scene where community is formed. Form is a category subtly describing the relationship between the individual and the community. According to Gombrowicz, it also serves to deepen the individual's awareness, enrich the individual's cognitive horizon, and create a new humanism. But twentieth-century phenomena such as political parties which resemble criminal gangs, the power of propaganda in social engineering of massive-scale terror or bigoted masses surprised and disoriented Gombrowicz's contemporaries. Indeed, twentieth-century social and political phenomena escaped the tools that Gombrowicz had at his disposal.

In the late 1930s, the subject of Italian and German fascism appeared several times in Gombrowicz's texts. During his trip to Italy in 1938, the writer passed twice through Venice, spending in this city several days.[8] The trip from Rome to Venice was described in three articles published in 1938 in *Czas*, *Polish Memories* (written in Argentina in the late 1950s), and *A Kind of Testament* (written in France in 1968), respectively. In these texts, Gombrowicz cited other episodes or returned to the same events but showed them differently. For instance, in one of the articles in *Czas*, Gombrowicz recalls meeting on the train two Italian pilots who wanted to show him around Venice but got lost at night. They were extremely gentle soldiers who declared their aversion to war. In *Polish Memories*, written in the 1950s, Gombrowicz mentions a group of airmen whom he had met on the train from Rome to Venice, with whom he talked all night and arranged to meet the following day at St. Mark's Square. When they met, Gombrowicz asked them whether, if Il Duce ordered them to bomb the square, they would execute Mussolini's order. The pilots said without hesitation that they would follow Mussolini's order.[9] I'm not interested in which version of the anecdote is closer to the truth; perhaps in both cases we are dealing with fiction. What is important, however, is that in 1938 Gombrowicz portrayed Italian soldiers as milksops and pacifists, indifferent to the official militarism and imperialism of Mussolini's state, while after the war he emphasized their fanaticism.

As far as his own perception of Italy is concerned, Gombrowicz expresses different opinions in newspaper articles than he does in *Polish Memories*. In the 1938 text, he betrayed his fascination with something "most wonderful" in the atmosphere of Rome, which he described as "a special technique of collective life at the same time lively and relaxed, and smooth, shiny." This "special technique of collective life" was characterized by "profound natural refinement" linked with "extraordinary sophistication."[10] In *Polish Memories*, by contrast, he writes that in "that pure, pellucid Latin climate" of Rome one could feel "something turbid and monstrous." The newspapers

> carried shrill praise of the Berlin-Rome Axis, and the stench of blackmail and betrayal – for me, the conspiracy between Italy and Germany meant the betrayal of Europe – dominated the streets, Mussolini's speeches, the fascists' songs, and even in the soldier games played by the brats in front of the Villa Borghese.[11]

He even mentions a Pole who, buying a portrait of Mussolini in a Roman kiosk, complains that Poland could also use a leader like this.[12] Why did Gombrowicz not say anything in his 1938 newspaper articles about "something turbid and monstrous," which he remembered so well after many years? Why did he not hint at the German-Italian "betrayal of Europe"? Commenting on the behavior of the Polish admirer of Mussolini, Gombrowicz claims that "it was difficult to make anything out in the mists of those times." "[I]t was unclear who was lying, who was bluffing, and who was genuine. Contours were blurred and boundaries washed away."[13] Apparently, Gombrowicz is also talking about himself. He was not familiar with international politics, he was not interested in the internal affairs of the totalitarian states, "contours were blurred and boundaries washed away." Facts such as Mussolini's invasion of Abyssinia and further conquest of this country in 1935–1936, the overt military involvement of Italy and Germany in the Spanish Civil War since 1936, or the systematic strengthening of links with the Third Reich, provided much to think about. But the author of *Ferdydurke* probably did not care too much about it, especially since fascist Italy and its dictator compelled admiration and sympathy not only in the ranks of the National Democracy (Narodowa Demokracja, ND) but also among the Sanation's (Sanacja) elites.[14] Official Polish-Italian relations were very good in the years 1937–1938. Warsaw eagerly accepted the conquest of Abyssinia and expressed understanding for the Italian-German intervention in Spain. Rome had hoped that Poland would join the Anti-Comintern Pact (signed in November 1936).[15] There were a lot of cordial declarations and gestures. For instance, in May 1937, Marshal Edward Rydz-Śmigły was given a Roman Sword by the Italian army, while Foreign Minister Józef Beck paid an official visit to Rome on March 6–11, 1938.[16] Interestingly, Gombrowicz and Beck both stayed by the Tiber at the same time, but Gombrowicz does not mention this fact in his newspaper articles, in *Polish Memoirs,* nor in *A Kind of Testament.*

The different perceptions of Italian Fascism by foreigners constitute the subject of Gombrowicz's article "Swawolnymi stopy po Rzymie" (Light-footed through Rome). There is, Gombrowicz claims, no objective truth about Italy under Mussolini. Everyone sees what the ideology that they profess makes them see. Gombrowicz does not stop before the paradox according to which in Italy "98 percent of the phenomena... defy all ideological or political affiliation."[17] He considered that Italian fascism did not really stand out against the background of other political systems and its black legend was created by people averse to it, especially leftists or liberal foreigners. Gombrowicz commented on the "extraordinary bliss" of the population.[18] He disagreed with those who claimed that "oppression and terror were painted on the faces of the passers-by in the street." On the contrary, the Roman people were cheerful and happy and when there was an official parade or celebration, "then everyone can enjoy as much as they can the brilliance and magnificence, shouting and cheering with enthusiasm."[19]

Gombrowicz limited himself to mentioning the expressions of support for the fascist regime by the masses; he ignored all other questions and doubts. In fact, the formula adopted earlier of a tourist essay did not allow an in-depth reflection on totalitarian regimes. Although Gombrowicz uses a playful tone in relation to Mussolini, he did not intend to formulate any allegations of a political or ethical nature to act as a defender of human and civil rights or as a critic of imperialism. Toward fascism, he adopted a reserved attitude tinged with kindness, refusing to repeat the accusations against the dictatorship made by liberals, socialists, and supporters of democracy. In the late 1930s in the Polish press there was a fair share of Mussolini and Hitler apologists. The members of the National Democracy and the National Radical Camp praised the economic and social achievements of fascism and national socialism. The Sanation also tended toward totalitarian patterns, bringing to life the Camp of National Unity (Obóz Zjednoczenia Narodowego, OZN), a political party of nationalist nature, in 1937. In the literary weekly *Pion*, which was funded by state authorities, writer and journalist Ferdynand Goetel (creator of the Sanacja party's name—the Camp of National Unity) published in mid-1938 a series of articles in which he praised the regimes created by Hitler and Mussolini. He contributed to the book *Pod znakiem faszyzmu* (Under the Banner of Fascism), which appeared at the end of that year, in which he rebuked the critics of right-wing totalitarianism, placing great hopes in it and announcing its triumph.[20] Goetel encouraged Poles to build "a fascist Poland" and concluded that the "starting point must be the awareness, however, that nothing that is opposed to the good of the nation is immutable and inviolable. This starting point means admitting to fascism."[21] The nationalist agitation did not make any impression on Gombrowicz; indeed every form of fanaticism appeared to repulse him. Toward fascism, however, he adopted a cautious and expectant attitude. A skeptic and a relativist, he could not find a foundation that would allow him to take a firm stand against the totalitarian dictatorship.

Gombrowicz was not interested in politics, neither as an intellectual project nor as a social practice. For him, it was a domain of insincerity and false pretenses, a subtopic that he found futile. According to him, a writer should not enclose himself in any philosophy or ideology. Belonging to a political movement, subordination, discipline was by definition hostile toward art; art implied liberation from constraints, patterns, and routines. To be an artist is "to force himself into contradistinction" and "force" readers to "confirm it."[22] Any involvement in politics, and thus the adoption by the artist of the role of a party tool, propagandist, officer, or publicist must result in the denial of art. Even Miłosz's *The Captive Mind* raised Gombrowicz's objections since Gombrowicz found Miłosz's book too immersed in the political struggle and thus secondary, schematic, and helpless against reality.

According to Gombrowicz, literature is not a suitable means for exposing political enemies or mobilizing the masses. By contrast, by its very
nature, it takes the side of the individual and defends freedom from
the aggressive collectivism of totalitarian movements. From this standpoint, wrote Gombrowicz, "one page of Montaigne, a single Verlaine
poem, or one sentence by Proust is far more anti-Communist than the
accusing choir which you represent. They are free and therefore they
are liberating."[23] Gombrowicz did not use words like "freedom" and
"liberation" in a political sense. Did he not proclaim that "the artist is a
form in motion?" "In contrast to a philosopher, moralist, thinker, the-
ologist"—this enumeration could well include a politician—"the artist
is endless play, ... endless shifts take place within him and only he can
oppose his own movement to the movement of the world."[24] It is not by
accident that the list of roles that Gombrowicz opposed to the one of an
artist did not include politicians. Art and politics are, in fact, infinitely
distant from each other.

In the second half of the 1930s, when many artists made clear political choices, Gombrowicz did not feel the need to engage on either side,
believing that political entanglement would constitute a particularism
harmful to his work. He saw his writing as an autonomous activity,
the aim of which was to discover the individual and not get involved
in the struggle for the realization of the objectives set by this or that
ideology. Gombrowicz's reluctance to political engagement led him to
refrain from expressing opinions, even in the moments when it seemed
necessary to take a stand. While in Rome, he preserved the attitude of
a tourist satisfied with the observation of only the surface of life. In the
case of the agony of Austria, he mustered up a little more interest in
the political situation, nevertheless he remained faithful to the formula
which he later verbalized as "never write 'about Berlin,' 'Paris,' only
about oneself ... in Berlin and Paris."[25] In Vienna and Rome, he also
wrote about Gombrowicz in Vienna and Rome.

In the article "Schuschnigg i ząb" (Schuschnigg and a tooth), published
also in *Czas* in 1938, Gombrowicz described the indifference of the inhabitants of the city in the moments that decided the fate of Austria.[26]
In *A Kind of Testament*, written in the mid-1960s, Gombrowicz recalled
his return from Italy and the view of the crowds of Austrians in Vienna
greeting Hitler after the Anschluss. What is striking is the difference of
perspective on this subject in the *Czas* articles of 1938 and in *A Kind
of Testament*. In the 1938 article, Gombrowicz wrote about the mood of
the inhabitants of the Austrian capital on February 24 when Chancellor Kurt von Schuschnigg gave his speech responding to the dictates of
Hitler requesting incorporation of the country into the Third Reich. In
his address, Schuschnigg stated emphatically that Austria is Germany's
equal and wishes to maintain its independence at any price.[27] Gombrowicz ascertained the total calmness of the citizens of Vienna and the lack

of violent or even more emotional reactions. "It is difficult to pronounce and make it clear how tired, how profoundly shocked I was by the city's terrible acceptance of its fate." He noticed the decay of political ties:

> No one really knew anything. Everything seemed to be done somewhere up there, beyond particular men and in the dark. Nobody got involved in anything. No one knew what other people thought but almost everyone was dependent on others, waiting for the judgment of the mass, but the mass was again dependent on individual people. And this tiring formation of people through the mass and of the mass through people lasted and did not want to find a resolution and this indecisiveness of people created a terrible anti-historic procrastination.[28]

A dialogue with a Viennese woman followed in which she expressed more interest in her visit to the dentist and her tooth that was about to be extracted than the unfolding events. In conclusion, Gombrowicz expressed his amazement at how the Viennese, showing "anti-historic procrastination," could within a few weeks turn into enthusiastic advocates of "the annexation" of their country to the Third Reich. In the same issue of *Czas*, the results of the poll organized by the Nazis after the Anschluss were announced in which 99.75 percent of the citizens were in favor of the incorporation of the country into the Reich. In Vienna, half a percent of the citizens voted against the Anschluss.[29] Gombrowicz adopted an attitude of an observer mainly interested in the spectacle that unfolded before his eyes. He was disappointed by the actors who remained passive and apathetic, and on the stage there was "discretion, silence, peace." Instead of showing civic involvement, they played the role of private people; even during the dramatic speech of Chancellor Schuschnigg saying "no" to Hitler, they manifested "terrible politeness and courtesy." However, Gombrowicz does not delve into their motivations, he does not investigate their political or moral positions and attitudes, and he has nothing to say about the European context of the loss of Austrian sovereignty. Gombrowicz has chosen the strategy of an ignorant tourist for whom the only source of knowledge about the political situation in Europe was not even newspapers but the headlines of agency reports. He did not see any "symptoms of commotion" and he mocked the journalists who were prophesizing it. Soon he stopped being interested in the subject when he left Vienna for Rome. Gombrowicz also applied the strategy of a politically ignorant "tourist" in his early years in South America. In the *Diary*, he recalled that he enjoyed the freedom of the Argentinians after "the stifling fury of nationalists." "It was pure pleasure in those first years," he wrote,

> knowing nothing of Argentina, knowing nothing of the parties, programs, leaders, newspapers, to live like a tourist.... but wasn't

Argentina one of my predestinations, since as a child in Poland I did everything I could to march out of step in the parade?[30]

After many years, Gombrowicz recalled in *A Kind of Testament* his encounter with Vienna on the way back from Italy. Gombrowicz's reaction is egocentric: the fanaticism of the crowds and the nationalist mobilization of Poland and of the whole of Europe spoil the writer's plans. He was returning from Italy relaxed, free, and triumphant; meanwhile, because of the annexation of Austria, "Poland had once again to lock itself in, like a fortress, to believe in itself, to love itself! And from every country there came the panic-stricken fury of threatened peoples."[31] Gombrowicz was irritated by the intensification of the collectivist trends, diminishing the status of the artist in society. In a climate of aggression, mobilization, and tribal hatred, the importance of autonomous art — and that was the only thing Gombrowicz was interested in — dropped almost to zero. "In all events," he writes in *A Kind of Testament,* "I understood one thing: *Ferdydurke* was doomed to failure and myself with it."[32]

The topic of Nazism appeared in the *Diary* in 1958 in the entry on Gombrowicz's stay in Tandil. The inscription on the wall praising the "martyrs of Nuremberg" provoked the writer to comment on Hitler. He wrote about the psychological aspect of the political tactics of the dictator who became the master of extremism. Constantly crossing the accepted limits, he imposed the impression of his own power on the masses. When the masses believed this hoax, the Führer was magnified "to incredible dimensions," became "a Giant," a suprahuman, a god who did not have to abide by any human law and customs anymore.[33] Gombrowicz is not interested in Nazism as such, its ideology and practice, but only in one aspect of the phenomenon—the emergence of the political power of the dictator elevated to the top by the people. Gombrowicz is satisfied with only this one fragment, leaving the consequences of Hitler's elevation aside. The comments on Hitler are part of a longer discourse on the fabrication of deities by people. When there is no God, says Gombrowicz, arguing with atheists, the advocates of universalism, we should accept this spontaneous process of formation: the birth of a divinity or semi-divinity out of the people themselves. Such demigods, imperfect, and so at the same time close to the people, could help them get out of the "accursed universalism" and restore their "salutary concreteness."[34] Thus, he returns to the dreams of a human church:

> If I could have forced myself to acknowledge this *deity* [underlined in the original] — and not concern myself anymore with absolutes and just feel above me, not high, barely a yard above my head, the play of creative forces, born of us as the only attainable Olympus — and to worship this.[35]

The example of Hitler's elevation to the heights of "a deity" is a proof that these "interhuman gods," called and endowed with power by the terrestrials themselves, can quite easily become a catastrophe for humanity. Besides, Gombrowicz does not hide the danger, admitting that

> man, as such, does not have much to say in this new, suprahuman, dimension. People begin to pile up. Pressures are created. A shape arises having its own reason and logic. The idea exists merely for the sake of appearances; it is the façade behind which the possession of man by man takes place, creating itself first, and only later asking about its meaning.[36]

After World War II, the metaphor of "a man possessed by a man" sounded really diabolical and Gombrowicz, with all his indifference to history, could not pretend he did not hear it.

Two years later, Gombrowicz wrote of a memory from his trip to Italy in 1938 and an Austrian Nazi's monologue on the train, prophesying the triumph of this movement across Europe. This fanatic was an example of "possession of man by man," expressed in total compliance with Nazi ideology, in complete submission to the "blind forces of the collectivity," the abandonment of thinking.[37] Gombrowicz recalled his defensive reaction involving the withdrawal to his own "I," providing protection against gibberish, screaming, lying, and the terror of the crowd.

In an entry from the late 1950s, what is striking is the unceremonious quality with which Gombrowicz writes about the dynamics of the secular society. "I," he says, "of course, do not see why modern metaphysical anxiety could not express itself in the adoration of man, if God is lacking."[38] Then he writes about the spontaneous "process of elevating one person at the cost of others" and

> the thrust upward, even if it elevates just one person, even if it is the most absurd and unjust, will be an absolute condition of Form; it will also mean the creation of a higher sphere within humanity, dividing it into levels; from the bosom of the common people will come a more noble kingdom, which, for the inferior, will be both a horrible burden and a magnificent elevation. Why do you refuse to honor the accidental world of — if not gods, then demigods — that issues from us?... Doesn't this phenomenon possess divine attributes, which are a result of interhuman power, that is, superior and creative, in relation to each of us separately?[39]

Gombrowicz's project of a humanist utopia of a human church does not contain any guarantees that if released or unbridled, the forces which will trigger the emergence of a new social elite—the demigods—"a more noble kingdom," will not want to establish an oppressive system based on violence, fear, and aggression. "The adoration of man" is a sufficiently important goal, not to count too scrupulously its cost. The writer always distanced himself from collectivism. Recalling Martin Buber, he wrote that on the ruins of Western individualism and Eastern collectivism, manipulating the abstractions of nation, social class, and country, a new vision of man will be born in relation to another concrete man.[40] It seems, however, that Gombrowicz's human church, promising rebirth through "the discovery of man himself, as the decisive and naked power," is another name for anthropocentrism, one more attempt to overcome nihilism, that is, the depreciation of the most important values.[41] Gombrowicz's optimism was diminished by the awareness that people are able not only to create people-demigods, it is equally easy for them to reach the state of "possession of man by man." In the human church there is no God but evil does not intend to leave. There is no reason for which a person would not become the devil to their neighbor.

Gombrowicz returned to Europe in April 1963. After a stay in Paris in May, he went to West Berlin on a fellowship from the Ford Foundation. In July or August, he was invited for an interview by a Polish journalist, Barbara Witek-Swinarska, on the basis of which she wrote an article "O dystansie, czyli rozmowa z mistrzem" (On the Distance, or a Conversation with the Master). The author accused Gombrowicz of disregard for the Polish victims of the German occupation. It was the editor of *Kultura* who told Gombrowicz about the article, warning him against the attempts of communist propaganda to discredit him.[42] He advised Gombrowicz: "You need to be most careful in your statements regarding politics. The anti-German hysteria runs extremely deep in our countrymen."[43]

It is impossible to determine the state of Gombrowicz's knowledge about World War II before his return to Europe. This subject does not really appear in the *Diary*. *Pornografia* is not a novel about the occupation. What did the author of *Ferdydurke* know about the Jewish Holocaust, the German terror against the East Slavic nations? One can only assume that his knowledge of the subject remained at the South American level — superficial. Gombrowicz was separated from Europe not only by the ocean but also by the indifference of the Argentinians toward those events. Juan Perón's regime in the years 1946–1955 was sympathetic to Nazism, and many war criminals settled in Argentina, which consistently rejected extradition requests.

The memories of Nazism in the *Berlin Diary* are marked by several phenomena: the Berliners' memory, the Poles' memory, and Witold Gombrowicz's memory. It all started with Witek-Swinarska's article. Gombrowicz denied the opinions the journalist claimed he had, both in the *Diary* and in the letter to the editor of *Życie Literackie* and other national magazines. In both texts, he included an eager declaration that

"I condemn sharply" Hitler's crimes and have "the greatest respect for the unprecedented sufferings of Poles during the last war."[44] Those statements show Gombrowicz's concern. Even before he was attacked by the national press for accepting the Ford fellowship to West Berlin, it took only a mention in "Dziennik transatlantycki" (Transatlantic Journal)[45] for a Warsaw columnist to deny Gombrowicz literary rank and compare him to Nazi propagandists defaming Poland.[46] Then came Witek-Swinarska's article and an indignant letter from Ludwik Hieronim Morstin to *Trybuna Ludu*. These voices could not be dismissed, although there was no doubt that this was the reaction of the Communist regime to the fresh pamphlet by Gombrowicz called "Tandeta" (Trumpery), attacking the cultural policy in Warsaw. However, the anti-German attitude was one of the few points where the *vox populi* resonated with the communist propaganda. The trauma of war and occupation was still fresh in Poles' minds, and they were worried about the status of the Federal Republic of Germany, which was challenged by all the major parties. So his arrival in West Berlin meant that the writer became the target of attacks and propaganda and at the same time provoked negative reactions from a part of the public opinion in whose eyes he was fraternizing with the enemy, challenging the patriotic Decalogue and national solidarity. Not without significance was the status of Berlin as a border city dividing the communist bloc and Western Europe. The crises happening there could have resulted in a global conflict. The last such crisis occurred in 1961 when Germany's communist authorities divided the city with a wall and barbed wire. Berlin became a trap to Gombrowicz who always valued highly the autonomy of the artist and avoided personal involvement in political conflicts. While he managed to defeat Paris by charging daringly at it, exposing its senility, over sophistication, futility, and had fun doing it, Berlin put up resistance. Argentinian nature, youth, exuberance, nudity, allowed him to unveil the shameful secret of Parisians who did not know how to cope with the greatness of their city, "and so they walk around this Spirit of theirs like field hands tending their milk cows and selling their milk. Paris, yes, a palace, but they gave the impression of being the palace servants."[47] If Paris stood wide open before Gombrowicz, Berlin proved difficult to access. The writer defined his attitude toward France without much difficulty. In Berlin, he was confronted with the memory of the Polish-German past, which he could not set aside, which he could not ignore. He was reminded about this by the voices coming from Poland, specifically Stanisław Zieliński and Witek-Swinarska.

The *Berlin Diary* is chaotic, nervous, marked by tension, and devoid of the lightness and humor that characterize his Parisian memories. The reader gets the impression that Gombrowicz does not know how to cope with this German and Berlin experience, that he retreats under its pressure, that it proves too much for him. And he knows it. At one point he writes, "Instead of my being an alert observer here, I prefer to tell my dreams. I am sleepy... I have been asleep ever since I left Argentina."[48] This definitely does not apply to his stay in Paris, but Berlin was already too close to Poland, Małoszyce, Bodzechów, his childhood, and he perceived this proximity as the closing of a cycle, as a harbinger of death.[49] Sleep was one of his metaphors. Elsewhere he spoke of debilitation and weakness, which did not allow him to face "the stony foreignness of Europe." He, a faithful European, and at the same time already an Argentinean, saw his home continent as "an alien planet."[50] Gombrowicz defended himself against this new experience, emphasizing his Argentineness and ahistoricity.[51] He fished out individual elements, such as hooks for hanging convicts in a former Nazi prison, a hook stuck in the wall in a painter's studio, hands (washed too often), hands (criminal?, in a gesture resembling a Nazi salute), and feet (maybe used to crush someone's throat). But his attention was not directed toward the elderly veterans who took part in the war, but toward young people who did not have and did not want to have anything to do with Nazism.[52]

The beginning of the 1960s was important for the German memory of Nazism. As Tony Judt writes, many Germans born during the war or immediately after did not know who their fathers were. Schools did not teach anything about German history after Hitler's rise to power. This period was generally taboo in family conversations. In the early 1950s, the demand for a general amnesty for Nazi war criminals found broad support in the public opinion of the Federal Republic.[53] It did not happen, but the prosecution of war criminals was sluggish. If there were trials, the courts pronounced very lenient sentences with many defendants being acquitted. It was not until 1958 that a national institution prosecuting Nazi crimes was established in Ludwigsburg. In December 1963, the authorities commenced the first trial of those accused of crimes in Auschwitz to be held on German soil. Twenty-two officials of the Auschwitz-Birkenau death camp were put on trial. The testimony of 270 witnesses reminded the Germans of the most drastic aspects of Nazi terror that had been concealed.[54] In the eyes of young people who came to the fore in the 1960s, the Federal Republic of Germany "emanated complacency and hypocrisy."[55] An important event was the kidnapping of Adolf Eichmann, one of the war criminals responsible for the Holocaust, from Argentina in 1960 by Israeli intelligence. His trial in the years 1961–1962 was widely discussed and commented on throughout the world. The following year Hannah Arendt published her book *Eichmann in Jerusalem: A Report on the Banality of Evil.* Gustav Herling-Grudziński's commentary on this publication appeared in the January-February *Kultura* in 1964.[56] Reading Herling's article made Gombrowicz realize that the genocide was made possible thanks to the collaboration of an enormous number of ordinary people, that the "demon of our times" has the face of an ordinary man who, in favorable circumstances, like Eichmann, can become an ardent performer of a criminal program, can become "the enemy of the human race."

This does not mean that Gombrowicz gave in completely to the pressure of the signs of the past that were attacking him, that persistently reminded him of his ties with the collective. Gombrowicz cites the opinion of the poet Max Hölzer, which was rather common not only in Germany but also in Europe. "Where has our genius gone," asked Hölzer,

> we had so many people in philosophy, in art,...and today, I ask you, where has this race of *grands seigneurs* gone to, our literature keeps rehashing the war and Hitler and politics, nothing but democracy's settling of accounts with dictatorship, this is what brilliance has been reduced to.[57]

Hölzer was therefore inclined to understand Nazism as a local event of passing significance. In his view, returning to the subject of Nazism is futile, does not bring anything new, probably because everything has already been said on the topic and the subject should be regarded as exhausted. For the sake of the contemporaries, the memory of Nazism should be sent to the museum. Dwelling on the past weakens the spiritual strength of entire nations. Gombrowicz himself was not far from this view. In his answer to Witek-Swinarska in November 1963,[58] he wrote about a mountain of corpses obstructing the Poles' view of Germany. He associated the Poles' tendency to think about the war with their inclination toward nationalism.[59]

The next part of the *Diary,* starting with Gombrowicz's arrival in Berlin, did not appear until the September issue of *Kultura* in 1964. The nine-month break was caused by the writer's illness and his hospitalization. In May 1964 he returned to France. The tone of his retort to Witek-Swinarska is essentially different from the tone of the Berlin *Diary.* In November 1963, six months after arriving in West Berlin, Gombrowicz was reluctant to undertake the subject of Nazism evoked by the national journalism. The concept of the mountain of corpses obstructing the Poles' view of Germany demonstrates the lack of the writer's orientation in terms of the forms of fixation of war experiences in the Poles' memory. Apparently, he did not realize that the phrase "mountain of corpses" is understood literally in Poland. The postwar films from the concentration camps liberated by the Allies showed piles of unburied corpses several meters high. It is very doubtful whether it was possible to see these films in Argentina, where the sympathies for fascism were still alive, and Perón's regime protected German Nazis. In his *Diary,* resumed nine months later, he no longer makes this kind of error. In general, the memory of Nazism became one of the main themes. And there are plenty of reasons for that. In the first half of the 1960s, those in

Germany who wanted to marginalize or forget Nazism were reminded about it. The discussion about German responsibility for Nazism re-emerged and it is this discussion to which Hölzer refers. This problem would reveal itself with full force in a few years during the students' protests in the Federal Republic of Germany.

In the Berlin fragments of the *Diary*, Gombrowicz admitted that he could not break free from the memory of the past. He wrote about his "Polish soul,"[60] and almost solemnly declared that the idea of forgiveness for German crimes in Poland is alien to him. But at the same time he adopted a universal perspective, recalling that Nazism was not an isolated phenomenon, that the blame for the crimes burdens all of mankind. The Berlin fragments of the *Diary* are concluded by a metaphorical argument:

> I had to take on all those crimes, just as if I had committed them. I became Hitler and I had to accept Hitler's presence in every dying Pole and the fact that he still existed in every living Pole. Condemnation, scorn, this is not the way, this is nothing...the eternal revulsion to crime simply extends its life... One must swallow it. One must eat it. Evil can be overcome, but only in oneself. Nations of the world: do you still believe that Hitler was only a German?[61]

It seems that the process of Gombrowicz's thought implies the following steps: the Nazi crimes were preceded by the transformations of the European civilization and its transition to modernism, with its nihilism and decreed end of all values. Depriving the existing world of sense, values, and morality allowed Hitler to come up with his murderous plan.[62] But there is more, Nazism and its crimes mean exceeding a certain threshold, a permanent transformation of the image of man. Hitler cannot be shut down in history books, and he cannot be nullified through the recitation of martyrological spells. There is no place for national historical politics or the guarding of individual interests because the crimes of Nazism have become a part of human nature and we all carry the burden in ourselves. Going back to the era before the genocide is impossible.

We do not know whether Gombrowicz knew Karl Jaspers's 1946 book *The Question of German Guilt* (Die Schuldfrage),[63] but it is very likely that his German interlocutors informed him about this famous text. Jaspers pondered on the question of the phenomenon of war guilt in the face of genocide committed by the Germans. He argued that the traditional understanding of guilt is too narrow and proposed a new interpretation of responsibility. In addition to criminal guilt, says the philosopher, there are other types of guilt: political, moral and metaphysical. The conceptual grid conceived in this way creates a situation of universal responsibility for evil. Each person is responsible for the actions of political power and is obliged to defend the norms of the natural law and the law of nations. The moral responsibility excludes the justification of acts committed on the orders of superiors. It is one's own conscience, says Jaspers, and one's bond with friends and neighbors, brothers caring for one's soul, that constitutes the superior instance. Finally, all people are joined by bonds of solidarity, under which everyone should feel responsibility for all the evil and injustice on earth, especially for crimes committed in their presence or with their knowledge. A person who does not do everything in their power to stop this evil, who in the face of persecution is not on the side of the victims, draws the metaphysical complicity on themselves. In the face of crimes committed against the one or the other, or if physical living requirements have to be shared, "among men the unconditioned prevails—the capacity to live only together or not at all,... — therein consists the substance of their being."[64]

The requirement for universal responsibility common for Jaspers and Gombrowicz is related to the conviction about the nature of evil. Real and concrete, it does not come from the outside world but lives in every human being. It is so expansive that it constantly threatens the well-being of everyone. Kołakowski says, "there is no case so noble, that it cannot be forged into a murder weapon, there is no idea so good, that we cannot, by devil's instigation, harness it for the evil."[65] This does not lead to a dilution or reduction of the perpetrators' liability for specific crimes. The years of Nazism proved, however, how men eagerly respond to the call of evil, how evil is fused in us with humanity itself.

The statement of the durability of the evil unleashed by Nazism had consequences for Gombrowicz's reflections. It seems that the Berlin confrontation with the memory of Nazism challenged the interhuman church utopia and especially the faith in the spontaneous emergence of demigods from among people who were supposed to fill the axiological void after the death of God.

Notes

1 Translated from Polish by Katarzyna Klepacka.
2 In the 1930s in Poland, the words "totalizm" and "totalistic" were used. They referred to fascist (Italy), national socialist (Nazi Germany), communist (the Soviet Union), as well as the Polish ONR. The word "totalitarianism" appeared in the Polish language after World War II.
3 Gombrowicz, *Skamander*, 264–84.
4 Gombrowicz, *Skamander*, 270.
5 Ibid., 269.
6 Gombrowicz, *Ferdydurke* (Borchardt), 80.
7 Gombrowicz, *Diary*, 237.
8 The travel stamps of border controls in Gombrowicz's pre-war passport in the Museum of Literature at the Adam Mickiewicz Institute in Warsaw (Department of Manuscripts, ref. 165, 2) help establish the stages of his travel. Gombrowicz traveled with Stanisław Brochwicz-Kozłowski, scribbler, visitor of the coffeehouse Ziemianska at Gombrowicz's table. Brochwicz

did not hide his fascist sympathies and his anti-Semitism. See Gombrowicz, *Wspomnienia polskie*, *Kronos*, 48–51.

9 Gombrowicz, *Memories*, 191.
10 "Wjazd do krainy włoskiej (Wspomnienia z podróży)," *Czas*, No. 110 (1939) reprited in "Czytelnicy i krytycy. Proza, reportaże, krytyka literacka, eseje, przedmowy," Gombrowicz, *Varia 1*, 123.
11 Gombrowicz, *Memories*, 189.
12 Ibid., 190.
13 Ibid.
14 The Sanation (Sanacja) was a political movement in the interwar period, prior to Józef Piłsudski's May 1926 Coup d'état, that came to power in the wake of the coup. It took its name from Piłsudski's aspirations for a moral "sanation" (healing) of the Polish body politic. The movement functioned until his death in 1935, then split into several competing factions.
15 The Anti-Comintern Pact was an anti-communist pact concluded between Nazi Germany and the Empire of Japan on Nov. 25, 1936. It was directed against the Third (Communist) International.
16 Borejsza, *Mussolini*, 215–18, 233–39.
17 "Swawolnymi stopy po Rzymie," *Czas*, No. 209 (1938) in *Varia 1*, 127.
18 Ibid., 125.
19 Ibid.
20 Urbanowski, *Pisma polityczne*, 146.
21 Ibid., 147.
22 Gombrowicz, *Diary*, 43.
23 Ibid., 22.
24 Ibid, 575.
25 Ibid., 628.
26 "Schuschnigg i ząb (Schuschnigg and a tooth)," *Czas*, 101 (1938) reprinted in *Varia 1*.
27 Batowski, *Rok 1938*, 190.
28 Gombrowicz, *Varia 1*, 116.
29 Based on the information published in *Czas*, 101 (Apr. 12, 1938).
30 Gombrowicz, *Diary*, 627.
31 Gombrowicz, *Testament*, 69.
32 Ibid.
33 Gombrowicz, *Diary*, 362.
34 Ibid., 358.
35 Ibid.
36 Ibid., 362–63.
37 Ibid., 477.
38 Ibid., 357.
39 Ibid., 358.
40 Ibid., 25.
41 Ibid., 26.
42 Giedroyc, letter to Gombrowicz ca. Sept. 26, 1963, in Kowalczyk, *Jerzy Giedroyc*, Vol. 9, 545.
43 Giedroyc, letter to Gombrowicz, Oct. 21, 1963, in Kowalczyk, *Listy*, 553.
44 Gombrowicz, *Diary*, 653.
45 See *Kultura*, 7–8 (1963), 189–90.
46 Zieliński, "Gombrowicz w Jordanie," *Kultura*, 11 (1963); Juliusz Mieroszewski ("Renesans w połn") and Konstanty Jeleński ("Pokajanie Picassa i zdrada Gombrowicza") defended Gombrowicz. Both texts appeared in *Kultura*, No. 10 (1963). The reprint of Zieliński's, Jeleński's, and Mieroszewski's texts appear in *Varia 2*.

47 Gombrowicz, *Diary*, 619.
48 Ibid., 639–40.
49 Ibid., 628–29.
50 Ibid., 659.
51 Ibid., 634.
52 Ibid., 635.
53 Wóycicki, "Spór o niemiecką pamięć," in Buras, *Spór o niemiecką pamięć*, 15–16.
54 Jarausch, *Po Hitlerze*, 476.
55 Judt, *Powojnie*, 492.
56 Herling-Grudziński, 195–96.
57 Gombrowicz, *Diary*, 640.
58 "Dziennik transatlantycki," *Kultura*, 12 (1963), 194. The answer to Barbara Witek-Swinarska was included in the last Paris fragment of the *Diary*.
59 Gombrowicz, *Diary*, 652.
60 Ibid., 659.
61 Ibid., 660.
62 Safranski, *Zło. Dramat wolności*, 237; Kołakowski, "Etyka bez kodeksu," in *Kultura i fetysze*, 152–54.
63 Confirmation that he was familiar with works by the German philosopher is in the *Diary* and in *Kronos*.
64 Jaspers, *Question of German Guilt*, 26.
65 Kołakowski, "W piekle" in his *Czy Pan Bóg*, 126.

15 Gombrowicz-Schulz

From Duel to Double[1]

Jean-Pierre Salgas

In 1961, Éditions Julliard published a volume of Bruno Schulz's stories entitled *Traité des mannequins* in its French series "Lettres nouvel." In the same year, Witold Gombrowicz wrote in his diary: "Schulz: self-destruction in form, the drowned madman. I: burning desire to use form to get at my 'I' and reality, the madman in revolt."[2] In this essay, my intention is to focus on the Gombrowicz-Schulz relationship. Indeed in France, until recently, Gombrowicz scholars were in general uninterested in Bruno Schulz—perhaps he was too Jewish? Further, specialists in Schulz often ignored Gombrowicz—perhaps he was too Polish?[3] Here I attempt to discuss the impact of Schulz on Gombrowicz, tracing the history of their relationship while dividing it into different periods. However, I do not intend to restrict myself to their relationship while Schulz was alive, which lasted five years from 1934 when they first met to 1939 when Gombrowicz left for Argentina. Indeed, Gombrowicz's relationship to Schulz became as important, or even more important, after Schulz died. Gombrowicz's wife Rita confirmed that her husband spoke of Schulz every day. Neither do I intend to limit myself to the *explicit* relationships between them. My aim here is to broadly reconstruct a dialogue that took place in their lifetime, but also posthumously, including one that was "subterranean." Moreover, I am convinced that beyond the personal relationship between these two writers, this reconstruction will shed light on part of Poland's destiny during the twentieth century.

To begin, I would like to draw attention to two aspects of the Gombrowicz-Schulz relationship. First, before 1939, when Gombrowicz left for Argentina, and 1942, when Schulz was shot and killed by a German Gestapo officer in Poland, these two young writers "struggled for recognition" from each other. Thus, their relationship may be read within the Hegelian master-slave dialectic. Within that context of mutual recognition, Gombrowicz saw himself as "more Jewish" than Schulz, who, in Gombrowicz's view, retreated into the spheres of art and Polish culture. In Hegelian terms, it was easier for Schulz to fraternize with the "master" than it was for him to do so with the "slave."

Second, Gombrowicz was constantly viewing art and Poland (as a nation) from the perspective of his relationship with "Bruno," who became his "double," his "dybbuk."[4] Moreover, as I suggested earlier, in this transit from "duel" between master and slave to "double," one encounters true reflections about the "Polish question." To use Gombrowicz's words in his 1960 prologue to his novel *Pornography*, I am convinced that the Gombrowicz-Schulz relationship "bears a stronger relationship" to the "destiny" and "recent history" of Poland.[5]

Prologue: "A Kind of Internal Pogrom" (1926)

Under Józef Piłsudski's administration, there were political clashes between the "Endecja"[6] and the "Sanacja."[7] At the same time, poets who belonged to the Skamander group[8] were unable to perceive "reality," but simply followed the "isms" of the moment, dreaming of the possibility of restoring the Parnassus or world of poetry in Poland. Gombrowicz, for his part, fraternized with the Jewish people within the fragmented Polish society.[9] According to Gombrowicz, his friendship with the Jewish community began to blossom in the Ziemiańska Café and in the end led him to consider himself "King of the Jews."[10] But "the King of the Jews" continued to have a difficult relationship with his subjects for obvious reasons. On the one hand, he was not Jewish; on the other hand, the Jews were, at that time, a persecuted minority in Poland. One may also argue that these difficult relationships can be explained simply because *we are talking about Gombrowicz.*

The asymmetry that continuously marked the Gombrowicz-Schulz relationship is startling. It may be seen in the first texts these authors wrote even before they met; namely, in the short story "The Memoirs of Stefan Czarniecki" ("Pamiętnik Stefana Czarnieckiego") that appeared in Gombrowicz's *Memoirs of a Time of Immaturity* (*Pamiętnik z okresu dojrzewania*, 1933) and in Schulz's *The Cinnamon Shops* (*Sklepy cynamonowe*, 1934).[11] While Schulz, the high school teacher from Drohobycz, depicts in his stories a dream-like vision of the shtetl on a "dead temporal track," Gombrowicz endowed his hero with a dual genealogy. Stefan Czarniecki, Gombrowicz's hero, not only gives his name to the title of the 1926 story but also endows the first sentence of *Polish Memories*[12] with a significant autobiographical dual identity as Czarniecki-Goldwasser. Indeed, Stefan Czarniecki is an individual at the crossroads of two messianisms: "my father was well-bred to the marrow of his bones—my mother was also well-bred, but in a different sense, in the Semitic sense."[13] Referring to his son, the father claims, "He's going to suffer terribly when he grows in awareness; I wouldn't be surprised if at that point something happens within him along the lines of an inner massacre."[14] Stefan wonders: "What awareness was he speaking of, and what massacre? And in general—what ought to be the coloration of a rat born of a black male and a white female? Ought it to be mottled?"[15]

In 1926, in the Poland that emerged after the partitions, Gombrowicz found himself in between worlds: "between" Polish and Jewish; "between" nobility and the people; "between" nationalist temptations (this becomes a theme in *Ferdydurke*); "between" gender identities; and last but not least, as a writer, he is also in "between" styles. Indeed, to "be between" is a Jewish mode of being—even without necessarily being Jewish. "These were the first 'between,' which subsequently multiplied until they almost constituted my country of residence, my true home," he wrote at the end of his life.[16] Schulz identified himself in the author of "The Memoirs of Stefan Czarniecki" to the point that he decided to travel from Drohobycz to Warsaw to meet him. Gombrowicz wrote:

> He kept showing up in order to find confirmation in me, for me to furnish him with the Outside without which an inner life is condemned to a monologue—and he wanted me to use him in the same way.[17]

Gombrowicz became acquainted with this man of "small" stature, who was nonetheless a talented artist, in 1934. Although he advocated for Schulz against his critics, Gombrowicz was not very impressed with his literary texts which he found too poetic, too Kafkaeske for his taste. Gombrowicz commented, "Bruno adored me but I did not adore him."[18] The two men were "friends" because they shared the same enemies, but they belonged to different social classes. "He was of the Jewish race," Gombrowicz explained. "I was from a family of Polish gentry."[19] They were friends, but not "brothers." The relationship was of dominant and dominated. In 1961, Gombrowicz wrote that Schulz was "Someone almost completely unknown to me."[20]

The "Dispute Over the Doctor's Wife from Wilcza Street" (Spór o doktorow z Wilczej, 1936)

At the basis of the very unique relationship that linked these two writers—a relationship that Gombrowicz described in 1961 as a "fiasco" rather than a "symbiosis"[21]—is the fictional dispute that Gombrowicz published in the pages of the literary monthly *Studio* in July 1936 at the request of its editor, Bogusław Kuczyński. By means of a "duel," very much in the Hegelian "master-slave" tradition, Gombrowicz forced the writer from Galicia to take refuge in Polish Form, literally *"stealing"* from Schulz what Gombrowicz would later refer to as the Jewish "attitude to Form."[22] Thus, Gombrowicz challenged Schulz to defend himself against the dismissive opinion of a doctor's wife whom Gombrowicz supposedly met by accident on streetcar 18 near Wilcza Street in Warsaw. "Bruno Schulz," Gombrowicz has her concluding, "is either a sick pervert or a poseur, but most probably a poseur. He's only pretending."[23] Gombrowicz said to Schulz, "Your form is manifested *in excelsis*! Get back down to earth!"[24] A prisoner of his own "mug,"[25] in his response to Gombrowicz, Schulz escaped from the seeming confines into which Gombrowicz had ensnared him by means of rhetorical contortions that appear more typical of the Polish form:

> I hate the doctor's wife from Wilcza Street...the pure distillate of a doctor's wife, the textbook case of a doctor's wife or simply of a wife...though on an altogether different plane I find it difficult to resist the charm of her legs.[26]

In this response, Schulz appears as if possessing a "Janus-like duality."[27] Thus, when Gombrowicz urges Schulz to take a stance against the doctor's wife, Schulz suggests a separation of sexuality and intellect and takes refuge in "lofty" culture. In other words, "expelled from life," Schulz takes refuge in art. "You have reversed roles,"[28] Gombrowicz claimed. Schulz, in turn, mocks the "great humanist."[29] In the next issue of *Studio*, Gombrowicz published a text admitting that he learned from his "chain of indiscretions."[30] He explained why he decided to take up this duel with Schulz and why Schulz lost. In Gombrowicz analysis, Schulz was "not able to take a position toward the trivial, tasteless incident with the doctor's wife."[31]

Far from suffering, and unlike Stefan Czarniecki, Gombrowicz could play with every identity, every form, as well as art. Thus, using his shrewd Polish logic, Gombrowicz believes himself to be more "Jewish" than Bruno Schulz. In Gombrowicz's portrayal, Schulz turns out to be less "Jewish"; rather, he is frozen in his mug as a "gnome" of Drohobycz, fascinated by Polish culture, and wishing to integrate himself into it, a wish that was certainly granted if we take into account that in 1938 he was awarded the Polish Academy of Literature's prestigious Golden Laurel award.[32] Through this "duel," the forces of "Immaturity" confront those of "Form," which Gombrowicz encounters again in *Ferdydurke*. Indeed, Gombrowicz confronts Polish Forms not only in the novel but also in public space. We have Bruno Schulz's reaction to this "duel" in a letter to his friend, Andrzej Pleśniewicz: "An insignificant thing; I was surprised that they took it so seriously."[33]

Bruno's Presentation (1938)

Bruno Schulz overcame the "dispute over the doctor's wife from Wilcza Street" and became an exceptional exegete of Gombrowicz's *Ferdydurke*. It "made a stunning, dizzying impression on me.... Gombrowicz is really great," wrote Schulz to Romana Halpern on November 16, 1937.[34] One can perceive in what has remained of Schulz's correspondence the progression of his passion for the book—Gombrowicz gave it to Schulz before giving it to anyone else—as well as in his protests against those critics who wanted to suggest that Gombrowicz was his disciple. Schulz designed the cover illustration for the first edition of *Ferdydurke* issued by Roj Publishers and is the author of two drawings of duel situations published in the body of the text. Above all, Schulz was the first to proclaim to the world the importance of Gombrowicz's *Ferdydurke*, thus exhibiting an impressive disregard for what had happened in the pages of *Studio*. Schulz's lecture on *Ferdydurke*, given in Warsaw when Gombrowicz was in Rome, was later printed in *Skamander* in July-September 1938. Schulz claimed:

> Our literature has long been unaccustomed to phenomena so overwhelming, to literary discharges on the scale of Witold Gombrowicz's novel *Ferdydurke*. What we are dealing with here is an extraordinary manifestation of literary talent, a new and revolutionary method and form of novel, and finally, a fundamental discovery: the appropriation of a new sphere of spiritual phenomena, a vacant strip of no-man's land where previously there was nothing but the gambollings of irresponsible word-play and nonsense and puns.[35]

Schulz believed that Gombrowicz transcended both Proust and Freud, inasmuch as Gombrowicz appeared to have written a novel of both the *ego* and *superego*. In Schulz's view, "Gombrowicz came to them from the side of pathology—his own,"[36] providing "an inventory of the backyard, the outhouse, the self."[37] In addition, Gombrowicz, in Schulz's words, "has put on show the embriology of forms."[38] Indeed Schulz's lecture on *Ferdydurke* appears to be a sort of two-headed manifesto, a declaration of the two "conspirators" from Warsaw and Drohobycz, as if Schulz had incorporated Gombrowicz and allowed him to speak through him.[39] The lecture sealed the manifesto of the two "musketeers" for an avant-garde that will be broken by the German-Soviet pact—murder and exile—although in the end Schulz could not resist a passing shot at Gombrowicz, reproaching him for relying on the public's taste that "in the intermonadic medium we term 'opinion.'" This was probably an allusion to "The Doctor's Wife from Wilcza Street."[40] And just as Schulz read a presentation on Gombrowicz's *Ferdydurke*, Gombrowicz wrote an article on the occasion of the publication of Schulz's *Sanatorium Under the Sign of the Hourglass* (*Sanatorium Pod Klepsydrą*, 1938).

The Jewish Relationship to Form (1954)

> My attitude to Poland is a consequence of my attitude to form... A hundred years ago, a Lithuanian poet forged the shape of the Polish spirit and today, I, like Moses, am leading the Poles out of slavery to that form.[41]

In Poland, the "author of *Ferdydurke*" became in 1947 the "author of *Trans-Atlantyk*," and then again in 1956 that of *Ferdydurke* when it was reissued in Poland. In these, he attempted tirelessly to continue waging the anthropological and aesthetic battles of his texts by other means—political. His struggle was against the heroic "masses" in favor of national atheism, proposing a different relationship to form which was based on a clear assessment of the Immaturity of the country and its place in the global interhuman Church (with emphasis on the "inter" or in-betweenness). Hence, we find in his *Diaries* innumerable addresses, receptions, and speeches to the Polonia of Buenos Aires, as well as lectures, readings, commentaries on publications, biographical flashbacks, and polemics with London or Warsaw. Moreover, as if it were a new version of Adam Mickiewicz's *Books of the Polish Nation and Pilgrimage*, Gombrowicz's *Diaries* reverses Mickiewicz's allosemitism.[42] Of the two protagonists and their mimetic rivalry, it may be necessary to upset the hierarchy. Thus, like the Gonzalo of *Trans-Atlantyk*, Gombrowicz can play with every identity: for example, he turned the painful experience of Stefan Czarniecki into a strength.

I believe one can see here the effect of the *interiorization* of the dialogue that Gombrowicz pursued with Schulz "posthumously," continuing in a "subterranean" but unceasing manner until 1969 when Gombrowicz passed away in Vence. Moreover, after his murder, Bruno Schulz became Gombrowicz's intimate "double," his *dybbuk*, in Argentina and then in Europe. From this relationship, we can detect a hundred direct and indirect traces before the beginning of the *Diary* in 1953; for example, in his attempt to obtain recognition from Martin Buber. In 1954, Gombrowicz resumed his reflections on the "Jewish question" which he had begun with "The Memoirs of Stefan Czarniecki" and the "duel" of the articles in *Studio* in 1936. Hence, in his *Diary*, Gombrowicz compares the Jewish "suicide-duel against his own form" with that of Frédéric Chopin, who, in the Polish Pantheon, is on a par with the three romantic poets (Adam Mickiewicz, Juliusz Słowacki, Zygmunt Krasiński), Kościuszko, and Copernicus, the unquestionable national hero. "The Jewish way of the cross is the same as Chopin's," writes Gombrowicz.[43] The Jew is "in-between" and knows it, unlike the Pole who does not even want to consider it.

Indeed, Gombrowicz credits to the heroes of the Polish national Pantheon the same positions that he would have liked to see Bruno Schulz endorsing in the formal duel of 1936, and not only in his lecture on *Ferdydurke* under the mask of friendship. Being "the King of the Jews," Gombrowicz might well have drawn from his real ties to Bruno Schulz before the war in their community of "conspirators"[44] of Form, the principle of the "Filistria" utopia that he suggested for all minor European cultures—something we might today equate with Édouard Glissant's "creolization." What is more, the "dispute" in *Studio* in 1936, where the writers' intimacies are subject to the social game of "mugs," could well provide the paradoxical abridged model of Gombrowicz's battle against Poland. Thus, the criticisms that Gombrowicz leveled against Schulz—that he takes refuge in art—are taken up later by Gombrowicz, amplified, and this time directed against the post-war writers of a divided Poland (Poland and Polonia) which he scorned from Buenos Aires. Gombrowicz accused them of failing to take reality (that is to say, immaturity) into account and for not having enough literary autonomy since they were prisoners of a national and "poetic" unreality.[45]

"A Prince Travelling Incognito" (1961)

Gombrowicz returned to the theme of the "Jewish relationship to form" in *Polish Memories* (1961), this time in an autobiographical manner. He exposed this theme in three stages: the game of the squire's and Jew's "mugs" in the Polish countryside; the arrival of the young squire at the university in 1923 (we may argue that this corresponds to the genesis and structure of "The Memoirs of Stefan Czarniecki"); and his entry into literature and the immediate support of Bruno Schulz, Artur Sandauer, and Józef Wittlin. He wrote, "Always and everywhere the Jews were the first to sense and to understand my work as a writer. It was so clearly pronounced that I sometimes wondered if a drop of their blood did not flow in my veins."[46] He then explained:

> they often feel themselves to be a caricature.... This tension in the Jew's relation to form; the fact that it torments him so, or renders him laughable, or humiliates him; the fact that a Jew is never fully himself in a way that a peasant or a squire is himself, thoroughly comfortable in a form he has inherited from preceding generations... all this made the Jews fascinating to me. For that was what I was striving for in my art—to bring out people's struggles with form....[47]

Moreover, Gombrowicz was convinced that this Jewish world represented "one of our best opportunities to devise a new species of Pole with a modern form capable of facing up to the present day."[48] In other words, it is time to make Poland a little more Jewish, to make it a kind of Argentina where identity is non-identity, to remake the country of "in-between" as it once was not so long ago. There is something in "Jewishness" that can revive the Polish nation that is engulfed in kitsch.

As mentioned earlier, Gombrowicz referred to Schulz in his *Diary* in the same year that Schulz's *Traité des mannequins* appeared in French.[49] Gombrowicz presented Schulz as an "untempered masochist" who "was ejected from life,"[50] but also as an "artist" most worthy to sit in the circle of the highest intellectual and artistic aristocracy in Europe. "No one, however, was more generous than Bruno.... No one ever supported me in so heartfelt a manner, no one ever delighted in me, ever stoked each and every one of my thoughts the way he did."[51] Moreover, in *Polish*

Memories, Gombrowicz recounted Schulz's first visit to Słuzewska Street, his provincialism, masochism, their misunderstandings, Schulz's enthusiastic reading of *Ferdydurke*, and the visit to Witkiewicz. "He has remained what he was," claimed Gombrowicz, "a prince travelling incognito."[52] Moreover, once again, Gombrowicz pursued the "master-slave" dialectic and applied it to their relationship, continuing the formal duel of the 1930s beyond death and genocide. "He was born to be a slave. I was born to be a master."[53] "He liked me to attack him."[54] He is the master that Schulz looks for while Gombrowicz considers himself "inferior" [55] to his novel. Again and again, there appeared in Gombrowicz's works two versions of Schulz: Dr. Bruno, the "conspirator," who is "experimenting with a certain explosive material called Form"[56] (who did the presentation on *Ferdydurke*) and Mr. Schulz, the Polish writer (the one from *Studio*). To put it in another way: his Jewish friend, who lives "in-between" versus the oppressed Jew, subjected to the norms of Polish society at that time.

Epilogue: "When We Lived in Drohobycz" (1965)

In his *A Kind of Testament. Conversations with Dominique de Roux* (1968), a book written with the "Western public"—that is to say French public—in mind, and in no way a "testament" as the English translation suggests. What a bad posthumous title indeed; this book is in no way a book for death. In *Testament*, Gombrowicz returned to his relationship with Schulz, this time both explicitly and implicitly. The latter can be seen when he asserted that Poland had caught up in the rivalry between two messianisms and would have a future only if it took part in a suicide-duel against its own form. This was an attitude that, in Gombrowicz's view, characterized the Jewish culture, the culture of the "in-between" or "Filistria." Finally, but not least, Schulz appears also "subterranously" in Gombrowicz's great novel *Kosmos*, where the ultimate Polish-Jewish bequest is represented by the character Leon Wojtis. Leon's main feature consists in his many linguistic inventions, among them the word "berg" that does not exist in Polish and which Leon uses in multiple combinations.[57] Indeed, Konstanty Jeleński underlines how much, in this case, the writer made an anthropological use of the language. In Chapter 8, Leon (between Epicure and Offenbach) remembered his experiences of twenty-seven years ago and decided to go from Zakopane to Drohobycz in Galicia, from the city of the Polish intelligentsia to the shtetl. "One time," Leon claims,

> when we lived in Drohobycz, a truly sumptuous actress came to town for a guest performance, a lioness no less, and I accidentally touched her little hand on the bus, so, young man, frenzy, madness, wild excitement, do it again, but it's out of the question, impossible.[58]

Thus, we may argue that in Drohobycz, the city of Bruno Schulz, the only contact of Leon with the Other took place. In this sense, it is significant that Jeleński saw in Leon's character Gombrowicz's double or Doppelgänger. After this single contact, Leon returns to his solitary pleasures. Therefore, we may conclude that, in Drohobycz, Schulz's posthumous triumph over Gombrowicz took place, the triumph of the "incognito prince," who, after the war, took up residence in the body of the fallen squire. In the end, it turns out that the actress deceives "the wife of the doctor of Wilcza street."

Post-scriptum: Schulz "Between" Isaac Bashevis Singer and Philip Roth (1976)

The American writer Philip Roth, who edited the "Writers of the Other Europe" for Penguin, wanted to include Schulz's in this series. Having learned that Isaac Bashevis Singer[59] wrote a rave review of Schulz's *The Street of Crocodiles* in 1963, Roth interviewed the Yiddish writer in November 1976, two years after Singer received the Nobel Prize for Literature 1978, one day in November 1976. The interview is included in Roth's book *Shop talk*.[60] "The more I read Schulz—maybe I shouldn't say it—but when I read him, I said he's better than Kafka,"[61] claims Singer. Roth approves of Singer's statement but insists on the differences between these two authors. Then, a dozen pages of conversation follow and Roth asks Singer to comment on the opposition between Yiddish and Polish writers during the interwar period ("Though the truth is," Singer claims, "they had no choice and we had no choice").[62] Moreover, Singer discusses at length the psychological complexes that dominated Jews in Poland at the time. To get his point across, he describes a situation that he experienced in a subway with the Yiddish writer S, "who had a beard"; as Singer adds, "at this time, forty years ago, very few people had beards."[63] To some extent, this scene is reminiscent of the narrative about the doctor's wife from Wilcza street. Central to the exchange between Singer and Roth is the question of language—question that never surfaced when Gombrowicz talks about Schulz, and which adds, in America, an additional depth to the issue. Towards the end of the meeting, Roth reminds Singer of a sentence from the latter's 1963 article about Schulz: "If Schulz had identified himself more with his own people, he might not have expended so much energy on imitation, parody, and caricature."[64] This sentence presents the Polish language as a choice rather than an imposition—an obvious fact for Gombrowicz but it appears that Schulz was not able to perceive it in that way. Singer explains why he believes Schulz wrote a kind of parody rather than writing "serious novels." He claims:

> I think basically he developed this style because he was not really at home, neither at home among the Poles nor at home among the

Jews. It's a style that's somewhat characteristic also of Kafka, because Kafka also felt that he had no roots.[65]

"I would rather have liked to have seen him as a Yiddish writer. He wouldn't have had all the time to be as negative and mocking as he was."[66] In other words, in the name of a national, atavistic, conception of Jewish identity, Singer regrets that Schulz was too "in between," becoming thus a Polish writer. Roth, for his part, praises Schulz's "in-betweenness"; for Roth, Schulz's writing is clearly "Jewish," where for Singer it appears that Schulz is not "Jewish enough." Precisely because of his "in-betweenness," Schulz, in Gombrowicz's view, cannot identify 100 percent either with Jewishness or with Polishness, as he points out when theorizing the Jews' relationship to Form in 1954, when revisiting his Polish youth in Argentina.

Paradoxically, because he raises the question of language, Philip Roth is perhaps unknowingly more Gombrowiczian that Gombrowicz in his *Diary* of 1961. Gombrowicz appears to have forgotten the "Witold" from 1954; but he will recover that "Witold" in 1965. Whereas Gombrowicz is critical of Schulz for being more "Polish" than "Jewish," Roth believes that Schulz's capability of thinking in terms of "rootlessness" while being engulfed within Polish form, including art, indicates the presence of this specifically Jewish creative tension.

Notes

1 This article was translated from the French by Silvia G. Dapía.
2 Gombrowicz, *Diary*, 528.
3 In the French editions of these two writers, it is very difficult to reconstruct their dialogue with accuracy. Thus, for example, the references of the texts of one are never given correctly in the notes of the texts of the other. See my *Les trois mousquetaires*.
4 *Translator's note*: a "dybbuk" in Jewish mythology is a malicious possessing spirit who takes up residence in a living body and leaves the host body once it has accomplished its goal, sometimes after being helped.
5 Gombrowicz, *Pornografia* (Hamilton), 10.
6 *Translator's note*: "Endecja" was the right-wing "National Democracy," a Polish political movement opposing the partitions. Led primarily by Roman Dmowski, it viewed Germany as the greatest threat to Poland, favored an accommodation with Russia, and envisioned a homogenous Catholic Polish state. It was supported by the majority of the Polish diaspora because of its alignment with Britain and France during World War I. With independence and the birth of the Second Republic, it adopted a policy of Polonizing the country's ethnic minorities including Germans in the west and Ukrainians and Ruthenians in the east. The movement came to an end after the German invasion of Poland in 1939.
7 *Translator's note*: "Sanacja" was a Polish political movement led by Józef Piłsudski who believed Russia to be the greatest threat to Poland, raised a legion of Poles to fight with the Austro-Hungarian Empire, and envisioned a multi-ethnic Poland in the tradition of the Polish-Lithuanian

Commonwealth. Sanacja came to power following Piłsudski's May 1926 *coup d' état* when he advocated a "sanation" (healing) of the Polish body politic. Following his death in 1935, Sanacja fragmented into competing factions.

8 *Translator's note*: "Skamander" was a group of Polish experimental poets created in 1918. Influenced by the neoromantic movement, they attempted to divorce poetry from its traditional historical function of promoting Polish patriotism and supported the use of commonplace language to make poetry more accessible to the public.

9 Gombrowicz devotes only a single line to Bruno Schulz, particularly to Schulz's *The Cinnamon Shops*, in his *Diary* of 1955. See Gombrowicz, *Diary*, 160, 520. For Schulz's place in twentieth-century Polish-Jewish literature, see Sandauer, *Polish Writer of Jewish Descent*, esp. 74 for Gombrowicz. Sandauer coined the term "allosemitism" for analyzing non-Jews' attitudes toward Jews.

10 Gombrowicz, *Memories*, 178.

11 Bruno Schulz's collection of short-stories *Sklepy cynamonowe*, whose literal translation is "Cinnamon Shops" is in English-speaking countries most often referred to as *The Street of Crocodiles*.

12 "'I was born and raised in a most respectable home': This ironic sentence, which begins one of my short-stories—'The Memoirs of Stefan Czarniecki'— may also serve as an opening for these present recollections." Gombrowicz, *Memories*, 2–3.

13 Gombrowicz, *Bacacay*, 25.

14 Ibid., 21.

15 Ibid.

16 Gombrowicz, *Testament*, 28.

17 Gombrowicz, *Diary*, 520.

18 Ibid.

19 Ibid., 522.

20 Ibid., 520.

21 Ibid.

22 Gombrowicz, *Memories*, 178.

23 Schulz, *Letters*, 117.

24 Ibid., 119.

25 *Translator's note*: the Polish word "gęba," the slang word for a "face," is translated by Danuta Borchardt into "mug." As she explains, "'gęba,' or the 'mug,' is a metaphor for destructive elements in our relating to one another." See Borchardt, "Translating Witold Gombrowicz's *Ferdydurke*."

26 Schulz, *Drawings*, 122.

27 Ibid.

28 Ibid., 124.

29 Ibid.

30 Gombrowicz, *Varia, Dzieła zebrane*, X, 203–7.

31 Schulz, *Drawings*, 128.

32 "Gombrowicz was fascinated by a question, namely, the value of art for the petty bourgeois, the fool, the idiot. He was able to see literature from outside, to ask questions about its sociological status, while Schulz was living in a fragile ivory tower (of cinnamon?) that he did not want to leave, not even for a moment." Zagajewski, *La trahison*, 192.

33 Schulz, *Dziela zebrane. Tom 5*, 117.

34 Schulz, *Correspondance et essais*, 197.

35 Schulz, "Ferdydurke," 25.

36 Ibid., 29.

37 Ibid., 28.
38 Ibid., 29.
39 Gombrowicz re-appropriates Schulz's voice in Gombrowicz, *Testament*, 64–65.
40 Schulz, "Ferdydurke," 32.
41 Gombrowicz, *Diary*, 44.
42 *Translator's note*: "the practice of settling the Jews apart as people radically different from others" is from Bauman, "Allosemitism," 143.
43 Gombrowicz, *Diary*, 99.
44 Ibid., 526.
45 Using "Immaturity" in this sense, Gombrowicz suggests that they did not take reality into account because they did not take into account immaturity, that is, "potential." Rather, they took something frozen in time, without considering the future, as if it were the only reality.
46 Gombrowicz, *Memories*, 182.
47 Ibid., 178–79.
48 Ibid., 180.
49 Gombrowicz, *Diary*, 519.
50 Ibid., 523.
51 Ibid., 521.
52 Gombrowicz, *Memories*, 114.
53 Gombrowicz, *Diary*, 522.
54 Ibid., 526.
55 Gombrowicz, *Testament*, 66.
56 Gombrowicz, *Diary*, 527.
57 *Translator's note*: Borchardt claims: "Another of Leon's oddities was the word berg. It does not exist in the Polish language and I left it untranslated in the English. In its multiple permutations it occurs in *Cosmos* more than one hundred times, as a noun, a verb, an adverb, etc. Leon not only uses it as a masturbatory word but also gives it other, though related, meanings, some of which I translated as 'penalberg,' 'lovey-doveberg,' 'pilgrimageberg.'" From "Translator's Note," Gombrowicz, *Cosmos* (Borchardt), ix.
58 Ibid., 141.
59 Singer was born in 1904 in Radzymin, near Warsaw.
60 A collection of Philip Roth's conversations with Primo Levi, Aharon Appelfeld, Ivan Klima, Isaac Bashevis Singer, Milan Kundera, and Edna O'Brien. In addition, the book contains a discussion with Mary McCarthy, a memoir of novelist Bernard Malamud, and essays on Philip Guston and Saul Bellow.
61 Roth, *Shop Talk*, 79.
62 Ibid., 82.
63 Ibid., 87–88.
64 Ibid., 84.
65 Ibid.
66 Ibid., 85. On all these issues, see Magris, *Lontano da dove*; Casanova, *Kafka en colère*; Serra, *Italo Svevo*. Schulz claims: "The world at that time was circumscribed by Franz Josef I. On each stamp, on every coin, and on every postmark his likeness confirmed its stability and the dogma of its oneness. This was the world, and there were no other worlds besides, the effigies of the imperial and royal old man proclaimed." From: *Sanatorium*, Wieniewska, transl.

16 The Politics of Performing Gombrowicz in Communist and Post-Communist Poland

Allen J. Kuharski

Throughout the period of Communist rule in Poland (1945–1989), various political and cultural factions sought to gain legitimacy by being associated with the works of Witold Gombrowicz in both print and performance. These factions ultimately represented a broad spectrum of Polish cultural and political life (reform-minded communist, secular democratic socialist, Catholic leftist, neo-liberal, nominally apolitical, and pacifist/anarchist), with the exceptions of the extremes of the Stalinist left and the nationalist right. The theatrical performance of Gombrowicz in communist Poland in particular was a complex and paradoxical phenomenon that has deeply inflected the subsequent normalization and canonization of the writer's work in the post-communist period. While the publication of Gombrowicz's writing in Poland remained erratic and conflicted through 1989, the theatrical performance of his works by the 1970s became a centerpiece of the contemporary Polish repertory, following a series of notable student productions and the first Polish professional staging of *The Marriage* in Warsaw in 1974.

For the publication of Gombrowicz in Polish during the years of Communist rule, the primary stewards of his work were the dissident editors of the Instytut Literacki/Institut Littéraire in Paris (commonly referred to simply as *Kultura*, the name of their highly regarded monthly cultural review), led by Jerzy Giedroyc. Giedroyc was eventually joined in this work by Rita Labrosse Gombrowicz, the writer's French Canadian widow and literary executor, following the writer's death in 1969. *Kultura* itself represented a specific political position in the Polish post-war diaspora: a combination of advocacy of principles of secular socialist democracy with categorical rejections of both pre-war Polish nationalist politics and Soviet-style communism. *Kultura*'s cosmopolitan, liberal, inclusive politics were in agreement with Gombrowicz's own politics, particularly as articulated in his *Diary 1953–1969* (originally published in serial form in *Kultura*). This political position moved from the arena of progressive dissident intellectuals such as Gombrowicz and Giedroyc living and publishing abroad to the center of Polish cultural and political life with the end of communist rule in 1989. There is a consistency of political thought over time in Gombrowicz's writing, which has been honored in varying degrees by those seeking either artistic or political legitimacy through association with his work in performance.

On this score it is useful to bear in mind that the essence of theatrical performance work is *collaboration* between artists, and that both artistic opportunity and prestige comes from the quality of one's collaborators—a process that at best is *mutual*. The fundamental principle of creative/professional collaboration in theater has a parallel in political alliances and coalitions, which are most meaningful when they are similarly both *free* and *mutual*. Compromised or coerced versions of either artistic or political collaboration are always possible, and the principle of freedom in both arenas depends upon the right to choose one's partners along with the option to refuse or withdraw from a given relationship. Theater, like politics in a free society, is based on the generation of *elective communities* of both makers and target audiences. Gombrowicz as a theater artist was ambitious and highly selective in his artistic collaborators, and as a public intellectual extremely scrupulous in his choice of political alliances. After his death, such decisions became the responsibility primarily of Giedroyc and especially Rita Gombrowicz.

The "normalization" of Gombrowicz on the stages of communist Poland began exactly ten years after the successful launch of his plays in Western Europe in the 1960s, with a momentum that ultimately reached many other parts of the world. Over time, Gombrowicz has emerged as Poland's most-produced playwright abroad, with *Ivona, Princess of Burgundia* by far the most widely performed of his plays. As such, performances of Gombrowicz's work since the 1960s have assumed an ever more significant role in representing Polish culture globally, which has repeatedly demanded a response from the country's political leadership both at home and abroad. Stage adaptations of Gombrowicz's prose works, always a significant part of the writer's history in performance abroad, also became increasingly common in Poland starting in the mid-1970s. The combination of the proliferation of stage performance with the restrictions on the circulation of Gombrowicz's work in print in Poland resulted in a shift in the cultural transmission of his work in the 1970s and 1980s, with significant Polish audiences having ready and often primary access to his work via live performance instead of the printed word. The impact of Gombrowicz in performance versus published text was further amplified by the increasing number of radio and television versions of his plays and various dramatizations of his prose broadcast in Poland in the 1970s and 1980s.

Gombrowicz in Poland before 1974

Before the 1970s, Gombrowicz's status as a banned expatriate writer largely followed patterns familiar in countries with authoritarian governments. While Gombrowicz was living in Argentina, West Germany, and France, his works were first published in Polish in Paris by *Kultura*, with Giedroyc and Konstanty Jeleński becoming Gombrowicz's early promoters in Western Europe. Alongside BBC Radio and Radio Free Europe, *Kultura* was a stalwart Cold War institution heavily supported by the United States government and its West European allies. It was a long-standing thorn in the side of Poland's communist leadership and these organizations often coordinated their efforts. Under theater critic Martin Esslin's leadership, for example, BBC Radio 3 produced the first professional production of Gombrowicz's *The Marriage* in the English language, which was then broadcast internationally (and possibly to Poland) in 1969. Gombrowicz–who knew no English–heard the BBC radio version in France shortly before his death that year, his only experience of a full performance of any of his plays. Smuggling publications of banned writers into Poland (including many translated from other languages, especially Russian) was among *Kultura*'s top priorities. Alongside Czesław Miłosz and Gustaw Herling-Grudziński, Gombrowicz was among the most notable Polish literary talents writing for *Kultura* at the time.

An opening in Gombrowicz's relations with communist Poland took place in 1957–1958, a fleeting period of "thaw" in cultural life, during which a limited number of his works appeared in print in official Polish editions with his approval, including the plays *Ivona*, *The Marriage* (first published in Spanish in Argentina in 1946) and *Trans-Atlantyk* (published in Paris by *Kultura* in 1953). During this time, the *auteur* director/designer Tadeusz Kantor tried unsuccessfully to obtain Gombrowicz's permission to direct the world premiere of *Ivona* with his independent experimental company Teatr Cricot-2 in Kraków. At the same time, the director Tadeusz Byrski, a dissident Catholic leftist with life-long ties with Czesław Miłosz, unsuccessfully sought permission to direct the world premiere of *The Marriage* at his theater in Kielce. Gombrowicz made it clear that he wanted the first Polish productions of his plays to be in Warsaw and done by a major classical company rather than by a provincial or avant-garde one.[1] As a result, *Ivona* had its world premiere at Warsaw's prominent Teatr Armii Ludowej (People's Army Theater, today known as Teatr Dramatyczny) located in the city's Soviet-style Palace of Culture, in a production directed by Halina Mikołajska, a future dissident and leader of the Solidarity movement. Mikołajska's production was broadcast on Polish television. Significantly, the program for the 1957 production included excerpts from Gombrowicz's *Diary*—a subtle by-pass of the larger ban on the publication of that text in Poland (approximately 25,000 copies of the program were distributed).[2]

By 1958, censorship in communist Poland returned to earlier patterns, and neither the publication nor the performance of Gombrowicz's works would be allowed until years after his death in 1969. In 1960, the director Jerzy Jarocki in collaboration with the designer Krystyna Zachwatowicz mounted an underground student production of *The Marriage* at the Gliwice Polytechnic University in Upper Silesia (the first staging of the play), which was closed by the authorities after four performances. Both Jarocki and Zachwatowicz would each play a significant role in future productions of Gombrowicz both in Poland and abroad (and in Jarocki's case, this would also include a number of major productions in Poland after 1989). The professional stage premiere of *The Marriage* would later take place in Paris in 1964, directed by the Argentine Jorge Lavelli and designed by Zachwatowicz. While successful in launching Gombrowicz as a playwright in France and Western Europe, this production was undeniably avant-garde in concept and style. The young Lavelli did not allow Gombrowicz to attend rehearsals, and Gombrowicz (then living near Paris), in turn, never attended a performance, even though he was charmed by Zachwatowicz.[3]

Here the variety of artistic vision and political positions that sought to claim pride of place in introducing Gombrowicz to the Polish stage is already evident: dissident secular leftist but theatrically mainstream (Mikołajska); progressive Catholic with theatrical roots in Stanislavsky and the rigorous interwar acting innovations of Juliusz Osterwa and his Reduta Theater (Tadeusz Byrski, who was also an early supporter of Jerzy Grotowski); secular pacifist anarchism combined with visually driven avant-gardism (Tadeusz Kantor); a sophisticated hybrid of Stanislavsky, surrealism, and the Polish avant-garde within the context of communist Polish institutional theaters (Jarocki). Zachwatowicz's *auteur* design work profoundly shaped the early productions she worked on, and linked the work being done in Poland with Western Europe. The protean role of student theaters in communist Poland is also apparent, notably in the setting of a provincial polytechnic institution rather than a prominent university or drama school in Warsaw or Kraków. While Kantor and Byrski were publicly frustrated in their attempts to introduce Gombrowicz to the postwar Polish stage, his writings nevertheless proved a private inspiration for many such "secret sharers" in Polish theater at the time. These included the work of director Jerzy Grotowski and his artistic partner dramaturge Ludwik Flaszen with the Laboratory Theater in Opole and Wrocław through 1982. In Flaszen's words, "One of Grotowski's secret masters was Gombrowicz (I considered him my overt master)."[4]

Jarocki and Zachwatowicz's historic staging of *The Marriage* in Gliwice was followed in the early 1970s by a series of ground-breaking student productions of Gombrowicz's work that at times enjoyed significant financial and institutional support for production costs as well as national and international touring expenses, even while the ban on full professional production was enforced by the authorities and the Gombrowicz estate. Between 1971 and 1976, Teatr STU (founded in 1966 by students of the Kraków State Drama School) performed *Polish*

Dreambook (*Sennik polski*), a collage of texts by various Polish authors (particularly the classic Romantic playwright/poets Adam Mickiewicz and Juliusz Słowacki) that included excerpts from Gombrowicz's novel *Trans-Atlantyk*. According to Kathleen Cioffi:

> STU wanted to show that contemporary Poles were still under the influence of stereotypes that were formed in the nineteenth century, and to question the power that these stereotypes still seemed to exert over Poles' thinking about themselves. ... In *Polish Dreambook* STU was engaged in an examination of the national myths of Poland, an examination which revealed both the beauty and the grotesquerie of those myths.[5]

Cioffi's analysis clearly reveals both why *Trans-Atlantyk* bolstered the larger themes of the production and how aptly it would counterpoint the works of the nineteenth-century Polish Romantics.

Teatr STU originated as one of communist Poland's elite student theaters, and as such it received generous government subsidies for performing productions on numerous domestic and international tours. In addition to touring in Poland, *Polish Dreambook* was performed widely in Western Europe, Latin America, and Iran years before the end of the general ban on professional productions of Gombrowicz's work in Poland. The company's tours in Latin America in particular were remarkable, representing Poland in major international festivals in Bogotá, Caracas, Santo Domingo, and México City between 1973 and 1976.[6] The only language into which *Trans-Atlantyk* had been translated at this point was Spanish, and the performances were done without supertitles on tour, so it remains an open question how much foreign audiences comprehended Gombrowicz's text or its significance. At the same time, Teatr STU anticipated Jarocki and Kantor's subsequent work in creating an aesthetic of freely inspired collage of various authors and texts. It also benefitted from the generous state subsidies that Kantor scorned. Like Kantor, Grotowski and other innovative Polish theater of this era, Teatr STU's heightened and poetic performance style was strongly physical and visual in non-literal ways, making the work more accessible to international audiences without a common language. The government-funded international tours by Teatr STU in the 1970s represented a significant form of cultural diplomacy targeted at student-aged audiences around the world. Having Gombrowicz in the mix of this work was clearly seen as desirable in representing Poland to best advantage abroad.

Another notable example of this early student work is Jarocki's *Acts* (*Akty*), a sprawling dramatic "anthology" production at Warsaw's State Drama School (Państwowa Wyższa Szkoła Teatralna; PWST) in 1972. Jarocki's text for the production consisted of four "acts," one each from Stanisław Wyspiański's *The Wedding* (1901), Witkacy's *The Mother*

(1924), Gombrowicz's *The Marriage* (1946), and Sławomir Mrożek's *Tango* (1964), performed in chronological order. This structure in effect enshrined *The Marriage* as one of the definitive works of Polish twentieth-century drama when there was yet to be a single professional production of the play in Poland. *Acts* was originally the diploma production of an extraordinary cohort of future stars in Polish theater and film that included Ewa Dałkowska, Jadwiga Jankowska-Cieślak, Marek Kondrat, Ryszard Major, and Jerzy Radziłłowicz. The production toured with the annual American College Theatre Festival (ACTF) in the newly built Kennedy Center in Washington, DC, in 1972—as such it was the first performance of Gombrowicz by Polish actors on tour abroad. The next time that Polish actors would perform a work by Gombrowicz on international tour in the English-speaking world would be in 2000, when Teatr Provisorium & Kompania made its first of several tours of the United States performing an adaptation of *Ferdydurke*. Though *Acts* was performed without supertitles, *The Marriage* was already in print in English in Louis Iribarne's translation. *Acts* was Jarocki's second pass at staging *The Marriage;* photos and documentation from the production are regularly included in overviews of Jarocki's work in Poland today.[7] Jarocki and Zachwatowicz reunited to collaborate on the Swiss premiere of the play at Zürich's prestigious Schauspielhaus later that year, presumably with the tacit cooperation of the Polish authorities. It would still be two years before the duo would mount the full Polish professional premiere of the play in Warsaw in 1974—on the same prominent stage in the city's Palace of Culture where the world premiere of *Ivona* took place in 1957. Five years after his death, Gombrowicz's wish to have *The Marriage* first performed in Warsaw in a large institutional venue was fulfilled, though Jarocki's production could no more be described as "classical" than Lavelli's in Paris in 1964.

An undeniable part of this tacit official support of such cultural diplomacy in this period was paradoxically to claim Gombrowicz as a Polish writer abroad even while the professional performance and publication of his works remained severely restricted in Poland itself. These mixed signals from communist Poland's cultural and educational authorities undoubtedly reflected the internal political divisions that dogged the country's cultural leadership throughout this period. These divisions were evident over the course of the Gomułka regime (1956–1970) as well as the subsequent Gierek government (1970–1980). The desire of elements of the more liberal Gierek leadership to embrace Gombrowicz's work was reflected in their early willingness to permit the performance of the writer's work by student groups before having an agreement with Rita Gombrowicz allowing professional stagings.

Audiences seeking ambitious student theater in Poland in the 1970s were able to attend *Retrospective* (*Retrospektywa*, 1973), a production by Teatr 77 in Łódź, which daringly used passages from Gombrowicz's

Diary as a point of departure for a piece as innovative as environmental and interactive performance as it was challenging politically. According to Kathleen Cioffi:

> [*Retrospective*] was staged as an art gallery opening to which people requested invitations rather than tickets. With the invitation some excerpts from Witold Gombrowicz's diary which were given to the audience members [...]. The audience was supposed to read the material by Gombrowicz and to think about it before coming to the opening. [...]
> [After the first part of the performance] the audience [was] asked to cast ballots which were given at the door. These contained one of the following two questions:
>
> 1. In casting off everything that, according to W. Gombrowicz, is degenerate in form, and in this way compromises us, humbles us, deprives us of individuality, and so in casting off, for example, our "convulsive history," do we obtain the chance of full self-realization?
> 2. [Or]—do we lose ourselves?

Each audience member is supposed to mark "TAK" ("Yes") or "NIE" ("No") on his/her ballot and then go upstairs to a different room depending on his/her answer.[8] Alongside this flowering of student theater using Gombrowicz's texts, the 1960s and early 1970s saw no further professional performances of Gombrowicz in Poland, the period of his first significant fame abroad.

The increasingly fluid categories of "student," "alternative," and "professional" theater in the 1970s helped nurture the long-term careers of artists first begun in universities or drama schools. The flourishing of student and alternative theaters often took on a political role as well. In the words of Kathleen Cioffi:

> ... alternative theatre served as an early warning device that signaled what was to come in Polish politics. ... during the early seventies ... before KOR[9] or Solidarity existed, [student theaters such as] Kalambur, STU, 8th Day, and [Teatr] 77 helped shape the consciousness of the generation of young intellectuals who would become active in KOR, and later in Solidarity.[10]

The same was also emphatically true of Lublin's Teatr Provisorium, which became particularly associated with Gombrowicz over time. All of these student theaters later suffered in various ways after the declaration of martial law that targeted the Solidarity movement in Poland in 1981. Halina Mikołajska, for example, the director of the world premiere of Gombrowicz's *Ivona* in 1957, and an outspoken member of both KOR (Komitet Obrony Robotników; Workers Defence Committee) and Solidarity (Solidarność), was imprisoned for her political activities.

What is striking in this picture is the diversity of artistic practices and political thinking in the supposed monoculture of a Soviet-style centralized authoritarian state, along with the broad geographical distribution of the artists. None of these directors fit the mold of a conventional Communist fellow traveler in the 1950s, a nonconformity that became more pronounced in each over time. It is also important to note that the earliest of these struggles to "brand" Gombrowicz on the Polish stage were consciously curated by the writer himself and began even before his reputation as a playwright was established outside of Poland.

Theatrical Dissent and "Normalization": 1974–1989

A theater-goer in Warsaw in 1979 was likely to have seen director Zbigniew Wróbel's stage adaptation of Gombrowicz's 1938 novel *Ferdydurke* at Teatr Studio, adjacent to Teatr Dramatyczny in the Palace of Culture. Teatr Studio was Warsaw's showcase experimental theater at the time, and was under the artistic leadership of the director/designer Józef Szajna, a career-long member of the Polish Communist Party, and best known abroad for his historic collaboration with Jerzy Grotowski on the Laboratory Theater's *Akropolis* in the 1960s. *Ferdydurke* was performed more than 200 times over the course of four seasons, with a total audience of over 55,000 people,[11] straddling the years of the rise of the Solidarity movement and the declaration of martial law in Poland in 1981. If that same theater-goer wanted to read the novel, however, they would have been forced to obtain a rare surviving copy of its pre-war first edition, discretely acquire a smuggled copy published in France, or request special permission at the University of Warsaw library to see a copy of the original edition from the locked case of banned books.

Among those who attended *Ferdydurke* at Teatr Studio at the time was the author of this article, who had read the text in Eric Mosbacher's English translation published by Grove Press in the 1960s. It was this American visitor's first experience of Gombrowicz in performance in particular, and of Polish theater in general. As with Mikołajska's *Ivona* or the Jarocki/Zachwatowicz production of *The Marriage*, Wróbel's *Ferdydurke* was performed on one of the stages located in the landmark Palace of Culture.

Around the same time, sixty students preparing for Poland's university-qualifying exams (the *matura*) in one of Warsaw's high schools shared a single copy of the first edition of the book to prepare for questions on modern Polish literature that included the text. That 40-year-old copy of the novel was similarly shared by several years of students in the school, illustrating the wide circulation of the text in spite of the official ban on its postwar publication.[12] High school teachers at the time had some freedom in what texts they could assign in their schools for the exams, and clearly elements of the educational establishment were content to tolerate this. Significantly, after the late 1950s, the concern of the Polish communist authorities was less with the content of the novel than with restricting the general circulation of publications from its dissident publisher in Paris.

In a unique historic compromise in the 1970s between the Polish communist authorities and Rita Gombrowicz, the official publication of Gombrowicz's writings in Poland remained blocked in accordance with the writer's will, while performance rights were permitted starting in 1974. The historic source of conflict between Gombrowicz and Poland's communist authorities began with his relationship with *Kultura* and remained unresolved as a result of passages in his *Diary* that were directly critical of both the system of Soviet communism and of the fundamentals of Marxist philosophy. Gombrowicz's charge to his wife before his death was that not one word of his work was to be published in Poland until every word was allowed without exception. The conflict over these passages in the *Diary* continued through the late 1980s when the prestigious Kraków literary press Wydawnictwo Literackie in 1986 published Gombrowicz's collected works in a large multi-volume edition in both hardcover and paperback with the offending passages of the *Diary* cut in flagrant violation of a contract with the Gombrowicz estate. Rita Gombrowicz publicly denounced the edition in 1987 as a corrupted version of the original text and in violation of the contract the press had signed. While the Wydawnictwo Literackie edition was nevertheless released in Poland at the time and remains highly visible in libraries and used bookstores, in the eyes of Rita Gombrowicz it was an illegal publication—ironically mirroring the official view of the communist authorities of the text's original provenance in the pages of *Kultura* in Paris.

This historic stand-off was significantly mitigated in the arena of the theatrical performance. Following the strategic advice of Jerzy Giedroyc, Rita Gombrowicz agreed to permit the public performance of her deceased husband's work even while the ban on publication remained active, thereby permitting his work to be shared with Polish audiences while holding to the integrity of the printed version of his texts. This move on her part was artistic and political rather than financial in motivation: the significant royalty income earned by the performance of Gombrowicz's plays in Poland in the 1970s and 1980s was paid into Polish bank accounts in her name in the country's "soft" currency (meaning that the funds could not be transferred abroad or converted into currencies outside the Soviet bloc). As a result, Rita Gombrowicz, who was unable to travel to Poland at the time, earned no royalty income from the over 100 professional Polish stage productions of her husband's writing between 1974 and 1989. The earnings were instead shared with Gombrowicz's surviving family in Poland.[13] On the other hand, the live performance of Gombrowicz's works reached hundreds of thousands of Poles during this politically and culturally critical period in spite of the ongoing official ban on the publication of his works.

The immediate impact of this unique compromise was reflected in the Polish professional premiere of Gombrowicz's last play *Operetta* which took place in Łódź in 1975. Directed by Kazimierz Dejmek, the production was performed 153 times over five seasons with total attendance of over 87,000—still the largest audience in Poland for any stage production of Gombrowicz's work to date.[14] There was also a political significance to Dejmek directing *Operetta*: he was earlier unwittingly cast in the role of dissident artist when he directed the historic 1967 production of Adam Mickiewicz's Romantic classic *Forefathers' Eve* (*Dziady*) at Warsaw's National Theater, which was shut down after pressure from the Soviet Union and helped spark a cascading political crisis that came to be known as "the events of March '68." The closing of Dejmek's *Forefathers's Eve* provoked student protests, and the brutal suppression of the students by the Gomułka regime at the time had repercussions for the emerging student theater movement as well as for Polish theater broadly, as did the subsequent fall of the Gomułka government in 1970 and its replacement by the more tolerant leadership of Edward Gierek. While Dejmek lost his position as artistic director of the National Theater after the closing of *Forefathers's Eve*, as a result he assumed a symbolic oppositional role in Polish theater and political history.[15]

In the late 1970s, Tadeusz Kantor was enjoying his first years of international success with *Dead Class*, which was freely inspired by several texts by avant-garde writers from interwar Poland, and included motifs from Gombrowicz's *Ferdydurke* and *The Marriage*. Among other distinctions, *Dead Class* won a Fringe First Award in Edinburgh and an OBIE (Off-Broadway Theater) Award for Best Production after Kantor's first tour to New York City. *Dead Class* ultimately became the most widely performed Polish theater production of all time abroad, with over 1,300 performances in at least twenty countries between 1975 and 1990.[16] Significantly, Kantor considered himself the embodiment of Polish theater as an artistically and politically autonomous expression, independent of the Polish communist state and the constraints placed on official institutional theaters such as Teatr Studio in Warsaw. Perhaps most significantly on this score, *Dead Class* was performed in the Olympic Arts Festival in Los Angeles in 1984, where Kantor's company was the only representative of the entire Soviet bloc to perform in spite of a boycott of the Olympics that year in protest against the American response to the Russian invasion of Afghanistan in 1979 which included an earlier American boycott of the Moscow Winter Olympics in 1980. The historic success of *Dead Class* was arguably Kantor's artistic vindication after being denied the chance to direct the world premiere of *Ivona* twenty years earlier. More meaningfully, with *Dead Class* Kantor became an acclaimed theatrical *auteur* in his own right, and as such assumed an artistic position alongside Gombrowicz rather than as a more conventional theatrical interpreter of his plays.

In 1979, audiences in festivals in France, Belgium, Germany, and Austria were also able to attend a touring Polish production of *Operetta* by Teatr STU.[17] It, and other student theaters, by this time had carved out an unprecedented institutional niche between the technically non-professional category of student theater and Kantor's alternative company model, and enjoyed huge popular success in Poland in the 1980s and after.[18] While Kantor's company ironically did not survive the director's death in 1990 (the year following the end of communist rule in Poland), Teatr STU successfully made the transition to professional life in post-communist Poland, with many of its members (in particular Mikołaj Grabowski, Jan Peszek, and Jerzy Stuhr) moving on to major professional careers and positions of professional leadership in post-communist Polish theater through the first two decades of the twenty-first century. The careers of Grabowski, Peszek, and Stuhr have all been strongly linked to the performance of Gombrowicz in the post-communist period.

A wave of stage adaptations of Gombrowicz's fiction took place on Polish stages in the 1980s. The most significant of these was Mikołaj Grabowski's 1981 production of *Trans-Atlantyk* at the Teatr Stefana Jaracza in Łódź. The production was a critical success in spite of its life being limited by the martial law crisis, and it launched Grabowski's subsequent career as one of the most prolific directors of Gombrowicz's work (a total of sixteen productions thru 2018, including seven adaptations of *Trans-Atlantyk* alone). After his early start with Teatr STU, Grabowski went on after the end of communism to join the faculty of the Kraków State Drama School and for several years held the position of artistic director of the prestigious Stary Teatr in Kraków, one of post-communist Poland's two designated "national" theaters.

A variation of the history of Teatr STU in the 1970s was the work of Teatr Provisorium, a dissident student theater based at the Marie Curie-Składkowska University in Lublin. In 1976, Provisorium staged a groundbreaking stage adaptation of *Ferdydurke*, performed with the title *In The Middle of the Road* (*W połowie drogi*), under the direction of Janusz Opryński. An archival copy of the typewritten text of the adaptation carries the dated approval stamp of the local government censor.[19] Provisorium's character as an openly dissident student theater with strong ties to KOR and later the Solidarity movement limited the group's opportunities for international touring at the time, though their work was tolerated through 1981. The company's members were aggressively targeted by security forces after the declaration of martial law by the Jaruzelski regime in Poland in 1981, with two members imprisoned and later forced to emigrate to the United States. The company carried

on in a diminished way through the 1980s and early 1990s, and subsequently enjoyed a significant rebirth when it merged with the independent company Kompania Teatr. Since the 1990s, Janusz Opryński
has enjoyed an active career as a director both within and outside that
company, and has also long functioned as one of the artistic directors
of the annual Theater Confrontations Festival in Lublin (*Festiwal Kon-
frontacje Teatralne*), today a well-funded international event descended
from an earlier festival dedicated to student and alternative theaters in
which the young Teatr Provisorium regularly performed.

Gombrowicz in Post-Communist Poland after 1989

This "normalization" of Gombrowicz in Polish theater under communism was followed by a period of official canonization in both print
and performance in post-communist Poland, with the writer's work
eventually becoming a standard part of the country's university placement examinations as well as of the training of students in the country's
state-supported professional drama schools. A biannual international
theater festival in Gombrowicz's honor was established in Radom in
1993, and a professional theater in Gdynia was named for him in the
early 2000s. Museums devoted to his life and work now exist in both
Poland and France, the latter with major financial support from the
Polish government. Among the observations of the centennial of Gombrowicz's birth in Poland in 2004 was the largest international conference in the history of the Jagiellonian University up until that time.
This took place in the wake of the explosive growth of both theatrical
production and scholarly publication devoted to Gombrowicz's work in
Poland after 1989.

The new status of Gombrowicz as an official international calling card
of post-communist Polish culture was exemplified by the historic version
of *Ferdydurke* performed by Teatr Provisorium & Kompania Teatr of
Lublin between 1998 and 2013. In addition to record-setting domestic touring (a total of 138 domestic tours to seventy-four Polish cities,
along with three different versions for television), the company toured
to twenty-three foreign countries, performing versions of the production
in both Polish and English.[20] The company's international touring over
the years was regularly subsidized and promoted by official Polish organizations such as the Polish Cultural Institute. In the end, Provisorium/
Kompania's *Ferdydurke* became the most widely performed single production of Gombrowicz as measured by the number of performances,
total audience, and breadth of national and international touring (this is
apart from Kantor's *Dead Class*, for which Gombrowicz served as one of
several sources of inspiration and motifs rather than as performance text
per se; the domestic Polish audience for Dejmek's *Operetta* surpassed
Ferdydurke, but the production also never toured abroad). Provisorium/

Kompania followed the success of *Ferdydurke* with a spirited adaptation of *Trans-Atlantyk* in 2004—which also enjoyed a substantial life on tour in Poland and abroad. Thus, the Lublin-based dissident student theater of the 1970s together with Gombrowicz became a theatrical emblem of post-communist Poland's new cultural freedom well into the twenty-first century.

The paradox of Gombrowicz today is that this supremely nonconformist writer has become required reading by high school students, and stagings of his work constitute a regular part of the curriculum in Poland's drama schools. At the same time, the Polish political right has at times attempted to remove Gombrowicz, and *Trans-Atlantyk* in particular, from the reading list for the *matura*, but without success—other than inspiring a spike in sales for the novel. An authoritative two-volume biography of the writer by Klementyna Suchanow was published to critical acclaim in 2017.[21] As this goes to press, Poland is governed by a right-wing government, and productions of Gombrowicz regularly play without restriction or controversy (some quite original and distinguished, some not), with recent productions of both *Ivona* and *The Marriage* in repertory at Warsaw's National Theater, with Lithuanian director Eimuntas Nekrošius's staging of *The Marriage* definitely in the avant-garde spirit of Lavelli and Jarocki. Gombrowicz today enjoys a secure place in the "classical" repertory as well as in the work of experimental artists in Poland and elsewhere.

But there is something not quite right with this latest normalization of Gombrowicz in Polish theater and society, which coincides with a low ebb in the performance of his work in other countries. His life, writing, and theater are the products of turmoil, both personal and political, and this turmoil is both his subject and what energizes his work. His most consistently popular work is *Ivona*, which was written and largely ignored in pre-war Poland, but roared to full theatrical life twenty years later. The moment the play first appeared, Poland was a mix of complacency and anxiety on the eve of the upcoming war.

Gombrowicz was always ready to provoke discomfort, and after seemingly winning the battle in contemporary Poland the next significant chapter for his work in the theater may ironically require finding a profoundly *insecure* place to flourish.

Notes

1 Byrska, Byrski and Milosz, *Korespondencja*, 34–35.
2 Based on attendance numbers from the archives of Instytut Teatralny, Warsaw.
3 Gombrowicz, *Dziennik 1961–1966*, 192; Gombrowicz, *Gombrowicz en Europe*, 133–35.
4 Flaszen, *Grotowski & Company*, 211.
5 Cioffi, *Alternative Theatre*, 115, 117.

6 Chudziński and Nyczek, *Teatr STU*, 181–84.

7 Guczalska, *Jerzy Jarocki*, 82–83, 241–42; Kubikowski and Płoski, *Reżyser*, 203.

8 Cioffi, *Alternative*, 131.

9 Komitet Obrony Robotników (Workers Defence Committee) was an early political coalition of Polish intellectuals and workers that deeply influenced the later Solidarity movement.

10 Cioffi, *Alternative*, 225–26.

11 Performance and attendance numbers are from *Almanach Sceny Polskiej* (Warsaw: Polska Akademia Nauk, Instytut Sztuki, Wydawnictwa Artystyczne i Filmowe).

12 Anecdote shared by Prof. Maria Olszewska, director of the Center for the History of Drama (Pracownia Historii Dramatu) at the University of Warsaw, about her experiences as a high school student in the 1970s, Feb. 21, 2018.

13 Details concerning Rita Gombrowicz, Giedroyc, and royalty payments for performances in Poland from personal interview with Rita Gombrowicz in Paris, Aug. 25, 2017.

14 Performance and attendance numbers are from *Almanach Sceny*.

15 For a critical overview of how "the events of March '68" following the closing of Dejmek's *Dziady* impacted student theaters, see Szpakowska, "Po Marcu," in *1968/PRL/Teatr*.

16 Kuharski, "Theatre of Witold Gombrowicz," 5.

17 Chudziński and Nyczek, *Teatr STU*, 184.

18 Cioffi, *Alternative*, 149.

19 Archives of Teatr Provisorium, Centrum Kultury, Lublin.

20 Performance data courtesy of Jacek Brzeziński, archives of Teatr Provisorium, Centrum Kultury, Lublin.

21 Suchanow, *Ja, geniusz*.

17 The Editorial Adventures of a Writer without Readers[1]

Klementyna Suchanow

When Witold Gombrowicz wrote *Trans-Atlantyk*, he was forty-six years old and, as he confided in his *Diary*, "people over forty [are] killing themselves off slowly, each year one year older."[2] By late 1948, he was depressed, fearing he would end up nothing more than a clerk in the Banco Polaco in Buenos Aires. World War II was over, ending his artificial separation from his homeland, but the Sovietization had begun in Poland. The doors to publishing were closed to authors of whom the government did not approve, those like the provocative Gombrowicz. Writers who remained abroad during the war and did not, or could not, return to their native land were placed on the government's forbidden list. Bartering one's soul for a three-room apartment and the possibility of selling copies of one's work might appeal to some, but this "deal" did not tempt Gombrowicz.

Gombrowicz's travels had taken him through latitudes that at first liberated him from the perils of war and social conventions. However, now he saw that the moves had only tied his hands, leaving him unable to publish in the familiar language of his youth. He dreamed of gaining a reputation by translating his first novel, *Ferdydurke*, when published in 1937. A list of Polish reviews of his work is preserved in the archives of the Insytut Badań Literackich, some prepared by him in French. He also mentioned in his correspondence with Bruno Schulz the possibility of a translation, but the war intervened destroying his plans, but not his aspirations.

Once the war was over, a decade after his initial inquiries about translation, his efforts again concentrated on France. Gombrowicz worked with a group at the Café Rex to translate *Ferdydurke* into its first Spanish edition that appeared in Buenos Aires in 1947. What is less known is that he also attempted a French translation with the help of random French people residing in the city. Although this did not materialize, in the first half of 1949, at the recommendation of René Marill Albérès, Gombrowicz sent the Argentinean edition of *Ferdydurke* to several French publishers. Albérès was the author of several books on the history of twentieth-century Western European literature. In his *Bilan littéraire du XXe siècle*, he explained the narrowing of literature to the

Western perspective as the result of a lack of access to books from other parts of Europe, the realization of which already made him unique.[3] Gombrowicz met him in Buenos Aires at the Institut français d'études supérieures and it is no doubt due to Albérès's appreciation of the post-war literary market that he lent his encouragement to the Pole.

In contrast to Poland, there was considerable continuity in the French publishing world during the wartime occupation. To survive, the majority of firms simply submitted to censorship. Gaston Gallimard placed the legendary *Nouvelle Revue française* into the hands of the noted French fascist and Nazi collaborator Pierre Drieu la Rochelle, so it would remain available. Despite his wartime collaboration, Gallimard remained the most prestigious publisher in postwar France, publishing works by Albert Camus, Jean-Paul Sartre, Franz Kafka, Ernest Hemingway, and Jack Kerouac.[4] It was to him that Gombrowicz wrote in December 1949, yet he was in for another disappointment. At Gallimard, the publisher gave the book to Roger Caillois to review. Following his return from Argentina after the war, Caillois spent twenty years, beginning in 1948, employed in a department of UNESCO. At the same time, he also worked for Gallimard, creating the well-known series Croix du Sud which introduced Latin American writers worldwide. The boom he provoked began with *Ficciones* by Jorge Luis Borges in 1951. While in Argentina, Caillois was involved with the literary circle revolving around Victoria Ocampo and publication of the journal *Sur*. Gombrowicz fell into disfavor with Ocampo after he injudiciously ridiculed her and her journal. Caillois was Ocampo's ex-lover and kept man in Buenos Aires during the war.

Knowing he would not receive a fair review, Gombrowicz wrote to Gallimard:

> Mr. Marill Albérès informed me of your decision to provide my novel *Ferdydurke* to Mr. Roger Caillois, who's a Latin American reviewer at Gallimard. I must confess, this decision disheartened me. Mr. Caillois' mentality, philosophy, temperament are totally opposed to mine, and it's logical he'll not become a fan of my book (he knew it already and I was told he didn't like it).[5]

Gombrowicz clarified that he sent a Spanish copy for practical reasons, but emphasized that he was a Polish author and therefore Caillois might not have the requisite competence in that field to provide a serious review. The final decision rested in the hands of Raymond Queneau.

Gombrowicz's fears proved correct. His old friend Paweł Zdziechowski described the way Gombrowicz was treated:

> I was at Gallimard, I talked to R. Queneau himself, the issue is unfortunately dealt with in a negative way. Q. is amused and enthralled

with the accuracy of your secret intelligence, because it's true what you told him in your second letter, that the reviewer of *Ferdydurke* was this guy whose name I don't recall right now. His report is negative – I pressured him and asked about eventual chances that Gallimard can change its decision. He said that chances are none. So we should forget about Gallimard.[6]

Gallimard was also running a Russian series, under the supervision of Louis Aragon, called "Littératures soviétiques." But there was no room for Gombrowicz since he was not "soviétique." But that was not the end. Gombrowicz also sent his work to Plon, Corrêa, and Julliard. The latter was established in 1942 by René Julliard, another Vichy collaborator, who published an official paper supporting the expropriation of legal status from the Jews.[7] This also led to frustration. At Corrêa they swore they did not receive the book. Although the initial news from Plon was positive and *Ferdydurke* made it to a second stage of review, this too ended without success.

Gombrowicz was also in touch with Antoni Słonimski, who moved between Great Britain and France and held a high position in UNESCO, headquartered in Paris. Unfortunately, by the time Słonimski received Gombrowicz's letter he had left the agency. Despite beautiful UNESCO declarations about building a literary translation program which would help to bring works by writers from peripheral languages onto the broad commercial market,[8] the circle of nations and languages taking part in the cultural-exchange program Translatorum narrowed as the Cold War developed. Jerzy Giedroyc, editor of the Polish émigré journal *Kultura* in Paris, concluded, "Unfortunately, neither I nor my friends can do anything because Poles are completely unrecognized by UNESCO."[9]

There was a program for translations from Arabic countries and from Latin America,[10] but no similar program for writers from behind the Iron Curtain – Czech, Romanian, and Polish works would be less available than Punjabi, Tamil, and Bengali. The dominant language would be English, with only a very trifling number of foreign literatures (from one to three percent). In 1958, for example, there were 463 translations from English and only 28 from Spanish and 5 from Polish.[11] Other writers in exile assimilated to foreign languages to help their careers: Samuel Beckett turned to French because English limited him,[12] other factors motivated the Russian Vladimir Nabokov and his compatriot Arthur Adamov, for whom French was a first language, as with the Romanian Eugene Ionesco. But Gombrowicz resisted Giedroyc's suggestion that he convert to French, feeling too comfortable in Polish and not imagining being able to play as much with another language. Further, Polish better reflected his philosophy: a peripheral language providing him greater freedom and distance.

The letter about Gallimard's decision arrived soon after director Jean-Louis Barrault returned to France from his theater tour in Latin America. Gombrowicz met him at his performance in Buenos Aires, where they had an opportunity to talk. The conversation and the contact appeared promising. By late 1950, Gombrowicz tried again, sending the French translation of *Ślub* in mimeograph form to two prominent authors. One went to André Gide with a special dedication: "Here, Mr. Gide, is a book that needs your support."[13] A second went to Jean-Louis Barrault. Neither replied.

At that time, the Polish cultural attaché in the United States, Czesław Miłosz, was seeking "manuscripts of new Polish theater plays worthy of translation into English."[14] He saw an opportunity in the International Student Theater Library, which was loaning plays to student companies, and in the United Nations Theater, the task of which was to "propagate international rapprochement by staging plays from different nations." He had in mind Polish writers living abroad, a select group including Jarosław Iwaszkiewicz, Antoni Cwojdziński, and Gombrowicz's friends from the prewar table at the Ziemiańska cafe in Warsaw, Stefan Otwinowski, Tadeusz Breza, and the young Stanisław Dygat. As a poet, Miłosz thought that "the elite reads Kafka, etc., so Schulz and Gombrowicz should make it." But soon he added:

> actually, Gombrowicz not so much, because he's too Polish and his name, everything that's Slavic smells like hell, a few years ago they published lots of Soviet books and cried over the brave Slavs. Here... Slavs are Russia, that Poles, Czechs and Serbs are different doesn't penetrate their consciousness.[15]

The correspondence between Jerzy Andrzejewski and his British agent, who was trying to convince Gombrowicz to modify his name for English readers, illustrates the same problem. Andrzejewski replied to Elaine Greene, an literary agent with MCA London:

> I quite understand the difficulties arising in connection with my name for English readers, though I doubt if they are any bigger than those arising for Polish readers with British names. I have been thinking what to do and the fact is that I should like to eat the cake and have it, that is, to keep my name as near its original version as possible and yet do something to help the British reader pronounce it. I am afraid your proposition to call me 'Adrewski' is not quite a happy one, since it turns me into a Russian, which is, in my case, a slight exaggeration to say the least.[16]

Aside from his publishing frustrations, Gombrowicz's attempts to have his works staged in theaters, originally begun in prewar Poland, met with repeated failure. He began thinking of the theater before his initial play *Ivona, Princess of Burgundia* was published in 1938. First, he approached Ludwik Solski, a prominent director. Solski mentioned Gombrowicz's name in an interview with the journal *Teatr*. At that point, the play was titled *Filip* and it appeared on a list of modern plays under consideration for the 1936–1937 season. Because of cast and technical problems, none of the avant-garde authors Solski mentioned was staged. Immediately after, Gombrowicz contacted another theater entrepreneur and director, Adolf Szyfman from Teatr Polski in Warsaw. As a result, *Iwona* was being considered for the 1937–1938 season, but it did not materialize. However, it appeared that the 1939–1940 season would definitely become the first to introduce modern writers on Polish stages with the names of Iwaszkiewicz, Czechowicz, and Karpiński appearing in the program. Who knows whether, if not for the war, 1942 or 1944 would have been the time for launching Gombrowicz? Instead, in 1947, ten years later, Gombrowicz remained in limbo.

Maria Kuncewiczowa, a Polish writer in exile in London, was at that time in touch with Gombrowicz, whom she believed to be a genius. She was also a vice president of the Pen Club until 1946, and beginning in 1950 president of the International Pen Club Center for Writers in Exile in London. Kuncewiczowa expended much effort helping Gombrowicz. She presented *Ślub* to an experimental theatre company whose director was a woman and reported that she "read your play and was very impressed, full of compliments, but she thinks that in Great Britain it will not work out, 'too little substance in it' – so much for London tastes."[17] On the other hand, a prewar friend in New York City, Litka de Barcza, the author of bestsellers under the pen name Alexandra Orme, had an agent named Mavis McIntosh who was representing John Steinbeck and John Irving, among others. Her first reader reacted to Gombrowicz's book with "repulsion."[18] When Litka wanted to approach the director Erwin Piscator, his wife, as Litka explained it, "insulted me, the old bitch, and slammed the phone straight if not into my nose then in my ear, I was speechless."[19] In London, Kuncewiczowa tried Peter Brook, a "very young boy with Russian origins,"[20] whom she considered a most talented director, but warned Gombrowicz that he tended to keep texts for a long time. The problem among British theater people was that they did not know French and were afraid of what Kuncewiczowa branded "continental symbolism." Similarly, in the United States "intellectuals in theater, as an audience, look for entertainment" or "inspiration."[21] Irritated, Kuncewiczowa encouraged Gombrowicz to send *Ślub* to a competition, but Gombrowicz replied "without much optimism" because, as he said, "I never received an award in my life."[22] Meanwhile, the rejection list grew longer and longer.

By this time Gombrowicz felt overwhelmed, he had no money even to pay for more copies of the translations of *Ferdydurke* and *Ślub* or for postage. Litka tried to sell the play in Hollywood through film composer Bronisław Kaper, again to no avail. At the same time, in his room on Venezuela Street, Gombrowicz received the disheartening news that there were no possibilities of publishing in Polish. "[T]he situation is totally catastrophic. There is absolutely no Polish publishing house abroad."[23]

Marian Kister, Gombrowicz's former publisher in prewar Warsaw, who established Roy Publishing, told the discouraged Pole "with his peculiar cynical approach" that

> to get to local readers I can use two ways: 1) by handing over sums of $150 at least...[and] 2) if the critic is a woman and I feel ready enough, I can go to bed with her.[24]

There were some Polish exile titles, usually those focusing on the military in World War II and published in London, which appealed to a rather more conservative part of the Polish diaspora after the war including former ministers, generals, and so on.

Finally, a new journal appeared on the horizon in Paris created by demobilized soldiers. Some of them established their own community, living and working together. Their journal, *Kultura*, revolved around Eastern European political questions regarding the war, geopolitics, studies of communism, and analysis of the political situation in Poland. When Gombrowicz communicated with its chief editor, Jerzy Giedroyc, in 1950, he was asking what to do with his novel *Trans-Atlantyk* and his play *Ślub*. Because of communist censorship these could not be published in Poland. Giedroyc replied that he was not interested in the play, but could publish excerpts from the novel. With this small step the long-standing collaboration between them began. Gombrowicz complained to Giedroyc, "If not for this stupid postwar situation, I would be already famous. I need to wait six or eight years more."[25]

Gombrowicz believed that history played havoc with his career. He vacillated between desperation—he was already into his fifties—and growing aspirations since he was certain of the value of his works, but becoming increasingly impatient with the lack of opportunity to prove it. He was quite correct when he spoke about six or eight more years. What finally brought his work to light was the French translation of *Ferdydurke*, which, as had been the case with its Spanish version from 1947, resulted from the author's insistence and the passion of his supporters. The French publication of *Ferdydurke* came about thanks to François Bondy, a critic and journalist. A Jew with German-Hungarian origins who had lived in Prague and attended Italian and French schools, Bondy knew Spanish. When approached by Józef Czapski, his feeling was that "all those most important for Polish people must be Polish" and wrapped up in assertions about their unknown geniuses. So "when he mentioned a great writer," wrote Bondy, "totally unknown in France, living in Argentina – his name being Gombrowicz – I thought immediately Well, well! then I ignored it." He put aside the Spanish copy of *Ferdydurke* and the book remained on his bedside table until he fell sick one day and took up the book to read its first page. "I started in," recalls Bondy, "and I was truly shocked. I was amazed by the first chapter. …I was amazed by this tone, style, as well as the directness and the irreverent way of putting things straight in your face." He immediately shared his discovery on the pages of the journal *Preuves* in October 1953,[26] but the French publication of *Ferdydurke*, in a new translation by Roland Martin (working with Gombrowicz) under the pen name Brone, appeared five years later, in 1958, with Julliard. The English translation by Eric Mosbacher, published by MacGibbon in London and by Harcourt Brace in New York City, appeared in 1961. The long years of desperately seeking fame only to find continued frustration because of the varied politics of publication finally came to an end. Gombrowicz was on his way to international acclaim.

Notes

1 This article was adapted from Suchanow, *Gombrowicz. Ja, geniusz.*
2 Gombrowicz, *Diary*, 46.
3 Albérès, *Bilan littéraire*; Albérès, *La révolte*; Albérès, *Jean-Paul Sartre*; Albérès, *Histoire du roman*.
4 Gombrowicz refers to Albérès's recommendation in his letter to Gallimard on Dec. 7, 1949, all letters from Gombrowicz Archive unless otherwise indicated.
5 Letter, Gombrowicz to Gallimard, June 9, 1950.
6 Letter, Zdziechowski to Gombrowicz, July 28, 1950.
7 The official Vichy journal of the French government from Oct. 28, 1940. Its history is described by Lamy, *René Julliard*, 59.
8 Lewin, "Antoni Słonimski."
9 Giedroyc and Parnicki, *Listy*, 110.
10 Unesco Translation Programme, Unesco/ALT/865, document from Sept. 4, 1956.
11 For statistics, see Jégouzo, *Histoire*. Also *Records of the General Conference of the United Nations Educational and Scientific and Cultural Organization*; personal folder of Antoni Słonimski in the UNESCO Archives in Paris (PER/REC. 1/51) and documents relating to this period from the same source (boîte 444).
12 Beckett, *Letters*, July 9, 1937.
13 Testimony by Rússovich in Rita Gombrowicz, *Gombrowicz w Argentynie*, 143.
14 For the report by Czesław Miłosz from Dec. 1946, see *Raporty dyplomatyczne*, 88.
15 Andrzejewski, Miłosz and Ross, *Listy*, 86.
16 Letter, Jerzy Andrzejewski to Elaine Greene from 1959, Archiwum Muzeum Literatury, letters by Jerzy Andrzejewski 1938–1981, file 1585, 59.
17 Letter, Kuncewiczowa to Gombrowicz, Nov. 24, 1950.
18 Letter, de Barcza to Gombrowicz, Dec. 6, 1950.
19 Letter, de Barcza to Gombrowicz, Dec. 7, 1950.

20 Letter, Kuncewiczowa to Gombrowicz, Mar. 13, 1953.

21 Ibid.

22 Letter, Gombrowicz to Kuncewiczowa, Dec. 6, 1950, Zakład Narodowy imienia Ossolińskich, file 16412/II, 200.

23 Letter, Zdziechowski to Gombrowicz, July 28, 1950. Zdziechowski recommended that Gombrowicz contact the Catholic publisher Veritas in London. Gombrowicz wrote on this issue to Tymon Terlecki, but Terlecki decided it made no sense to show *Trans-Atlantyk* to Veritas. Footnoted information in Terlecki, et al., *Listy*, 45.

24 Letter, Ryszard Augenblick to Gombrowicz, Nov. 24, 1947.

25 Letter, Gombrowicz to Giedroyc, no date, Gombrowicz Archive.

26 Bondy, "*Ferdydurke*," 97–98.

Bibliography

Archival Source

Archives of Teatr Provisorium, Centrum Kultury, Lublin.

Archivo General de la Administración, Alcalá de Henares, Spain.

Gombrowicz, Rita. Interviewed by Allen J. Kuharski in Paris, France, August 25, 2017, in possession of Prof. Kuharski.

Gombrowicz, Witold. *Ferdydurke*, manuscript of the translation of with associated other materials. CO737, Box 1, Folder 19. Antón Arrufat Papers. Rare Books and Manuscript Library, Princeton University Library.

Olszewska, Maria. Interviewed by Allen J. Kuharski in Warsaw, Poland, February 21, 2018, in possession of Prof. Kuharski.

Witold Gombrowicz Archive, Beinecke Rare Book and Manuscript Library, Yale University, New Haven, Connecticut.

Published Sources

Ahmed, Sara. "Affective Economies," *Social Text*, Vol. 22, no. 2 (2004), 117–39.

———. *The Cultural Politics of Emotion*, second edition (Edinburgh: Edinburgh University Press, 2014).

Aira, César. "Prologue" to Osvaldo Lamborghini's *Novelas y cuentos* (Buenos Aires: Ediciones del Serbal, 1988), 7–16.

———. *La guerra de los gimnasios* (Buenos Aires: Emecé, 2006).

Albérès, René Marill. *Bilan littéraire du XXe siècle* (Paris: A. G. Nizet, 1971).

———. Histoire du roman moderne (Paris: Albin Michel, 1962).

———. *Jean-Paul Sartre* (Paris: Universitaires, 1953).

———. *La révolte des écrivains d'aujourd'hui* (Paris: Corrêa, 1949).

Almanach Sceny Polskiej (Warsaw: Polska Akademia Nauk, Instytut Sztuki, Wydawnictwa Artystyczne i Filmowe, annual editions).

Andrzejewski, Jerzy, Czesław Miłosz, and Barbara Riss, eds. *Listy 1944–1981* (Warsaw: Wydawnictwo Biblioteka Więzi, 2012).

Attridge, Derek. *The Singularity of Literature* (London: Routledge, 2004).

Balderston, Daniel. "Estética de la deformación en Gombrowicz y Piñera," *Explicación de Textos Literarios*, Vol. 19, no. 2 (1990), 1–7.

Barral, Carlos. *Memorias* (Barcelona: Ediciones Península, 2000).

Bartoszyński, Kazimierz. "Kosmos i antynomie" in his *Teoria i interpretacja* (Warsaw: PWN, 1998), 282–331.

Basch, Linda, Nina Glick Schiller, and Christina Szanton Blanc. *Nations Unbound: Transnational Projects, Postcolonial Predicaments and Deterritorialized Nation-States* (Amsterdam: Gordon & Breach, 1994).

Bataille, Georges. "Attraction et répulsion: I. Tropismes, sexualité, rire et larmes, II. La structure sociale" in Denis Hollier, ed. *Le Collège de Sociologie: 1937–1939* (Paris: Gallimard, 1995).

Batowski, Henryk. *Rok 1938 – dwie agresje hitlerowskie* (Poznań: Wydawnictwo Poznańskie, 1985).

Bauman, Zygmunt. "Allosemitism: Premodern, Modern, Postmodern," in Bryan Cheyette and Laura Marcus, eds. *Modernity, Culture, and "the Jew"* (Cambridge: Polity Press, 1998).

———. "Culture in a Globalised City," *Occupied London*, 3 (July 2008).

Bazán, Osvaldo. *Historia de la homosexualidad en la Argentina: De la Conquista de América al siglo XXI* (Buenos Aires: Editorial Marea, 2004).

Beckett, Samuel. *The Letters of Samuel Beckett, Volume 1, 1929–1940* (New York: Cambridge University Press, 2009), Letter of July 9, 1937.

Benjamin, Walter. *The Arcades Project* (Cambridge, MA/London: Harvard University Press, 1999).

Berlant, Lauren. *Cruel Optimism* (Durham, NC: Duke University Press, 2011).

Berressem, Hanjo. *Lines of Desire: Reading Gombrowicz's Fiction with Lacan* (Evanston, IL: Northwestern University Press, 1998).

Bhambry, Tul'si. Interview with Danuta Borhardt, n.d., www.asymptotejournal.com/interview/an-interview-with-danuta-borchardt/ (accessed 26 May 2018).

Bielecki, Marian. *Interpretacja i płeć: Szkice o twórczości Gombrowicza* (Wałbrzych: Wydawnictwo Państwowej Wyższej Szkoły Zawodowej im. Angelusa Silesiusa, 2005).

———. *Literatura i lektura. O metaliterackich i metatekstowych poglądach Witolda Gombrowicza* (Kraków: Universitas, 2004).

Blanchot, Maurice. *The Space of Literature* (Lincoln: University of Nebraska Press, 1989).

Bloom, Harold. *Anxiety of Influence: A Theory of Poetry* (New York: Oxford University Press, 1997).

Bondy, François. "Ferdydurke," *Preuves*, no. 32 (October 1953), 97–98.

Borchardt, Danuta. "Translator's Note" in Witold Gombrowicz, ed. *Ferdydurke* (New Haven/London: Yale University Press, 2000).

Borejsza, Jerzy W. *Mussolini był pierwszy* (Warsaw: Czytelnik, 1989).

Borges, Jorge Luis. *Labyrinths: Selected Stories & Other Writings*, Donald A. Yates and James E. Irby, eds. (New York: A New Directions Books, 1964).

Bourne, Randolph. "Trans-National America," *The Atlantic Monthly*, no. 118 (July 1916), 86–97.

Bradatan, Cristina, Adrian Popan, and Rachel Melton, "Transnationality as a Fluid Social Identity," *Social Identities: Journal for the Study of Race, Nation and Culture*, Vol. 16, no. 2 (2010), 169–78.

Brennan, Teresa. *The Transmission of Affect* (Ithaca: Cornell University Press, 2004).

Brodsky, David. "Witold Gombrowicz and the 'Polish October,'" *Slavic Review*, Vol. 39, no. 3 (1980), 459–75.

Buras, Piotr, ed. *Spór o niemiecką pamięć. Debata Walser–Bubis* (Warsaw: Centrum Stosunków Międzynarodowych, 1999).

Burzyńska, Anna. *Anty-teoria literatury* (Kraków: Universitas, 2006).

———. *Dekonstrukcja i interpretacja* (Kraków: Universitas, 2001).

Byrska, Irena, Tadeusz Byrski, and Czesław Milosz, *Korespondencja* (Warsaw: Instytut Badań Literackich Pan Wydawnictwo, 2017).

Casanova, Pascale. *Kafka en colère* (Paris: Seuil, 2011).

Chudziński, Edward, and Tadeusz Nyczek, eds. *Teatr STU* (Zielona Góra: Młodzieżowa Agencja Wydawnicza, 1982).

Chwin, Stefan. "Gombrowicz i Forma polska," afterword to Witold Gombrowicz, *Trans-Atlantyk* (Kraków: Wydawnictwo Literackie, 2004).

———. "Gombrowicz, my i Niemcy" in Jerzy Jarzębski, ed. *Witold Gombrowicz nasz współczesny* (Kraków: Universitas, 2012).

Cioffi, Kathleen M. *Alternative Theatre in Poland: 1954–1989* (Reading: Harwood Academic Publishers, 1996).

Cioran, Emil. *Cahiers 1957–1972* (Paris: Gallimard, 1997).

Compagnon, Antoine. *Le démon de la théorie. Littérature et sens commun* (Paris: Éditions du Seuil, 1998).

———. *Les Antimodernes: de Joseph de Maistre à Roland Barthes* (Paris: Gallimard, 2005).

Cordingley, Anthony, ed. *Self-Translation: Brokering Originality in Hybrid Culture* (London/New Delhi/New York/Sydney: Bloomsbury, 2013).

Cromby, John. *Feeling Bodies: Embodying Psychology* (Basingstoke: Palgrave Macmillan. 2015).

Damasio, Antonio. *Looking for Spinoza. Joy, Sorrow, and the Feeling Brain* (London: William Heinemann, 2003).

———. *The Feeling of What Happens: Body and Emotion in the Making of Consciousness* (New York: Harcourt Brace, 1999).

De Bruyn, Dieter. *Literary Polemics in/on Polish Modernism: The Case of Gombrowicz and Schulz* (Gent: Slavica Gandensia, 2008).

Delaperrière, Zob. M. "Marginalność i trasgresja: Gombrowicz i Genet" in Jerzy Jarzębski, ed. *Witold Gombrowicz nasz współczesny. Materiały międzynarodowej konferencji naukowej w stulecie urodzin pisarza Uniwersytet Jagielloński – Kraków, 22–27 marca 2004,* (Kraków: Universitas, 2010), 471–83.

Deleuze, Gilles. *Dialogues,* Hugh Tomlinson and Barbara Habberjam, transl. (New York: Columbia University Press, 1977).

———. *Essays Critical and Clinical,* Daniel W. Smith and Michael A. Greco, transl. (Minneapolis: University of Minnesota Press, 1997).

———. *Nietzsche and Philosophy,* Hugh Tomlinson, transl. (New York: Columbia University Press, 1983).

———. *Présentation de Sacher-Masoch* (Paris: Éditions de Minuit, 1967).

———. *Spinoza: Practical Philosophy,* Robert Hurley, transl. (San Francisco: City Lights Books, 1988).

Deleuze, Gilles and Félix Guattari, *A Thousand Plateaus* (Minneapolis: University of Minnesota Press, 1987).

———. "May '68 Did Not Take Place" in David Lapoujade, ed., Ames Hodges and Mike Taormina, transl. *Two Regimes of Madness* (New York: Semiotext(e), 2007), 233–36.

Deonna, Julien A., Raffaele Rodogno, and Fabrice Teroni. *In Defense of Shame: The Faces of an Emotion* (New York: Oxford University Press, 2012).

Dobrowolski, Jacek. *Sztuka człowieka nowoczesnego* (Warsaw: Narodowe Centrum Kultury, 2015).

Domańska, Ewa. *Historie niekonwencjonalne: refleksja o przeszłości w nowej humanistyce* (Poznań: Wydawnictwo Poznańskie, 2006).

Dominiak, Zbigniew. "Rozmowa z Jerzym Jarzębskim o odnalezieniu pierwszej wersji Operetki Witolda Gombrowicza," *Tygiel Kultury*, Vol. 2 (1996), 62–66.

Dover, Kenneth James. *Homoseksualizm grecki* (Kraków: Homini, 2004).

Dzikowska, Elżbieta Katarzyna. (2004) "Koń by się uśmiał – o kulturowych kolizjach w niemieckiej recepcji Gombrowicza" in Elżbieta Skibińska, ed. *Gombrowicz i tłumacze* (Łask: Oficyna Wydawnicza Leksem, 2004), 85–102.

Engels, Friedrich. *The Condition of the Working Class in England*, D. McLellan, transl. (Oxford: Oxford University Press, 2009).

Enright, D. J. "Dancing the Polka," *The New York Review of Books*, June 15, 1967 www.nybooks.com/articles/1967/06/15/dancing-the-polka/ (accessed 26 May 2018).

———. "Witold Gombrowicz," *Presència*, March 15, 1965.

Flaszen, Ludwik. *Grotowski & Company* (Holstebro, Denmark: Icarus Enterprise Publishing, 2009).

Franczak, Jerzy. *Poszukiwanie realności: światopogląd polskiej prozy modernistycznej* (Kraków: Universitas, 2007), 279.

———. *Rzecz o nierzeczywistości. "Mdłości" Jeana Paula Sartre'a i "Ferdydurke" Witolda Gombrowicza* (Kraków: Universitas, 2002).

Freixa Terradas, Pau. *Recepción de la obra de Witold Gombrowicz en la Argentina y configuración de su imagen en el imaginario cultural argentine* (2008). http://diposit.ub.edu/dspace/bitstream/2445/42056/3/Gombrowicz-Argentina-Freixa-tesis-castellano.pdf (accessed 3 February 2017).

Freud, Sigmund. "Dostoyevsky and Parricide" in James Strachey, ed. *Complete Psychological Works*, collaboration with Anna Freud. Volume XXI. (London: The Hogarth Press and the Institute of Psycho-Analysis, 1961), 177–96.

———. "Mourning and Melancholia," in Joan Riviere, transl. *Collected Papers* (London: Hogarth, 1956), Vol. 4, 152–70.

———. "Uwagi na temat pewnego przypadku nerwicy natręctw" in Zygmunt Freud, ed. *Charakter a erotyka* (Warszawa: Wydawnictwo KR, 2014).

Gall, Alfred. *Performativer Humanismus: Die Auseinandersetzung mit Philosophie in der literarischen Praxis von Witold Gombrowicz* (Dresden: Thelem, 2007).

Gamerro, Carlos, Rubén Mira, Victoria Noorthoorn, and Alejandro Tantanian, "Una teoría del montaje de Osvaldo Lamborghini," *Une terrible beauté est née* (Dijon: Les Presse Du Reel, 2011).

Gasparini, Pablo. *El exilio procaz: Gombrowicz por la Argentina* (Rosario: Beatriz Viterbo, 2007).

Gasyna, George Z. *Polish, Hybrid, and Otherwise: Exilic Discourse in Joseph Conrad and Witold Gombrowicz* (London: Continuum, 2011).

Giedroyc, Jerzy. *Autobiografia na cztery ręce*, Krzysztof Pomian, ed. (Warsaw: Czytelnik, 1994).

Girard, René. *Evolution and Conversion: Dialogues on the Origins of Culture* (London: Continuum, 2008).

Giroud, Vincent, *The World of Witold Gombrowicz 1904–1969: Catalog of a Centenary Exhibition at the Beineke Rare Book and Manuscript Library* (New Haven: Beineke Rare Book and Manuscript Library, 2005).

Głowiński, Michał. "Komentarze do Ślubu," *Gombrowicz i nadliteratura* (Kraków: Wydawnictwo Literackie, 2002).

Goddard, Michael. *Gombrowicz, Polish Modernism, and the Subversion of Form* (West Lafayette: Purdue University Press, 2010).

Goethe, Johann Wolfang von. *Goethes sämmtliche Werke: in vierzig Bänden, mit 40 Stahlstichen. Bd 10* (Stuttgart: Cotta'schen Buchhandlung, 1871).

———. *Podróż włoska*, trans. into Polish by Henryk Krzeczkowski (Warsaw: Państwowy Instytut Wydawniczy, 1980).

Goffman, Erving. *Piętno: rozważania o zranionej tożsamości* (Gdańsk: Gdańskie Wydawnictwo Psychologiczne, 2007).

Gombrowicz, Rita. *Gombrowicz en Europe* (Paris: Denoël, 1988).

———. *Gombrowicz w Argentynie* (Kraków: Wydawnictwo Literackie, 2004).

———. *Gombrowicz w Europie: Świadectwa i dokumenty 1963–1969*, Oscar Hedemman and Maryna Ochab, transl., Jerzy Jarzębski, ed. (Kraków: Wydawnictwo Literackie, 1993).

Gombrowicz, Witold. *A Guide to Philosophy in Six Hours and Fifteen Minutes*, Benjamin Ivry, transl. (New Haven: Yale University Press, 2007).

———. *A Kind of Testament*, Dominique De Roux, ed., Alastair Hamilton, transl. (Champaign, IL: Dalkey Archive Press, 2007).

———. *Bacacay*, Bill Johnston, transl. (New York: Archipelago Books, 2004).

———. *Bakakaj* (Kraków: Wydawnictwo Literackie, 2013).

———. *Cosmos*, Danuta Borchardt, transl. (New York: Grove Press, 2005).

———. *Cosmos and Pornografia*. Eric Mosbacher and Alastair Hamilton, transl. (New York: Grove Press, 1985).

———. *Diary*, Lillian Vallee, transl. (New Haven, CT: Yale University Press, 2010).

———. *Dzieła*, Jan Błoński and Jerzy Jarzębski, eds. (Kraków: Wydawnictwo Literackie, 1986–1997), 15 vols.

———. *Dramaty* (Kraków: Wydawnictwo Literackie, 1986).

———. *Dziennik 1961–1966, Dzieła zebrane* (Paris: Instytut Literacki, 1986), VIII.

———. *Dzienniku 1957–1961* (Kraków: Wydawnictwo Literackie, 1997).

———. *El casamiento*, Witold Gombrowicz and Alejandro Rússovich, transl. (Buenos Aires: EAM, 1948).

———. *El casamiento*, Alejandro Rússovich and Witold Gombrowicz, transl. (Buenos Aires: El cuenco de plata, 2010.

———. "Ferdydurke," *Skamander*, Vol. LX (1935), 264–84.

———. *Ferdydurke* (Buenos Aires: Editorial Argos, 1947).

———. *Ferdydurke*, Erich Mosbacher, transl. (London & Boston: Marion Boyards, 1979).

———. *Ferdydurke* (Warsaw: Towarzystwo Wydawnicze "Rój," 1938).

———. *Ferdydurke*, Danuta Borchardt, transl., Susan Sontag, intro. (New Haven: Yale University Press, 2000).

———. *Ferdydurke*. Anna Rubió and Jerzy Sławomirski, transl. (Barcelona: Círculo de Lectores, 2005).

———. *Ferdydurke*, Włodzimierz Bolecki, Jerzy Jarzębski and Zdzisław Łapiński, eds. (Kraków: Wydawnictwo Literackie, 2007), Vol. II, 277–83.

————. *Ferdydurke. Dzieła zebrane* (Paris: Instytut Literacki, 1982), Vol. I.

————. *Ferdydurke: Novela* (Buenos Aires: Editorial Argos, 1947).

————. *Ferdydurke: Pisma zebrane II*, Włodziemierz Bolecki, ed. (Kraków: Wydawnictwo Literackie, 2009), 67.

————. "Fragmenty powieści" [Fragments of the Novel], in Włodzimierz Bolecki, ed. *Ferdydurke. Dzieła zebrane* [Complete Works] (Kraków: Wydawnictwo Literackie, 2007).

————. "Jaki jest sens Ślubu," *Varia* (Paris: Instytut Literacki, 1973), 519–20.

————. *Kosmos, Dzieła zebrane* (Paris: Instytut Literacki 1970), Vol. IV.

————. "Łańcuch nietaktów," *Varia, Dzieła zebrane* (Paris: Wydawnictwo Institut Litteraire, 1973), Vol. 10.

————. *List do ferdydurkistów: wywiady, odpowiedzi na ankiety, listy do redakcji czasopism* (Kraków: Wydawnicwo Literackie, 1995).

————. "Niedole zakopiańskie," *Czas*, no. 57, February 27, 1938.

————. *Opowiadania. Dzieła zebrane* (Paris: Instytut Literacki, 1982), Vol. XI.

————. *Polish Memoirs*, Bill Johnston, transl. (New Haven: Yale University Press, 2004).

————. *Pornografia*, Alastair Hamilton transl. (London: Penguin, 1991).

————. *Pornografia*, Danuta Borchardt transl. (New York: Grove Press, 2009).

————. *Pornografia, Dzieła zebrane* (Paris: Instytut Literacki 1982), Vol. III.

————. *Pornographie*, Walter Tiel, Renate Schmidgall, and Gesammelte Werke, transl., Rolf Fieguth and Fritz Arnold, eds. (München; Wien: Carl Hanser Verlag, 1984), Vol. III.

————. *Possessed: The Secret of Myslotch: A Gothic novel*, J. A. Underwood, transl. (London: Boyars, 2000).

————. *Publicystyka, wywiady, teksty różne 1939–1963* (Kraków: Wydawnictwo Literackie, 1996).

————. *Testament. Entretiens avec Dominique de Roux* (Paris: Gallimard, 1996).

————. *Testament. Rozmowy z Dominique de Roux* (Kraków: Wydawnictwo Literackie, 2012).

————. "The Statue of Man Upon the Statue of the World," in *Conrad under Familial Eyes*, Zdzisław Najder, ed. and complr., Halina Carroll-Najder, transl. (Cambridge: Cambridge University Press, 1983).

————. *Trans-Atlantyk* (Kraków: Wydawnictwo Literackie, 1988).

————. *Trans-Atlantyk*, Nina Karsov and Carolyn French, transl. (New Haven: Yale University Press, 1995).

————. *Varia 1: Czytelnicy i krytycy. Proza, reportaże, krytyka literacka, eseje, przedmowy* (Kraków: Wydawnictwo Literackie, 2004).

————. *Varia 2* (Kraków: Wydawnictwo Literackie, 2004).

————. *Varia 3. List do Ferdydurkistów. Wywiady, odpowiedzi na ankiety, listy do redakcji czasopism*, Barbara Górska and Marian Rola, eds. (Kraków: Wydawnictwo Literackie, 2004).

————. *Walka o sławę* (Kraków: Wydawnictwo Literackie), Vol. 1 (1996), Vol. 2 (1998).

————. "Witold Gombrowicz o swoim odczycie w Teatrze del Pueblo," *Kurier Polski*, August 23, 1940, 5, reprinted in W. Gombrowicz, *Publicystyka, wywiady, teksty różne 1939–1963* (Kraków: Wydawnictwo Literackie, 1996), 299–302.

——. *Wspomnienia polskie, Kronos* (Kraków: Wydawnictwo Literackie, 2013).

Goodstein, Elizabeth S. *Experience without Qualities: Boredom and Modernity* (Stanford, CA: Stanford University Press, 2004).

Grimstad, Knut Andreas. "Co się zdarzyło na brygu Banbury? Gombrowicz, erotyka i prowokacja kultury" transl. Olga Kubińska, *Teksty Drugie*, no. 3 (2002).

——. "Gombrowicz's 'Gender Trouble' or The Problem of Intimacy in Possessed," *Gender and Sexuality in Ethical Context*, Vol. 5 (2005), 222–53.

——. "L'homoérotisme sublimé, ou comment maîtriser le passé polonaise," *Gombrowicz – une gueule de classique?* Małgorzata Smorąg-Goldberg, ed. (Paris: Institut d'études slaves, 2007), 231–41.

Grinberg, Miguel, ed. *Evocando a Gombrowicz* (Buenos Aires: Galerna, 2004).

Guczalska, Beata, *Jerzy Jarocki: artysta teatru* (Kraków: Państwowa Wyższa Szkoła Teatralna im. Ludwika Solskiego/Oficyjna Wydawniczo-Poligraficzna "Agat-Print" s.c., 1999).

Hartling, Linda M. and Tracy Luchetta, "Humiliation: Assessing the Impact of Derision, Degradation, and Debasement," *The Journal of Primary Prevention*, Vol. 19, no. 4 (1999), 259–78.

Hardy, Thomas. *Tess of the d'Ubervilles* (Delhi: Oxford University Press, 1988).

Harnesberger, Jill. *Sovereignty and Experience: Walter Benjamin and Witold Gombrowicz: The Redemptive Violence of Allegory and the Interhuman Church* (Saarbrücken: VDM, Verlag, 2009).

Heidegger, Martin. *Being and Time: A Translation of Sein und Zeit*, Joan Stambaugh, transl., D. J. Schmidt, revised (Albany: State University of New York Press, 2010).

——. *Contributions to Philosophy (Of the Event)*, R. Rojcewicz and Daniela Vallega-Neu, transl. (Bloomington: Indiana University Press, 2012).

——. *The Fundamental Concepts of Metaphysics. World, Finitude, Solitude* (Bloomington: Indiana University Press, 2012).

——. *Pathmarks*, W. McNeill, ed. (Cambridge: Cambridge University Press, 1998).

——. *The Fundamental Concepts of Metaphysics. World, Finitude, Solitude* (Bloomington: Indiana University Press, 2012).

Herling-Grudziński, Gustav. "Demon naszych czasów," *Kultura*, no. 1–2 (1964).

Hermans, Theo. *The Conference of the Tongues* (Manchester: St Jerome, 2007).

Heydel, Magda. "Angielskie wersje Ferdydurke – strategie przekładania nieprzekładalnego" in Elżbieta Skibińska, ed. *Gombrowicz i tłumacze* (Łask: Oficyna Wydawnicza Leksem, 2004), 103–15.

Holmgren, Beth. "Witold Gombrowicz w Stanach Zjednoczonych" in Ewa Płonowska-Ziarek, ed. *Grymasy Gombrowicza. W kręgu problemów modernizmu, społeczno-kulturowej płci i tożsamości narodowej*, J. Margański, transl. (Kraków, Universitas, 1998), 331–44.

——. "Witold Gombrowicz within the Wieszcz Tradition," *The Slavic and East European Journal*, Vol. 4 (1989), 556–70.

Husserl, Edmund. *Vorlesungen zur Phänomenologie des inneren Zeitbewusstseins* (Tübingen: Max Niemeyer Verlag, 1928).

Hutchinson, Phil. *Shame and Philosophy: An Investigation in the Philosophy of Emotions and Ethics* (New York: Palgrave Macmillan, 2008).

Jagielski, Sebastian. *Maskarady męskości: pragnienie homospołeczne w polskim kinie fabularnym* (Kraków: Universitas, 2013).

Jarausch, Konrad H. *Po Hitlerze. Powrót Niemców do cywilizowanego świata 1945–1995*, Jacek Serwański, transl. (Poznań: Wydawnictwo Nauka i Innowacje, 2013).

Jarniewicz, Jerzy. "Frazes i frazeologia w angislim przekładzie Transatlantyku, czyli tu właśnie cisną mnie buty" in Elżbieta Skibińska, ed. *Gombrowicz i tłumacze* (Łask: Oficyna Wydawnicza Leksem, 2004), 191–200.

Jarzębski, Jerzy. "Gombrowicz: ucieczka z rodzinnego domu" in his *W Polsce czyli wszędzie* (Warsaw: PEN, 1992), 19–37.

———. *Gra w Gombrowicza* (Warsaw: Państwowy Instytut Wydawniczy, 1982).

———, et al. *Korespondencja Witolda Gombrowicza — walka o sławę: korespondencja* (Kraków: Wydawnictwo Literackie, 1996).

———. "Literatura polska pod znakiem Gombrowicza," *VVAA: Lektury polonistyczne* (Kraków: Universitas, 1997).

———. "Operetka jako garderoba duszy," *Odra*, no. 9 (1996) 58–66.

———. *Podglądanie Gombrowicza* (Kraków: Wydawnictwo Literackie, 2001).

———. "Pojęcie 'formy' u Gombrowicza," in *Gombrowicz i krytycy* (Kraków & Wrocław: Wydawnictwo Literackie, 1984), 313–46.

———. "Pytania do Ślubu," *Podglądanie Gombrowicza* (Kraków: Wydawnictwo Literackie, 2000).

———. *Witold Gombrowicz: nasz współczesny* (Kraków: Universitas, 2010).

Jaspers, Karl. *The Question of German Guilt* (New York: Fordham University Press, 2001).

Jay, Martin. *Downcast Eyes: The Denigration of Vision in Twentieth-Century French Thought* (Berkeley: University of California Press, 1994).

Jégouzo, Joël. *Histoire du fonctionnement de la reception de l'oeuvre de Witold Gombrowicz en France 1953–1971* (Paris, 1991).

Jeleński, Konstanty. "Od bosości do nagości: o nieznanej sztuce Witolda Gombrowicza," *Kultura*, Vol. 10 (1975), 3–28.

———. *Witold Gombrowicz et Ferdydurke* (Paris: Julliards, 1959), 7–14.

Jerzak, Katarzyna. "Defamation in Exile: Witold Gombrowicz and E. M. Cioran" in Ewa Płonowska Ziarek, ed. *Gombrowicz's Grimaces: Modernism, Gender, Nationality* (Albany: State University of New York Press, 1998), 177–209.

Judt, Tony. *Powojnie. Historia Europy od roku 1945*, Robert Bartołd transl. (Poznań: Dom Wydawnictwo Rebis, 2013).

Juszczyk, Andrzej. "Apetyt na starość: uwodzenie, pożądanie i przemoc w 'Pornografii'" in Jerzy Jarzębski, ed. *Witold Gombrowicz nasz współczesny: materiały międzynarodowej konferencji naukowej w stulecie urodzin pisarza, Uniwersytet Jagielloński – Kraków, 22–27 marca 2004* (Kraków: Universitas, 2004), 316–27.

Kaliściak, Tomasz. "Statek odmieńców, czyli o marynarskiej fantazji Witolda Gombrowicza" in Ewa Bartos and Marta Tomczok, eds., *Literatura popularna. T. 1, Dyskursy wielorakie* (Katowice: Wydawnictwo Uniwersytetu Śląskiego, 2013).

Karpiński, Wojciech. "The Exile as a Writer: A Conversation about Sorrow and Joy" in John Glad, ed. *Literature in Exile* (Durham, NC: Duke University Press, 1990), 131–38.

Karst, Bronislawa Irene. *The Problem of the Other and of Intersubjectivity in the Works of Jean-Paul Sartre and Witold Gombrowicz* (Ann Arbor, MI: University Microfilms, 1989).

Kempf, Edward. "The Psychopathology of the Acute Homosexual Panic: Acute Pernicious Dissociation Neuroses,"in Edward Kempf, ed. *Psychopathology* (St Louis, MO: C. V. Mosby Co., 1920), 477–515.

Kłosińska, Krystyna."Zwrot analny," in her *Feministyczna krytyka literacka* (Katowice: Wydawnictwo Uniwersytetu Śląskiego, 2010).

Kołakowski, Leszek. "Etyka bez kodeksu," in *Kultura i fetysze: Zbiór rozpraw* (Warsaw: PWN, 1967).

———. "W piekle bez zmian (informacja własna)" in Leszek Kołakowski and Zbigniew Mentzel, ed. *Czy Pan Bóg jest szczęśliwy i inne pytania* (Kraków: Wydawnictwo Znak, 2010).

Kojève, Alexandre. *Introduction to the Reading of Hegel. Lectures on the Phenomenology of Spirit*, Raymond Queneau, assembled, James H. Nichols, transl., Allan Bloom, ed. (New York: Cornell University Press, 1980).

Kowalczyk, Andrzej Stanisław, ed. *Jerzy Giedroyc—Witold Gombrowicz: listy 1950–1969* (Warszawa: Spółdzielnia Wydawnicza "Czytelnik," 2006), Vol. 9.

Kraszewski, Charles S. "Witold Gombrowicz – Trans-Atlantyk" in his *The Romantic Hero and Contemporary Anti-Hero in Polish and Czech Literature: Great Souls and Grey Men* (Lewiston, NY: Edwin Mellen, 1998), 213–32.

Kristeva, Julia. *Powers of Horror. An Essay on Abjection,* Leon S. Roudiez, transl. (New York: Columbia University Press, 1982).

Kubikowski, Tomasz, and Paweł Płoski. *Reżyser: 50 lat twórczości Jerzego Jarockiego* (Warsaw: Teatr Narodowy, 2007).

Kuharski, Allen James. "The Theatre of Witold Gombrowicz" (Ph.D. dissertation, University of California at Berkeley/University Microfilms Inc., 1991).

Kühl, Olaf. *Stilistik einer Verdrängung: Zur Prosa von Witold Gombrowicz* (Berlin: Freie Universität, 1995).

Lamborghini, Osvaldo. *Novelas y cuentos* (Buenos Aires: Ediciones del Serbal, 1988).

———. *Tadeys* (Buenos Aires: Ediciones del Serbal, 1994).

Lamy, Jean-Claude. *René Julliard* (Paris: Julliard, 1992).

Langer, Susanne. *Mind: An Essay on Human Feeling* (Baltimore, MD: The Johns Hopkins University Press, 1967), Vol. 1.

Łapiński, Zdzisław. *"Ja, Ferdydurke." Gombrowicza świat interakcji* (Lublin: Wydawnictwo KUL, 1985).

———. *Przypisy*, in Witold Gombrowicz, *Bakakaj i inne opowiadania* (Kraków: Wydawnictwo Literackie, 2002), I.

Latour, Bruno. *We Have Never Been Modern*, Catherine Porter, transl. (Cambridge, MA: Harvard University Press, 1993).

Laurent, Maryla. "Język Gombrowicza, czyli całkowanie wieloznaczności" in Elżbieta Skibińska, ed. *Gombrowicz i tłumacze* (Łask: Oficyna Wydawnicza Leksem, 2004), 21–36.

Lawaty, Andreas, and Marek Zybura, eds. *Gombrowicz in Europa: deutsch-polnische Versuche einer kulturellen Verortung* (Wiesbaden: Harrassowitz, 2006).

Lefevere, Andre. *Translation, Re-writing and the Manipulation of Literary Fame* (London/New York: Routledge, 1992).

Levitt Peggy, and Nina Nyberg-Sørensen. "The Transnational Turn in Migration Studies," *Global Migration Perspectives*, no. 6 (October 2004).

Leys, Ruth. "The Turn to Affect: A Critique," *Critical Inquiry*, Vol. 37, no. 3 (2011), 434–72.

Lipińska-Iłłakowicz, Krystyna. "Gombrowicz i Ameryka: boje wydawnicze" in Jerzy Jarzębski, ed. *Witold Gombrowicz. Nasz współczesny* (Kraków: Universitas, 2012), 62–78.

———. "Miss America Goes Shopping: Perceptions of American Women in Poland in the 1920s and the 1930s." Paper, Fifth World Congress on Polish Studies, Warsaw, June 20–23, 2014.

Longinović, Tomislav Z. *Borderline Culture. The Politics of Identity in Four Twentieth-Century Slavic Novels* (Fayetteville, AR: University of Arkansas Press, 1993).

Lutostański, Bartosz. *Gombrowicz – Beckett, Beckett – Gombrowicz: A Comparative Inter-Modal Study* (Gdańsk: Gdańsk University Press, 2016).

Maerkle, Andrew. "Aernout Mik: Part I: Possession/Form." ART iT. www.art-it.asia/u/admin_ed_feature_e/jJ0Dd4MXy9RkPVAHgwYI/. Consulted on November 1, 2018.

Magris, Claudio. *Lontano da dove: Joseph Roth e la tradizione ebraico-orientale* (Bologna: Piccola Biblioteca Einaudi, 1989).

Mallarmé, Stéphane. *Selected Poetry and Prose*, Mary Ann Caws, ed. (New York: New Directions, 1982).

Mann, Thomas. *Der Zauberberg* (Frankfut am Main: Fischer Verlag, 1991).

Margański, Janusz. *Gombrowicz wieczny debiutant* (Kraków: Wydawnnictwo Literackie, 2001).

———. "Józio w piekle literatury," *Teksty Drugie*, no. 3 (2002), 7–21.

Markowski, Michał Paweł. *Czarny nurt: Gombrowicz, świat, literatura* (Kraków: Wydawnictwo Literackie, 2004).

———. "Facemaker" in M. Potocka, ed. *Witkacy: Workoholism* (Kraków: Bunkier Sztuki, 2009).

———. "O nudzie" in *Anatomia ciekawości* (Kraków: Wydawnictwo Literackie, 1999).

———. *Polska literatura nowoczesna: Leśmian, Schulz, Witkacy* (Kraków: Universitas, 2006).

———. *Powszechna rozwiązłość: Schulz, egzystencja, literatura* (Kraków: Universitas, 2012).

———. "Ręka kelnera. Esej o obsesji w literaturze" in Ryszard Nycz, Anna Łebkowska, and Agnieszka Dauksza, eds., *Kultura afektu—afekt w kulturze. Humanistyka po zwrocie afektywnym* (Warsaw: Instytut Badań Literackich, 2015), 215–52.

Marx, Karl. *Economic and Philosophic Manuscripts of 1844*, M. Milligan, transl. (Amherst: Prometheus Books, 1988), 77.

Massumi, Brian. "Notes on the Translation and Acknowledgements," in Gilles Deleuze and Felix Guattari, eds. *A Thousand Plateaus* (Minneapolis: University of Minnesota Press, 1987), xvi.

———. *Parables for the Virtual. Movement, Affect, Sensation* (Durham: Duke University Press, 2002).

Melville, Herman. *Billy Budd* (Oxford: Heinemann ELT, 1999).

Menninghaus, Winfried. *Disgust: Theory and History of a Strong Sensation*, Howard Eiland and Joel Golb, transl. (New York: State University of New York Press, 2003).

Mosse, George L. *Nationalism and Sexuality: Respectability and Abnormal Sexuality in Modern Europe* (New York: Howard Fertig, 1997), 23–47.

Ngai, Sianne. *Ugly Feelings* (Cambridge, MA: Harvard University Press, 2005).

Nowak, Leszek. *Gombrowicz: człowiek wobec ludzi* (Warsaw: Prószyński i Spółka, 2000).

Nussbaum, Martha C. *Hiding from Humanity: Disgust, Shame, and the Law* (Princeton, NJ: Princeton University Press, 2004).

Oklot, Michał. *Phantasms of Matter in Gogol (and Gombrowicz)* (Champaign & London: Dalkey Archive Press, 2009).

Oosterhuis, Harry, ed. *Homosexuality and Male Bonding in Pre-Nazi Germany* (New York/London: Routledge, London, 2010).

Pál Pelbart, Peter, and Gerko Egert. "Sharing Distance: On the Precarious Assemblage of Singularities and the Art of Collectivity. An interview with Peter Pál Pelbart," *Inflexions*, Vol. 8, "Radical Pedagogies" (April 2015), 239–49, here 242.

Paloff, Benjamin, *Lost in the Shadow of the Word, Space, Time, and Freedom in Interwar Eastern Europe* (Evanston, IL: Northwestern University Press, 2016).

Papoulias, Constantina and Felicity Callard, "Biology's Gift: Interrogating the Turn to Affect," *Body & Society*, Vol. 16, no. 1 (2010), 29–56.

Pessoa, Fernando. *The Book of Disquiet*, Richard Zenith, transl. (London: Penguin, 2002).

Phillips, Ursula. "Gombrowicz's Polish Complex" in Stanislaw Eile and Ursula Phillips, eds. *New Perspectives in Twentieth-Century Polish Literature: Flight from Martyrology* (Basingstoke: Macmillan, 1992, Studies in Russia and East Europe), 28–46.

Piglia, Ricardo. "¿Existe la novela argentina?," *Espacios de Crítica y Producción*, Vol. 6 (1987), 13–15.

———. "La novela polaca," *Formas breves* (Barcelona: Anagrama, 2000).

Pratt, Daniel. "Narrative and Form: Gombrowicz and the Narrative Conception of Personal Identity," *The Polish Review*, Vol. 60, no. 2 (2015), 7–20.

Probyn, Elspeth. *Blush: Faces of Shame* (Minneapolis: University of Minnesota Press, 2005).

Puig, Manuel. *The Kiss of the Spider Woman* (New York: Vintage Books, 1991).

Pym, Anthony, and Horst Turk. "Translatability" in M. Baker and K. Malkmaer, eds. *The Routledge Encyclopaedia of Translation Studies* (London/New York: Routledge, 2005), 273–76.

Quiroga, José. *Tropics of Desire: Interventions from Queer Latino America* (New York: New York University Press, 2000).

Reckless, Walter. *The Crime Problem* (Englewood Cliffs, NJ: Prentice Hall, 1961).

Ritz, German. "Inexpressible Desire and Narrative Poetics: Homosexuality in Iwaszkiewicz, Breza, Mach and Gombrowicz," in Knut Andreas Grimstad and Ursula Phillips, eds. *Gender and Sexuality in Ethical Context: Ten Essays on Polish Prose* (Bergen: University of Bergen, 2005), 254–76.

――――. *Nić w labiryncie pożądania Nić w labiryncie pożądania: gender i p·leć w literaturze polskiej od romantyzmu do postmodernizmu* (Warsaw: Wiedza Powszechna, 2002).

Rock, David. *Authoritarian Argentina: The Nationalist Movement, Its History and Its Impact* (Berkeley: University of California Press, 1995).

Romanelli, Sergio. *Gênese do processo tradutório* (Vinhedo: Editora Horizonte, 2013).

Rosset, Clément. *Le réel. Traité de l'idiotie* (Paris: Les Éditions de Minuit, 2004).

Roth, Philip. *Shop Talk: A Writer and His Colleagues and Their Work* (Boston: Houghton Mifflin Harcourt, 2001).

Rugoff, Ralph. "A Man of the Crowd," in Aernout Mik and Stephanie Rosenthal, eds. *Dispersions, Aernout Mik* (Cologne: DuMont Literatur und Kunst Verlag, 2004).

Ruppel, Richard. "Joseph Conrad and the Ghost of Oscar Wilde," *The Conradian*, Vol. 23, no. 1 (1998), 19. http://digitalcommons.chapman.edu/english_articles/78/.

Rússovich, Alejandro. "El otro idioma de Witoldo," *Clarín*, July 25, 1999.

――――. *Palabras encontradas* (Buenos Aires: Bibliográfika de Voros, 2010).

――――. "Russovich o Gombrowiczu," *Teatr*, Vol. 9 (1995), 10–12.

――――. "Sobre esta traducción," in Witold Gombrowicz, ed. *El casamiento*, Alejandro Rússovich and Witold Gombrowicz, transl. (Buenos Aires: El cuenco de plata, 2010).

Safranski, Rüdiger. *Zło. Dramat wolności*, Ireneusz Kania, transl. (Warsaw: Czytelnik, 1999).

Salgas, Jean-Pierre. *Les trois mousquetaires: Witkacy, Schulz, Gombrowicz, Kantor* (Nancy, France: Musée des Beaux-Arts & Fage, 2004).

Sandauer, Artur. "Gombrowicz and Politics," in Edward Rothert, transl. *Polish Perspectives*, Vol. 29 (1986), 33–39.

――――. *On the Situation of the Polish Writer of Jewish Descent in the Twentieth Century* (Jerusalem: The Hebrew University Magnes Press, 2005).

Schulz, Bruno. *Collected Stories*, Madeline G. Levine, transl. (Evanston: Northwestern University Press, 2018).

――――. *Correspondance et essais critiques et romans* (Paris: Denoël, 1991).

――――. *Dziela zebrane. Tom 5. Księga listów* (Gdańsk: Slowo/obraz terytoria, 2016).

――――. "Ferdydurke" Paul Coates, transl., *Literary Studies in Poland*, Vol. X (1983), 25.

――――. *Księga listów* (Gdańsk: Słowo/obraz terytoria, 2002).

――――. *Letters and Drawings of Bruno Schulz*. Walter Arendt, transl. (New York: Harper & Row, 1988).

――――. *Sanatorium under the Sign of the Hourglass*. Celina Wieniewska, transl. (Wilmington, MA: Mariner Books, 1997).

Sedgwick, Eve Kosofsky. *Between Men: English Literature and Male Homosocial Desire* (New York: Columbia University Press, 2016).

――――. "Anality. News from the Front" in Jonathan Goldberg, ed. *The Weather in Proust* (Durham, NC: Duke University Press, 2012).

――――. *Epistemology of the Closet* (Berkeley, CA/London: University of California Press, 2008).

———. "Męskie pragnienie homospołeczne i polityka seksualności," *Krytyka Polityczna*, no. 9/10 (2005).

———. *Touching Feeling: Affect, Pedagogy, Performativity* (Durham, NC: Duke University Press, 2003), 35–65.

Sedgwick, Eve Kosofsky, and Adam Frank, eds. *Shame and Its Sisters: A Silvan Tomkins Reader* (Durham, NC: Duke University Press, 1995).

Serra, Maurizio. *Italo Svevo* (Paris: Grasset 2013).

Seyfert, Robert. "Beyond Personal Feelings and Collective Emotions: Toward a Theory of Social Affect," *Theory, Culture & Society*, Vol. 29, no. 6 (2012), 27–46.

Shaw, Deborah. "Deconstructing and Reconstructing 'Transnational Cinema,'" *Contemporary Hispanic Cinema* (April 2013).

Smorąg-Goldberg, Małgorzata, ed. *Gombrowicz, une gueule de classique?* (Paris: Institut d'études slaves, 2007).

Sontag, Susan. Foreword in Witold Gombrowicz, *Ferdydurke* (New Haven & London: Yale University Press, 2000), vii–xv.

Spacks, Patricia Meyer. *Boredom: The Literary History of a State of Mind* (Chicago & London: University of Chicago Press, 1996).

Spektor, Alex. "Between Mourning and Melancholy: Narrative Ethics in Fyodor Dostoevsky and Witold Gombrowicz," *Comparative Literature*, Vol. 66, no. 2 (2014), 186–207.

Spinoza, Benedictus de. *Ethics*, Andrew Boyle, transl., T. S. Gregory, intro. (London: Dent, 1959).

Stanislavski, Konstantin. *Creating a Role*, Elizabeth Reynolds Hapgood, transl. (New York: Taylor & Francis, 1989).

Stasiakievicz, Zofia. "Witold Gombrowicz in Spain," *The Polish Review*, Vol. 60, no. 2 (2015), 39–52.

Suchanow, Klementyna. *Argentyńskie przygody Gombrowicza* (Kraków: Wydawnictwo Literackie, 2011).

———. *Gombrowicz. Ja, geniusz* (Wołowiec: Wydawnictwo Czarne, 2017).

———. "Gombrowicz w oczach Argentyńczyków," *Argentyńskie przygody Gombrowicza* (Kraków: Wydawnictwo Literackie, 2005).

Svendsen, Lars. *Philosophy of Boredom*, John Irons, transl. (London: Reaktion Books, 2005).

Swoboda, Tomasz. *Historie oka. Bataille, Leiris, Artaud, Blanchot* (Gdańsk: Słowo/obraz terytoria, 2010).

Sykora, Luke. Translating Gombrowicz's *Pornografia*: An Interview with Danuta Borchardt, 2010. www.raintaxi.com/translating-gombrowiczs-pornografia-an-interview-with-danuta-borchardt/ (accessed 26 May 2018).

Szczuka, Kazimiera. "Gombrowicz subwersywny" in German Ritz, Christa Binswanger, and Carmen Scheide, eds. *Nowa świadomość płci w modernizmie* (Kraków: TAiWPN Universitas, 2000).

Szpakowska, Małgorzata. "Po Marcu 1968: Teatr Studencki," in Agata Adamiecka-Sitek, Marcin Kościelniak, and Grzegorz Niziołek, eds. *1968/ PRL/Teatr* (Warsaw: Instytut Teatralny im. Zbigniewa Raszewskiego, 2016).

Tardieu, Émile. *L'Ennui: Etude psychologique* (Paris: F. Alcan, 1903).

Tcherkaski, José. *Las cartas de Gombrowicz (Jorge Lavelli lo recuerda en una conversación entrañable)* (Buenos Aires: Siglo XXI/Catálogos, 2004).

Terradas, Pau Freixa. "Recepción de la obra de Witold Gombrowicz en la Argentinayconfiguracióndesuimagenenelimaginarioculturalargentino," doctoral thesis, http://diposit.ub.edu/dspace/bitstream/2445/42056/3/Gombrowicz-Argentina-Freixa-tesis-castellano.pdf.

Thompson, Ewa. *Witold Gombrowicz* (Katowice: Wydawnictwo UŚ, 2002).

Tomaszewski, Marek. "Trans-Atlantyk Witolda Gombrowicza po francusku" in Elżbieta Skibińska, ed. *Gombrowicz i tłumacze* (Łask: Oficyna Wydawnicza Leksem, 2004), 175–90.

———, ed. *Witold Gombrowicz entre l'Europe et l'Amérique* (Villeneuve d'Ascq: Presses Universitaires du Septentrion, 2007).

Tomkins, Silvan. *Exploring Affect: The Selected Writings of Silvan S. Tompkins*, E. Virginia Demos, ed. (Cambridge: Cambridge University Press, 1995).

Toohey, Peter. *Boredom: A Lively History* (New Haven: Yale University Press, 2012).

Toury, Gideon. *Descriptive Translation Studies and Beyond* (Amsterdam/Philadelphia: John Benjamins, 1995).

Urbanowski, Maciej. *Pisma polityczne "Pod znakiem faszyzmu" oraz szkice rozproszone 1921–1955* (Kraków: Wydawnictwo Arkana, 2006).

Vallee, Lillian. "Who is Gombrowicz?" in Witold Gombrowicz, Ferdydurke, and Eric Mosbacher, transl. (New York: Penguin, 1986), xviii.

Van der Meer, Jan IJ. *Form vs. Anti-Form: Das semantische Universum von Witold Gombrowicz* (Amsterdam: Rodopi, 1992).

Velleman, James David. "The Genesis of Shame," *Philosophy & Public Affairs*, Vol. 30, no. 1 (2001), 27–52.

Vertovec, Steven. "Conceiving and Researching Transnationalism," *Ethnic and Racial Studies*, Vol. 22, no. 2 (1999), 447–62.

———. "Transnationalism and Identity," *Journal of Ethnic and Migration Studies*, Vol. 27, no. 4 (2001), 573–82.

Warkocki, Błażej. *Homo niewiadomo: polska proza wobec odmienności* (Warsaw: Wydawnictwo Sic!, 2007).

———. *Pamiętnik afektów z okresu dojrzewania. Gombrowicz – Queer – Sedgwick* (Poznań & Warszawa: Wydawnictwo Naukowe Uniwersytetu im. Adama Mickiewicza, 2018).

———. "What a Shame! Memoirs of a Time of Queer Immaturity: Prologue," in Ryszard Nycz, ed. *Teksty Drugie*, Vol. 1 (Special Issue, 2017), 185–201.

———. "Zbrodnia inkorporowana. O konwencji "paranoicznego gotyku" w Zbrodni z premedytacją Witolda Gombrowicza," *Poznańskie Studia Polonistyczne, Seria Literacka* Vol. 30, no. 50, (2017), 237–58.

Wetherell, Margaret. "Affect and Discourse – What's the Problem? From Affect as Excess to Affective/Discursive Practice," *Subjectivity*, Vol. 6, no. 4 (2013), 349–68.

Wilde, Oscar. "The Importance of Being Earnest," Cecylia Wojewoda, transl., in Oscar Wilde, *Cztery Komedie*, Juliusz Żuławski, ed.; Włodzimierz Lewik, Janina Pudełek, and Cecylia Wojewoda, transl. (Warsaw: Panstwowy Instytut Wydawniczy, 1961), Vol. I.

———. *The Picture of Dorian Gray*, Andrew Elfenbein, ed. (New York: Pearson, 2007).

Winckelmann, Johann Joachim. *The History of Ancient Art* (Boston: Ticknor, 1872).

Witkiewicz, Stanisław I. *Insatiability. A Novel*, L. Iribarne, transl. (Evanston: Northwestern University Press, 1996).

———. *The Mother & Other Unsavory Plays: Including the Shoemakers and They*, Daniel C. Gerould, Christopher S. Durer, Jan Kott, and Hal Leonard, transl. and eds. (New York & London: Applause Theatre Book Publishers, 1993).

———. "The Shoemakers" in *The Madman and the Nun and Other Plays*, Daniel C. Gerould, Christopher S. Durer, and Jan Kott, transl. and eds. (Seattle & London: University of Washington Press, 1973).

———. "The Water Hen" in his *The Madman and the Nun and Other Plays*, Daniel C. Gerould and Christopher S. Durer, transl. and eds. (Seattle: University of Washington Press, 1968).

Wittlin, Józef. "Apologia Gombrowicza" in Zdzisław Łapiński, ed. *Gombrowicz i krytycy* (Kraków: Wydawnictwo Literackie, 1984), 83–92.

Wojtas, Paweł. *Translating Gombrowicz's Liminal Aesthetics* (Frankfurt am Main: Peter Lang, 2014).

Wóycicki, Kazimierz. "Spór o niemiecką pamięć" in Piotr Buras, ed. *Spór o niemiecką pamięć. Debata Walser–Bubis* (Warsaw: Centrum Stosunków Międzynarodowych, 1999).

Wyka, Kazimierz. "Tragiczność, drwina i realism" in his *Pogranicze powieści. Wydanie drugie poszerzone* (Warsaw: Czytelnik, 1974), 7–29.

Zagajewski, Adam. *La trahison* (Paris: Fayard, 1993).

Zaleski, Krzysztof. "Ślub Witolda Gombrowicza," in Zdzisław Łapiński, ed. *Gombrowicz i krytycy* (Kraków-Wrocław: Wydawnictwo Literackie, 1984).

Zerilli, Linda M. G. "The Turn to Affect and the Problem of Judgment," *New Literary History*, Vol. 46 (2015), 261–86.

Ziarek, Ewa Płonowska. *Gombrowicz's Grimaces: Modernism, Gender, Nationality* (Albany: State University of New York Press, 1998).

Zieliński, Stanisław. "Gombrowicz w Jordanie," *Kultura*, no. 11 (1963), reprinted in *Varia 2* (Kraków: Wydawnictwo Literackie, 2004).

Ziomek, Jerzy. "Solecyzmy w Ferdydurke" in his *Prace ostatnie* (Warsaw: PWN, 1994), 221–38.

Żółkoś, Monika. *Ciało mówiące* (Gdańsk: Słowo/obraz terytoria, 2001).

Index

For Product Safety Concerns and Information please contact our EU
representative GPSR@taylorandfrancis.com
Taylor & Francis Verlag GmbH, Kaufingerstraße 24, 80331 München, Germany